D0711691

BASIC TRAINING FOR HORSES

English and Western

BASIC TRAINING
FOR HORSES
English and Western

———◆———

ELEANOR F. PRINCE

GAYDELL M. COLLIER

With a Foreword by Dave Jones

Drawings by E. F. Prince

Photographs by the authors
unless otherwise credited

BROADWAY BOOKS

NEW YORK

BROADWAY

A previous edition of this book was originally published in 1979.
It is here reprinted by arrangement with Doubleday.

Basic Training for Horses. Copyright © 1979 by Eleanor F. Prince and
Gaydell M. Collier. All rights reserved. Printed in the United States of
America. No part of this book may be reproduced or transmitted in any
form or by any means, electronic or mechanical, including
photocopying, recording, or by any information storage and
retrieval system, without written permission from the publisher.
For information, address: Broadway Books,
a division of Random House, Inc.,
1540 Broadway, New York, NY 10036.

Broadway Books titles may be purchased for business or
promotional use or for special sales. For information, please write to:
Special Markets Department, Random House, Inc.,
1540 Broadway, New York, NY 10036.

BROADWAY BOOKS and its logo, a letter B bisected on the diagonal, are
trademarks of Broadway Books, a division of Random House, Inc.

Visit our website at www.broadwaybooks.com

First Broadway Books trade paperback edition published 2001.

The Library of Congress Cataloging-in-Publication Data has cataloged
the previous edition as:
Prince, Eleanor F.
    Basic training for horses.
    Bibliography: p.
    Includes index.
       1. Horses—Training.   1. Collier, Gaydell M.
  II. Title.
SF287.P77   1989   636.1'0888   88-33436
       ISBN 0-385-26238-8

25 24 23 22 21 20 19

FOREWORD

I was very flattered, when, some time ago, I was asked to write this Foreword. To be asked to do a Foreword is a great compliment, for the authors of this book have read my writings and liked them well enough to single me out of the crowd.

There's a lot involved in writing a Foreword. The first thing one must do is to read the book he's doing the Foreword for. When the galley proofs of this one arrived, I was amazed at the size. This is one big book.

Galleys aren't easy to read. There are all sorts of corrections on them and some of the stuff isn't too clear. A guy might speed read through all this but I found myself using my magnifying glass so I could savor every word.

I found what I was looking for; compassion and understanding. Without these, such a book is a dead mechanical thing. The authors convey the feeling that they really care for horses and are extremely concerned that you who read it share their feelings.

Now, let me say this. I don't always agree with these gals. I have my methods and they have theirs. I had a lot of fun disagreeing with some of the things they wrote about.

I'm an ole cowboy. Can't you see me starting a colt with a bareback pad and riding side-saddle? Heck, Will James and Charlie Russell just turned over in their graves! When I start a colt, I pull up my chaps, pull down my hat, and "git on."

But the early horse masters would have liked such a method. The thought is good. Professor Rarey, the great old English horse master, would have been high with his approval.

The authors are very thorough. The person who buys this book, be he novice or professional, will find material well worth reading. Many western trainers now use dressage methods, and all this is extremely well covered.

A colt can be trained if the rider ropes him, manhandles a saddle on him, and goes for a ride. But a great many colts are spoiled by such crude methods. The slow, precise, humane way of doing things is far better, and you're told how to do it in this book.

A part I really liked was the advice to "spice up the training"—to make things interesting for the colt so he'll want to work. This is valuable advice. Too many trainers consider themselves teachers in the strictest sense of the word. They drill-drill-drill! The horse puts up with this drudgery day after day, week after week, and month after month. Nothing—animal, horse, dog, human—cares for drudgery. Making work enjoyable for the colt is very necessary.

Someday I'd like to know both authors well, for they're my kind of people. It's easy to see that they both love horses and are serious about training them. Their sincerity comes through loud and clear. Such folks are my friends.

Dave Jones

ACKNOWLEDGMENTS

For their kind assistance—whether in providing information, helping with photos, or in other ways—we are grateful to Dave Jones, Charlotte Brailey Kneeland, Sandy Whittaker, Leslie Turner, Margaret Smith, Woodson Tyree, Dorothy R. Feldman, Helen Lund, John Galbraith, Fred and Frank Collier, Kathryn G. Hanaford, Ellin K. Roberts, the Wyoming Travel Commission, the University of Wyoming Photo Service, our husbands—Bill Prince and Roy Collier, and our many other friends—both human and equine—who have helped to make this book possible.

Eleanor F. Prince
Sodergreen Ranch, Buford,
Wyoming

Gaydell M. Collier
Backpocket Ranch, Sundance,
Wyoming

CONTENTS

Part II   Basic Training

Part III   Basic Advanced Training

Part V Corrective Training and Special Problems

INTRODUCTION

Training is discovery. To train a horse is to discover his nature and to develop his abilities.

Every time a trainer and a prospective equine pupil first confront each other, they stand at the head of a new road, down which they'll have to travel together. There may be roadsigns and trail markers; there may be stretches of well-worn macadam; but somewhere along the way they will have to break trail and pick their way among the rocks.

That's why, if you ask six horsemen how to train a horse, you'll probably get six different answers. Ask any one of those horsemen how he trained six horses, and, chances are, you'll still get six different answers.

There are many ways to train a horse, and a good trainer is sensitive, innovative, and flexible. In *Basic Training for Horses: English and Western,* we present training methods that have proved effective for us, and we offer ideas that we hope will challenge you to discovery—to training your horse creatively. This book is closely correlated with *Basic Horsmanship: English and Western,* carrying through what the student has learned as a rider to what he can apply as a trainer. The case studies and examples of ways to deal with different problems should serve as continual reminders that there is no one way, or best way, to train a horse.

In working with horses, there is always a challenge ahead. If you are thinking about training your horse, what will you have to know? Do you really want to? Are you able to? Above all, should you?

To be successful, a trainer should have:

First, an innate and deep-seated love and respect for horses, and

Second, a certain amount of knowledge of and experience with horses.

Patience, common sense, and willingness to work hard are also of top importance. With these as starting points, how can you decide whether or not you should be a horse trainer? Or, a better question would be: How can you tell whether or not you should train this particular horse? Unless you are a professional trainer, experienced and equipped to handle any horse that comes your way, there is going to be a dividing line between horses you will be able to train and those you shouldn't attempt. In many cases, after a reasonable evaluation, you'll be able to tell, even before you begin, whether or not to tackle that particular horse. Certainly, after several sessions and a re-evaluation, you should know whether or not to continue.

How to make this evaluation is discussed in Part I, Chapter 1. But first, let's take a close look at this animal called "horse." Just what kind of critter is he?

Part I

———◆———

THE ART OF TRAINING

THE PSYCHOLOGY

OF TRAINING HORSES

A horse is an individual. He has his own set of physical characteristics that in some measure conform to or deviate from a breed standard. He has an individual temperament and disposition, and his background and environment have touched him in special ways. He may be wary, friendly, crafty, playful, lazy, ornery. He is himself.

But a horse is also a member of a genus and a species, and as such he has certain characteristics in common with every other horse. A working knowledge of these characteristics and behavioral traits helps the trainer to avoid mistakes and gives him the advantage he needs to progress gently but firmly in training.

Horse Psychology

GENERAL CHARACTERISTICS OF THE HORSE

Horses are gregarious; they are social animals who prefer the company of their own kind to living or traveling alone. In the wild state, on the range, or in pastures, horses will form groups and move around together. If a horse must live alone, he will usually develop a strong, friendly relationship with some other creature—perhaps a dog, cat, or goat, or even man. It is a kindness to make sure that your horse has a companion if he has no other horses for company.

Within each group or herd, horses establish their own hierarchy or pecking order. If a new horse joins the group, there will be a lot of bickering and turmoil until the place of the new arrival is determined. If he is a youngster, his place will probably be near the bottom of the pecking order —he will defer to the other horses, letting them have the choicest pasture or hay, drinking only when they have finished.

Each horse is individual, but, like people, horses share common characteristics. For instance, they are gregarious and form groups as they graze. (Courtesy Wyoming Travel Commission)

Horses are subject to jealousy, especially concerning food, and especially when their self-determined pecking order is violated by humans. When you have several horses in a stable, they should all be fed at the same time and in the same order. Sometimes jealousy and restlessness can be avoided by feeding the horses always according to their own hierarchy.

Horses are naturally athletic. They need plenty of exercise. When unrestricted, they move around constantly, traveling over a wide area. Sometimes they run or race, apparently just for the joy of it. Horse owners have an obligation to see that their animals get enough exercise, either running loose in a large field or pasture, or through daily exercise on the longe line or under saddle. Failure to provide sufficient exercise is one of the greatest misdeeds committed by today's horsemen.

Horses have excellent memories. And they learn to associate ideas— they learn that good actions bring rewards, bad actions evoke punishment. Because of these traits, horses develop habits quickly and easily. Repetition of desirable actions forms a desirable habit. And, unfortunately, undesirable actions are quick to develop into bad habits.

Together, these qualities of memory and association are tremendously important to the trainer. They can work for him or against him, depending upon whether the habit learned by the horse is considered to be desirable or undesirable.

Horses are sensitive to touch. Because of this sensitivity, they learn to recognize and respond to the lightest of aids. Breeds with "hot" blood—horses of Thoroughbred and Arabian breeding in particular—are generally more sensitive than the "cold" breeds and react more quickly or strongly to a stimulus. For example, a very sensitive animal will immediately lift his foot if touched on the pastern, even without having been conditioned or taught to do this. A cold-blood may sometimes need a stronger stimulus, such as a tap, before he'll lift his foot. But this difference in sensitivity is only a matter of degree.

Because of their innate sensitivity, horses are most successfully trained when they are led, rather than forced, into good behavioral patterns.

Horses have excellent hearing, incorporating a range of frequencies. Because of their sensitivity to sound, they react to unnatural, sharp, or loud noises. They also respond to tones of voice—it isn't what we say but how we say it that registers. A soothing tone reassures a frightened horse; an exclamatory tone brings immediate attention.

A horse's eyes, set on either side of his head rather than in front, enable him to see a wide panorama. What is interesting and important to the trainer is that the horse sees a different picture on each side. A trainer should work with a horse both from his left side and his right side so that the animal can get used to seeing the picture with either eye. If a horse is fearful of a strange object, such as a lawnmower in his path, he should be led past it from both directions.

When grazing, horses can see both far and near. Often they can distinguish movement in the distance but cannot see what is actually causing the movement. Their natural response to this situation may be to run, since, from earliest times, their basic reaction to danger is to escape by flight. It is wise for the trainer to remember this when he takes his green horse out on the trail for the first time. Vision is of prime importance in recognition. Your horse knows you in your work clothes, but he may have an entirely different reaction to you when you appear in a slicker or Sunday-go-to-meeting dress.

Horses have a wonderful sense of rhythm, a fact that can be used to the trainer's advantage. They love music, and some horses step in rhythm to the band when ridden in a parade.

Horses are imitative. Seeing one of their members wander to a different patch of grass, the rest of the herd will likely follow. If one horse in a stable becomes a weaver (shifts his weight back and forth in rhythm) through boredom, he will probably be copied by the rest of the horses—enough to make any trainer seasick.

What about intelligence? A horse's brain is like his stomach—small in relation to his body size. However, the brain has many convolutions of the surface, and the horse should not be considered stupid. Most of what he learns is by rote, and he learns that well. In effect, everything we do with a horse is training, whether it's leading him through a gate, picking up his feet, or saddling and bridling him. When a trainer is consistent in his actions, the horse learns the proper behavioral pattern.

Most obstacles to training are psychological rather than physical. A trainer can't bluff his horse. The sensitive trainer persuades his horse—he doesn't enslave him. Persuasion brings willing obedience; enslavement creates resistance requiring constant correction and reinforcement. As Xenophon states in his treatise *On Equitation* (400 B.C.), ". . . What the horse has to do under compulsion, he does not understand. Such actions are not beautiful, any more than if one were to teach a dancer by whipping and spurring. For there is apt to be far more ugliness than grace about the actions of either a horse or a man who is subjected to such treatment. But he must follow the indication of the aids to display of his own free will all the most beautiful and brilliant qualities."

YOUR HORSE IN PARTICULAR

With these general characteristics in mind, take a close look at your own horse. As an individual, he exhibits a collection of traits that must be considered before training begins. The type of training he will receive depends, at least in part, on his health, conformation, temperament, disposition, age, sex, and training history. Consider these in the light of your training goals for this particular horse: Are you teaching a foal to like people and to behave in a mannerly fashion? Or teaching the basics to a green two-year-old? Or training an older horse for a specific type of work, such as roping calves or dressage?

These considerations will influence the methods you use, the equipment you work with, and the timing for your overall training program.

First of all, how old is your horse? A youngster has neither the patience nor the attention span of an older animal. A younger horse requires training methods that differ greatly from methods used for an older horse, and the younger horse's special needs are best met by short, frequent lessons. On the other hand, a horse that has lived free until maturity (over five or six years) may not be mentally or physically conditioned to work—he enjoyed his freedom for too many years. At this age, the horse may resent work and set up mental barriers. This isn't to say that he cannot be trained—only that it's an entirely different story from training a foal. In-between horses require still other methods.

Is your horse sound and in good health? Is he glossy, alert, and raring to go? Then he is most apt to be receptive and ready to learn. A weak or unthrifty animal, on the other hand, will not be eager and alert in your classroom. Although he may seem tractable, he'll be able to think only of his misery and discomfort, and so will be slow and unresponsive. It isn't fair to try to train sick or "poor" animals—nor is it worthwhile. The stress would be frustrating and detrimental to both you and your horse. A trainer's first job is to see that his animal is in good health.

What kind of temperament does your horse have? Is he excitable? Alert? Lazy? Flighty? Calm?

With an especially excitable horse, your methods and movements must be very quiet, patient, and firm. Care should be taken to feed an adequate grain and hay ration, as well as to provide optimum training conditions—dry ground, good weather, absence of any interference from nearby horses or other distractions. Probably more time should be spent on ground training than would be necessary with a calm, quiet horse.

On the other hand, if your horse is especially phlegmatic, the initial stages of training can usually proceed more quickly. Later training, however, may take more time, in order to encourage energetic gaits and sensitive responses.

Temperament should also be considered in more advanced training for specialized work—an excitable animal might make a brilliant show horse for some classes, but would be unsuited to competitive trail riding or pleasure classes.

Does your horse have a friendly disposition? Or does he display antisocial tendencies, preferring to be left alone? It seems that horses who like people generally are willing and want to please. Horses that dislike or distrust people are often more rebellious or difficult. Most horses, of course, fall between the extremes. And, like their trainers, they are subject to moods and notions that may temporarily affect their disposition.

The sex of your horse also has a bearing on behavior. It is more difficult to keep the attention of a stallion than of a gelding or mare. Some mares can be inattentive, even downright ornery, during estrus or heat periods. Geldings are usually more even-tempered and willing to work, and therefore may be a better choice for a beginning trainer to work with.

Conformation may influence training. Some horses are congenitally less able to flex at the poll, or to achieve collected or extended gaits. A horse must not be asked to do what is physically impossible for him. Some horses may tend toward stiffness and therefore require more suppling and conditioning before they are physically able to perform certain exercises. Gaits and action should also be considered—high action means unnecessary expense of energy and quicker fatigue for a trail horse, and it would be foolish to try to train a horse with a long, low, swinging stride to perform in park horse classes.

Intelligence is an important ingredient in training. Some horses catch on quickly and seem to enjoy new learning experiences; others require endless repetition of basic exercises. Some horses are smart in a crafty sort of way and always seem to have some new trick up their throatlatch. They can present the trainer with a real challenge.

What kind of training background or history does your horse have? Is he gentle? Has he been halter-broken? Does he allow you to pick up his feet? Or has he run loose all his life, with no handling or restraint? This last case, especially if the horse is an older animal, calls for a different method of training, usually requiring the firm understanding of an experienced horseman.

Most difficult for the trainer is the horse that requires retraining. The bad habits or vices that the horse has acquired must be supplanted by good behavior. This unlearning and relearning can be a long process. If the bad habits have become deeply ingrained over a long period of time, it is possible that retraining may never be entirely successful. Again, this is a job for an experienced horseman.

Trainer Psychology

EVALUATING YOURSELF

There is nothing more satisfying than the feeling of being "one" with your horse, especially when you have trained him yourself. This feeling can be attained only by working together patiently, firmly, intelligently, and with love. Don't take the training of horses lightly. It's hard work. There's no easy road or magic formula to produce a finished animal—or even a safe one. Taking on the task is a commitment in time, patience, and sensitivity.

QUALITIES AND ATTRIBUTES DESIRABLE IN A HORSE TRAINER

First of all, of course, is a genuine love of horses. This alone generates a desire for harmony with your horse and a desire to learn all you can about horses and horsemanship.

Next, consider your sense of responsibility. Are you willing to work— really work? Do you have the self-discipline to keep regular work hours? In winter as well as summer? Despite rain, heat, hail, and sleet? Training an animal demands regularity; it's not something you do only if everything else is out of the way.

Training takes thought, too. It's important to plan ahead to map out an intelligent program and schedule. Keep up with current ideas and equipment; be familiar with time-honored theory. Do the names Xenophon, Newcastle, de la Guérinière, Caprilli, Podhajsky, Monte Foreman, Arthur Konyat, Dave Jones, and William Steinkraus mean anything to you? They should. Plan to develop your own library of horse books and periodicals—and use it.

How do you rate on patience, self-control, and perseverance? You'll need all three in grand measure. Fly off the handle at every turn, and your horse will soon be ready only for bucking fits at the neighborhood rodeo.

You'll need to be sensitive, consistent, and confident. You'll need to know when to be firm but not harsh, when to reprimand, when to reassure. A sensitive trainer knows when a horse has had enough, when to push a little more.

You should be alert and capable of paying great attention to detail— no skipping steps here and there, no ignoring of developing quirks or problems. You'll find that some horses are so full of tricks and experiments that you'll need to use all your wits to stay ahead of them.

Above all, you'll need to be flexible. Each horse is different, and you will have to choose your methods to fit the horse.

A word about physical characteristics—you can't discount them. Whether you are tall or short, fat or thin, agile or elderly—all should be taken into consideration, not so much as limiting factors but more as guiding ones. Take extra care in your training to compensate for any physical attribute that may present a problem. Take mounting, for instance: A very agile person, capable of mounting quickly and easily, will probably not have to do as much on-the-ground preparatory work as a less athletic person. But with that extra groundwork, the horse should be equally safe to mount by the less-agile trainer.

Some men insist that women are not strong enough to train horses, especially stallions. Let's look at what (we think) this really means: Using these particular methods, a girl is not strong enough to train this particular horse. This may well be true. There are horses that require such strong handling that not even many men should attempt to train them. On the other hand, using different methods, that same stallion might be ideal training material for a girl who is knowledgeable and experienced. We have been training, using, and handling stallions as studs for over twenty years with a minimum of problems because we insist on discipline.

One of the main points of this evaluation is to help you decide— before ruining a horse or becoming injured yourself—whether or not you should attempt to train a particular horse, given a particular set of circumstances. Horses are not marshmallows. Because of their size, strength, and quick reactions, they are potentially dangerous animals. Safety for horse and trainer is our most important consideration.

EXPERIENCE AND ABILITY

Ability and experience are related in that your ability generally improves with experience—up to a point. There is simply no substitute for experience in working with horses, but everyone has to start somewhere. The more you are around horses and work with them, the more your "horse sense" develops. You begin to get the feeling of the horse. As you become more sensitive to his personality, you begin to anticipate difficulties before they happen and are better able to cope with them when they do. You develop confidence and consistency.

A trainer should be an exceptionally good rider, able to use his aids independently and in conjunction with one another. To attempt training before one can ride well is a self-defeating job. It is too easy to confuse a horse when you don't have your own body under control. You should be able to transmit confidence to your horse, not uncertainty. Mutual confidence is the starting point for successful training.

If this is the first horse you have ever trained, spend time observing him and caring for him. Improve your riding ability by riding many horses. Become familiar with the equipment you plan to use, and practice using it on a horse that is already trained to it. Read books and magazines about horsemanship and training; books can't take the place of practical experience, but they can answer questions and save experimentation.

Many people tend to be somewhat timid when first working with horses. Again, familiarity—experience—should give them confidence. Work often with your horse, without rushing, without feeling, "I've got to train this horse by St. Patrick's Day." Alois Podhajsky, former director of the Spanish Riding School of Vienna, held as his motto the saying, "I have time," and he recommended the motto to anyone training a horse. This holds true also with bold or overconfident horse-owners who tend to rush training. For them, it will also help to plan ahead, write down a schedule, and then stick with it.

Take into consideration, too, that no one is at his best every day. If it's an off day, don't try to introduce something new that may test your patience and upset your horse; instead, review what the horse has been doing well. Avoid mistakes rather than try to bull through them.

YOUR TIME AND FUNDS

It often seems, with time and money, that the less you have of one, the more you need of the other. If you're short on time, you might better spend the money to have someone else train your horse. If you're short on money, you may have to work with a minimum of equipment and make-do facilities: Plan to take extra time to compensate. But no matter how you cut it, you'll still need an adequate supply of both. Let's consider them separately.

Time: How much time does it take to train a horse? How much time daily; how much time overall? As always, with horses, this is variable—some horses may have a very short attention span and you might do better with very short lessons spread over a longer period. But as far as your own time is concerned, if you can't spend at least forty minutes a day, seven days a week, you had better think again about this whole project.

Here's why: Horses are creatures of habit. They learn by repetition. When you are regular in your training habits, they know what to expect. They're ready to go to work. This in itself is a training aid that saves time and sets the atmosphere for learning.

And, depending on the age and temperament of the horse, you can't expect to work too long at a time: With a very young horse, five to ten minutes may be as much as you can spend at first in actively training (not counting time for grooming, cleaning up, and so on). In other words, you can't make three hours a day on weekends replace daily weekday sessions. It won't work. You'll notice a setback even skipping one day.

When it comes to long-range time, if this is your horse, you probably plan to ride him for years to come—and really, since riding is training, you'll be training him as long as you have him. But if you're looking at a specific goal, such as training a two-year-old for riding, again you have many things to consider: his temperament and physical development, how much groundwork and previous training he has had, where and how you plan to ride him, and so on and so on.

Now, some professional trainers expect to take a green or unbroken horse and have him ready for you to ride in a month. And they do. Owners expect it and they often don't want to pay for any more than that. But these trainers are expert riders, they have the equipment, they have the facilities, they have the help, and they are being paid to take personal risks. Some take shortcuts—often rough shortcuts—in their training to produce results within a prescribed time limit. But it's these shortcuts that make future problems for the owner, especially if he is not capable of carrying on the training the moment his horse comes home.

So let's not worry about the quick-do professionals here, or confuse them with the professionals who insist upon regular, unrushed training. If you own a horse and plan to train him, you certainly must love horses and plan to make them a part of your life. Be rigorous with yourself in demanding a schedule, but don't set any time limit for "when you'll stop training." It's a continuing, developing project, and once you have some experience under your belt, you'll begin to have a general idea of the time elements involved for you, under your particular circumstances.

Concentrate more on enjoying your horse, whether ground training or riding, and coming to know him better. Concentrate on giving him a solid, basic education that will stand as a basis for any future specialized training. Above all, concentrate on developing a safe horse, safely.

Next, consider funds. If you already own a horse for pleasure riding, you're well aware that horses take money. You already know about the grain, hay, pasture, supplements, shoeing, and vet bills. You're aware of incidentals such as your own clothes and special tack when going to shows or on trail rides. But when you talk about training, you have even more expenses to think about. You'll need a certain amount of equipment, and, even keeping this to a minimum, it still adds up. When training, you'll have to keep your horse handy to work with—this may mean feeding more hay than if he's left out on pasture or on the range. You'll have to feed grain and supplements enough to keep your horse in top-notch physical condition—good health and regular exercise are important considerations in training. You'll need training facilities that, depending on what you already have and what you're going to need, may involve some constructing, remodeling, adding on, repairing, or fencing. Take a good look at the financial side of the project before you begin—it may save disappointment later.

YOUR FACILITIES AND EQUIPMENT

Suitable, adequate facilities and equipment make your training job easier, sometimes quicker, and often better. Take a good look at what you have, keeping in mind your training project. Few people achieve an ideal training setup, but by comparing yours with the ideal (see Chapter 2), you'll be able to see how you can adapt your facilities, what problems you can live with, which ones you'll definitely have to do something about. As to equipment, you'll have to decide how much is indispensable, what you can put off getting for a while, what you can do without and still be effective.

GOALS

A good trainer probably never considers one of his horses as perfectly trained, but he is always working in this direction.

Clarify your training goals, both long-range and short-range. Ask yourself why you want to train this horse or any horse (if the only answer that comes to mind is To Save Money or To Make Money, you're already in trouble). One continuing, long-range goal in training a horse is to make him a joy to ride and own.

More specifically, your goals can help you in planning your training routine. Are you training a horse for a trail ride or contest? Your training will involve conditioning, rating, working alone and in company with others. Are you training a youngster? You'll want to concentrate heavily on basic education.

Some goals to think about:

Training the horse to be

- well-mannered, free from vices—he should allow his feet to be handled and his teeth to be looked at
- responsive and obedient
- quiet, calm, secure in your presence
- balanced, supple
- willing and enthusiastic
- versatile—the result of a solid, basic, well-rounded education. He should go well under English or Western tack, work nicely on the trail or in the ring

Discovering the horse's aptitudes and abilities for advanced work—perhaps in dressage, hunting, roping, cutting, or some other field

Learning

- to understand horse psychology
- about proper nutrition and management—to balance feed, care, and exercise to keep the horse in top physical condition
- to be a sensitive, understanding teacher

Colonel Podhajsky says that our horses are our teachers. How true! Each horse is different, and each provides us with a new experience.

Principles of Training

Effective, sensitive training requires an understanding of horse psychology in general, and of the individual horse to be trained in particular. The principles of training are founded upon this basic knowledge.

Training is accomplished by means of repetition, reward, and punishment. The way in which these elements are used—in conjunction with each other and as applied to each individual horse—denotes the character of the training and reveals the character of the trainer. When training is at its best, a horse learns by the repetition of actions and exercises that earn him a reward.

Ideally, any vices or bad habits may be prevented by avoiding any mistakes in handling and training. Anything and everything a trainer does with a young horse is training—whether greeting him in the stable, leading him out to water, or picking up his feet. A trainer must always give himself the time to do any specific job correctly and consistently.

REWARD AND PUNISHMENT

Before going further, let's take a close look at what is meant by reward and punishment. Both are strong terms that imply action, even strong action. When training horses, however, we usually think of reward and punishment not as concrete actions, but rather as relative conditions. For instance, pressure, as when giving a leg aid, may be considered punishment; release of that pressure is reward.

The effect of punishment or reward must be measured against three factors: first, the character and sensitivity of the individual horse; second, the degree of his training; and third, the specific action in question, whether desirable (meriting a degree of reward) or undesirable (meriting a degree of punishment). A sensitive horse may feel well rewarded by a kind word where a less sensitive animal may be immune to words or caresses, needing a bite of food to make an impression. A well-trained animal will respond to the slightest pressure from leg or rein, where a green horse may need a great deal of pressure before he will respond. The degree of punishment or reward must always be decided with both the individual horse and the specific action in mind.

It's important to consider, when working with a horse that has never been handled or been around humans, that he will have to be conditioned to understand that a pat or caress *is* praise. It will not necessarily be a pleasant sensation to him. Time may have to be taken to condition him to accept the pat as a desirable effect, possibly by patting him while feeding grain or cake, and talking gently and soothingly at the same time.

Use of punishment or reward must always be immediate, or the value is lost. If a horse performs an exercise correctly, an immediate caress and "Good boy!" will let him know he has behaved well. To delay the reward would be to lose the opportunity—the horse may never realize he accomplished the proper action, and therefore be less inclined to repeat it. When necessary punishment is delayed, the horse does not connect the punishment with the act. Not only will he be inclined to repeat the undesirable action, but also the seemingly unwarranted punishment may cause confusion, fear, or loss of confidence in his trainer.

Both punishment and reward can of course go beyond subtle, relative conditions to concrete actions, and under these circumstances, the degree of severity is a primary consideration. Horses are much like people—most respond better to praise than to chastisement, though chastisement is sometimes necessary. The sensitive trainer will be as generous as possible with praise, using punishment only when necessary.

Training is discovery. The sensitive trainer takes pains to discover the many ways in which he can reward an individual horse, thereby gaining the horse's confidence and desire to please. He tries to discover also which punishments are both suitable and effective, choosing always the mildest and briefest form of punishment *that is effective* for that particular horse under that particular circumstance.

Simple, effective rewards include a gentle pat on the neck and speaking in a soothing, pleased-sounding manner. For many horses, this type of praise is sufficient, and stimulates them with a further desire to please. A free walk (letting the horse walk with a very long rein) is relaxing and rewarding; so is taking the horse out on the trail after a session of ring work. In some cases, when a horse has performed an exercise correctly, the best reward may be to stop the lesson and lead him back to the barn. A tidbit —a piece of carrot or apple, a lump of sugar, a pellet of range cake—may be an effective reward for some horses, but the practice of hand feeding can lead to problems (more about this later).

Be generous with praise and be quick to reward any good performance. It is too easy to take the good for granted.

Punishment can often take the form of simply withholding the reward. If a sensitive horse has come to expect a pat on the neck or a free walk as a reward, he will notice its absence and attempt to behave in such a way that will reinstate the reward. Other mild punishments include the reprimand, "No!" (this can be devastating to some horses if spoken too harshly), or repetition of an exercise or of an aid until successfully obeyed and the reward has been earned.

If a stronger punishment is needed, one method is to halt the horse and keep him in place for several seconds or minutes, depending on the nature of the problem. His attention is captured, and he realizes that he'd rather move and behave as directed than be restrained. This is especially effective with a playful, spirited animal.

An active punishment is to speak sharply ("No!" or "Bad!"), combined with a slap on the neck with the open hand. Although the slap is not painful, the sound of it, along with your displeased voice, leaves the horse no choice but to understand your meaning. Other punishments that may occasionally be necessary are use of stronger aids (including spurs), pushing the horse into stronger forward motion, or one quick, effective use of crop or whip.

It is important for the trainer to know what form of punishment to use, and then to administer it immediately and calmly. Poorly administered punishment—too strong, ineffectual, or poorly timed—is probably the greatest cause of failure for beginning trainers. It is better not to punish at all than to do so too late or too strongly.

A horse will not understand the reason for the punishment if it occurs more than a second or two after the transgression; it must be dealt with instantly and in a manner that will not result in your loss of control. A trainer should never punish in anger or bad temper—this can only result in loss of confidence on the part of the horse as well as the loss of the pleasant atmosphere of training that should be of paramount importance.

Try to make peace with the horse as soon as possible after any punishment is given, thereby restoring and increasing his confidence. One way to do this is to ask him to perform an exercise that he enjoys and does well; then you may reward him and proceed on a positive note. It is vital for good training to keep and promote a horse's confidence.

HAND FEEDING

Hand feeding is a practice that can be a great aid to the trainer or that can lead to an accumulation of vices. Professional trainers have differing opinions on whether or not to give horses tidbits—some encourage it, with caution; others make it an adamant rule never to hand feed a horse.

Hand feeding generally implies giving a lump of sugar, a piece of carrot or apple, or a pellet of range cake to a horse from your hand. This can be very helpful in catching horses that run loose in a large pasture or on

Hand feeding can be an aid to catching horses in a pasture, but it can produce problems, too. This girl could be in a dangerous position if the youngsters began crowding and pushing to get to the food.

the range, because they know that there will be an immediate reward in coming to you. Hand feeding can help you gain the confidence of a frightened or shy animal, and in this way be a positive training aid. Some horses are not particularly sensitive to a caress or spoken praise—to reward them for a correctly performed exercise, a tidbit may be necessary to make them want to repeat the desirable action.

The trouble comes when a horse begins to demand treats. Wanting the tidbit so badly, he may begin nosing or nipping, or may even behave in an ill-tempered manner when the treat is not forthcoming. He behaves, in fact, like a spoiled child. If, when he acts this way, he is appeased by a treat, he is in effect being rewarded for his misbehavior. He loses all respect for the trainer and may develop serious and dangerous vices such as charging, biting, or kicking.

Hand feeding, then, is a practice that must be approached carefully. Its success or failure depends on the character of the individual horse. It can be a great aid, but always use it sparingly. Be alert; if you detect signs of greediness and overinterest in the treat, discontinue this method of reward. But be sure to replace it with another kind of reward.

CONFIDENCE, RESPECT, AND DISCIPLINE

A horse must have confidence in his trainer; he must know that the trainer will treat him fairly at all times, never punishing when the horse does not understand. A trainer must work constantly to keep and to increase a horse's confidence if the training is to proceed successfully.

Confidence is built through love, sensitivity, and consistency. A trainer must be consistent in the way he asks for an exercise, the way he corrects a mistake, the way he reacts to the horse's personality. Horses live by habit, and they come to expect certain results from certain actions. This attribute is a great help to the trainer, who can use it as a road to quicker, easier training if he retains the horse's confidence—that quality of knowing what to expect.

Respect is as necessary an ingredient for successful training as is confidence. Any horse that does not naturally respect humans must be taught to do so before training can proceed at all. Today, lack of respect is most often found among backyard pets who have actually become backyard pests; such horses are often more difficult to train than those that have had little contact with humans. Often, a backyard pest was raised from a foal when it seemed cute for him to nibble at people or to play tag. A thousand-pound horse that nips or runs over people is far from cute— he is downright dangerous, and his playful little quirks may develop into serious vices.

Discipline is as necessary for a horse as it is for a child. An undis-

A thousand-pound horse that nips or runs over people is far from cute. . . .

ciplined animal becomes unruly and dangerous. Ideally, discipline is attained by continual correct action—if every action of the horse is rewarded or gently corrected, the horse grows up in a naturally disciplined manner, having both confidence in and respect for his handler.

Of course, the ideal is usually a shining light in the distance, leaving us with some foggy problems right here at hand. Discipline is one requisite for respect—the horse must know that unruly behavior will be corrected. He must discover that it is more pleasant to behave properly.

One aspect of discipline applies as much to the trainer as to the horse —keeping a regular schedule. Again, this takes advantage of a horse's tendency toward habit. If he is in the habit of working at a particular time, he is mentally conditioned and ready to go when that time comes. The training session will proceed more smoothly and easily than if the horse must be pulled from some other activity or even a rest period, in which case a certain amount of time must be spent in simply convincing him that he must now go to work.

Schedules are designed to suit the particular horse to be trained. The young student horse is like a first-grade child; he has a short attention span and learns much by repetition. He should be worked often for short periods of time. He must learn how to learn, as well as to perform what is asked of him. A more experienced horse has learned how to concentrate and can therefore benefit from a longer lesson period.

Both the new trainee and the experienced student should be protected from boredom. Training requires repetition, but lessons should be kept varied and interesting. Ways of doing this are discussed in following chapters.

THE AIDS

The aids are signals given to a horse to help him understand what is expected of him. The natural aids include voice, hand (rein), weight, and

leg. Artificial aids are extensions of the natural aids and are used to reinforce the natural aids. For instance, spurs are reinforced leg aids; the whip
or crop may reinforce either rein or leg. Martingales may be considered
artificial aids that restrain more than they reinforce.

The trainer works to develop sensitive, refined aids. Watch the performance of a well-trained horse and rider—use of the aids is so refined as
to be almost imperceptible.

The aids in themselves are a system of reward and punishment. As
mentioned above, pressure may be considered as punishment; release, as
reward. The pressure of a rider's calves against the horse's sides signals the
horse to move forward. As he does so, the pressure is released.

Of course, the horse must learn to respond to these pressures. This is
done by means of the increasing aids. Pressure is first given very lightly,
then increased until the horse begins to respond. In some cases, it may be
necessary to reinforce leg pressure with the smart smack of the crop
behind the girth. When the desired act is performed successfully, the horse
is rewarded, and again the act is asked for lightly and sensitively. The
horse soon learns to respond to sensitive aids.

Take another illustration: teaching the horse to respond to rein signals. To train a green horse to turn, it may be necessary to pull his head
around with the leading or opening rein. Gradually, he learns to respond
to the lightest movement of a finger on the rein (direct reining).

IF A HORSE DOES NOT RESPOND TO THE AIDS

There are several reasons why a horse will not perform, and it is up to
the trainer to understand the reason before attempting to apply corrective
measures.

1. *Lack of understanding.* The horse does not understand what is expected of him. The trainer may be asking for more than the horse is mentally capable of obeying, most likely because the trainer is rushing his
training, or not building logically, step by step. Sometimes a horse does
not understand a command or an aid because it is ambiguous: The trainer
must learn to give his aids clearly and without conflicting overtones. The
clearer the trainer can be—the more precise the stimulus he gives—the
easier it will be for the horse to understand and therefore to obey. A
trainer must never punish a horse for failure to perform because he does
not understand. The failure to obtain response rests entirely with the
trainer. He must clarify his own methods until they become under-
standable.

2. *Good spirits.* A healthy animal—especially a youngster full of
good spirits—may sometimes want to play rather than to work. Either the

trainer must channel these spirits into the right path, or he must give the horse the proper outlet for his energies, perhaps providing an exercise area or pasture to play in before the training session. Maintenance of a definite schedule is especially helpful in handling this type of horse because it clearly defines the work period. Even so, a horse will sometimes evade the trainer through an excess of good spirits.

3. *Poor health.* A horse in unthrifty condition cannot perform properly if indeed he can perform at all. A trainer's first concern is to make sure his animal is in top physical condition and then to keep him that way. This requires a healthy balance of feed, exercise, and rest, and should include a checkup by a veterinarian to determine problems due to internal parasites, disease, or injury.

4. *Physical inability to perform.* A horse should not be asked to perform an exercise that is physically impossible for him. This is not as obvious as it may at first seem. Training develops a horse physically as well as mentally, building up muscles and improving suppleness and balance. A horse must be physically conditioned to bend and flex; he must build up the muscles in his hindquarters to be able to either collect or extend himself; he must learn to balance his weight during different movements both with and without a rider. The trainer must understand the horse's physical capabilities. Any attempt of the horse to perform an exercise approaching the present limits of his capabilities should be amply rewarded.

5. *Lack of attention.* If the training area has distractions—other horses, playing children, noisy traffic—a horse may have his attention anywhere but on the trainer, and therefore ignore signals or commands. It is the trainer's job to find a work area where concentration is possible, and then, through mild corrective action, insist on keeping the horse's attention during the work period.

6. *Fear or uncertainty.* The fault here is with the trainer or with the horse's earlier handling. Apparently the horse has been punished when he has not understood what was expected of him. He is confused and unhappy, afraid that no matter what he does, he will be punished. Under these circumstances, the trainer's first job is to restore confidence, giving great attention to rewards.

7. *Intentional disobedience.* When the trainer is sure that a horse is intentionally disobeying—not failing to perform because of misunderstanding, playfulness, physical or mental incapability, fear, or poor health—he must take immediate corrective action. He must be firm and clear with the horse, making him understand that evasion, rebellion, or disobedience get him nowhere and are not to be tolerated. At the same time, the trainer should examine his own methods carefully to determine whether he is at fault, either fully or partially. Rebellion and evasion are most often reactions to treatment by the handler. Sometimes an owner will send his horse to a trainer because he has become "mean and unmanagea-

ble." The owner fails to realize that his own insensitivity, poor judgment, or lack of knowledge of the horse's nature have caused the problem. The trainer has a difficult job of retraining, for he must first gain the horse's confidence. The owner is in even more need of training than the horse, but this is often a difficult and delicate subject to broach.

Remember that horses are not naturally mean. (Any exceptions to this are notable because they are so rare.) They are inherently timid, inclined to run from danger or unpleasantness. When unable to run, however, because of man's restraint, they resort to bad habits in retaliation.

However, it seems that resistances are natural in almost all training circumstances. Perhaps the horse is testing just how far he can go, how definite are the limits set up for him, how much he can get away with. Just as he must find his own place in the hierarchy of a horse herd, so he must establish his place in relation to you, his trainer. He must find out, and continually reassure himself, that you give the orders. When this is a pleasant relationship, he will usually do his utmost to please you.

Learn what makes a horse tick. It's your first and foremost requirement as a trainer.

CHAPTER 2

GENERAL CONDITIONS

OF TRAINING

Facilities and Care

A happy horse is usually a willing, receptive horse. Therefore it behooves us, as trainers, to be very concerned about the animal's well-being. Proper feed, care, and facilities will help to keep the horse in a receptive frame of mind.

Most of us must adapt existing facilities rather than plan new ones. If you are planning on training a horse, probably you already own one or more horses that you ride regularly for pleasure. Now perhaps you're planning on buying another horse to train for a particular purpose, or you've had your mare bred and are awaiting the foal. With this new member of the family, you may have to expand your facilities.

There are several factors to consider in training a horse that may be somewhat different from simply owning and riding one, especially if you are involved in elementary training. The type of training facilities you need will depend to some degree on the way you plan to keep your horse. There are many different ways to care for a horse, from keeping him continually housed to keeping him out on the range year-round except for brief spurts of riding activity. You will have to make arrangements that are most convenient for you and that will allow you to do the best possible job with your horse.

GENERAL CONDITIONS IN EAST AND WEST: HOW DO THEY AFFECT YOUR HORSE?

To oversimplify, kinds of horse care may be broadly divided into Eastern and Western, stemming from differences in the type of country and use of the animal.

The wooded hills and country roads of the East, together with a wetter, lusher climate and smaller acreage necessary to support one animal, are conducive to small pastures, riding rings, and stables. Eastern horses are generally used for recreation; therefore they are most likely to be kept in a place convenient to the owner and to be ridden often. Pleasure riding may take the form of hunting, hacking along the scenic back roads, or, where this is limited, practice in the ring or over a jump course leading to culmination in horse shows and meets. Because space is so often a factor, many horses are kept stalled continually except for controlled exercise such as riding or longeing. Eastern horses grow up in the midst of human handling and companionship; they learn from the beginning that people are the source of their food, exercise, and comfort.

On the other hand, the open spaces of the West, where many acres of sparse vegetation are needed to support a single animal, provide a natural, free habitat where horses can pretty much take care of themselves. They are used for work in many cases, and even the pleasure horse has inherited the general care-situation of his cowhorse brothers. Living in large, uncontrolled areas, Western horses are brought in only as they are needed—when the cattle must be moved, or when the horses themselves are to be branded, castrated, or halter-broken. Usually the Western horse's first experiences with humans are unpleasant, setting a threatening and wary pattern in his mind.

Both of these situations, however, along with the many in-between and combination conditions, have their advantages and disadvantages. Let's consider these briefly.

Eastern horses are generally kept close to home; they are conveniently on hand and waiting for you when you're ready to work with them. (Of course, many horses are kept at riding stables of various kinds, but under these circumstances, any training you do at a boarding stable will probably be advanced enough to preclude the need for any training area but the ring provided.) But the convenience of constant stabling is offset by the disadvantage of the horse's need for exercise. Taken directly from the stall, the horse will be brimming with energy—posing a problem for the trainer. What young horse will settle down to work when he's longing to run and kick up his heels?

Further, failure to exercise a horse sufficiently is one of the horse owner's most common failings. He may neglect routine exercise even though he may be well aware of correct feeding and sanitary stabling. As explained in Part V, Chapter 1, lack of exercise causes boredom and frustration, leading to vices such as weaving and cribbing.

Another problem with stalled horses is that they have no opportunity to encounter and become accustomed to regular outdoor phenomena on their own. They are more likely to be fearful of and shy at strange objects or situations; sudden movements made by rabbits, birds, or flying papers; noises made by passing trucks or motorcycles; and unusual weather conditions such as wind or hail. Training these horses for the trail may require a lot more time and patience than is required for a Western outdoor horse.

Western horses, growing up free in open country, exercise themselves and develop good feet and legs and excellent wind. Generally they are healthy and strong, well able to fend for themselves. They establish their own place among the hierarchy of horseflesh they live with and are naturally gregarious. They are accustomed to conditions on the range and so adapt more easily to trail riding than the stalled horse does. Their instincts are usually good, and they will naturally avoid dangerous terrain and situations if allowed to do so. Many riders trust to their horse's judgment to take them safely through problem situations.

Disadvantages here stem from the horse's early fear and distrust of humans: It may take many more hours for the Western trainer to gain his horse's confidence than for his Eastern counterpart to do so. Unless a trainer plans to use the "enslavement" method of training, he must first win the horse's confidence before effective training can proceed. This horse, taken out of his natural environment, should be offered pleasant surroundings and much attention and praise from the human who is now taking the place of his equine friends. The trainer should be especially careful to avoid giving any cause for punishment. The Western horse, unless roughly trained, is usually relatively free from vices, except perhaps for being hard to catch.

Which system is better? No doubt, the ideal would combine features of both: large pastures, allowing natural feeding and plenty of fresh air and exercise, with enough pleasant contact with humans to ensure the horse's trust, confidence, and respect. If the trainer is aware of the shortcomings of the system he must work with, he will take steps to correct or counteract them. He will make sure his stalled horse has adequate exercise before a training session; he will work patiently with his range colt to establish a bond of confidence. He will take the time to do what needs to be done.

FEED AND MANAGEMENT

No matter where you and your horse live or what kind of situation you have, the correct balance of feed and exercise is important: Don't stuff your horse just because he has started to work. Causing founder or azoturia (Monday morning sickness) is not a kindness. Any changes in a horse's diet should be made slowly, over a period of several days, sometimes weeks. Feed a variety of grain and nutritious, well-cured, sweet-smelling hay. Water, salt, and other minerals should be adequate for the animal's good health.

It pays to take pains to ensure your horse's comfort in his surroundings—a comfortable, airy shelter and a large, safe place to exercise. He will be more content if he can be near other horses, or at least be provided with substitute companionship.

Regular, complete grooming is an important step in the training process and is necessary for the well-being of any horse. When you finish with the initial training of your horse, he should be in shape to enter a halter class. In fact, he should be in better form after training than before, since muscling and overall condition are improved.

A horse is only as good as his feet and legs. Check his feet for stones and other foreign matter before and after each training session. This in itself is good training, as any horse should learn early to allow his feet and legs to be handled.

YOUR HORSE'S LIVING QUARTERS

Training is a daily affair. Under some circumstances, a trainer may work with a horse three or more times a day. Therefore it is essential to keep the horse nearby during any training period. In some cases, this is the normal state of affairs; for a range colt, it will be a radical departure from what he's used to. What are the main considerations when keeping a horse relatively confined?

Health, safety, comfort, and convenience should be considered, and these should include proper exercise, feed, and care. A horse capable of taking care of himself on the range will nevertheless need special consideration in a corral.

Any horse undergoing training should have some sort of shelter. This can be an open shed that he may use if he wishes; it may be a well-appointed stable, or something in between. You'll save time and frustration if you have some area where you can keep the horse inside during bad or wet weather—it's hard to put a saddle on an ice-coated horse!

The ideal would be a large (at least twelve feet by twelve feet), airy (but not drafty) box stall with a dirt floor. Wooden flooring holds dampness and absorbs bacteria from urine; concrete floors are hard on feet and legs. In any case, stalls should be well bedded, well ventilated and frequently cleaned. There's no need to heat your stable—horses do better without extra heat, provided that they are not subject to drafts. Doors, gates, corridors all should be wide enough to allow the horse to pass through with room to spare—it is easy for a horse to injure himself by banging a hip or leg against a doorjamb. It would be nice to have running water available in or near the stable area, but you can get by with hauling water.

Safety is important, and all aspects of safety should be considered both for your horse and yourself. Look over the stall for loose or rotten boards or wires, both on the walls and the floor. Check for nails, splinters, and other protrusions. Be aware of danger spots where a horse might catch a foot, or even put his head through and catch it when he tries to come back—horses panic easily and may injure themselves by pulling or throwing themselves when actually the danger is minimal. Flooring should be nonslippery; this can be a problem in winter if snow balls up on the horse's feet.

Consider fire hazards and take precautions—proximity to water, fire extinguishers on the walls that everyone knows how to use, "NO SMOK-ING" signs that are rigidly enforced. If your stable shares a garage area, special care should be used to keep the garage free of oil cans, rags, and the like, and to be sure the stable is well ventilated.

Avoid tight, narrow, or otherwise cramped space that you and your horse must work in or walk through. Giving yourself and your horse enough room—overhead and all around—is always a good safety precaution.

Pastures, paddocks, corrals, yards, and pens should all be subject to the same safety check. These areas should be well drained and not too rocky. Junk, old cars and parts, and abandoned rolls of barbed wire are potential traps that can catch a horse's feet and legs, causing breaks or other serious injury. We know of one valuable and well-trained horse that bled to death when he caught his foot in some half-buried barbed wire; one of the barbs cut a near-the-surface digital vein in his pastern. Watch too for culs-de-sac in pastures and corrals where a small or timid horse could be trapped and kicked, injured, or even killed by a bigger, more dominant animal.

Wire fence is a problem no matter how you look at it—woven wire becomes a trap for feet and legs; barbed wire can cause deep, ragged cuts and atrocious scars. Most Western horses learn to respect barbed wire, but a lot of them are scarred for life because of it. Never put a range colt into a wire paddock until he becomes calm and manageable; keep him instead within slab, board, round metal, or corral-pole enclosures.

In some cases, it is best for a horse in training to be kept alone, away from other horses. More often, a horse will be more relaxed and comfortable if he can rest after the training session with congenial companions. When introducing new horses it is often best to let them become acquainted across a stout pole fence before putting them together in one corral. Even then, trouble may occur, depending upon their dispositions, until their pecking order has been established.

YOUR TRAINING AREA

If you've ever tried to lead an untrained stallion through a pasture of soft-eyed mares, or if you've ever tried to walk a big, semihalter-broken gelding down a dusty road in a windstorm, you'll know that in most cases, your training area should be adjacent to your horse's living quarters. The only time this might not apply is if all the horses you handle are already halter-broken and reasonably well mannered. Proximity of training area and stable allows you a safe walk from one area to the other, relatively free of potentially disastrous situations—and this is important because avoiding mistakes, as we discussed in Chapter 1, is infinitely better than trying to correct their results. Even if something does go wrong, the horse is still confined within barn, alleyway, or corral, and is not likely to precipitate a calamity.

Also important is for your tack room to be close to the training area, or at least for you to have a convenient place to keep tack during the training session, so that it is off the ground and out of the way but still readily available.

Of course, it would be ideal to have an uncluttered indoor arena with stalls and alleyways, two riding rings (small and large), tack room, and grooming area. But you can make your facilities work for you, usually with a minimum of cost, if you think it out imaginatively.

What exactly do you need?

First, an indoor grooming area, unless you live where the rain never falls and the wind never blows and there's no such thing as snow. This can be the horse's stall, if the stall is fitted with crossties, an alleyway in the barn, or any other place where crossties may be affixed and where there is enough space to give you plenty of room around your horse. Crossties are important, both for your convenience and safety, and as a simple training aid—it's easier to teach a horse to stand still if he can't roam all around. The grooming area should be—at first—a place where the horse feels secure and comfortable and where outside distractions are minimal. Later, it may be well to groom the horse in busier areas where he can become accustomed to noise, pets, wheelbarrows, and the like, but at first you want to encourage confidence, security, and calm. Your grooming area should include a convenient shelf for the tools, or you may arrange a portable grooming kit.

Second, you need a small corral or ring with high sides. Ideally, this would be between 35 and 45 feet in diameter. The corral must be small enough to insure control and high enough to discourage jumping. If the walls are solid—perhaps built of slabs or boards—distractions will be kept to a minimum and the horse will have nowhere to put his attention but on his trainer. Most trainers prefer this small corral to be round, so that the horse can't zero in on the corners, but square will do. The important thing is not to start your training in too large an area, thereby leaving yourself open to loss of control, and leaving your horse open to the development of such unpleasant vices as running away with the longe line or lead rope. Horses are usually less excitable when enclosed, so again, the small corral is important.

Third, you need a large, well-fenced riding ring. The regulation size is 120 feet by 60 feet, which is nice if you have room for it. The ring should be large enough so that a green horse can canter or lope in balance. If it is too small, the young horse has difficulty in balancing his own weight, and even more difficulty in adjusting to the weight of a rider. Also, a full-sized ring encourages forward movement and the development of a long, free stride. If there's no help for it—if the largest ring area you have is still too small—help your horse to adjust to the smaller circles by longeing him, first without, and finally with, a rider. Also, you could start your canter on straight lines the length of the ring or in a larger but well-fenced pasture. Begin riding in larger areas as soon as you feel safe in doing so.

The ground of both the large and small training areas should be flat and soft so that the continual impact will not produce leg ailments such as splints. Of course, it should not be a mud wallow either—if yours is the kind of soil that turns to taffy after a prolonged rain or during spring thaw, you'll have to avoid faster work until you have firmer footing. At any rate, keep your training area free of stones, and if you have to plow it up several times a year to unpack the dirt, do so. Indoor arenas may get very dusty—you'll have to wet them down frequently or you may try putting down a two-inch to three-inch layer of sawdust (in some areas you can get sawdust free for the hauling from a sawmill). For an even better footing, sawdust and oil is springy yet firm, and there is no dust. Most rings, especially the indoor arenas, may need leveling occasionally. You should not let the "track" become a trench.

If you are planning to train any animal that isn't halter-broken, you'll need one more piece of built-in equipment. We're not talking about foals here, but any horse that is old enough and big enough to be stronger than you are—and he doesn't have to be very old before he gets to that point. A horse must be halter-trained before you can work any further with him. For this purpose you need a stout post or upright set in concrete. Some trainers have a special corral with a snubbing post in the center. If one of the wall posts of your small corral is planned for this purpose, it would work very well. The horse must learn from the beginning that he can't get away—you must have an unmovable, unbreakable post and strong halters and ropes.

Equipment
for Early Training

There is a great variety of equipment designed for training horses. Some items are basic and useful; a lot are gimmicks that insecure trainers use instead of proper training. Most trainers use standard equipment such as halter, lead rope, snaffle bit and bridle, and a saddle. And each trainer uses more specialized equipment that works especially well for him: perhaps a longe line and whip, longeing cavesson, Spanish hackamore, surcingle, elastic side reins, long reins, and a variety of bits. Some training devices may be used with success by professional trainers who have the know-how and experience to apply the device to correct a retraining problem; the same device used by an amateur on a young horse might be a fatal mistake.

Having a variety of basic equipment and knowing how to use it can help make training sessions proceed smoothly and quickly. Quality equipment is a great aid in training. At the same time, many of us don't have the money to rush out and buy a lot of expensive equipment no matter how good it is or how much we think we need it. You can substitute some items for others, or you may be able to make or adapt your own versions.

To be useful, all equipment must be subject to a three-point check:

1. It must be strong.
2. It must fit and be comfortable.
3. You must know how to use it.

Only strong equipment is safe, and no piece of equipment is stronger than its weakest point. It must be comfortable to the horse; if it causes discomfort, the desired effect of the equipment will be lost. New tack should be broken in slowly or it could rub sore places on the horse's flesh. And it must fit: Know how to fit any piece of equipment properly. Poor fit either causes discomfort or destroys the effectiveness.

If a piece of equipment is new to you, try it out first on a horse trained to its use. Or, if this isn't possible, try it out on a calm, experienced horse before using it on the young recruit. The point is that you should know what you're doing before using your trainee as a guinea pig. For instance, using a longe line looks easy when you watch a professional with a trained horse. But we've seen beginners get so wound up in the line that they couldn't even stand up. This might be a hilarious show with a wise, patient old horse at the end of the line, but with a youngster, it could be disaster. And tying you both up in knots won't help the training process.

*Try out new equipment on a quiet, experienced horse . . . beginners can get
all wound up in a longe line.*

YOUR BASIC TRAINING EQUIPMENT

Halters. Halters come in rope, webbing, and leather; rope halters are
sometimes called Johnson halters, for a company that makes them. All
varieties should fit the head snugly but not tightly (you can choose among
several sizes and make further adjustments on the horse). It's dangerous
to leave a halter on when turning a horse out to pasture: The horse could
catch the halter on something, or, if it's loose enough, catch his own foot
in it and not be able to undo himself. Leaving a halter on continually can
be uncomfortable for the horse and can leave him with rubbed areas and
unsightly scars.

Rope halters may shrink when wet, causing discomfort or real torture
and injury if left on a horse during a rainstorm. We soak and dry rope halters before adjusting them on the horse to avoid this possibility.

Wide web halters are good because they're strong, won't shrink, have
less tendency to rub, and can be washed. They're neat and come in a
choice of colors. However, they're usually not as quick and easy to buckle
on as the rope halters, and some are not as adjustable. Web safety halters
are now available; they are designed to release if they become caught, and
may be left on hard-to-catch horses.

Most leather halters won't rub once they're broken in and the stiffness is gone. They are most durable if well cared for, but will break with age if they are allowed to dry out and crack. Good oil and elbow grease keep them strong, supple, and elegant-looking.

Lead ropes. For training, your lead rope should be at least ten feet long and have a very strong snap. Use a heavier rope than you would use for an ordinary lead. A three-quarter-inch cotton rope is a good size and will not burn you or your horse.

Longeing equipment. For longeing you'll need a surcingle or saddle pad, a longeing cavesson or hackamore (yes, you can use a halter or bridle in some cases—we'll go into this later), two longe lines, and a longeing whip. Elastic side reins can be a big help when first asking the horse to feel restraint on his mouth. We'll cover this equipment in detail in Part II, Chapter 2.

Spanish hackamore. The hackamore is a type of bitless bridle that controls the horse through pressure of the noseband on the bones of the nose; it also applies pressure under the jaw. Correct adjustment and fit of the bosal are important; the effectiveness of the hackamore is greatly reduced if it is incorrectly fitted. The bosal should be from three-quarter inch to one inch in diameter, fitting snugly around the muzzle, and resting on the prominent nose bones above the nostrils. The reins are attached above the heel knot.

Bits and bridles. Training bits should be thick and fairly heavy, with either full or half cheeks to keep the bit correctly centered and prevent its sliding through the mouth. The purpose of your training should be to produce a sensitive, responsive mouth, and this can best be done with a mild bit. Curbs, spades, and other bits with nonmovable parts and long shanks have no place in the initial stages of training.

The breaking or mouthing bit consists of a large round bar with an attachment of small movable pendants in the center. These encourage the colt to mouth his bit, which in turn helps to produce a sensitive mouth. The mouthing bit can also be of snaffle construction, with the pendants hanging from a small center ring.

Other useful bits in the early stages of training are the egg butt bit, the hard rubber-mouth snaffle (bar type), and snaffle varieties of the dee bit.

Saddles. A training saddle should be light in weight and should fit the horse's back. By avoiding undue discomfort at the outset, training will progress more smoothly.

The felt saddle pad is ideal for training because it is lightweight, versatile, strong, and pliable; because it conforms to the animal's shape, it doesn't pinch or rub. It is shaped like an English saddle, but without a tree. Made of three-quarter-inch felt, it is reinforced with leather at obvious pressure points. The strong wide girth (made of heavy duck or webbing) is attached through the saddle so as to go completely around the horse like a surcingle, thereby preventing problems, such as the stitching coming loose. The ends of the cinch are heavy leather. (The girth should be replaced when old, as the webbing material can rot when it becomes hard and sweat-laden.) The pad comes equipped with safety stirrup bars so that the stirrups may be easily removed.

An English saddle, with felt or sheepskin pad, is useful for early training, provided it fits the horse's back properly. A horse with wide withers needs a saddle with a wide tree and gullet. If the gullet is too narrow, the saddle can roll to the side, frightening the horse or causing discomfort or sores. Although the type of English saddle is generally immaterial, be cautious about using either the McClellan saddle or military-type English saddle, both of which were designed for narrow withers and therefore tend to roll easily on some horses.

Because a horse's back muscles must be developed to carry weight, we prefer a light saddle for early training. However, if a Western saddle is all you have, it can be adapted. Use adequate padding—felt or wool blankets—but not so much that the saddle tends to slip sideways. Tie up loose saddle strings so that they won't flap or get caught in other tack. Remove the rear cinch until the horse is reasonably used to being cinched up—if tight, the rear cinch may tend to encourage a green horse to buck; or, if it is loose, the horse may accidentally catch a foot when kicking at a fly. A roping saddle, with low, wide horn and cantle, is preferable for training because it is easier and safer for quick mounting and dismounting, and this in turn encourages the horse to stand quietly.

Use blankets or saddle pads of wool or felt. Avoid foam-rubber pads, as they tend to retain moisture and cause saddle sores.

Surcingle. The surcingle or training roller is a cinchlike band—usually made from padded, reinforced webbing—equipped with rings and dees so that side reins, crupper, overchecks, and so on may be attached easily. The more expensive surcingles are leather-covered. It fastens around the barrel, and should be buckled snugly as far forward as possible. Surcingles or cinches that work back on the barrel can end up as bucking rigs—and that is not our goal!

CARE, STORAGE, AND SAFETY

Safe tack is of prime importance. It is safe when it fits and when it's clean and strong. Start with good equipment—it's better to make do with less than to buy cheap tack.

As tack is used, it must be inspected regularly, especially around girths and other pressure points. Check leather parts that crease or wear, such as where the bit attaches to the headstall, where cinches are attached to dee rings, and where stirrup leathers are creased to hold stirrup irons. Check you longeing cavesson and longe line for strength.

Part and parcel of this regular inspection should be regular cleaning. Leather should be sponged and saddle-soaped, then treated with leather conditioner. Metal parts, including stirrups and bits, can be cleaned with steel wool if dirt doesn't yield to a soap and water scrubbing. Wash longe lines and web or string girths in warm, soapy water (but try to keep leather parts from getting wet).

When a piece of equipment becomes old or worn, replace it. Don't take chances with training equipment. If it's going to break, it will do so at the worst possible time—when the horse is acting up or is frightened. When equipment breaks under these circumstances, the horse learns a lesson you didn't intend to teach. If the longe line breaks and he runs off, he's sure to try it again. Worse, if you're mounting a spooky youngster for one of his first rides and the cinch breaks, you're likely to be injured, and there will be a long haul retraining the horse.

Check everything. Some bridles are constructed with screws where the leather creases to hold the bit. One day, when a student was riding her three-year-old filly alone on the trail, the bit suddenly fell out of the horse's mouth. The screw had worked loose and the leather simply unfolded and let go of the bit. If the filly hadn't been trained to stop immediately on the word "Whoa," a bad accident could have occurred. We know of another case where the curb shank of a grazing bit cracked and then broke off when the horse was being ridden; again the horse stopped on command.

Store your tack in a special room or area where horses can't get to it (they love to chew on saddle strings or reins), and where raccoons, mice, cats, and chickens won't be tempted to use it to nibble on, curl up under, hop around over, or lay eggs in. Each saddle should have its own rack; each bridle, its own hook. Avoid nails as bridle-hangers, though; the leather will keep better and fit better if it is stored over a rounded hanger such as a wood block cut from a post about four or five inches in diameter. Or, if nothing else, an empty tin can will do. Leave leather reins hanging straight down or loosely looped. If you must tie or knot leather reins or lines when using them, always untie the knots so that the reins may be stored flat; if knots are allowed to stay, the leather will be kinked and damaged, and the reins will no longer lie flat against your horse's neck. Saddle racks can be handsome, store-bought affairs, or they can be made from wooden boards or poles.

Before You Begin Training

The process of training is a relationship-in-progress between the trainer and the horse. Two conditions of this relationship must always be present before basic training can proceed properly—they must be established before any attempt at training begins, and, if they are ever lost, they must be re-established before training can continue. These conditions are:

- •The horse must trust you and have confidence in you.
- •The horse must respect you.

Inherent in these conditions, of course, is the implication that you warrant the horse's trust and respect.

In some cases, these conditions will be ready-made or quickly established in your relationship, and training may begin almost immediately. In others, the establishment of confidence or respect may take weeks of your time before actual training begins. What will you have to do?

Before going further, let's clarify terms and distinguish between foals and other horses. Foals and weanlings are babies and must be handled as such. Even yearlings demand a different type of handling than the 2-to-3-year-old. We'll consider training these youngsters later.

Different again is training an older, mature horse, if you're starting right from scratch. Training such animals (and horses with special training problems) usually requires professional knowledge, experience, and equipment. This will be considered in Part V.

Most horses, although they may be halter-broken and handled as foals, receive the major part of their training when they are old enough to ride. For clarity and continuity, we'll assume your horse is at least 2½ or 3 years old—still young and immature, but old enough to be ridden lightly.

DEVELOPING CONFIDENCE AND RESPECT

Your first job here is to evaluate your horse, as we discussed in Part I, Chapter 1. Spend some time observing him. See how he reacts to humans in general, to you in particular, and to other aspects of his environment. Is he afraid? Fearless and sassy? Friendly but frivolous?

A young Western range colt needs to gain confidence; he needs to learn that humans can be friends. Keep him in a corral by himself and visit him several times a day. Feed him and work with him yourself. You are taking the place of the herd leader, giving him the leadership and companionship he no longer is getting from his friends. Some horses will conform readily to the new situation, while others will be wary of all new experiences and require more initial gentling. Your horse should become accustomed to your voice and start coming to you for an occasional tidbit (grain cube, carrot, or apple) or a caress. If he becomes nippy, don't feed tidbits; instead, stroke his neck and talk pleasantly to him. He will learn to associate the tone of voice and the pats with a reward, and this already sets a good pattern for your training lessons. Make no demands upon the animal until you feel that he has accepted you and looks forward to your frequent visits.

Usually the young horse that is used to human companionship will not need this initial gentling. However, some of these horses may have become too bold, or may have developed bad manners. In this case, respect must be taught, and you would do better to start with halter and rope rather than visit the horse loose in his corral or paddock.

What it comes down to, then, is establishing control, both physically and psychologically, through patience, love, firmness, and consistency— not through force and fear. As you develop your horse's confidence and trust, you are gaining psychological control; as you develop his respect for you, you are gaining physical control. Both confidence and respect should be developed together: Never sacrifice one for the other.

Your first step in the establishment of this control is to be able to lead the horse and to tie him. He must respect the lead rope. Until you have this control of the horse's head, you cannot proceed with training, or even with gentling. Most Eastern horses and many Western horses will already be halter-broken when you begin working with them at this age. If this is your first experience with training a green youngster, it would be best for you to be sure your horse is halter-broken when you get him (of course, he will be if you raised him yourself from a foal), or to have an experienced horseman help you with these initial stages. It is vitally important that the youngster learn he cannot get away from you—and that he doesn't *want* to break away—when you hold the lead rope. He must be absolutely convinced that you and your equipment are invincible! (Nonsense, of course, but you must nevertheless convince the horse that it is so.)

How? That is what halter-breaking is all about.

HALTERING

As you gain experience in working with different horses, you will begin to get the hang of doing the right thing at the right time to avoid creating problems. Some horses will work well one way; some will need a different approach. Gradually you'll find the method that works well for you, as long as you stay flexible enough to meet each varying situation.

Let's assume that the young gelding you've just acquired is friendly, pleasantly dispositioned, and fairly calm. You've taken some time to get to know him and he'll come over to you to have his ears scratched. He has decided to trust you. Perhaps he's already had some halter-training when he was a youngster, but you don't know for sure. When all goes as it should—and it sometimes does—you might proceed like this (of course, you'll be working in the small corral):

Hold the halter in your left hand, and when you visit with him, let him sniff at it while you stroke his neck and rub his ears and head. Moving slowly and talking gently, gradually move the halter around his head and neck, rubbing it against him and finally slipping it in place. A rope halter is good for this purpose because it is strong and quick and easy to fasten.

Now, either that was a simple, easy thing to do—and in most cases it is, if you've prepared properly—or he shied away, threw his head, or otherwise didn't let you get the halter on at all. Supposing the worst, let's give it another try. If he's a range colt, he may have been roped but never haltered. You may do better to hold the lead rope around his neck and then halter him. Many horses respect the feel of the rope against the neck and will stand still.

Still didn't get the halter on? You should know by now whether a little more patience will turn the tide or whether you've got bigger problems. Don't spend forever at this stage. The time for easy going is back there when you're first starting. If you did your preliminary groundwork and you still make several unsuccessful attempts, the horse figures he's got your number. You'll have to get him haltered now or he'll lose respect for you and you'll be encouraging him in the wrong direction. You may be able to get someone to help you, especially someone experienced. You may be able to work the horse into a more confined area, but if you're inexperienced yourself, this could be dangerous. Some horses will simply have to be roped and snubbed down and you go from there (see Part V), but this is usually the case only with older range horses. Probably everything went just fine, and there you stand with your haltered horse.

LEADING

Always remember that the order of these basic, pretraining steps will vary according to the horse you're working with. Many horses—especially those Eastern-trained—will learn quickest, easiest, and most painlessly for all concerned, in the order we're prescribing here. But some will require complete halter-training before you can begin to lead them successfully. Experience and common sense will guide you.

Use a long, heavy lead rope as described under Equipment for Early Training. Attach it to the halter ring (you may find it more convenient to have the lead rope already attached when you halter the horse). Hold the bight of the lead rope in a serpentinelike fold as shown in the illustration. Never hold the rope in loops around your hand or wrist—if the horse were to spook and run, the loops could tighten around you, and you could be dragged (and this could do far more to frighten and harm your horse from

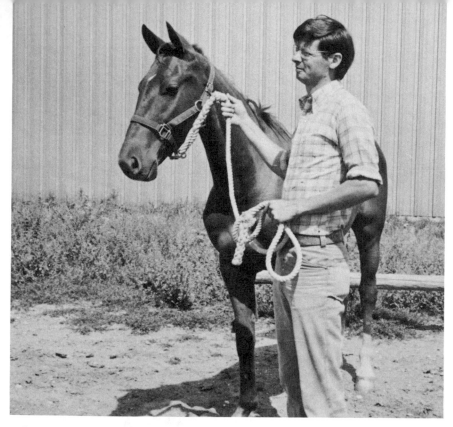

When training your horse to lead, use a long, heavy lead rope and carry the bight folded in your left hand.

a training aspect than if he simply got away from you in a small corral). The reasons for the long, heavy rope are several:

•The extra length gives you an advantage if the colt should shy or spook: By using your thigh or hip for leverage, you have a much better chance of holding him.
•The extra thickness gives you a firmer grip.
•If it is cotton, it won't burn if it slips through your hands a little, and, if the colt gets a leg over it, it won't burn him (be sure to use gloves if the rope is anything but cotton).
•Using a longer lead gives you more maneuverability—you'll find it works better than a longe line when you first start the horse longeing.
•A heavy rope has more stability, won't flap in the wind, and gives the horse the definite knowledge that you're there and have a hold on him.

We do nothing but lead the horse for the next two days, depending, of course, on his reactions. He's learning a lot here, so although this may seem simple to the point of simplemindedness, consider what's involved.

Teach the young horse to walk along briskly beside you.

First, your consistency sets the pattern of the training sessions. He will be continually reassured by your praises and pats when he obeys or does as you wish. He becomes attuned to your voice, learning the tone of praise indicating he is pleasing you and doing well. He'll begin looking for this. He finds that these lessons—short and undemanding—can be pleasant, something to look forward to.

Second, he is learning vocal commands. Although "Walk" and "Whoa" are the only two words he'll need to know at first, both are important. Further, he is learning the language that will be used later in longeing and riding. Again, consistency.

Third, he is learning physical commands. At first just a tug on the halter, these will later develop into a full range of aids.

Fourth, he is learning how to concentrate. That's why your beginning lessons must be short and frequent. He's used to listing with the wind, so to speak—letting his attention wander to whatever goes by. Now he must learn to pay attention to you. For the first time, he is learning to do as you want him to, rather than to do what he pleases.

Stand by your horse's left shoulder; hold the lead rope in your right hand close to the halter (but not restricting his head unduly), and hold the bight of the lead in your left hand. To go forward, give a gentle tug forward and say, "W-a-l-k." Give the physical and vocal commands simultaneously. Draw out the word "Walk" to make it distinctive and easily distinguishable from the short, sharper "Whoa!" The tone of your voice and the way you speak are important: Keep them consistent. Your voice should be firm and loud enough for the horse to hear and to be kept alert, but don't shout.

If the horse doesn't want to move forward at first, he probably doesn't understand what you want him to do. Encourage him by moving his head sideways toward you—he'll have to take a step to keep his balance and,.

when you praise him for this, he'll usually move on with you. Avoid tugging straight forward, as this rarely helps and can degenerate into a pulling contest.

Go a few steps and stop the horse by tugging toward his chest and saying, "Whoa!" When he stops, repeat the word to him several times so that he associates it with stopping and standing still. And of course praise him, pat him, make much of him. One of the most important words for your horse to learn is "Whoa." If a green horse is frightened when under saddle, the command "Whoa!" is familiar and reassuring; it gives him something definite to do (assuming that his reaction to the command is automatic); and it is a safety factor for both horse and rider.

Continue to lead the colt around the corral, varying the number of steps between "Walk" and "Whoa" so that he doesn't anticipate the commands. From the very start, teach him to stand when you face him and to move out when you are beside him. Encouraging him to walk briskly will help to keep him alert, and a good, fast walk is desirable no matter how you plan to use your horse.

These first lessons in leading should last about five minutes, but should be repeated six to eight times during the first and second days. When the colt leads fairly well, move to his right shoulder and lead him from the off side. Although leading from the left is correct, he should learn to lead willingly, briskly, and calmly from either side. There may be times when you will have to lead two horses at once, or when for some reason it is most desirable to lead from the right. Further, it will be easier to teach your horse to longe in both directions if, from the beginning, he is used to seeing you on either side.

When he leads well at a walk in both directions and stops readily, it is time to lead at the trot. It is helpful to have an assistant when you first begin: He can walk behind the colt to encourage him to trot on. Say "Trot" in a short, brisk tone, tug forward on the halter, and begin trotting yourself, even if you're jogging in place. Praise him and repeat "Trot" several times when he trots with you. If he doesn't move on, try clicking to him in a regular trotting rhythm. If you are alone and the colt doesn't understand what you want, you may try flicking the bight of the lead rope around behind you to his hindquarters. However, it's hard to aim and have the rope flick him in the right place. Further, the colt tends to move his hindquarters away from you so that he is two-tracking instead of moving forward. A training whip is especially useful to encourage the colt to trot: Its long stock and short lash let you touch the colt on the hindquarters without pushing him out of line. It often helps to plan the trotting part of his first lesson so that he is heading downhill, toward the barn, or toward a favorite buddy. Keep him alert and he will be more apt to move forward briskly.

A training whip, held in the left hand, may be used to encourage the colt to move forward without pushing him out of line. Here a longe whip is used, the lash held with the stock; it can be turned with a slight wrist movement to touch the colt low on the hindquarters. (Photo by Sandy Whittaker)

TEACHING TO STAND TIED

With some colts, you'll have to teach them to stand quietly when tied before you can proceed with the lessons in leading. As with all phases of training, there are many ways to accomplish the task.

Attach a long lead rope or lariat rope to the colt's halter, pass it around your snubbing post, and hold one end in a serpentinelike fold as shown. The long rope and leverage of the post give you control. You can give and take as necessary, while you calm him by speaking to him and stroking him. Work up toward the post by shortening the rope.

When he accepts this calmly and will stand quietly by the post, it is time to tie him. To make this arrangement especially safe and useful, set a strong inner tube around the post about 4½ to 5 feet from the ground. If a colt is tied to the inner tube rather than to a solid object, the resulting elasticity helps to prevent any muscle strain on his neck and also helps to keep halters and ropes from breaking when he pulls back. The tube should be high enough so that the colt won't get his foot over the rope if he rears,

When teaching some horses to stand tied, you may need the extra leverage and control provided by passing a long lead or lariat rope around your snubbing post. (Photo by Sandy Whittaker)

and so that any strain on his neck and shoulders comes from above—if a horse's head is tied low and he sets back, he can injure his neck and shoulder muscles.

Tie the lead rope to the inner tube with a nonslip, quick-release knot. You'll want to be able to release the rope immediately if something goes wrong. (It's wise to carry a pocket knife when working with horses and ropes—you'll probably never need it, but if you do, there won't be time to run to the house to rummage for one.) Tie him short: About 3 feet of combined inner tube and rope should be plenty—too much rope leaves the situation wide open for tangles or disaster.

The colt will probably set back, either pulling or rearing, fighting against the rope. Using the inner tube gives you several advantages in this battle:

•The tube gives and takes with the horse and is strong enough to withstand his most violent efforts.

•The give-and-take action is gentle rather than sudden: Ropes,

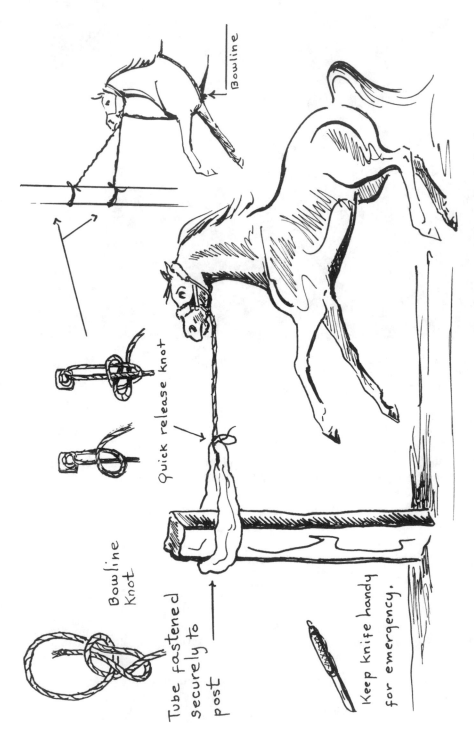

Bowline

Quick release knot

Bowline Knot

Tube fastened securely to post

Keep knife handy for emergency.

In teaching the colt to stand tied, use a quick-release knot and keep a knife handy.

buckles, and halters are much less likely to break than if the colt sets back against a solid upright.

•The tube itself acts as a training aid, encouraging the colt to move forward: When he relaxes and steps forward, pressure is released. He learns to move forward to avoid pressure.

•Tying to an inner tube is a safety factor for the colt. He can't break his neck or strain his muscles, as is possible if he suddenly comes to the end of an immovable rope and post.

Tie to the inner tube as often as is necessary until you're sure the fight with the rope is over. He may then be tied to a solid upright. Never tie a horse to horizontal corral poles or fence boards; it is too easy for them to break or come loose, which will frighten him. A horse running with a pole tied to his lead rope—perhaps with nails protruding from the ends—will most likely result in catastrophe for himself, his stablemates, or a luckless human bystander.

LEADING FROM HORSEBACK

When a colt respects the rope, you may lead him from horseback beside an older, steady horse that he knows and likes. Some trainers like to begin their training in this way, but they are experienced in dallying the rope around the horn of a Western saddle and in managing two horses at once. For less experienced trainers, or for anyone who doesn't have a Western saddle, it's better to let this training come after the other.

Begin working in the corral. Lead the colt in both directions and from both sides of the experienced horse. Hold the lead rope (use a long-length lead) in one hand, keeping the colt's head even with the older horse's shoulder. Or hold your reins and the bight of the lead rope in one hand as you lead with the other. Make sure the rope is free and uncoiled—don't let it catch around your hands, legs, or on any part of the saddle. If all goes well in the corral, proceed into a larger pasture and work at "Walk," "Trot," and "Whoa."

Leading from another horse has several advantages.

•The colt becomes used to seeing you and hearing you from a different position—above him. This will help when you begin to ride him.

•The older horse will help do the training—use the word commands as you did leading him on foot, and the older horse will set him an immediate example.

•The colt will become used to working with you and paying attention to you in larger unconfined areas—again, this will be a big help when you begin riding him.

•It's easier on you—you'll be able to trot for a longer time than you could on foot.
•The variety of your lessons keeps the colt interested and more alert.

For more on this subject, see "Ponying" in Part II, Chapter 7.

GROOMING

Thorough grooming before each training lesson is an important ritual. Regular grooming helps establish a sense of companionship between you and your horse. It sets you both in the proper frame of mind for a training session: You'll find your horse to be much more receptive than when starting in cold. Grooming is an important health aid for your horse, keeping him clean, improving muscle tone, stimulating his circulation, and promoting a show gloss that's good for both of you. It lets you keep a close eye on his condition—you'll watch daily for scratches, soreness, foot problems, or other irregularities that should have attention. Regular, thorough grooming is in itself an important part of training—your horse learns to stand quietly and patiently, to tolerate handling all over his body, including his feet, and to become used to people moving around him from all angles. Now that the colt has learned to stand quietly when tied, you're ready for the first grooming session.

The most convenient arrangement for grooming is use of the crosstie. This consists of two ropes with snaps on the ends, tied to two posts about eight to ten feet apart. To adjust the crosstie to the correct length, the ropes should meet in the center. Both snap into the side halter rings. In this way, the horse will have some head freedom, but will be able to take only a step or two forward, back, or to the side. However, you'll be able to move freely around him, encouraging him to stand quietly right from the beginning. You want the horse to look forward to these grooming periods; they should be a form of reward and relaxation.

Keep your grooming tools clean and neatly arranged in a readily accessible place close to the grooming area. You may find it most convenient to use a grooming tool box with a carrying handle so that you can take it wherever you wish. Clean water should be available, either in a bucket or at a nearby faucet. At this stage, your tools should include a curry comb, brush, hoof pick, mane comb, and cloth.

At first, your grooming procedures will differ somewhat from the regular grooming of an experienced horse. Because your colt has a lot to get used to, it's best to start slowly and work up to the regular grooming procedure.

Begin, for the first day or two, with no tools at all. Using only your hands, stroke him and rub him all over, proceeding slowly and gently, and talking to him continually. Run your hands down his legs gently, but firmly enough so that he knows what you're doing. Use caution. Now is the time that you'll find out his ticklish spots, or particularly sensitive areas. Keep an eye on his ears, especially as you work toward his hindquarters and hind legs. Although he's used to your patting his head and neck, this is something new. As always, work from both sides. If he is especially sensitive under the belly, work toward this area gradually, a little more each day, until he accepts it completely.

Usually, grooming begins with a curry comb, and eventually this is the tool you'll use first. But for now, start with a brush, accustoming him to the feel of that tool for several days before using the curry. When your colt seems calm and unconcerned under your hand, go ahead with the curry comb. Use a rubber or plastic comb—these are humane and safe, and both do a good job. The metal curry comb can cut the skin or can be very uncomfortable on thin or sensitive horses. It has its place, but not for inexperienced youngsters. Use the curry comb only on fleshy parts of the body.

Work the curry comb in a circular motion, starting behind the head and progressing down the neck, front to rear and top to bottom, first on one side, then the other. Begin lightly to accustom the horse to the feel of the tool and the motion against his body. Gradually work up to using it vigorously: The purpose of currying is to help circulation and to bring dirt, dried skin particles, and any other foreign material to the surface.

Brushing comes next in the regular scheme of things. There are many types of brushes: a stiff brush for mud or caked manure; the all-purpose dandy brush, neither stiff nor very soft (this is the brush to have if you're starting with just one); the soft-fiber brush (usually white) for finishing the horse (bringing out the shine and removing dust); and the plastic brush, which can be used while washing the horse to encourage lather and to rub down to the skin. Some trainers brush as they curry, using brush in one hand and curry in the other. Although perfectly acceptable with an experienced horse, this may make an unschooled animal nervous. One thing at a time is more relaxing.

The purpose of the brush is to sweep away the dirt left on the surface by the curry comb, and to smooth and condition the hair. Use the brush vigorously with long, sweeping strokes as soon as the green horse seems calm enough. At first, of course, go gently. It's especially important to move slowly and carefully around your colt's eyes and ears. He can easily become headshy if you are rough or careless, or if you rush what you're doing.

Most green horses object to having the tail handled or brushed. At first just use your hand; as you rub over his body, move back over his croup and down his tail, reassuring him as you do this. He'll probably tuck his tail in and hold it tightly against his body. Gradually pull it to the side, a little at a time and brush gently or simply run your fingers through it. Never stand behind the horse to do this—always work from the side; this is a safety precaution for you and more reassuring for the horse, because he can see where you are. Work for short periods, gradually prolonging the time you hold the tail as the colt learns to relax.

Generally, clawing your fingers to separate the hairs, followed by brushing, is the best way to care for mane and tail. Combs are made of metal and plastic, but should be used with care, since they can pull out the hair. A dog grooming brush can give a nice finish to the job.

Use a soft cloth to wipe around the eyes and to wipe out the nostrils. Rubbing with a small, soft cloth gives a final polish as well as conditioning the colt for the movement of the saddle blanket and other odd things humans use on horses. Of course, waving a cloth in front of a green horse's eyes can have a startling effect, so go easy when using it on his face. It's best to get him used to rubbing all around the face and head with your hand alone before using a cloth.

HANDLING THE FEET

Daily foot care is a regular and important part of the grooming operation. All horses should be mannerly in allowing their feet to be handled. Most will be shod at one time or another; almost all will need to be trimmed occasionally. Prepare them for such eventualities right from the beginning. Further, if you are using a horse, his feet should be checked daily—or more often—for pebbles or bits of wood caught in the frog, for cracks developing in the hoof wall, or for other problems.

For your first grooming sessions, don't plan to use the hoof pick. All you want to do now is to get the horse used to handling. Begin now to set the pattern for each grooming session. The establishment of a routine— working first with the left fore foot, then left rear, right fore, right rear (or any order convenient to you)—and the consistent use of a word command such as "Up" or "Hup" will be reassuring to the green horse. He soon knows what to expect and will be more likely to co-operate.

Begin by rubbing your hands down his legs, especially handling the lower legs and fetlock area. Some horses will lift their foot just at a touch. Be ready to hold the hoof if this should happen; praise him, and let the hoof down gently. Hold it just for a few seconds at first and avoid dropping it or letting him pull away quickly: Dropping the hoof makes the horse reluctant to lift it again for you.

Chances are that it wasn't so easy. Or sometimes a horse will lift three of his feet in rotation for you with no trouble, but the fourth might seem

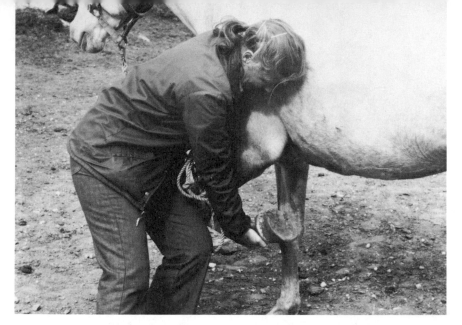

If a horse is reluctant to pick up a foot, you may have to lean or push against his shoulder to shift his weight. (Photo by Sandy Whittaker)

nailed to the ground. Most likely it will take you several days of handling before the colt is relaxed to your touch. (We know of horses that took months!) Remember that giving you his foot is like giving you part of his security. His feet help him to flee enemies; naturally, he's reluctant to surrender the means of flight.

When you think he is ready, first make sure he is balanced correctly before you ask for his hoof. If he has three feet arranged in a line and you ask him to pick up the fourth, you're going to have trouble. Run your hand down his leg as usual and encourage him to lift his foot on word and physical command (perhaps "Hup" and lifting gently under the fetlock). If he is reluctant, lean against his shoulder to shift his weight to the other leg and lightly squeeze the tendon above the fetlock (increase pressure here if he's still slow to pick up his foot). Be firm but not rough.

When the horse quietly lifts his hoof on command, and is secure and well enough balanced that he doesn't mind your holding it for more than just a few seconds, begin using the hoof pick gently. Gradually, of course, he should work up to having the foot held for minutes at a time so that he can be trimmed, rasped, and, if necessary, shod. Training the horse to be co-operative is your job, not the farrier's.

Any kicking or violent acts of aggression should be handled immediately and with knowledgeable force. Preventing vices from becoming ingrained is vitally important. Sometimes an experienced horseman will recognize a threat and stop the intended disobedience before it happens. Let the horse know you are displeased. Say "No!" and slap him on the side of the rump. Take care that you are in a safe position when administering your justice, but any action you take should be immediate. Most horses will not resent chastisement.

Remember, though, that the problem is most likely yours rather than the horse's. His natural instinct is to kick if he is hurt or frightened. Introduce new things gradually, be gentle and soothing, and praise by voice and hand whenever he is on the right track. If correction is necessary, be consistent and immediate: Always give the least corrective action that is effective.

If your colt is reluctant or slow to co-operate in picking up his feet, work with him again after his training session. He will have rid himself of his excess energy and be more in the mood for co-operation.

Usually a green horse is not shod; watch to see that his feet are wearing evenly and that they stay in healthy condition. Use of hoof dressing will keep hoofs moist and will guard against their becoming cracked and brittle. Buy prepared dressing or make your own concoction of one-third bacon grease (straight from the frypan), one-third neatsfoot oil, and one-third pine tar. It won't hurt to make a somewhat larger proportion of bacon grease, if you've got it to spare. The neatsfoot oil can be pure (more expensive) or neatsfoot oil compound (less expensive and just as effective). Paint the goo on with a brush, beginning at the coronary band (if the horse is shod, don't put dressing around the nail holes; it could loosen the nails). As with everything, work slowly when introducing this operation. Some horses that are quiet for the hoof pick come apart when they first see the brush (besides, it smells funny). Always be alert.

Safety

Working with horses can be dangerous. Usually with experience comes a basic understanding that helps you to avoid dangerous situations. Much of this involves learning a horse's natural reactions to various situations—in other words, learning to think like a horse. Most potentially dangerous situations and conditions can be prevented by use of a little common sense and forethought, a willingness to go easy and avoid rushing, a sharp eye to catch problem areas when they first show up, and a consistently alert manner.

We are concerned about safety because accidents are so easily come by in working with horses, and in most cases could so easily have been prevented. Take the time to think about what you are doing and how you are doing it. It's a shame to ruin your (or your child's) love of horses through an unnecessary, unfortunate incident that may cause injury. And it's equally sad to have some injury to your horse cause disappointment or even loss of the animal.

The issue of safety will recur throughout this book in specific situations, and several aspects of safety have already been discussed earlier in this chapter. Much of your own safety in working with horses can be summed up by saying:

- Learn to anticipate your horse's actions.
- Give yourself and your horse enough room.
- Use strong equipment.
- Don't rush.
- Stay alert.

Get in the habit of putting away any equipment you use in a stable; if you leave a pitchfork leaning against the wall of a stall, trouble is bound to follow. Dress safely; avoid dangling straps or sashes or scarves that could become caught in tack or that could frighten a young horse. Avoid holding ropes or longe lines in such a way that you could become entangled.

Safety is an attitude. Consider all eventualities and try to proceed in such a manner that if something went wrong, you would be in the best possible position to deal with it.

In short, *think*.

Part II

BASIC TRAINING

CHAPTER 1

FOAL TRAINING

The arrival of a new foal in the family should be an exciting and happy occasion. You've planned for the event—perhaps for years ahead of time —by careful selection of a stallion, proper care of your pregnant mare, and sanitary management at birth. The foal is healthy, the mare content: Mission accomplished and all's well.

Or is it? Have you thought ahead on how to work with the foal? How to begin the training—right now—that will eventually develop a mature, responsive, and well-mannered horse? Early handling of the foal, when done carefully and knowledgeably, can be the easiest, most effective training you will ever give. The few minutes spent daily with the foal at this early age can save days, weeks, even months of gentling and conditioning later. Why? Because the baby is so small and easy to control now, and because his nature is so open to influence before he learns to take flight with his dam and to be continually wary. A foal is naturally curious; by taking advantage of his inherent curiosity, we can turn his latent tendency to fear us into friendly confidence. We can hope to develop his nervous energies into calm, willing receptiveness. What he learns now in his relationship with humans will carry over throughout his life, unless it is deliberately destroyed by rough, thoughtless handling. For the trainer, the opportunity is too good to miss!

Facilities and Management, East and West

The general conditions under which your horses are raised will have a bearing on your training methods. On some Western ranches, especially the larger spreads, the foaling mares are left to take care of themselves. Under natural conditions, they generally foal late, perhaps between mid-April and mid-June, when the weather is mild. Generally such births are uneventful, if the mare is healthy and experienced, and the foal benefits from clean grass, open air, sunshine, and exercise, to develop quickly and become healthy and strong. In these cases, the youngster grows up in conditions similar to those of a wild horse, and with similar basic reactions. Of course, if something should go wrong, the foal (or both foal and mare) could be lost; such conditions, therefore, would not be considered for valuable stock. Similarly, poor pasture, bad weather, and lack of sufficient minerals in the feed could affect the foal adversely, and perhaps cause stunted growth and weak constitution, which could lead to the onset of disease, deformed bone structure, or the development of other abnormalities. Under natural conditions, even healthy, well-grown foals receive little or no handling until weaning time, when they are separated from their dams. The double trauma of weaning and halter-breaking can set patterns of suspicion, distrust, and rebellion that are difficult to break.

Despite such obvious problems, however, natural methods are not without their advantages. If the weather is sunny, dry, and mild, and if the mare is healthy and experienced, some breeders may prefer to have their foals born in a small, grassy pasture. In this way, they gain the advantage of cleanliness, sun, and open air, while a close eye can be kept on the foaling process. A nervous, wary, or shy mare—especially if range-bred—may be more relaxed in the open than in a foaling stall, and if so, the birth will be quicker and more comfortable for her, and probably better for the foal. An experienced breeder will be aware of these factors, and also will know if there are any symptoms of impending problems.

Today, in both East and West, wherever horses are raised with consideration of value, the mare is usually brought under shelter to foal. Generally, to compete in shows, it is desirable to have early foals—thus they will be more fully grown when competing within their classes. A young horse is considered to be one year old on January 1 of the year following his birth—whether he is actually twelve months old (born in January) or five months old (born in August). In most of the country, January, February, and March are cold, wet months, requiring proper shelter for the foaling mare. And of course, having the mare confined where she can be closely watched allows the breeder to monitor the birth to be sure all goes well, and to give the foal such immediate attention as is desirable, such as disinfecting the navel and umbilical cord and drying the foal in cold weather.

Confinement, however, produces its own problems. The pregnant mare needs exercise. If she is in good physical shape to the outward eye, she is probably in good physical condition within. This means easier, safer foaling.

What, then, is a good management plan, adaptable to your conditions?

Many brood mares run in large pastures, especially in the West, often with a mixed herd of mares, geldings, and young stock. As foaling becomes imminent, it is wise to keep the brood mares in a smaller pasture, separate from the geldings. Most geldings are not intentionally mean, but they are curious: They worry the mare during foaling and may chase a new foal to see him better. This may cause the foal to run through a wire fence, to get trampled, or to be injured by falls or kicks from other horses.

After the foal is born, the mare is brought into her foaling stall so that she feels at home and comfortable in it before giving birth. The stall should be at least twelve feet by twelve feet, preferably somewhat larger, and it should be very carefully checked over for danger points—splinters, protruding nails, and the like. The stall should be deeply bedded with clean straw. For complete information on foaling care and procedures, please consult the section on recommended reading.

After the foal is born, the routine remains much the same. Mare and foal are confined to the stall at night; during the day, depending on the weather, they are let out to exercise in a small adjacent pasture. If shelter is available in the pasture, they may spend more time outside. Climate and weather determine whether or not the pair should be stabled. A foal is a rugged little individual, needing sunshine and exercise to develop properly. But care during particularly cold, wet, or windy weather will promote his early growth and hardiness.

Care should be taken in preparing the small pasture for mares and foals. If possible, the fencing should be of pole or board construction. Barbed wire is particularly dangerous to foals. If you have no choice, at least tie aluminum pans or rag strips to the wire fence at fairly close intervals. It will help the youngster to see the fence more readily, and make it easier for him to avoid it when running and playing. One electric wire will teach the baby respect for the fence without hurting him, and will make him more wary of all wire fences. There should be extra poles or boards around the bottom of a foal fence. Youngsters will often lie down next to a fence and rise on the other side of it, causing panic, injury, or even death if the mother can't reach the baby and the problem is not discovered in time. (This can also happen to a foaling mare. Mares will often lie down next to a fence and the baby is born on the other side. In many such cases, the baby dies if not rescued immediately.)

While mares and foals exercise in the small pasture, the youngsters learn to handle themselves and enjoy playing together. If possible, it is convenient for the babies to get acquainted with other horses over the fence; then when the mare and foal are released to the larger pasture, there are few, if any, incidents. Some geldings protect a mare and foal, keeping other horses away and making sure the baby is not interfered with. Unless you are sure of this kind of relationship, however, it's best to keep mares and foals separate from other horses until the foals are strong and experienced enough to handle herd life.

The First Twenty-four Hours

How can we capitalize on the distinctive features of the foal's temperament? We know that the foal is unable to focus his eyes clearly during his
first twenty-four hours of life. Because of this, he has no fear of the odd
two-legged animals around him. Right away, then, is the golden opportunity to handle him thoroughly and to let him become accustomed to your
touch and the sound of your voice. You may even slip a halter on the foal
for a few minutes; don't leave it on, however, as he may put a foot
through it in his wobbly efforts to rise. Also, his baby skin is tender, and
the halter can chafe around the cheekbones.

Always remember to use moderation—too much handling will discourage the dam from taking an interest in her foal. Immediately after
foaling, the dam should have the opportunity to satisfy her maternal instincts in privacy. The foal is hers.

The First Two Weeks

A foal is naturally curious. You will find that if you kneel a short distance away from the youngster and speak gently to him, he will come to
you, sniff, and even try to nuzzle. All of this early contact with the baby
will develop his confidence in you and discourage his natural tendency to
flee.

The foal will take cues from his dam. If she is gentle and unafraid of
humans, the baby too will be relaxed and interested in your presence. But
even if the mare accepts you and the family without concern, strangers
may upset her. If you allow visitors, have them view the foal quietly, one
at a time, with you in attendance. Groups of people, standing around and
talking loudly, will make the mare nervous and overprotective. She may
crowd the baby into the corner away from the people, and of course he
will pick up her nervousness. Because every bit of handling received by
the foal is training, we want to eliminate unfortunate incidents and
mishandling right from the start.

On the first day after foaling, groom the mare, stroking her and talking constantly. This allows the baby to become used to your voice and to
having you move about the stall. Of course, you will keep the stall clean
and well bedded, working slowly and quietly to avoid startling the baby.
After these preliminaries, you may start on the foal. Gently and slowly
herd him toward a corner of the stall closest to his mother. Junior will be
small and still wobbly; hold him by putting your left hand around his chest
and your right around his hindquarters. When he is standing quietly,

A horse's natural curiosity can be a great help to the trainer. This foal is willing to let himself be touched. The other horses, curious about him, can become acquainted over the fence; when the pair return to the larger pasture, there will be less likelihood of the foal being chased if the other horses are already used to him.

release your right hand and stroke the foal, concentrating on his head. You may find it necessary to use your body and right leg to brace (not squash!) the baby. This bracing position is also helpful when trying to halter the foal.

After showing the halter to the foal, caress his neck with it and let him sniff it; then very gently slip it on. You may need several tries—just be careful not to excite him. It is wise to have the lead rope attached to the halter, but do not try to lead him. Just put the halter on, tell him he's wonderful, pet him around the ears and along his neck, and take it off again. Handling Junior in this way, ten minutes a day for about two weeks, should be all you need to make him used to the halter and to human contact. Toward the end of the two-week period the foal can wear his halter for an hour or two. But be sure that the halter fits snugly, and do check him often.

Try to keep ideal conditions present whenever handling the foal. For instance, don't attempt to work with him if the dam is upset. When weather conditions are poor and the baby feels especially flighty, attempt only what you feel confident of accomplishing.

Early Hoof Care

After the initial period of handling the foal, there will probably be a lapse of a month or more before you begin a scheduled and more complete training program. Generally this depends both on the weather and on your plans for showing mare and foal during the summer. May or early June is a good time to begin more intensive training. During the interim, however, you'll see him daily, perhaps to bring mare and foal under shelter at night, perhaps only to visit him in the pasture.

Right from his first week, keep an eye on his feet and legs, making sure they are developing properly. Many foals have crooked legs at birth, but they straighten quickly. In our area, crooked legs are often a sign of phosphorus deficiency; we make sure our pregnant mares have sufficient phosphorus, and, if the foals are crooked-legged, an extra phosphorus supplement will usually correct the problem within a few weeks. Your veterinarian will be able to tell you if there are mineral deficiencies in your area.

It is often necessary to trim and level the foal's hoofs within a few days after birth, and to keep close watch afterward. Knowledgeable trimming will ensure development of good, straight bone structure in the pasterns and legs. Unfortunately, this usually frightens the foal, but at his small size, two people can accomplish the job quickly, gently, and easily. The foal learns early in life that there are times when there's no sense in fighting, since humans are so much stronger than he is: It's a lesson with merit, one he will remember later when the tables have turned on strength and size.

Halter Training, Handling, and Grooming

When the time has come to make a more complete job of halter training, set up a daily training program. Baby will probably be at least a month old, strong now, and sure on his feet. Whether you have one foal or several, the new routine can be arranged in a logical, time-saving way.

Decide where you will work: Perhaps you have several small outdoor pens to which you can assign a mare and foal. In a large corral, tie the mare to a convenient upright; each mare and foal should have their own special place. The foals will follow their dams into the pen or to their own area, but they can all become elusive at times. Your first aid in avoiding problems with the foal is to keep the mare quiet and content: Give her hay to occupy her thoughts, and always work the foal nearby. Plan to work with each foal in turn: When mare and foal know what to expect, your job is easier.

Now to catch the foal. If you've been working with him and visiting him all along, this will be no problem. Probably he'll come to you and offer to put his head in the halter.

If a foal has never been haltered before, or if he is feeling playful or ornery, you might have more trouble. Never chase or lunge at the foal to catch him; this will only make him harder to catch next time. Whether the mare is in a small pen or tied in a larger corral, the youngster will proba-

Holding a foal with a lead rope. This method can save trouble if the youngster doesn't come up to you readily. He may circle around you for a minute but will soon quiet down so that you can halter him. Never chase a foal, lunge at him, or rope him. (Photo by Sandy Whittaker)

bly try to get between her and the wall. This is to your advantage, as you can catch the baby over or around the mare simply by putting the lead rope around his neck. Hold both ends of the lead rope in your left hand, keeping it low. As the youngster pulls against it, or tries to get away, you can hold him easily, letting him circle around you, and keeping him from ducking or rearing out of your reach. The rope can't become tangled or twisted on him, even if he turns and ducks around inside the loop. It usually leads to a short longeing session before he quiets down near his dam. Then run your right hand from the top of his rump gently forward to his head. Rub his head and ears with your hand, then with the halter; let it slip over his nose as you feed him grain from a shallow pan. Try to make the experience pleasant, and don't hurry. There are times when you have to be forceful, but even so, work slowly and talk quietly; your quiet control will be both commanding and reassuring. The baby must learn that you are boss, but he should learn this as pleasantly and painlessly as possible.

If the foal is especially difficult to catch, leave the halter on him—fit it carefully so that it is snug but not tight; *check him often.* Leave a short rope (eight to twelve inches) tied or snapped to the halter. This is not long enough to tangle or interfere with his movements, but is easy to catch and hold.

When you have the foal haltered, snap on the lead rope if you did not have it already attached to the halter. Do not tie him. Hold the shank in one hand and caress the foal with the other. Give more attention to the body and legs than you did at the time of foaling.

When you are able to stroke the foal completely, then try picking up his feet. By running your hand down the back of his front legs and the front of his back legs, you encourage him to pick them up. Be satisfied with lifting the foot and setting it back down immediately. The foal will panic if you try to hold up a foot for any length of time. It is better to begin slowly and to gradually increase the time you hold the foot and the height to which you raise it.

Next introduce a brush to the foal and gently brush him. Later a curry, hoof pick, and rasp can be added to the grooming implements.

Teaching to Lead

When the foal takes the halter quietly, it is time to teach control through the lead shank. The following method of teaching him to lead has been most successful for us; it lessens revolt in the foal and minimizes the possibility of injury to the handler or animal.

Work either in the stall with the dam, or outside in the place you have arranged. Hold the halter shank in the left hand; your right hand can touch the croup, if necessary. Give a light forward tug on the lead shank and say, "W-a-l-k." The tone and sequence of your signals are important; physical pressure should come first, then the verbal command (later the verbal command will be unnecessary). Give the commands firmly and clearly in a normal tone of voice. Be consistent in tone, sequence, and action.

If the foal will not move forward, use your right hand on the croup to push him gently. When he takes a few steps going around to the left, move to his other side, take the halter shank in your right hand, and try the same procedure to the right. The foal will become used to seeing you on either side and will learn to handle easily in either direction. Praise him freely.

When the foal responds to forward pressure on the lead shank, begin leading him in the accepted fashion—handler on the horse's left or "near" side; hold the lead rope in your right hand about a foot from the halter and carry the slack or bight of the rope folded in your left hand. Encourage the foal to move around in both directions, but this time do not switch to the foal's right (or "off") side. Stop frequently with an abrupt tug to-

ward the chest and smartly (but quietly) clip out the word "Whoa!" Be
sure to pet and praise him each time he responds; he should learn when
you are pleased. In later stages of training you cannot always touch him to
reward him, but he will know when you are pleased if he's conditioned to
a certain expression of praise and a pleased tone.

Know when to stop the training. The foal has a very short attention
span and when bored or tired will kick, bite, or become stubborn and
unhappy.

Keep in mind too, even at this early date, that you want your horse to
be versatile and safe; orient your training to this general goal. Although
you'll be working mainly from the near side when leading, work enough
from the off side also so that the foal will be comfortable in seeing you on
his right. A horse that is upset when being led from the off side can become dangerous on the trail or when being led with another horse: He
may push you or stumble on your heels in his efforts to get over to your
right.

When you are able to halter your foal easily, groom him completely,
and lead him near his dam in both directions, it is time to teach him to
lead in a straight line. At first, he'll learn to move with his mother, later
away from her. These first lessons will be easier if you have an assistant to
help you. However, with a little more planning, you can work quite well
alone.

If you have an assistant, let him lead the mare two or three times
across an area and back in a straight line; have him make left and right
turns and stop often. Lead the foal behind his dam in a follow-the-leader
plan (if you are working alone, you'll have to skip this step). Then begin
leading the foal alone along the same route. Don't expect him to go too far
or to do too much. You may be able to lead him straight away from his
dam two or three times, or even just once. The important thing is to be
consistent and to use the physical and verbal commands. These signals
used in the beginning of your training will be remembered when you start
to longe him, and your carry-over instruction will be consistent. If this is
your first try at training a horse, this practice will help you to become consistent and more confident with each foal you handle.

If the foal is inclined to balk, or if he becomes frightened, take the
halter shank in your left hand and use your right on the foal's rump to encourage him forward as you talk gently and matter-of-factly. Stay at his
shoulder while he walks forward; do not walk in front of him at any time.
On no account should you plant yourself in front of the foal and pull on
the halter; this will encourage him to set back and will present a tug-of-
war situation.

If he should rebel or become frightened, he may pull back from you.
Be firm and hold him, but don't pull against him. Speak to him in a matter-of-fact tone, and stroke him when he steps forward to you again. It is

Using the come-along to help a foal learn to walk forward on cue from the halter. First encourage him to move in circles around you. When he does so willingly, urge him forward in straight lines.

important at this stage to retain his confidence; in addition, you are now teaching another lesson. The big pull was all his idea and it got him nowhere; therefore he can have no resentment against you. When he steps forward again, he is praised, and all is well. Further, he learns that you are stronger than he is—a happy thing for him to learn at this stage, since he'll remember it when he's grown.

Another way to help a foal to walk forward is with a come-along (see picture). Use a cotton rope about fifteen feet long. Loop it around his rump (not under his tail!) and run the end through the halter or hold the end in your right hand. Tug gently (or with more pressure if needed) on this rope as you give the verbal commands; continue to use the lead shank for direction. This way you are causing his hindquarters to push him along, rather than encouraging his forehand to pull him—just as, eventually, you'll encourage impulsion through the hindquarters.

If you have an assistant, he can walk to the side and behind the foal, urging him forward with a hand on his croup. Because you are leading the foal, you will give the commands; your assistant will help the foal to carry them out. The foal should learn that the human with the lead shank is his primary concern and the one to which he should give his attention.

Day by day, work the foal gradually away from the mare in straight lines and in several directions. When you have achieved a willing walk in

Teach the youngster to stand squarely and quietly as part of early training. At the John Gorman Arabian farm in Loveland, Colorado, the youngsters are ready to "show" at a moment's notice as the result of gentle, consistent, and affectionate handling.

all directions within sight of the dam, you may teach the foal to trot. This comes easily with confidence and daily work sessions.

Start the trot where you think the foal is most willing to go: for instance, toward his dam or one of his buddies, or down an incline. Tug on the lead shank and say "Trot!" in an excited manner that will not be mistaken for either "Walk" or "Whoa." You can also use a come-along for the first few times so that he learns what you want. Run beside his shoulder, even if you run in place; it is amazing what small signs the foal will pick up as clues. Encourage him to trot in straight lines as well as around a circle in either direction. Work gradually and consistently until he trots willingly uphill and away from his dam.

Train him also to stand squarely and quietly, with his handler beside him or in front of him. It takes only about five minutes each day for it to become so automatic that he will be ready to show at any time, either to prospective buyers or in the show ring. Stand beside him, square him up (see Part IV, Chapter 1), and say, "Stand." Each time he moves, begin again and gradually increase the time that he should hold his position. Don't expect too much at first—even a few seconds are worthy of praise. Face him to square him up, and eventually move back away from him, encouraging him to stand for longer periods. You can cue him by your position as you face him, and if he comes toward you, push the palm of your hand toward him and say. "Whoa! Stand."

After these lessons have been learned to your satisfaction, it will be necessary only to repeat them twice a week. Never neglect the foal's grooming; this is one of our best training aids and will remain so through his entire training.

Trailer Training

While the foal is small and willing to follow his dam, and while you are working with him each day, it's a good time to introduce him to the horse trailer. He should, of course, lead readily; and he should have arrived at a calm, receptive state of mind, ready for each new thing he is being asked to do or accept.

Before you begin any training, prepare the trailer for immediate occupancy. Park it in an enclosed corral, if possible, so that the foal may investigate it on his own. If it is not hitched to a truck, it should have the wheels blocked. The floor should be covered with matting or nonslip material, and the sides and front should be checked for protruding nails, screws, and splinters. We use burlap sacks to cover license plates, light fixtures, and other sharp protrusions outside the back of the trailer. Until a horse is used to stepping in and out, he may slide his rear hoofs under the trailer, either barking his cannon bones or causing more extensive injury. To prevent this, make a dirt ramp for step-up trailers. A good arrangement is to place a railroad tie up against the rear gates of the step-up trailer and to cover it with dirt; this also keeps the trailer floor from sounding hollow, a sound that is likely to frighten young and green horses.

If you have been using grain as a reward, it can be used as a bribe to help in loading, and as a reward in the manger; this gives the foal a good feeling about the trailer. Keep the grain ready, and have the doors tied open, the tailguard chains (or "butt chains") unhooked. Have your assistant lead the mare to the trailer; follow with the foal. The first time or two, it may be enough for the youngster to just stand near the trailer, to see the doors open and close, and, if the mare loads easily, to watch her step in and out. He will also become used to the sound her feet make on the floor.

When you are ready to try loading the foal, hold the mare (or tie her, if you don't have an assistant) close behind the trailer on one side. Bring the foal up beside the mare and start coaxing him in. You may step into the trailer to encourage him. Expect to go right in with him the first few times. The foal is small enough not to crowd you, and your presence will give him confidence. Do not tie the foal or close the tailgate—just let him stand and eat. Talk to him and stroke his neck.

If he will not follow you into the trailer and you feel it's high time he did, have two assistants grasp hands and literally push and lift his hindquarters right in. We have never known a foal to kick or put up much fuss at this handling. The assistants must, however, be firm and quick; it all happens so fast that the foal is in the trailer before he can think up a defense.

After standing in the trailer awhile, help the foal to back out. If he tends to rush, your assistants can put a hand on his rump to slow him. If he won't back out, which often happens when a young horse has been in a trailer for a time, stand in front of him and push him out. We usually walk the foal in and out several times at each daily training session until he enters and leaves readily.

Later, teach the foal to step up into the trailer and load by himself. When you feel he's ready, tie him and close the trailer door. A short ride once in a while is excellent training; take the mare along too. Be sure to have grain in the manger for his reward.

Although we tie a foal in the trailer, once he is calm and knowledgeable about loading, we do not tie him in the open unless we remain right there with him. In the open, it is too easy for a baby to rear back or fall sideways and hurt himself or even break his neck.

A suckling foal may be left loose in the trailer with his dam (who is tied), so that he can nurse or lie down. Of course, if the partition is solid, it should be removed; a simple bar partition will support the mare while still allowing the foal to nurse.

Showing at Halter

If you are proud of your breeding program, or if you have obtained an especially nice foal, you probably would like to show him. The prospect of showing your foal will encourage you to keep at and improve his conditioning and training. Please refer to Part IV, Chapter 1, for more on training to show at halter.

In most shows, when showing the current year's foals, the dam is allowed in the ring if the foal is still a suckling. She may even be led with the foal; however, the youngster will show to best advantage if he is fully trained and is used to being led away from his dam. Your home training— teaching the foal to travel in straight lines, to set up in show stance, and to trot beside you—will pay off now.

There are several classes available in most shows for the mare and foal: Foal Class (current year); Mare and Foal Class; Mare Class; and, in large shows, Futurities (foal is entered before being born, after the mare has been bred). Do not be tempted to enter classes such as the Mare and Foal Race (Dinner Bell Race) offered by some rodeos. Besides frightening the foal and inviting injury by some other mare or foal, such a class may undo all the good training you have accomplished, so that months will be required to restore the foal's confidence.

If the dam of your foal is a show mare, she will help her youngster by her calm, matter-of-fact attitude. If not, you may have your hands full with both of them. In the latter case, take excursions to small nearby shows or horsey get-togethers to prepare them for their exciting new experiences. It would not be necessary to show them at these outings, although if there is one, you could enter a Mare and Foal Class for practice; just the experience of a new place, different stall, unfamiliar horses, people, confusion, and strange smells is in itself training. Even the experienced horseman would not try to take the responsibility of two such animals alone; he'd want an assistant. Choose a helper who is knowledgeable, dependable, and sensible—one who is familiar with your animals and who will follow your advice on procedure. These first experiences should go off smoothly so that the stage is set for further successful showings.

When you travel to any show, take precautions against injury and disease—arrange for health and brand inspections, have shots given if necessary, check the stall for nails and other hazards, be careful about diet, and use your own water buckets. When leading the foal among vehicles, people, strange objects, and other horses, be alert for sudden moves. Let your assistant lead the mare; follow with the foal. In order to control the foal better when leading him in unfamiliar surroundings, we sometimes crosstie him between two people. This lessens the chance of upset or injury, and is especially good if the foal must be led by children. Do not leave mare and foal alone if they are tied in the open; if you leave them alone in a stall, check back often.

If you arrive before the show starts, you may be able to lead mare and foal into the arena. If this can be arranged, conduct your own practice showmanship class. Without the confusion and noise of an audience, you can check the footing and best placing for showing the foal to advantage. At the same time, he will see the stands and strange objects close to the arena, and feel the show atmosphere. Floodlighting can be especially frightening to the uninitiated. If the show is to be held inside under lights, try to let mare and foal experience the situation before they are actually showing. In some shows there is a band or canned music, although not usually during halter classes. We recently attended a national sale where both music and floodlights were used; even some experienced, mature horses panicked. Every new situation that can be experienced in advance will lessen your trials later.

Most judges take into consideration that foals are sensitive, explosive, inexperienced little bundles, and they expect some display of spirit or temper. Don't be surprised if all your training seems to fly out the window, but do prepare the youngster as best you can. Showing your foal at halter will give you a chance to see how he is progressing in size, conformation, condition, and training, compared to his peers.

Longeing for Foals

We do not longe our foals; we feel that it is unnecessary unless the foal is very restricted in his exercise. Because they are skittish and frolicsome, they get the idea that the longe line is for play. If they should plunge or rear and inadvertently go over sideways or backward, they can damage their neck muscles. Too much longeing at an early age tends to inhibit free action in the forequarters, and can fill the hocks.

Freedom to Grow

It is ideal for the foal to be with his dam and also with other frisky young animals, sleeping away the hottest part of the day, and galloping and trotting freely through his first summer. As he learns to handle himself on uneven ground, he develops good balance and muscling. Even so, it's important to keep an eye on the youngster. All our horses come in from pasture daily to be grained and checked over for injury. This daily contact with his two-legged friends helps the foal to grow in confidence and gentleness.

Weaning and After

Weaning can be a tough time for the foal. To be taken away from his mother at six to eight months of age is a heartbreaking experience. It may be easier for both foal and dam if the weaning takes place gradually and each becomes used to separation for increasing periods of time. More often, however, it must be a sudden process—especially on large horse farms and ranches, dam and foal may be separated one day, never to see each other again. (For suggestions on weaning—proper care, diet, precautions, and methods—see the recommended reading at the end of the book.) On top of this trauma, halter-breaking may begin immediately for the range-raised youngsters.

What special care or training can you give the youngster at weaning time? Misery loves company, so do provide a companion for your weanling. Other weanlings make good buddies; lacking them, perhaps a goat, calf, or old pony will help to ease the loneliness.

First, let's consider the problem of the foal that has been handled from birth. Even if he has run free for the summer, he has had good preliminary training and you've checked him daily: He has confidence in you and will be happy for your company. Now is a good time to reinforce your earlier training. Visit him often and review the lessons in leading that you taught during the summer. Don't be too demanding; do be lavish with praise. Frequent visits while he is confined will make life easier for him, and, later, for you. If you have a separate pasture for the weanlings, they may be turned out fairly soon, provided you have taken precautions to avoid injury by running against a fence. If the weanling must be turned back in with the other horses, you will have to keep him confined for a longer time, perhaps six weeks. In this case, his corral or paddock should be as large as possible to allow him to exercise freely, and your visits are especially important. If you feel he is too limited in exercise, you may teach him to longe at this time—work only at a walk and trot, and don't overdo.

The range-raised foal will have a more difficult time. If possible, the mares and foals should be brought in a week or more before weaning. Tie the mares and groom them while the foals are nearby, allowing the young-sters to get used to the presence of humans, to hear your voice, and to have pleasant experiences in their contact with people. In this way, you may be able to gain the foal's confidence and to slip the halter on without a major battle. Often, however, the youngster must be roped and the train-ing begun more traumatically.

At this point, your procedure depends upon several factors: the size, weight, and temperament of the weanling; your size and strength in com-parison to his; and the extent of your experience. You may use some of the suggestions on training foals outlined in this chapter; or you may need to complete the job of halter-breaking as explained in the next chapter. Most likely you'll use a combination of both. Even with foals you raised and trained yourself, you will need to use firmness and discipline as well as patience and praise to correct occasional youthful experiments in naughty behavior.

Undisciplined youngsters of this age may crowd you when you try to lead them, or try to rear and pull away from you. These problems should be corrected immediately if you are to keep their respect. The bigger the youngster gets, the stronger he becomes. If he learned when a baby that you are stronger than he is, any rebellion will be short-lived and quickly routed. If these are his first experiences in discipline, you'll have to be more convincing, especially if he has actually become stronger than you are, or is approaching that point.

Beware of using gimmicks and gadgets to make youngsters behave. Such items have no place in working with youngsters, and can only make problems worse. If you have serious behavior problems, re-evaluate your handling of the situation: Are you providing adequate exercise? Are you consistent in your correction and expectations? Are you praising the youngster sufficiently when he does something right? Some correctional suggestions may be found in Part V. You may do well to consult an experienced horseman for advice, before the situation gets out of hand. Avoid seeking help from someone not used to horses, in the hope that two heads are better than one; it is too likely that someone will get hurt. This is one more place where experience counts.

Yearlings

Yearlings should know how to stand and show at halter. They should lead willingly beside you at walk and trot, and they should be mannerly—pleasant and calm to work around, allowing their entire body to be groomed and their feet to be handled and held. They may be taught to longe, although longe periods should be short and limited to walk and trot —work sessions, not playtime. Much of the yearling's contact with humans should be quiet, pleasant, and undemanding: Visit him in his stall or in pasture, take him out on a lead rope, and provide companionship while he grazes. Beyond this, his time should be his own in which to grow and develop.

CHAPTER 2

LONGEING

Longeing, a phase of ground training, is one of the most important and most beneficial training methods used by horsemen today. It is also one of the least understood. Trainers may find it helpful to consider both the advantages and disadvantages of longeing.

By definition, longeing is an exercise in which the horse travels at the end of a longe line in a circle around the trainer. He moves at various gaits and in various stages of collection and extension on commands given by the trainer. Usually the trainer uses a longe whip to indicate or to reinforce his vocal commands, and to induce impulsion.

Except for foals, longeing can benefit horses of all ages and in all stages of training or retraining. Because such a variety of lessons can be taught on the longe, longeing is invaluable for conditioning, exercising, and for many facets of training. Its usefulness, however, depends upon the experience and expertise of the trainer. If a trainer doesn't understand the theory and the mechanics of longeing—if he doesn't understand what can be accomplished and how to accomplish it—the effects of longeing a horse can be either useless or detrimental. There is not much point in simply having your horse go round and round in a circle.

Theory of Longeing

WHY LONGEING IS HELPFUL

Work on the longe develops a horse both mentally and physically. Since all basic training proceeds step by step, building each succeeding lesson on a firm and broadening foundation, it is well to keep in mind one's overall training goals. What are we trying to produce in a horse? Generally, we hope to make our horse obedient, supple, calm, versatile, and willing. Specifically, what goals can we hold in mind as especially attainable through longeing?

Longeing is especially useful in teaching a young horse to be calm, to go forward freely, to respond obediently to simple commands, and to develop his attention span and learning capacity. Also, longeing strengthens a young horse's muscles and develops his balance and flexibility. With these goals in mind, then, let's consider in more detail what you can teach your horse on the longe.

Young horses must learn how to work. Like children, they have a short attention span and are easily distracted. Up to now you have worked with your horse for short periods, leading him, and teaching him the commands "W-a-l-k" and "Whoa!" He can now begin learning to work for a longer period. Daily work on the longe allows you gradually to build up the lesson time so that more can be accomplished. This will be a great aid when you begin riding him. Of course, you must be careful not to overdo: Avoid tiring the colt excessively or souring him on the whole experience.

Along with increasing the attention span, longeing helps develop his attitude. Even before the horse is old enough to ride, he learns that there are no-nonsense times when he is expected to behave in a certain way. He must learn obedience. Commands are given and he must learn that it is more pleasant to obey them than to rebel or goof off. Longeing is not a play time—it is the colt's introduction to work. It is an ideal way to teach this lesson because, although the youngster is under control, he is not hampered by a conglomeration of distractions—no weights to carry and get used to, no commands coming from overhead, no pressures and pokes around his body. He sees the trainer in his first and most natural relationship—on the ground, where he can watch him. The more he can learn this way, the better: Each new step that you introduce will build on a solid foundation; the most gradual of transitions will be effected. The horse will learn best when he is asked to learn only one thing at a time.

In elementary longeing lessons, the horse learns—or reinforces his knowledge of—the commands "W-a-l-k," and "Whoa!" and "Trot!" Teaching obedience to vocal commands on the longe offers the trainer three advantages: First, when the time comes to mount the youngster, the *new* experience he encounters will be the new location of the trainer and the weight he presents. The colt already understands the commands and therefore they act as familiar reassurances to him: One thing at a time. Second, the colt learns the physical aids from the voice commands and quickly makes the association. Third, there is a tremendous safety factor in learning the command "Whoa!" so automatically on the longe line that his instantaneous reaction is to stop. There are many times while riding a youngster that this automatic, ingrained response will prevent accident, injury, or an unpleasant experience resulting in a training setback.

Longeing also helps the young horse to develop physically. As he learns to manage his body when under outside control, he develops balance and rhythm. Working on various-sized circles in both directions develops his suppleness and flexibility. Trotting on the longe develops his muscles, especially in the hindquarters. This type of overall suppling and conditioning puts the young horse in better shape for riding.

Even after lessons under saddle have begun, daily longeing sessions can be of great benefit. For one thing, the youngster can work off excess energy and healthy exuberance on the longe before the trainer mounts. The longe has a settling influence, and the youngster will be more inclined to get down to work after a warmup longe session. Any kicks, bucks, or joy-of-living leaps can take place before you ride, thereby lessening the possibility of the colt unseating you or of any bad habit developing. Of course, the youngster should not be longed excessively because of high spirits. This would only give him sore muscles and encourage him to set up a resistance. As always, use discretion.

Longeing helps you to judge both the horse's mood and your own on that particular day. Is he willing and enthusiastic, or not quite up to par? Are you feeling irritable and upset because of a "final notice" you just received on a bill you paid two months ago? Longeing helps you to determine what can be accomplished during the day—whether a new lesson will go forward smoothly or whether it would be best only to review and stabilize your gains.

As soon as the horse responds well on the longe line, longeing becomes an excellent way to introduce anything new. New tack may be properly fitted and introduced on the longe, allowing the horse to become familiar with its feel and sound before weight or pressure is added. Cinches and girths need not be as tight for longeing as they must be for riding—so again, the horse is allowed gradual familiarization with the equipment. Longeing a horse near or through water, mud, strange objects, in rain or wind, will help him to accept the new and upsetting circumstance. We have had several horses in for training from dry-land farms who have been afraid of water and refused even to go through puddles. By longeing them next to, and finally through, puddles and across small ditches—with the longe whip to drive them forward and the longe line to maintain control—the phobia was soon overcome.

Horses that have been shod or reshod, especially if they are not free to run in a large pasture, should be longed before they are ridden. Especially if corrective shoeing has been done, or if comparatively different shoes are used (such as ice cleats), the horse should be allowed to adjust and rebalance himself to his new way of going without the hindrance of a weight on his back and constant direction from the legs and reins. Further, this is only a sensible safety precaution for the rider.

Longeing prepares a young horse for driving as well as for saddle training. Driving can be used either as a ground exercise to further prepare the horse for saddle training, or as an end in itself for harness work. A horse may be introduced to the bit while longeing, and further responsiveness to the bit can be achieved by driving.

One of the most important accomplishments of longeing is to teach the horse to move forward freely. (Photo by Sandy Whittaker)

The greatest accomplishment of longe training in the early stages is to teach the horse to move forward freely and calmly. More advanced training on the longe helps to stabilize and perfect the gaits, to improve rhythm and cadence, and to encourage extension and collection. Training for jumping can begin on the longe; by working over cavalletti, without a rider on his back, the horse feels free and can develop timing, balance, and confidence.

Problem horses—those that need retraining—can make much progress on the longe line in the hands of a sensitive and experienced trainer. A horse with bad habits such as bucking, rearing, refusing to move forward, and attitudes including sullenness, fear, or excessive spookiness need positive action on the longe line. Working in an enclosed area, the experienced trainer keeps the horse between his two hands, driving him up to the bit with the longe whip and maintaining control with the longe line. He is far enough from the horse to be out of the way if the horse is inclined to kick, strike, or bite, and this distance gives him ample time to anticipate, prepare for, and counteract any such shenanigans. The trainer must be experienced enough to know how to make the horse move up to the bit—to know what he wants the horse to do and how to get him to do it.

It is useful to teach your brood mares to longe, even if you don't train them to saddle. We longe our mares, at walk and trot only, immediately after breeding. This calms them and keeps them from straining, thereby improving the chances that they settle.

Some of the first lessons under saddle can be given on the longe line. Because the horse is under control of the trainer, the rider need do nothing at first but accustom his mount to moving under his weight. Then he can give the aids in conjunction with commands given by the longe trainer, and again, the horse learns with a gradual transition.

WHAT'S BAD ABOUT LONGEING?

The trainer must first of all know what he is trying to do. He should have a definite plan for training a horse in which longeing fits as one part of the overall pattern. What the horse learns on the longe line will be carried over to later lessons, all of which should be correlated. If your training steps are worked out in advance, you will be able to achieve continual gradual transition from one step to the next, avoiding any confusion on the colt's part and avoiding the necessity for retraining at a later day.

Confused trainers, or those unsure of what they are trying to accomplish, are apt to push a horse around in a circle to no purpose. The colt may learn to play on the longe, or gallop around madly, or take the whole matter into his own hands, so to speak, walking, trotting, and reversing as he is so inclined, and finally stopping altogether. The trainer must insist on obedience; to do this, he must work as much as the colt works, and keep alert and constantly active. He cannot dream, converse with bystanders, or allow his attention to depart over the hill.

The colt should learn to move forward freely. This means to move briskly, actively, even gaily. If he is allowed to plod, he will quickly lose interest and the whole exercise becomes valueless—you may as well buy a small grist mill, hitch up the horse, and at least grind some flour while he circles in endless boredom.

Too much longeing, also, can quickly sour a horse. If early exercises are too prolonged, his muscles will become sore and stiff and he'll resist the exercise all the more. Begin briefly and work up to lengthier lessons as muscles, attention span, and degree of learning develop to allow benefit from what you are teaching.

Understand the physical demands of working on a circle. The horse is expected to bend his spine along the curve of the circle he is describing. A small circle has a much greater curve than a larger one; therefore to work properly on a small circle, the horse must be supple throughout his body. He must be developed to attain this suppleness, especially working in both directions. Consider further: The horse's right legs and left legs, if he is bending correctly on the curve, are tracking in two concentric circles. His outside legs are moving on a larger circle than his inside legs: The outside legs are making a longer stride. The smaller the circle he is traveling, the greater will be the proportional difference between these two circles and therefore the greater difference in strides and proportional strain on the leg muscles.

Only a supple, well-trained horse can move at a faster gait on a small circle without interfering with himself. Too much work on a small circle or too fast work before the horse is developed for it will actually inhibit rather than encourage free forward movement. Especially for foals and yearlings, overdoing tight longe work can adversely affect young legs and inhibit free action.

The trainer should begin his longe work slowly, with short lessons, because he must maintain control (at first possible only on a short longe) without straining untrained muscles. His goal is to achieve as large a circle as possible without losing control. This is why an enclosed, small training ring is so important—it allows the animal to work on a larger circle because he cannot run out on the trainer's control. Eventually, as the colt develops, he will be able to work at faster paces on a smaller circle. He'll learn extension and collection as the trainer opens and closes the circle in conjunction with impulsion from the whip and control from the longe line.

Another problem of longeing concerns the roping horse. Some Western trainers say that once a horse learns to circle his trainer at the end of a rope, he will do the same thing when at the far end of a calf, circling around it instead of backing to hold it. We have not experienced this problem, but it should be considered by a trainer developing a roping horse. Even so, complete basic training of a horse should include the command "Stand!" If a horse takes it on himself to circle at the end of the rope, the commands "Whoa! Stand!" should stop him immediately. Several repetitions should permanently overcome any tendency by the horse to move in a circle unless asked to do so. Problems of this kind often develop simply because training is rushed and the horse becomes confused about the meaning of commands. It is best for any horse to have a thorough basic training, followed by several years of general use, before advanced work in any particular line is attempted. A roping horse, especially, should be old enough to stand the strain of roping, and should have exhibited some aptitude for the job during his general cattle work. Thorough grounding in all phases of basic training, with careful adherence to obedience to each command and insistence on unrushed, step-by-step progress, should make problems of this kind negligible.

WHEN SHOULD YOU BEGIN LONGEING A HORSE?

We generally begin longe training during the summer or fall after the colt becomes one year old. With care, and as special cases warrant, it can be started earlier; but the trainer should understand what problems are liable to develop. Even as a long yearling, legs and shoulder muscles can be damaged by too much or incorrect longeing.

When the horse has learned the basic lessons of obedience, calmness, and free forward movement on the longe, the lessons need be repeated only occasionally until he is old enough to ride and his training becomes more intensified. Except for the occasional review lessons, it is good for the youngster to be out on pasture where he has freedom to grow and develop.

If this is not possible, however, daily longeing will provide the exercise he needs. Take care to work equally in both directions and to avoid boredom by varying both content and location of lessons. There is always a temptation to begin riding too soon. Resist it. Some breeds mature faster than others, but as a rule, three years of age is soon enough to begin riding, and then the horse should be worked only lightly. Some trainers prefer to wait until the horse is four. As in all things with horses, don't rush. You'll find it's well worth the time to proceed gradually. By waiting—by not starting to ride too soon—you may find that the horse can give you many more years of use and companionship.

We continue longeing regularly until the horse is considered tractable and stable under saddle. At that time, we longe him occasionally as the situation warrants—perhaps in bad weather, as steps in advanced work on collection or extension, or to correct problems that might develop in way of going.

Mechanics of Longeing

LONGEING EQUIPMENT

The tack and equipment you will use for longeing depend upon the extent of the animal's education and, of course, on what you have available or can afford to buy. Often a trainer must improvise, use and adapt what he can. Some trainers prefer one piece of equipment over another because it fits in best with what they like. We'll try to pinpoint some of the advantages and disadvantages as we see them.

Web halter. Halters were discussed earlier under Basic-training Equipment in Part I, Chapter 2. Generally, a halter is not advised for longeing, but in some cases it is satisfactory or even preferable to a standard longeing cavesson. In these cases a well-fitted web halter is preferred to other types, because it is less inclined to slip or rub, because it has rings on the cheek pieces as well as underneath the chin (into which the longe line can be clipped), and because of its strength. Also, since it lies flat against the head, it is less in the way when used under other equipment.

The nylon cavesson with one type of elastic side reins.

Since the main object of longeing a brood mare that has just been bred is to keep her moving at a walk or a leisurely trot, the simple web halter is adequate.

It may be preferable to start a young or timid horse in a web halter. The heavier, fussier longeing cavesson can frighten or confuse such an animal, and it's usually best to introduce the heavier equipment gradually. Control, however, is minimal with a halter, compared to a longeing cavesson, because the line is clipped to the ring under the jaw instead of over the nose, and because the halter is not in a stable position on the horse's head, it can slip and move. Therefore it's important to work within an enclosed area unless the horse is tractable and well trained.

Nylon longe cavesson. This is a relatively new piece of equipment on the market, an inexpensive substitute for the standard longeing cavesson. In effect, it is a reinforced, padded-nylon halter with a fleece-padded noseband. There is a dee ring on top of the noseband, and some come equipped with dee rings on the sides. Since this piece of equipment is soft and flexible, and cannot be tightened into a stable position on the horse's head, it gives less control than the standard cavesson. It should not be used on problem horses. It does give more control than a halter, however, and when used correctly, it can be suitable for most needs.

Standard longe cavesson. This consists of headstall and noseband,

The standard longe cavesson.

made of quality bridle leather, with throatlatch and cheekpieces so that it is fully adjustable. It is heavily padded and should be adjusted tight enough to be in a stable, immovable (though not pinching) position on the horse's head. Its effectiveness is lost if it is loose enough to slip. This cavesson is equipped with dee rings on the sides and a swivel ring on the hinged steel noseband that aids in reversing the horse. When adjusted properly, it gives the trainer maximum control. Also, it helps to keep the horse's head turned in the direction of movement. The standard cavesson is especially valuable in the later stages of training to help promote flexibility and lateral suppleness. It is somewhat cumbersome, however, and can be uncomfortable for a young horse not used to headgear.

Longe line or longeing rein. Most longeing reins are twenty-five to thirty feet long with a swivel snap on one end and a hand grip on the other. They come in a variety of materials including nylon, cotton tubular web, and plain web. The better-quality lines are reinforced with leather at essential points. We prefer the web longe line because it is serviceable and heavy enough to be stable in our Western winds. Nylon lines will whip in the wind and are light enough to become tangled and knotted even without a wind. Wear gloves whenever you longe; if you longe bare-handed, the nylon line, especially, can slip and burn. A leather driving rein may be substituted for the normal longe line, but it is slow and cumbersome to buckle into the cavesson and it will tangle more easily than a line with a swivel clip. However, it is easy to hold and heavy enough not to twist. Be sure it is long enough for your needs. Very early longeing lessons can be taught with a cotton lead rope—the long, heavy lead discussed in the last chapter. This can be used until the horse understands the idea of longeing and will go willingly on the circle.

Longeing whip. The longeing whip consists of a five-to-six-foot stock with a six-to-seven-foot lash. Plastic-covered Fiberglas whips are quite adequate and take the weather very well; more expensive whips are steel-lined and covered with black thread. If you have a long driving whip, you can fashion a lash from a rawhide thong or braided hay twine. The purpose of the long lash is to reach the horse from the center of the circle as an extension of the trainer's arm. Most horses do not need to be touched by the whip, and some trainers insist that they never should be. However, some horses need the touch of the whip against the lower leg to wake them up or to enforce obedience. With practice, the whip can be made to snap behind the horse, and this is usually sufficient incentive to move him forward.

Training surcingle and felt saddle pad. Both of these items were discussed in Part I, Chapter 2. They are especially useful for early longe training because they are light in weight, have dee rings or places where reins can be attached, and have no parts such as saddle flaps to slap around and frighten the horse. Because of the way it molds to a horse's back, the pad stays in place even if the girth is not tight. This gives the colt a chance to become used to more gradual restriction around the girth than is possible when cinching the conventional saddle (sudden tightening of the girth can be a disturbing experience).

Spanish-type hackamore or bosal hackamore. This also was discussed in Part I, Chapter 2. We like the bosal hackamore for starting a colt, rather than the more widely used snaffle bit. The hackamore tends to keep the horse's nose from pointing in the air as he travels, thereby allowing you to obtain a better and more flexible head set. Use of the hackamore eliminates any possibility of a severe jab on the mouth if the youngster should become frightened and shy, buck, or rear; it gives the rider more control in the early stages of saddle training; and it is just plain convenient in later riding when the temperature drops to twenty-five degrees below zero. We want any horse we train to feel relaxed and work well in hackamore, snaffle, double bridle, and Western curb bit. (We do not use hackamore bits in longeing; these should not be confused with the Spanish-type bosal hackamore.)

When longeing with a hackamore, be sure to fit it properly—it should

Training Equipment

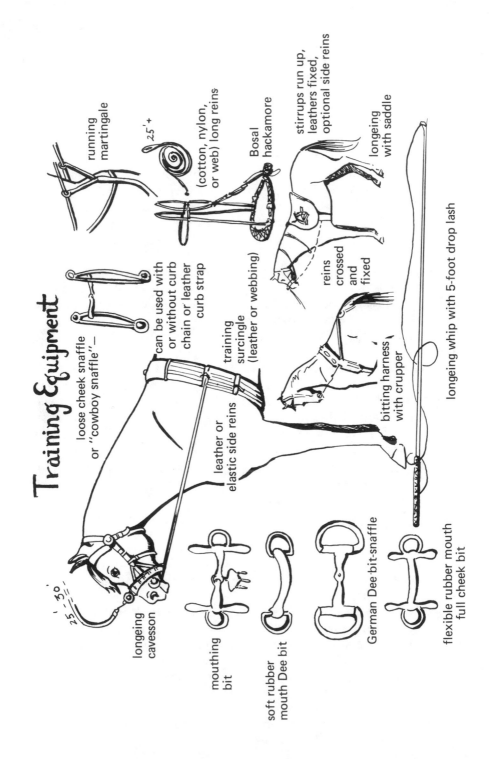

running martingale

25'+

(cotton, nylon, or web) long reins

Bosal hackamore

stirrups run up, leathers fixed, optional side reins

longeing with saddle

loose cheek snaffle or "cowboy snaffle"—

can be used with or without curb chain or leather curb strap

training surcingle (leather or webbing)

reins crossed and fixed

leather or elastic side reins

bitting harness with crupper

longeing whip with 5-foot drop lash

25' - 30'

longeing cavesson

mouthing bit

soft rubber mouth Dee bit

German Dee bit-snaffle

flexible rubber mouth full cheek bit

be snug over the nose bones (the two visible bones above the nostrils). When fitted too low, it will interfere with breathing and therefore be very frightening to the horse; when too high, loss of control will result. Reins are attached above the heel knot, and the longe line is attached to the heel knot loops.

Bits. Although briefly discussed earlier, bits deserve more attention in connection with longeing.

The mouthing bit (a thick bit with players or pendants hanging from the center) conditions the youngster to hold something in his mouth that he cannot spit out, and encourages salivation (a moist mouth improves responsiveness). This bit is used without reins. The youngster holds it in his mouth simply to become used to it. Some trainers prefer to use the mouthing bit only when the horse is standing, and switch to a plain snaffle when they begin longeing.

Other thick, heavy bits good for the early stages of training and longeing include the soft, rubber-mouth dee bit, the German dee bit snaffle, the flexible, rubber-mouth full-cheek bit, and the Fulmer full-cheek snaffle bit. These are designed with full cheeks or large dees and rings to keep them in position. They are both mild and effective, capable of developing a sensitive mouth and also of disciplining a youngster's rebellious whims. Some colts prefer a straight snaffle. For especially sensitive mouths, bits may be wrapped with rubberized elastic tape.

Bits are made of several different metals. We usually prefer stainless steel because of its all-round utility and economy. Bits with copper mouthpieces stimulate saliva, and are liked by some for this reason; however, since copper is expensive, a bit made wholly of copper would be prohibitive. Nickel plating is satisfactory as long as it does not flake off. Chrome plating is more expensive than nickel, but looks better and lasts longer. Chrome and nickel bits can be replated.

Bits come in different widths; be sure you get one that fits your horse's mouth. Some colts can use a 4-inch mouthpiece; older horses need 4½- or 5-inch bits.

TRAINING THE TRAINER: DO YOU KNOW HOW TO LONGE?

Even the best equipment isn't much good if you don't know how to use it. Longeing looks easy. But it takes practice and co-ordination to manage both longe line and whip properly, especially if the horse is unsure of what to do or feels like acting up. If you haven't longed before, don't start right out with a green colt; get some practice first.

The best way to practice is with an older, steady, well-trained horse that is experienced at longeing. He will walk and reverse calmly, and stop

Basic Position for Longeing

Handler wears gloves for protection and greater control.

Horse wears leg wraps and bell boots for protection.

Longeing over cavaletti - showing how to produce longer strides as the circle is enlarged.

3' 5' 7'

right
Correct bend in body - horse driven from behind.

wrong
haunches escaping - handler positioned Too far forward - no driving action.

Horse circles to left; hold arms out, left hand pointing to head, right hand to tail. You are "holding the horse between your hands."

immediately on the command, "Whoa!" Moreover, he'll be unconcerned if the longe line gets under his legs. You'll be able to concentrate efficiently on what you are doing rather than worry about what the horse is doing. If you don't have such a horse at hand, get someone to help you. One of the kids (con the little ones into it by having them pretend to be a horsey— they'll even trot for you), long-suffering husband or wife, bewildered Aunt Kate, bemused friend, anybody will do who can walk around in a circle holding the buckle end of the longe line.

Plan to begin by having the horse circle to the left: As you look at him, his head will be to the left, tail to the right. Hold your arms out, left hand pointing to head, right hand to tail: You are "holding the horse between your hands." This is the basic position for longeing.

Impulsion should come from behind the horse; therefore your right hand, pointing toward the tail, should be the one to hold the whip. Direction begins at the head—therefore the longe line goes from your left hand to the horse's nose. You can hold the entire longe line in your left hand, but control is often a bit quicker and smoother if you hold the bight of the longe line in the right hand along with the whip. Fold the bight in a serpentinelike arrangement so that it can slip through your hand or be taken up easily. *Do not coil it in loops around your hand or wrist.* If the horse should spook, the loops could tighten quickly around your hand and you could be injured or dragged.

As you ask your horse to walk, point with the whip toward his hocks (or behind the hocks). Let the lash trail on the ground. When you give the command to stop, raise the whip vertically as a signal. Practice both standing in one spot (turning with the horse), and walking in a smaller concentric circle, even with the horse's hip. As you walk, step toward the horse's hindquarters to increase the impulsion; as you stop, step forward toward the horse's shoulder—your position will help him to know what you want. The idea is for the horse to go around you, but we've seen the horse standing mystified as the handler backs around, longeing himself. Practice, and be clear in your mind what you expect.

The biggest problem comes in changing smoothly to have the horse circle to the right.

•First change the whip and bight to the left hand,
•then with the right, take the longe line as you give the command to reverse,
•pull his head to the right as you
•step left toward his hindquarters.

You won't ask the inexperienced colt to do this right away. Walk to his head and turn him around. However, you should know how to turn him efficiently—this is the point at which a lot of tangles occur. Always keep the longe line fairly taut—both for control and to avoid wrapping the

Raise the whip vertically as a signal to stop. (Photo by Sandy Whittaker)

horse's legs up in a knot. We watched one beginner wrap himself up in the longe line until he couldn't move—fortunately with a quiet, patient horse.

You will need to practice using the whip. You should be able to flick it along the ground, to make it snap, and to flick it lightly against the horse's lower leg. This may come easily if you are right-handed, when you hold the whip in your right hand; learn to do it equally well with the left. Do not attempt to touch the horse with the lash until you have practiced sufficiently (you may never need to touch him at all); if you're too close, the whip may wrap around the horse's leg and be pulled out of your hand, scaring him into a frenzy. Any movement asking the colt to move forward is made by flicking the whip sideways; continue to hold the whip low unless you are asking him to stop or reverse. Under no circumstances should you ever use the whip in a downward motion against the horse.

Some trainers prefer to let the bight of the longe line drag behind them instead of holding it folded in the hand. This is all right if you know what you're doing, but a beginner is too likely to become entangled and trip himself up. Keep everything up out of the way.

Elementary Longeing: The First Two Weeks

PRELIMINARIES—A THREE-DAY INTRODUCTION FOR THE COLT

Begin each training session with a thorough grooming. We've already discussed the importance of this grooming period—it holds true throughout the horse's life. Don't take shortcuts in training.

Fit the horse with a wide web halter and use the heavy training lead rope. Take him to your small, enclosed ring and do nothing but lead him and ask him to stop (as explained under "Leading" in Part I, Chapter 2). These lessons should be short (five to ten minutes), but they should be repeated six to eight times in these first two days. If the horse has had earlier training sessions, this should come easily and without any problem.

As soon as he seems comfortable with this procedure (perhaps after only one or two leading sessions, perhaps not until the second day), introduce the saddle pad (without stirrups attached) or longeing surcingle as you prepare for the leading lesson. You have time to work gradually, so play it by ear. If the horse seems spooky, begin simply by letting him see and smell the saddle pad and blanket; in later sessions, rub it gently over his neck, back, and rump. Then, later, place blanket and pad gently

Preliminary to longeing lessons, review exercises in leading, using the commands "Walk" and "Whoa" and giving a gentle tug on the lead along with the "Whoa" command. A halter may be used, but the hackamore may be introduced by the second day. (Photo courtesy E. F. Prince and Arabian Horse News)

on his back (start it well forward over his withers and slide it back to keep the hair in place), check the girth on the off side to be sure it isn't twisted, return to the near side, and fasten the girth only until it's snug. Too tight a girth at the outset will make the colt uncomfortable and later difficult to saddle. It may also make him pull back violently. Probably by the middle of the second day, you will be able to lead the youngster with blanket and saddle pad in place. If so, introduce the hackamore next session (or longeing cavesson). Place it on over the halter and tie the reins to the girth of the saddle pad or rings of the surcingle—they should be loose enough so as not to restrict his head, but should keep him from putting his nose to the ground. The lead rope will still be clipped into the halter; lead him this way to accustom him to the feel of the new headgear.

Remember, during the first two days of training, you will be giving the colt many brief training sessions. You have plenty of time to make gradual transitions, to progress so gently from one step to the next that the youngster is never disturbed. If by some chance you have an unusually timid or rebellious youngster to deal with, take another day—or two or three—to complete the lessons. There's no prize forthcoming in finishing any lesson by Tuesday at 10 A.M. The prize comes in treating each horse as the individual he is, and introducing each new point at the right time for him.

Toward the end of the second day, lead the horse in both directions at the area in which you plan to longe. Lead him on the approximate path that he will travel in longeing. This will prepare him for his first longeing lesson.

If all has proceeded smoothly, on the third day groom the horse as usual, and tack him up with blanket, saddle pad, and hackamore, if he has accepted this equipment in earlier lessons. If some part of the equipment has troubled him, you may take another day for leading, or you may go ahead with the preliminary longeing lesson and plan to introduce the troublesome equipment again later. We often start a colt on the longe with only a well-fitted web halter, simply because he is sufficiently aware of the heavier cavesson or hackamore to distract his attention from the trainer. We let him become used to the more cumbersome headgear during grooming or for a few minutes after longeing. Be flexible and innovative; every horse is different.

A word of caution: If you use hackamore or longeing cavesson without using a saddle pad or surcingle on which to tie up the reins, either remove the reins or arrange them so that they do not flap around where they could annoy or frighten the youngster or where he could step on them or get a leg through them. Crossing them over the neck and then knotting them under the neck is a good method.

If at all possible, arrange to have an assistant for the first longeing lessons. It will help to make the lessons go smoothly.

THE FIRST LESSON ON THE LONGE—"WALK" AND "WHOA"

Lead the colt to the longeing corral or ring and again repeat the "Walk" and "Whoa" lessons of the past two days, using the circle on which you will begin longeing him. Instead of using the lead rope, attach the longe line to the halter; but keep it serpentined in your hand so that your lead shank is the same length as usual. If you prefer, the long training lead rope can be used instead of the longe line for the first few lessons where you'll keep the circle small. Show the longe whip to the horse and let him smell it. Carry it as you lead him with the stock under your arm and the whip pointing back out of the way. He should become used to seeing it and it should not disturb him, especially if you have used the training whip to teach him to lead. If he seems at all concerned, hold the lash of the longe whip so that it doesn't drag.

When you are ready to begin longeing, ask your assistant to snap a second lead rope into the halter; he will walk with the horse, leading on the outside of the circle while you stand in the center. His sole function at this point is to help the horse understand what to do—to keep him moving on the circle and to keep him from turning in toward you. The assistant gives physical direction only if necessary, and he shouldn't speak at all. The colt's attention should be focused on you.

Start the horse to the left (most horses travel best in this direction). Have your longe line about ten feet long; control will be easier with the shorter line. Hold the horse "between your hands" and stand behind the girth area. Keep your line an even length so that the horse will move on a true circle. It should be fairly taut; there should be contact—even and gentle all the time—and the line should not droop or touch the ground. Hold the whip so that it is pointed up.

Say "W-a-l-k," give a slight forward tug with the longe line, take one step toward the horse's hindquarters, and point the whip toward his hocks (gently—you don't want the lash flying all over). Your assistant will lead him forward if he doesn't step out on the command. Repeat the word "Walk" and praise him so that he understands he is going correctly.

After half a circle or so, say "Whoa!," give a slight backward tug on the line, and raise the whip vertically. Again, the assistant will inconspicuously enforce the command, stopping the colt on the circle. Keep the whip vertical until you again give the command to walk.

Repeat the "Walk" and "Whoa" commands, varying the distance walked, the duration of the halt, and the places where you halt the horse. He should respond to your commands, not anticipate them. When you are ready to work to the right, walk to the horse (at a halt), unsnap the assistant's lead, turn the horse in a reverse toward the center of the circle, and

First longeing lesson: The colt has a hackamore on over the halter. The hackamore reins are tied loosely to the saddle pad, and the longe line is attached to the halter. No whip was used at first with this colt.

place him properly so that he is on the circle, this time to the right. The assistant will again be on the outside; have him snap in the lead rope. Repeat the lesson several times during the day, and don't be too quick to dispense with your assistant; the more the horse repeats the work correctly, the less likely there will be trouble.

Now, what if you don't have an assistant?

Your main problem will be to get the horse to understand that he is to work away from you; up to now he has been working next to you. He'll want to come toward you until he understands this new idea.

You may find that you have to use an even shorter line (three to four feet) and pivot on your right foot as you step backward with your left, tugging forward lightly to get the horse to walk around you. Remember, though, that impulsion should come from behind, so, as soon as possible, step back toward his hindquarters and encourage him to walk on by flicking the whip on the ground. Probably you'll have to walk too, to keep him moving (when he gets the idea, you can simply pivot). Give your commands as above, but be careful that you don't tug too hard on the longe line and pull him in toward you. If he hesitates, flick the whip behind him; if he cuts toward you, point the whip toward his shoulder. It takes co-ordination to encourage the horse forward with one hand on the longe line and the other on the whip, as well as to anticipate his hesitations, weavings, and assorted antics. Now, aren't you glad you practiced ahead of time?

Keep these lessons short and be lavish with praise when the horse goes correctly; until he understand what you want him to do, this will be very confusing and tiring for him. If you're having a lot of trouble, watch his feet for a minute: If each step he takes is ahead of the other hind or forefoot, he's trying. He's going forward, even if slowly. If each step is sideways or behind, however, you are not making progress. Try something a little different, or if at all possible, get an assistant.

Other problems to consider: Some very nervous youngsters and some old horses that have had unpleasant experiences may be nervous about (or afraid of) the whip. You may be better advised to do without it during the early stages of training. Use your arm, then, without the whip, raise it vertically on "Whoa," and swing it a little toward the horse's hindquarters on "Walk." Work with a shorter, flexible, willow-type stick before going back to the longe whip.

Some trainers like the horse to turn and face them on the command "Whoa" (rather than to halt on the circle). However, we want "Whoa" to mean halt; we do not want to attach any superfluous meaning to the word —no turns or other unnecessary movements. Otherwise "Whoa" has lost its meaning. Longe training should prepare a horse for riding, and certainly "Whoa" doesn't mean "Turn" when you are in the saddle. Be consistent.

You may occasionally see a bit of "flashy" longe work in which the trainer stands facing in one direction and lets the horse circle around him while he raises his arm over his head as though twirling a rope. This is a rather useless bit of exercise, and the horse can make a real fool out of the trainer when behind his back. If you're inclined to become dizzy in rotating with the horse, walk forward on a small circle concentric with the one the horse is making. This is necessary, anyway, in more advanced longeing, to allow the horse to make larger circles at a faster gait. You can still hold him "between your hands" without difficulty. Keep your attention on the horse if you expect to hold his attention.

THE NEXT THREE DAYS

Repeat the "Walk" and "Whoa" lessons three or four times a day for the next two or three days. During this time, depending upon the colt's grasp of the situation and resultant progress, you can expect to accomplish several things:

•The youngster should learn the longeing pattern well enough to walk willingly on the circle both to the left and to the right without the assistant leading him. He should be willing to work out at the end of the line, keeping it fairly taut, without cutting in or trying to run off.

•He should obey the commands "Walk" and "Whoa" fairly quickly.

•He should be introduced to wearing a hackamore (or longeing cavesson) and saddle pad (or surcingle), if he wasn't ready for them earlier.

•He should be working on a somewhat larger circle, perhaps with a radius of fifteen to eighteen feet.

If you are having problems—perhaps he's turning in on you or not traveling at the end of the line or refusing to go forward—remember that he's a beginner; perhaps he doesn't yet understand what you want. Are you being clear in your directions? Have an assistant help you through several lessons. If problems persist, see the later section of this chapter on how to handle them.

REVERSE

When the colt works well in the four accomplishments listed above, it is time to teach him to reverse. To become supple and muscularly developed throughout his body, it's important for him to work in both directions. Most horses, like people, have a favored side or direction, one on which they work the best. If allowed to do so, a horse can become extremely one-sided; if you've ever ridden such a beast, you'll know the problem. He'll turn willingly one way and hardly be able to bend his neck the other.

By now you know which side your horse favors. He works so well in that direction, and goes so easily for you, and it looks so professional, the temptation is to let him have his way rather than to work on the more difficult direction. Resist. Make a determined effort to work more on the side that needs it more.

Teaching the horse to reverse on the longe will help you to work more easily in both directions and to inject a note of variety into the lesson. Decide on a command that will not conflict with those you have already taught, or with "Trot" and "Can-ter," which are yet to come. We use a brief whistle—it is effective and seems to offer a change of pace to which horses readily respond. There are, of course, several ways to reverse a horse on the longe. We like the following method. As we suggested earlier, it's wise to practice and co-ordinate your signals before you try reversing an inexperienced horse.

Up to now, you have halted your horse on the circle, walked up to him, and turned him toward you into the new direction. Now start him on a short line (about eight to ten feet) in the direction he least favors—that way he will more readily make the change to the opposite direction. If he prefers to go left, let's say, start him on the small circle to the right. The whip will be in your left hand, while your right holds the longe line.

Simultaneously
> •whistle
> •tug lightly on the longe line toward your left hand,

Then,

> •switch your whip to the right hand and longe line to the left,
> •step quickly to the right, and immediately place yourself behind the girth area in the regular longeing position.

At first you will have to move several steps; later he will reverse on the circle and it won't be necessary for you to move around him. He should learn to reverse on the physical command alone; some horses will watch the whip and take their cue from it. Praise your horse generously as he is learning.

Vary your timing when asking for reverses (perhaps 3 circles left, then 1½ right, ½ left, 2 right), halting intermittently. Don't reverse in the same spot too often. As the horse becomes more adept, enlarge the circle he is working on; you'll find he turns more easily on the larger circle.

Reverses have another function: that of waking the horse up or regaining his wandering attention. Use a quick series of reverses as he goes ¼ circle or ½ circle. Of course, this should not be attempted until he thoroughly understands the command.

ABOUT WORD COMMANDS

When you were first working with your horse, leading him and teaching him to walk and to whoa, you spoke the word command clearly and without shouting because the horse was right there next to you. When longeing, however, with all that distance in between, you may unconsciously raise your voice or shout. You needn't—unless you're longeng next to a riveting plant. The horse hears very well.

In fact, shouting can be psychologically bad for you, the trainer. We've seen cases where the trainer gives a command and the horse is slow to respond. So the trainer repeats himself, louder, and again louder as though the horse out there is in need of an ear trumpet. Next thing you know, the trainer is giving every command in quadruplicate at the top of his lungs—and can't understand why the horse won't obey.

When a horse is learning a command, of course you will have to repeat it for him. When he understands what the word command means, give it once. Insist on obedience the *first* time. (Otherwise, what good is it?)

Give the command with authority, as though you expect it to be obeyed. (You do, don't you?) The tone will differ from a soothing "Easy —easy there," or a sharp "Bad!" or "Wake up!" But that doesn't mean it has to be loud. In fact, one teen-ager tried a special way of giving word commands when longe-training her temperamental and difficult filly—she enunciated clearly but spoke very quietly, almost a whisper. The filly began paying very close attention so that she wouldn't miss anything. The quiet way of speaking and handling helped to calm the filly and carried over beautifully in the first stages of saddle training.

Of course, some horses are too phlegmatic for this technique, but it brings up a good point: Be aware of what you are doing. Don't allow yourself to drift into bad or absurd training habits. Constantly re-evaluate —not only your horse's progress, but also your own. Train creatively: What is the best thing to do with this horse, this time?

TROT

When the colt will walk, stop, and reverse on signal and voice command in both directions, you may introduce the trot—probably around the fifth or sixth day of longe training. Usually the colt enjoys this and will trot readily.

Before asking for the trot, lengthen the longe line enough to allow him freedom to perform the faster gait. As he is walking on the larger circle, say "Trot!" briskly and flick your whip enough to make a noise. He will most likely trot right out. Keep your whip in the same position as for the walk.

It is easy to overcue when asking the exuberant youngster or high-strung animal for a faster gait. Such horses may need no more than the new command to encourage them to trot—a flick of the whip may send them leaping into a race. Use only as much aid as is necessary to produce the trot.

If the horse doesn't trot readily on the first command, repeat it, and this time step forward to snap the whip behind him. Praise him as he begins to trot.

Keep the horse in a trot for several circles. Strive for an even, energetic gait. Don't let him dog along.

Then say "W-a-l-k" and give a slight tug on the longe line. If he doesn't slow down, shorten the longe line until the circle becomes small enough that he has to slow to a walk. Don't keep repeating the walk command endlessly if he keeps trotting—instead, say "Easy" or something similar, repeating "W-a-l-k" just as he begins to walk. Then you can praise him for doing correctly. Keep your word commands clear and unmuddled; enforce obedience by action with longe line or whip. It will also help to slow the colt if you walk more slowly yourself, or just pivot; he may take some of his cue from watching the action of your legs. Also, you may step a bit closer to his shoulder rather than working behind the girth area.

Work in both directions and repeat the action of shortening the longe line until he understands and obeys the command to walk. Slowing the colt from trot to walk can be one of the most difficult parts of longeing. Another is when the colt breaks from a walk to a trot without command: You should reprimand him and immediately bring him down to a walk. These are critical points in your training. You are now setting his behavior patterns—he must obey you implicitly.

THE SECOND WEEK OF LONGE TRAINING

The colt is now acquainted with four commands: "Walk," "Whoa," "Reverse," and "Trot." During the next few days of training, you will be working for improved obedience and precision with these commands. Intermix them, vary the intervals between them, work in both directions. Be exacting in your signals and commands, and insist on obedience.

Encourage free forward movement. The horse should carry his head fairly low, moving in a calm, natural way.

Insist on the horse's attention. One way to do this is by regulating the length of longe line—the horse will be more attentive and try harder if you are close to him; he will be able to move faster if he is going on a larger circle farther away from you. A series of reverses also demands the horse's attention.

During the second week of longe training, you may gradually work for longer periods—perhaps twenty minutes or so twice a day.

If all is progressing smoothly, you may try a few more additions to the routine. The horse should now be wearing a web halter, over which the hackamore has been placed. The longe line has been attached to the halter; now tie it into the heel knot loops of the hackamore. The reins should still be tied to the saddle pad or surcingle—tight enough so that the horse can't touch his nose to the ground, but otherwise loose enough so as not to restrict his head. Attaching the longe line to the hackamore will give some additional control and encourage the horse to keep his nose down. He will get a better feel of the hackamore, which will prepare him for saddle training.

If the horse is calm at walk and trot, add the English stirrups to the saddle pad. At first leave them run up but arranged so that they will come down gradually as the horse moves. He will become used to feeling and

Introducing the bit. The colt wears a simple headstall under the hackamore and holds the bit—no reins attached—in his mouth. The longe line is now attached to the hackamore rather than to the halter.

seeing them bump around him. You may also tie on a burlap sack or slicker; tie them down well at first and later let them flap around more. Do this only as you feel it will be accepted with relative equanimity—do not rush.

If you have only a Western saddle, you may introduce it at this time. Make sure you have sufficient padding under it. Tie the stirrups down so that they don't flap (run a string through the stirrups and tie under the barrel). After the colt accepts the saddle quietly, you may remove the string.

Also, it is time for him to be introduced gradually to the bit. Make the introduction while he is standing at the crosstie for grooming and saddling. To prepare for it, attach the mouthing (or breaking) bit to a simple headstall (either split ear or standard) that has had noseband, browband, and reins removed. Dip the bit into warm water and then into sweet feed to

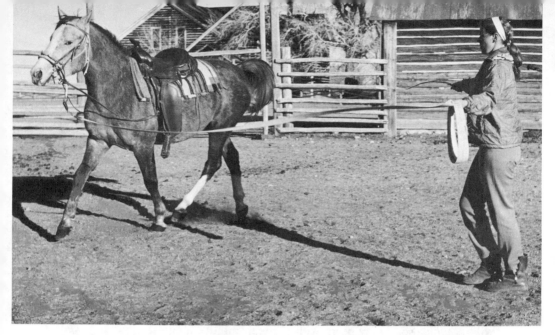

Introducing the Western saddle. Tie the stirrups together with a string at first, to keep them from flapping. Experienced trainers may prefer to hold the longe line in a coil as shown, or may even let the line drag—both methods are dangerous for beginners and should be avoided. (Courtesy E. F. Prince and Arabian Horse News)

make this introduction a pleasant experience. You may have to unbuckle and rebuckle the headstall, rather than put it on over his ears. Let the colt hold the bit in his mouth for just a few minutes at first. With the feed on it, most colts willingly take the bit and mouth it rather than try to spit it out.

If you don't have a mouthing bit, you can use a standard snaffle, perhaps wrapped with tape so that it is thick and very gentle. To encourage mouthing the standard snaffle, fit it low—about a half inch from the corners of the colt's mouth.

Each time you groom and saddle the youngster, let him hold the bit for a longer time. Eventually extend the time to his longeing lessons—he'll wear the abbreviated bridle over the web halter and under the hackamore.

WHERE LONGEING FITS IN

Let's take a minute now to consider how longeing fits in with your overall training pattern. Longeing is not an end in itself, it is a valuable training aid. Once the horse works well in the accepted longeing pattern—calmly, halting immediately on "Whoa"—he may begin other aspects of training: driving and suppling exercises (Part II, Chapter 3), and, if he is old enough, saddle training (Part II, Chapter 4). These different phases of instruction may proceed concurrently. By taking advantage of the different kinds of instruction, the horse's overall training is made varied and interesting.

Each phase of instruction—longeing, suppling, driving, and saddle training—complements the others and reinforces the basic knowledge you are imparting. For instance, the horse's understanding of his four commands to date—"Walk," "Whoa," "Reverse," and "Trot"—has been learned with the hackamore or longeing cavesson on the longe line. This understanding can be reinforced with the driving reins (with hackamore or snaffle bridle), followed by his first saddle lessons where he hears and feels the same commands as before but administered from a different direction (again with hackamore or snaffle bridle).

In other words, at this point in his training, he is readier for a variety of instruction than for more advanced work on the longe line, such as the canter. Further, the types of instruction may be varied and combined at will. A typical day may begin with a fifteen-minute longe session, followed immediately by a brief session under saddle. In the afternoon, the colt may go through some suppling exercises followed by a driving session. Throughout the day he is reinforcing his understanding of the commands while gaining a little in suppleness, responsiveness, flexibility, muscular development, and, above all, confidence.

With this in mind, then, we'll complete the discussion of longeing.

Problems Encountered in Longeing

It would be wonderful if training always proceeded so smoothly that no problems ever developed. Such utopia is pretty well nonexistent, however, so before going further, it's time to consider some of these problems and what to do about them.

TURNING IN TOWARD YOU

During the first stages of longeing, especially if you are working alone, the horse has a tendency to come toward you. He is used to walking next to you and feels that something is wrong with this different position. At first he may want the security and familiarity of being close to you; before long, he discovers that this is a good way to stop the exercises.

This can be frustrating for the trainer, especially if the horse seems to be winning. If possible, ask an assistant to help you until the horse understands what is wanted.

Part of the fault, however, may lie in your position in relation to the horse. Keep your body behind the girth area and snap your whip behind the horse to drive him forward. Use a short line and keep him moving.

To receive any benefit from longeing, the horse's spine should be curved along the arc of the circle he is describing. In the first photo, the horse is inattentive, incorrectly curved, and, if he were wearing a halter instead of a longeing cavesson, he'd be a prime candidate for running away. In the second photo, the horse is working: He is relaxed and supple, moving forward in good stride, attentive (note left ear), and tracking correctly on the circle.

When he starts to turn toward you, step toward him and point the whip at his shoulder (you may have to snap it). Say "No!" or "Bad!" and then repeat the command to walk. Be free with praise as he begins to go correctly. Continue to encourage forward movement. Anticipate his moves and be ready to shift your position and the position of your whip to counteract them.

TURNING TOWARD YOU AT THE HALT

It seems natural for a horse to turn and face you when he is asked to halt on the longe line. But, as mentioned earlier, allowing him to do so muddies and adulterates the meaning of the word "Whoa." He should learn to halt squarely. But how can you teach him this?

Because so many beginning horse trainers are somewhat experienced in training dogs, let's draw an analogy here. The problem is parallel to the dog trainer's problem of getting his dog to sit squarely beside him when he stops. Often the dog will sit out away from the trainer, or will face him, or will sit crooked. To correct the dog, the trainer indicates his displeasure ("No" or "Bad"), pushes the dog into the right position with his hand, and then praises him. The dog learns through repetition.

It's the same with your horse. When he stops and turns, immediately say "No!" and go to him. Move him onto his circle and make him hold the position for a moment; praise him; drive him forward again.

The most common trainer-mistake, here, also parallels that of the dog world. Beginning dog trainers often compensate for their dog's mistake. The dog sits wide and the owner steps over close to the dog, thereby "correcting" the position. Do not compensate for your animal's mistakes. Sure, it's easier for you to take three steps left or right and presto! the horse is on the circle again. But it doesn't train the horse. Make the horse stand or go where you want him to go.

BALKING

When a horse balks, he is refusing to go forward. This is a serious problem, because when it occurs, everything comes to a standstill. Nothing can be taught if the horse is not moving forward freely.

Most resistances of this kind stem either from overdoing some aspect of his training or from asking him to perform something of which he is physically or mentally incapable. To correct the problem, we must first find out why he balks.

Does he understand what you want him to do? If you have been rushing your training, he may be confused, especially with certain commands, or when traveling in one direction. Some beginning trainers create trouble for themselves by using the whip *on* the horse instead of as a directional aid—this adds the fear of the whip to the horse's confusion and is inexcusable on the part of the trainer. There is nothing for it but to start over. Have an assistant lead the horse until he is calm and understands what he is to do. Make sure you handle the whip correctly. Reward the horse lavishly when you gain forward motion. Repeat the lesson a few times, and then go right on to some other phase of training.

If you have been overdoing, it may be well not to longe at all for a few days. When you begin longeing again, make the lessons short, and vary them as much as possible.

But perhaps he is simply lazy and doesn't want to work: His habits must be improved. Work in an enclosed area, free of distraction. Drive him forward firmly with the whip. Keep the lessons short, however; his attention span will lengthen gradually and then more can be accomplished.

RUNNING OUT OR RUNNING AWAY

This problem is the natural outcome of the horse evading the driving force. He raises his head, grabs the bit (if he is wearing one) in his teeth, and charges away, in extreme cases, either pulling the longe line out of the trainer's hand or possibly dragging him, if he allowed the line to loop around his arm or wrist. With the longe line attached to a halter, the trainer is at a tremendous disadvantage in control.

Working within an enclosed, small training ring precludes the development of this problem. Important, both in the prevention and correction of running out, is proper use and adjustment of tack. Once a horse has run out successfully, he will try it again. Be prepared by using proper equipment: The standard longeing cavesson (with longe line attached to the ring on the top of the noseband) gives you a great deal of leverage; or attach the longe line to the hackamore instead of to the halter. Because the horse must follow his nose, you keep the runaway home when you maintain control of his head.

For added control, adjust the reins to keep the horse from pointing his nose up and out. Tie them shorter to surcingle or saddle pad girth, but do not overdo. Never pull the horse's head back so far that his profile is behind the vertical. As soon as the problem seems to be under control, release his head so that he can maintain the free forward movement that his training level warrants.

Always be aware of the reasons why a horse chooses a particular method of resistance. Re-evaluate your training methods and avoid boring him by too much repetition, tiring him with overlong lessons, or confusing him by asking him to do what he doesn't understand or is incapable of performing for some other reason. Prevention of the problem is always the best solution.

KICKING, BITING, REARING, CHARGING

Here are some tough-egg tactics that require immediate, intelligent correction. No matter how you raise your kids, you can't excuse your horse for dangerous misbehavior on the grounds that he had a difficult childhood. Restrain the horse by shortening the reins, thereby limiting the strength and speed of his undesirable actions. By driving him forward, you give him less opportunity to resort to his trick.

If the vice is ingrained—not simply an experiment that can be corrected through reprimand, adjustment of tack, and the impulsion of the whip—you must be able to deal further with it. This kind of corrective training should be undertaken only by someone experienced in handling horses.

When a horse kicks, charges, or bites, he should receive a swift, painful reminder with the whip that he would do better to work obediently. If he kicks at you, he should receive the reminder on the offending leg; if he bites or charges, on the nose or front legs. This is why the trainer should be experienced: He must have mastery of the whip so that there is no danger of injuring the horse's eyes; he must be able to anticipate the horse's actions and have enough co-ordination to meet them instantaneously; and he must have both the confidence and the wisdom to be unafraid but not endanger himself. Above all, he must dispense punishment dispassionately; he must never lose his temper, or he may aggravate the situation.

If the problem horse can be ridden, sometimes the combination of rider and longe trainer can really drive him forward and give him no chance to shy, kick, buck, or whatever.

Immediately after the reprimand, drive him forward, calm him, and praise him. Do not work too long.

TOO SPIRITED—TOO LAZY

The high-spirited horse must be handled differently from the lazy animal.

Try to calm the excitable horse. Work in an area free of distractions, and start him with a smaller circle so that there is less opportunity for him to run out. Talk to him continually in a calm, soothing tone. You may have more success letting him trot when you first begin the longeing sessions, and gradually bring him down to a walk. Do not wear him out, however, so that he starts fighting. Most high-spirited horses will fight endlessly, developing both sore muscles and a rebellious attitude that will result in your next longe session beginning on a negative note.

The lazy horse needs an energetic longe trainer, one who encourages through praise and who can maintain that necessary forward movement. Never let him lag at walk or trot. He must learn that the longe session means work and that he must produce. Here again, be careful about the length of your sessions. Make them short to begin with and increase them gradually, being careful not to overdo.

LEANING ON THE LONGE LINE—KEEPING THE LINE SLACK

When your horse makes a sloppy circle, not traveling out at the end of the longe line, try shaking the line a little to move him back; or snap the whip at his shoulder to keep him out on the circle. Keep him awake and drive him forward faster on a short line to make him use as large a circle as he can.

The horse that leans on the longe line presents the opposite problem. He may learn to lean on the longe because of boredom at going around and around endlessly. Keep him awake and alert, and keep lessons short. Give quick, repeated tugs on the longe line rather than a steady pull. Change commands more frequently, including an occasional series of reverses. And drive him forward so that he can't use the longe line as a crutch. If the problem persists, use two longe reins as described later in this chapter to gain control of his head. Some horses learn to overcome this habit when longed at liberty.

Intermediate Longeing

Once you have accomplished free forward movement, obedience to the four basic commands, and calm understanding of the longeing pattern, you have advanced beyond the elementary stage of longeing your colt. Now you may begin more serious work on stabilizing the gaits, and you may introduce a variety of new commands and experiences. As you adjust tack, you will begin to work on bitting the horse and on gaining more flexion at the poll. Although any work you do on collection and extension at this point will be rudimentary, good beginnings can be made, good behavior patterns set.

Most of your longeing lessons at this time will be planned in conjunction with other ground work and, if the horse is old enough, saddle training. There is such a wide range of training possibilities available to you now that you should be able to plan your lessons creatively, keep them interesting, and progress always on a positive note.

Take advantage of the colt's moods, your moods, weather and ground conditions, and other outside factors to aid, rather than hinder, your train-

The horse can learn to extend on the longe line.

ing sessions. If he's feeling doggy and tired, perhaps it's a good time to begin teaching him to stand or to come. If he's feeling frisky and it's a beautiful, fresh day, perhaps the time has come to introduce the canter or longeing over jumps. He's belligerent or feeling sassy? How about some heavy exercise longeing up and down hills? Or if you've just had a good rain, perhaps it's time to begin longeing him through puddles. And if your local celebration committee has planned a day of fireworks and aerial spectaculars, it's probably your cue for a very brief and quiet review session.

TEACHING THE HORSE TO STAND AND TO GROUND-TIE

Teach the horse to stand first at the crosstie and on the longe line; this training will carry over naturally to ground tying—the Western term that means the horse stands quietly wherever you leave him, with the reins on the ground. Teaching a horse to ground-tie usually takes little time, but it can be one of the most useful things you can teach a horse from the point of view of your convenience and his safety.

Ground-tie a horse *only* with Western split reins or *unbuckled* snaffle reins; to let closed reins dangle where the horse could catch his foot in them is to court disaster.

Begin his training after a longeing or riding session. Then the horse is ready, both mentally and physically, to stand quietly. Take the reins from his neck or untie them from the saddle pad and let them drop to the ground. Grasp both reins a few inches from bosal or bit and give an abrupt but not severe tug downward; at the same time say, "Stand." Make sure that he is standing squarely so that he is comfortable and less likely to move. Back away from the horse with one hand raised and palm facing him (or if the whip is handy, raise it in the same manner in which you stop the horse on the "Whoa" command). If he tries to follow you, step toward him and repeat the "Stand" command firmly. You may have to go back to him to return him exactly to his original place.

Move only a short distance away from him to begin with, wait a moment, then return and praise him. Gradually extend the distance and time. When he understands, begin moving around him; if he begins to step around to watch you, move him back into place as you repeat the command. Eventually you will be able to walk around him and even go out of sight for a few moments. When he accepts this, use the "Stand" command occasionally as a change of pace in longeing. Later, you may teach the horse to stand in areas of activity, noise, and confusion.

This training is valuable for a show horse, especially when showing at halter. You will be able to set him up and have him stand quietly and without fidgeting in the line-up; and the judge will be able to walk around him without upsetting him.

In conjunction with saddle training, dismounting occasionally and commanding your horse to stand will again provide changes of pace. As he becomes steady in his obedience to the command, try it out on the trail when the proper opportunity presents itself and when you can be sure of success in the venture. If you are riding with closed reins, *always* unbuckle them before ground-tying.

A horse that will ground tie is more versatile, pleasurable, and handy for his rider than one without this training. There will be a number of times when it seems necessary or convenient to leave the horse for a short time—whether on the trail, or even near the barn if there is no hitching post available—and you will be grateful that he has had this training. Remember that it is intended to be for a short time; don't expect the horse to stand indefinitely.

An added advantage of this training is the safety factor. If a rein is dropped while riding, a stand-trained horse will stop without becoming excited. And if he should become wound up in something—perhaps catch his foot in wire—he will be far less likely to panic than his untrained brother. His calmness will help him to extricate himself, or he will be more inclined to stand quietly and wait until someone comes to the rescue.

TEACHING THE HORSE TO COME

To relieve the horse from longe fatigue and boredom, teach him to come to you. This is a useful command, especially when used in conjunction with the horse's name—"Come, Ranger," or, better yet, "Ranger, come." Since it always means a kind word and pat, or even a tidbit, the horse finds it to be a pleasant experience and usually learns readily. It is a delight to be able to call your horse in from pasture, or to have him come to you from a corral full of buddies.

However, teaching the horse to come can make trouble for you in longe training unless you are aware of the possible problem and adjust your training accordingly. As we've discussed, the horse seems naturally

inclined to turn in toward you when halting on the longe line; this is something we want to avoid. Your clue in preventing this from happening in
conjunction with the command "Come" is to keep the meaning of "Come"
and that of "Whoa" separate and clear.

Do not try to teach the horse "Come" too soon. He must first have a
good understanding of the longeing pattern, and his obedience to "Whoa"
must be correct and immediate. When you are ready to introduce the new
command, halt the horse and let him stand for a few seconds. Then say,
"Ranger, come," and give a gentle pull on the longe line. Reel him in toward you, repeating "Come" until he is directly in front of you. Praise and
pat him.

Be sure you don't compensate for your horse by stepping up to him as
he comes to you. It would be better to back away a little and make him
come up to you.

Be sparing in repeating this command, or he may begin turning toward you, hoping and anticipating that the next command will be "Come."
Or he may try coming in toward you whenever he wishes to stop the lesson, thinking he will be praised for doing so. Return him to the circle if he
tries this, and reinforce obedience to the basic commands.

LONGEING THROUGH WATER AND NEAR FRIGHTENING OBJECTS

Horses that are raised on the range or that run free in large pastures
have no fear of crossing water, of stepping into snowdrifts or mud, or of
being near cattle and other farm animals they are used to. Backyard and
stable-raised horses, on the other hand, sometimes have an unreasoning
fear of simple, everyday objects or situations, even wind or rain. A squealing pig can send some horses into a panic, while those from dry-land
farms are sometimes terrified of water. Longeing your horse through or
near the things that bother him is a safe and satisfying way of handling the
problem. But of course he should be well trained in the basic longeing pattern before you consider introducing problems.

Since you will probably anticipate trouble when introducing these
worrisome objects or conditions, be sure to adjust your tack so that the
horse can't run out on you. Shorten the reins to surcingle or saddle pad so
that he can't get his head and run off. If you feel you may need an assistant, anticipate this and prepare for it. Don't start something you can't
finish.

Begin longeing some distance from the object, gradually working
closer to it. If it is a puddle, work him past it in both directions, moving
closer until he must step into it. Use your whip to keep him out at the end

of the line. He may rush through or try to leap over it at first, but will gradually settle down.

You have a threefold advantage when introducing this type of problem on the longe line. You have control of the head, you have the forward-driving force of your whip, and you have the reassurance of your voice to calm and encourage him. If he should react violently, your control is in no way diminished. You can immediately drive him forward and reassure him with your voice. On the other hand, if you were riding the colt and he acted in this way, your efforts to stay with him might put him off balance, adding this fear to his other problems. Longeing is a great safety measure for both of you.

ADJUSTING TACK

So far in this section on intermediate longeing, we have been considering training that will add to the horse's versatility and overall confidence more than training that will increase his proficiency and improve his way of going. Now let's look again at what we hope to accomplish on the longe, and how to achieve it.

The horse moves forward freely and calmly in obedience to the basic commands you have taught. You can now think about introducing the action of the snaffle bit, as well as the idea of positioning the head, developing lateral and vertical suppleness and flexion, and improving rhythm, cadence, balance, and impulsion. How?

The trainer works toward these improvements by two means. The first is by adjustment of the tack; the second by his action of the longe line and whip. Although these points will be discussed more fully in the section on advanced longeing, the trainer can begin now to adjust the tack toward the accomplishment of these goals. Remember that your use and adjustment of tack during longeing parallels this use during the other phases of training —driving, suppling, and saddlework.

For now, the main adjustment you make will be the adjustment of the reins—these are called "side reins," as distinguished from long (or driving) reins, longe reins (use of two longe lines), and check reins (reins used in a bitting harness to help position the head). Up to now, you tied the side reins loosely. These reins have been attached to the hackamore, and the horse has been carrying a bit in his mouth with no reins attached.

You may begin with the hackamore reins; tie them somewhat shorter than before in order to encourage the horse to tuck his head and flex at the poll. But you will soon want to attach the reins to the snaffle bit instead. The snaffle is the most important bit the horse will wear: Most elementary and advanced training is learned by communication through the snaffle bit.

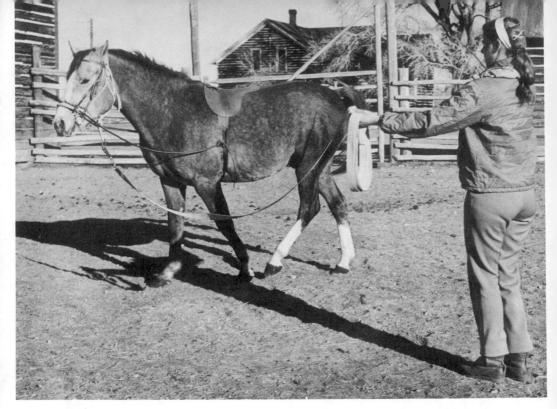

The side reins are shortened slightly to encourage tucking the head and flexing at the poll. The reins are still attached to the hackamore, but they may soon be attached to the bit. They are tied the same length; however, slack is taken up in the outside rein by the curve of neck and body.

Keep in mind the following principles when adjusting side reins:

•Tie them evenly. It is usually best to tie the reins the same length; if you wish the head to be turned toward the inside, it is preferable to obtain this tendency simply through the weight of the longe line. (Too much weight to the inside may make the horse's haunches swing out.) However, it is sometimes necessary or desirable to shorten the inside rein a little more than the outside rein. Never shorten the outside rein more than the inside one.

•Attach the reins to girth or surcingle in the position that best fits that particular horse. If the horse tends to fight and carry his head high, attach the reins low; if he carries his head too low, attach the reins higher on surcingle or girth.

•Shorten the reins very gradually. You want the horse to move forward into the bit, and therefore you want to encourage, rather than discourage, acceptance of the bit. Tying the reins too short or too low may frighten the horse or cause him to resist by rearing up and even going over backward. At this stage of training, you are developing the

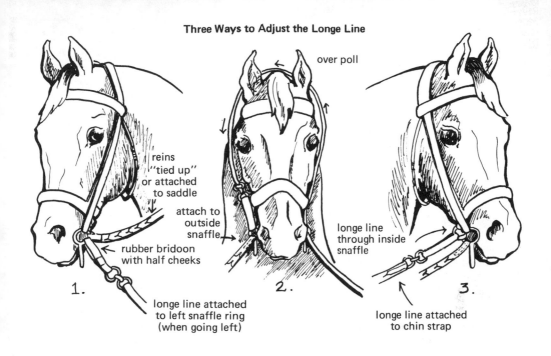

1. reins "tied up" or attached to saddle

rubber bridoon with half cheeks

longe line attached to left snaffle ring (when going left)

over poll

attach to outside snaffle

2.

longe line through inside snaffle

3.

longe line attached to chin strap

horse's mouth, not trying for extreme collection. Never tie the reins so short that the horse cannot flex his head further.

•Use side reins, or "tie up the horse's head," only when he is moving and being driven up to the bit. You are working for sensitivity and flexion: The horse should learn to reach for the bit. To tie up the horse's head while he's standing in the stall produces stiffness rather than sensitivity.

You may attach the longe line to hackamore or longeing cavesson, or, if the horse is tractable and ready for more contact with the bit, you may attach the line to the snaffle. There are several ways to do this:

1. Attach the line to the near ring of the snaffle. Ring guards or half- or full-cheeks should be used to keep the bit from being pulled through the mouth.

2. Run the line through the inside ring of the snaffle, over the horse's poll, and attach it to the outside ring of the snaffle bit.

Both of the above methods require the trainer to rearrange the longe line when changing direction.

3. Buckle a chin strap between the snaffle rings (under the jaw), and run a small ring over the chin strap. Attach the longe line to this ring. With this method, you need not rearrange the tack to reverse the horse.

As you can see from studying the illustrations, the three methods give a different emphasis to the feel of the bit. The first works more on one side of the horse's mouth; the second works more in the corners of the mouth; the third works more on the bars (the toothless space of the gum where the bit rests). By experimenting with the different methods, you will see how your horse reacts to the somewhat different action. Use this knowledge creatively to produce the best results.

What you continually hope for and work toward in longeing is for the horse to take the same light contact with the longe line that he will eventually take with the reins. This contact will keep the line fairly taut and elastic, neither too loose nor too tight.

Another method of tacking up uses two longe lines (longe reins). Attach the longe reins either to the side rings of the longeing cavesson or to the snaffle bit. (When side reins and longe reins are both attached to the snaffle, the side reins should be above the longe reins.) Use of the two reins will be discussed in more detail in the next chapter. This method is very effective because it gives better control of the hindquarters as well as of the head. It helps the horse to round his spine in the shape of the circle he is describing. (The outside rein is run through a side ring or stirrup iron, then around the lower part of the croup above the hock to the trainer's hand.) Using two reins in this way gives you the same contact with the horse's mouth as if you were riding him. You have control over the whole horse—an advantage over ordinary longeing.

CANTER

There is no rush to start the horse cantering on the longe line. As this gait tends to excite the youngster, it is easy for him to be carried away. Beginning the canter too soon can be a disadvantage to you, the trainer, because the horse will often readily break into a canter when you are trying to produce an animated or extended trot. However, the horse should learn the meaning of the word "Can-ter!" and he should be taught to canter on the longe before he is taught to canter under saddle. Be sure he is well trained in elementary longeing before you ask him to canter.

Incidentally, although Westerners generally prefer the word "lope," even Western trainers usually use "canter" when teaching the horse on the longe. "Lope" is too easily confused with "Whoa."

First, consider the problem of leads: A young and inexperienced horse must learn to balance himself correctly. Until he is supple through the spine, cantering properly on a small circle will not be easy for him; therefore it's important to keep the circle as large as possible. If he should begin to canter on the wrong lead, his spine will be bent in the wrong direction and he could interfere with himself, perhaps even stumble or fall. Often, then, the youngster winds up in a disunited canter in his efforts to balance himself (one lead in front; the opposite lead behind). You should know when a horse has taken the wrong lead or is cantering disunited so that you can immediately have him trot and begin again. (If you are unsure about the pattern of the gaits, please refer to basic texts listed under "Recommended Reading.")

We considered earlier that when on the longe, the horse's inside leg makes a smaller circle than the outside leg: Therefore the inside leg is taking a shorter stride. Because of this restriction on the inside leg, there is not always sufficient freedom for the youngster to strike off on the correct lead, and he goes wrong. How can you help the youngster to strike off on the correct lead?

Prepare for the canter by an adjustment of tack: Shorten the inside hackamore rein *slightly*. This will keep his nose pointed in the direction of movement—at least preventing him from turning to the outside—and encourage him to bend his spine along the curve of the longe circle, thereby helping him to balance and setting him up for the correct lead.

Before asking for the canter, pull the colt slightly into the circle, and then as you give the aids for canter, drive him forward on the circle again, thereby freeing the inside leg enough to make it easier for him to take the correct lead. This requires some expertise in handling the longe, but if you can master it, you will have less difficulty in getting your horse to strike off on the correct lead. Pulling him slightly into the circle before the canter has an added advantage: It helps to collect him just a little, which is good preparation for taking the canter. All of this follows through in teaching the horse to canter under saddle.

When ready,
> •put the horse into an energetic trot,
> •pull him into the circle a little,

and simultaneously,

> •say "Can-ter!"
> •let out the longe line,
> •flick your whip.

The two-syllable "Can-ter" differentiates the command from others you have given. You may have to repeat the sequence until the horse understands and obeys; or, if he takes the wrong lead, pull him in and repeat. Keep him in the canter for only a short distance at first, and gradually extend the time over several lessons.

When the colt is adept at all gaits, change your commands so that he can't anticipate a standard routine; keep him interested and alert. At the same time, you may begin pacing your horse—that is, lengthen the time at the trot and canter, working to keep him steady and regular in each gait. This preliminary gait-training forms good habits and saves time and frustration when you begin riding.

If you have trouble with the canter, especially in obtaining the correct lead, you may begin using two longe reins. At first, do a great deal of trotting to obtain the correct bend of the spine. The outside longe rein keeps the haunches from turning out. When you initiate the canter (as before) and have this added control of the haunches, he will strike out more readily on the correct lead and be less likely to canter disunited.

Be sure your circle is large enough. Very often the youngster starts on the correct lead but, because he can't balance himself on a full circle at the canter, he will begin to canter disunited. In this case, canter him for several strides, then bring him down to a trot. Repeat this until he is better balanced and co-ordinated.

LONGEING OVER INCLINES AND ROUGH GROUND

A horse may work beautifully on level, smooth ground and be completely at sea on rough or uneven footing. Longeing is a good way to introduce this new type of terrain, although a range or pasture horse is not generally bothered by this situation. Even so, trotting over plowed furrows, through sand, or on other types of uneven ground can be excellent exercise, developing both muscles and balance, encouraging a higher and more suspended action, and enforcing suppleness. The footing must be good, however; avoid rocky or slippery ground.

Longeing up and down inclines can be another good muscle-building exercise. Strive for an even, regular gait: The horse will learn to increase his effort when going uphill, let up when going down, and maintain a regular rhythm. Try for smoothness as he makes these changes. Later you may vary the pattern, cantering as he goes uphill, trotting or walking on the downhill side. Do not overdo these exercises, as they can really tire a horse's muscles. Give him enough rein to maintain balance.

If you have a horse that stumbles because of lack of attention—often a stallion or a barn-raised horse—longeing him over rough or pitted ground will teach him to watch where he's going.

LONGEING OVER POLES, CAVALLETTI, AND JUMPS

Even if you do not anticipate producing a jumper, your horse will be a better all-round athlete if he can maneuver over jumps easily and be able to anticipate and time his distances and heights. In endurance and trail riding, the horse is often required to jump low obstacles; his willingness and method are judged.

This type of longeing builds muscles, especially in the hindquarters, loin, and neck, and helps to supple the horse. He also gains in experience, confidence, and balance. Adjust your tack so that the reins do not restrict the horse's head; they should not interfere with the lowering or stretching of his neck.

At first lay just one pole on the ground; lead him up to it and let him investigate if he wishes; then lead him over it. Follow by longeing him over it at a walk, then at a trot. When he trots over it quietly, add several poles at a distance of 4½ to 6 feet, depending on the stride of your horse. He should step exactly in the middle of the space between the rails. You may place these poles in a straight line or in a circular pattern. If placed in a straight line, you will have to walk along with the horse so that he can keep moving forward in a straight line. If you place the longeing poles in a circle, be sure to make your circle large enough so that the horse will be able to take long strides. Short, choppy strides will defeat your purpose.

In any case, place the poles in such a way that the chance of the horse running out is minimized. Have the horse jumping *into* the corner of a ring or enclosure so that he can't run around the jumps on the outside. Use your whip to keep him from running out to the inside. You may have to rearrange the poles when changing direction.

It is useful to have enough control of the longe to be able to shorten or enlarge the circle at will, thereby controlling the exact spot at which the horse will take the jumps, or pulling him in to miss the jumps for several rounds. Be careful not to overdo. Three times a week for five to fifteen minutes a session should be the limit.

When you are satisfied with his progress, you may substitute cavalletti (not more than a foot high) for the poles, later adding a jump at the end. Keep your cavalletti and jumps low and broad. This will improve his balance, rhythm, and flexibility. As you vary combinations of jumps and cavalletti, the horse will learn where and when to take off, and how to lengthen or shorten his stride. He will improve in grace and boldness.

This is really advanced work and will be discussed more fully in Part II, Chapter 6.

LONGEING AT LIBERTY

Longeing at liberty means that no longe line is used: The horse works on the longe circle without direct physical control. The trainer stands in the center, gives commands, and uses his whip as before. This training should take place in an enclosed circular or square ring of the correct size. In most cases, longeing at liberty should be attempted only when the horse is obedient, willing, and knowledgeable on the longe line.

Some trainers like the results of longeing a horse at liberty and do a lot of it. Free of restraint, the horse learns to balance himself, to round his spine properly and more naturally. Correct longeing at liberty improves gaits, suppleness, and balance.

Generally it is effective with lazy horses, or horses that tend to lean on the longe line. Horses that require retraining due to unfortunate experiences with a rope or on the longe may do especially well at liberty; they learn to respond willingly and gain confidence. However, longeing at liberty is less well suited to exuberant youngsters or to horses inclined to run or rebel.

CHAPTER 3

SUPPLING, BITTING,

AND DRIVING

Developing Responsiveness

Something often seems to happen at this stage of training—after the first two weeks of longeing. The horse is going well and is calm and has learned his commands, so why are we dinking around? Let's zoom along with the training! What are we waiting for?

In English training, the result of this impatience tends to be a sudden concern to get the horse bitted and acquire a good head set. In Western training, it tends to getting him to rein well and put on a good sliding stop. Both can be accomplished at this point, true enough, but they can only be done in the wrong way: by taking shortcuts that indeed speed up the training but leave behind some major deficiencies.

Let's take a few pages here to consider these problems, to compare the various training means we have at our command, and to really understand what happens to a horse when we use one or another method of training.

Please understand that we are not implying criticism of trainers who use some of these methods knowledgeably—who have the experience to fit the method to the horse and who have a thorough understanding of the result. It is when understanding is less than perfect that these methods become dangerous, result in training setbacks, discomfort or pain for the horse, sometimes injury, and often a shortening of the horse's life of usefulness. Every trainer must work creatively with each horse he undertakes to train—but to be effective and humane, he must understand what he is doing.

HOW TO DEVELOP RESPONSIVENESS

Keep in mind your overall training goals. Probably they boil down to responsiveness on the part of the horse. If he is responsive, he'll react immediately to your slightest aids, and you will achieve harmonious horsemanship.

How can we develop responsiveness to our wishes? In order for a horse to respond to the aids, he must

•understand what the signal means,
•be physically and mentally able to comply,
•be ready to comply,
•want to comply.

Is all of this natural and automatic?

Most certainly not. In order to be responsive, the horse must be developed, through training, in each and every one of these areas.

So far we've been doing well at this: We've been building gradually on our basic foundation, letting the colt learn one thing well before he is asked to learn something new. He *understands*. We haven't rushed the training and we've rewarded him generously so that he enjoys the work and *wants* to please. We keep his attention so that when we ask him to trot or to halt, he is *ready* to obey this simple command. And we've kept the lessons short and simple, so that he has been physically and mentally *able* to obey, at least in intent if not in perfect execution.

But so far these have been simple commands, performed without a rider—a long way from the show horse that carries his head proudly and steps high, or the rodeo horse that scores and rates a calf and then stops on a dime, or the smooth-gaited pleasure horse that takes you willingly and comfortably on an eight-hour trail ride. How to get from hither to yon? How to make the horse ready to respond—constantly, always *ready;* completely, thoroughly, willingly *able* to react in harmony?

The key to responsiveness involves suppleness and sensitivity and balance; and these must build on the foundations of calmness and free forward movement that you have already begun to establish. We've mentioned these qualities in passing; now let's look at them more closely.

BALANCE

On his own in the wild, a horse is naturally balanced. Put a weight on his back and, once he becomes used to the weight, he can still balance himself naturally—so long as he can do what he wants to do and his volition is not interfered with (a packhorse following without a lead; a cutting horse in action). But put a weight on his back and expect him both to carry the weight and to respond to outside stimuli, and balance becomes a problem.

Here's why: A horse carries more of his total weight on his forehand than on his hindquarters; add a weight to that, and he carries an even greater proportion of this total weight on the forehand. But, as we learned earlier, impulsion must come from the hindquarters: If a horse is to be ready at any instant to obey the signals he receives—to turn, to spin, to move forward at a faster gait—he must learn to carry more of his weight on the hindquarters and thus be ready to apply impulsion.

Consider also how the weight of head and neck affects the horse. With that much weight out in front, the forehand acts somewhat as a fulcrum, and the head and neck balance the action of the hindquarters. If the horse is standing at rest, the farther his hind feet are under him, the lower his head must be to balance this. The racing horse, on the other hand, going at speed with his hind legs stretched out behind, also stretches his head out before. Because of the head and neck's function in balance, then, their placement is important for the proper execution of any given maneuver.

As the horse learns to carry more of his weight on his hindquarters, his center of gravity moves back. His hindquarters lower, his back arches, his forehand seems to rise higher, his neck and head rise and flex at the poll, and he tucks in his chin and relaxes his jaw. He's ready to move instantaneously into a canter or slide to a stop.

We find that head carriage is indeed important, for it affects balance and impulsion and therefore responsiveness.

SUPPLENESS AND MUSCULAR DEVELOPMENT

Getting the head and neck up into the proper carriage is an end result of proper training, not a beginning condition. It is the result of careful development of muscles, of intelligent suppling and conditioning. It does not come all at once, and some horses, because of their natural structure, are better able to achieve it than others. Further, it is not achieved alone: The entire body is involved as a unit.

Muscles stretch and contract with a degree of elasticity that improves with development. When a horse is supple, his muscles have achieved a degree of elasticity that allows him to respond—*with ease*—to the direction of advanced aids. But first of all, he must develop certain muscles to carry weight and, gradually, those that will allow him to carry more weight on his hindquarters. Acting throughout his body, the muscles that most need developing are in his neck and down through his shoulders, along his back, and along both sides of his abdomen.

When properly developed, these muscles allow the horse to arch and flex, and thereby to carry weight easily and move fluidly. On the other hand, if the head and neck are forced into collected position before this muscling and suppling have taken place, the attitude produces stiffness and a hollow instead of arched back, so that the horse cannot get his hindquarters under him. He becomes sore and stiff and most likely disinclined to work willingly. This is where we run into trouble with bitting rigs and head sets and what-have-you (it is wise to be suspect of all gimmicks in training; mechanical devices tend to give mechanical results).

Compare: Properly developed, the young horse learns to move forward freely with his head low, thereby stretching the muscles along the top of his neck and beginning to arch his back. As he improves in muscling and suppleness, he flexes more at the poll, arching both back and neck, and naturally raising his head carriage. Still moving forward with impulsion, he accepts the bit and learns to flex his jaw, to go into the bit willingly.

On the other hand, if the head is forced into position (whether by misguided use of bitting rigs, curb bit, or heavy hand), the tendency is exactly the opposite: The pull or force is aimed backward instead of forward. Impulsion is impaired, and the horse is more inclined to evade the bit or become hard-mouthed; his head and neck stiffen and develop resistance. Also, the wrong muscles of the neck become involved, which results in a tendency to look ewe-necked.

Hence the importance of muscular development and suppling at this stage—the importance of gradual, progressive training. Incidentally, the horse that receives this gradual conditioning and development will be in good physical shape for many years to come; his useful life will be far longer than that of the horse that was early rushed and strained and never allowed to realize his full physical potential.

The horse that moves with neck and back arched, his hind legs under him, his head tucked—balanced, supple, brilliant in his action—is moving the way a horse, impelled by excitement or good spirits, moves when on his own in a natural state. This brilliance can be *approximated* in the mounted horse by fear, anxiety, or extreme excitement (evident in many horse shows); it can be *attained* in the mounted horse through impulsion, balance, sensitivity, suppleness, and the willing generosity of a horse schooled with love and understanding.

SENSITIVITY

While developing balance and suppleness in the colt, we also work to develop sensitivity. The colt should become sensitive to the feel of the bit and the action of the reins, to weight and pressure changes on his back, and to the feel and action of the legs on and behind the girth.

Again, we hear at this point about the importance of bitting, of getting an easy rein, or making a mouth. And again, lack of understanding of how to go about this education produces some horrible examples of abuse to the horse, whether from a bitting harness, or "tying up the horse's head" in the stall to "soften" one side of his mouth at a time, or rough handling with a severe bit. This static or backward-pulling "bitting" results in either a hard, deadened mouth or one that is "panic-sensitive"—that is, that responds by extreme reaction (such as a sliding stop or a ninety-degree turn) to any pressure at all. The hardened mouth is produced by steady, unremitting pressure, with a side result that the horse learns to lean

Responding to aids of impulsion plus restraint, this horse demonstrates lightness by placing all his weight on his hindquarters, bringing his forehand off the ground. He is balanced and supple, and could be taught to perform a levade. The rider has given the reins as the horse's forehand came off the ground.

on the bit; the panic-sensitive mouth has been subjected to painful jabs, which have caused the horse to fear the bit.

So what is it we want?

The educated mouth responds to gradations, vibrations, and directions of pressure on the bit. These pressures, in conjunction with the leg and weight aids, act throughout the body to produce good "contact" and to result in clear communication: harmonious horsemanship.

Development of this degree of sensitivity can only be as gradual as the development of suppleness and balance: They are interrelated, and the horse must learn to seek the contact himself. We want him to reach for the bit with confidence and to feel our slightest desires through the reins.

The sum total of progress in balance, suppleness, and sensitivity (along with impulsion and willingness) is the development of lightness—the quality of responsiveness *with ease*. This requires a commitment in time, patience, understanding, and love. It is what advanced training is all about. But it must begin now.

Further Ground Training

The ground work we do at this stage of elementary training—suppling exercises and long-reining—is aimed mainly at developing responsiveness through suppling and muscling. At the same time, we reinforce earlier lessons in obedience, working toward increased precision. As the colt develops in suppleness and sensitivity, we are able to refine our aids, become less and less crude, more and more delicate.

This work—sometimes growing into actual driving in harness—combines with longeing and saddle training to establish a basic education and conditioning program that will benefit any young horse—whether his destiny holds show jumping, polo, hunting, cutting contests, roping, Saddle Seat riding, dressage, or any other aspect of the sport.

ELEMENTARY SUPPLING EXERCISES

Suppling the neck with a hackamore

The first exercise may be begun with a hackamore. Stand at your horse's head on the near side and hold the reins about six inches from the hackamore. Gently give little pulls or vibrations toward his chest, inducing him to relax at the poll and lower his head. Reward any indication of compliance with immediate praise and release of the pressure. Let him stand a minute and repeat. If he learns to give with the pressure—and is rewarded, each time he yields, with release—he will be more and more inclined to relax and flex in the direction you have indicated. This alone is a great stride forward. Repeat perhaps three or four times, be generous in your praise, and then move right on to something else.

It is easy to sour a horse with this type of exercise. At first be satisfied with small gains; it's better to give the exercises briefly, but repeat them several times during a day's lessons.

Next, holding the reins in the same way, give a lifting motion to gently raise his head. Follow with a downward pressure or motion to lower the head.

Then gently turn his head from side to side, first toward you, then away.

These simple exercises begin work toward vertical and lateral flexion. Remember that you are not simply turning the horse or yanking his head up and down—you are working for flexion with relaxation. You are applying light pressure and *inviting* the horse to yield to it. It's physically impossible to force it—the horse must do it himself.

Suppling the neck and mouth with a bit

After the horse has become familiar with the feel of the snaffle bit, repeat the exercises using the bridle reins. If he resists and pushes against the bit, give with him and begin again. Some trainers tie a snaffle bit to the halter and let the colt wear it in his stall, even while eating. This lets him get used to a bit without any pressure or stress being exerted.

This time, along with looking for relaxation and yielding at the poll, you are also looking for it in the lower jaw. The mouth will open slightly

Suppling with a hackamore.

and the tongue will move up. Always, in these exercises, relax the pressure or vibration as soon as the horse yields, and praise him generously.

There are several problems to watch for when working on these exercises. First is the possible tendency of the horse to move backward instead of to relax at the poll and jaw. So, continued emphasis on forward movement is important; it's one reason why we don't want to teach the horse to back too early in his training. The suppling exercises we're working on now will help him eventually to seek contact with the bit himself by going forward, by "going into the bit" with a flexed poll and jaw that will enable him to develop full sensitivity, balance, and communication. If at any time in these exercises the horse has a tendency to back, stop immediately and

Suppling with a bit.

move him forward. It may be necessary in such cases to do the exercises only when moving forward, either as described under "Suppling at a walk," or under saddle with the impulsion of the legs.

When you are working on lateral flexions (moving the head from side to side), make sure that the head remains vertical; it is easy simply to tip up the muzzle to one side or the other, rather than have the horse flex left or right at the poll. If you have trouble with this, or with direct flexions, you might try gently rubbing or pressing the poll with one hand while you work the reins with the other.

Suppling laterally. The same position may be used to supple the horse at a walk, turning him left and right.

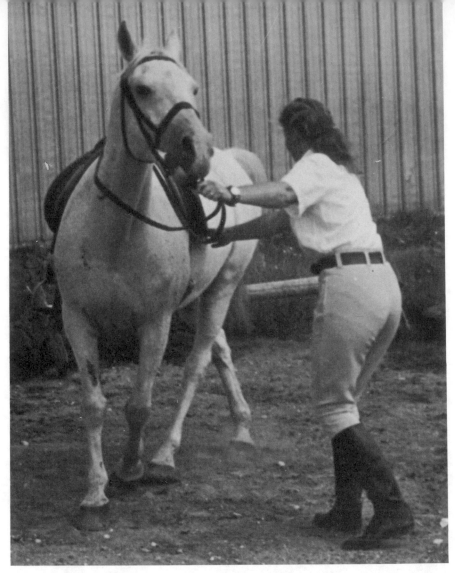

Suppling the hindquarters—note correct movement as near hind leg crosses in front.

Sometimes a horse will flex at the poll but not at the jaw. In this case, use one hand on each rein up close to the bit and gently work them (or use vibrations) back and forth until he relaxes his jaw. Stop immediately and reward him; then repeat. He should soon respond to the regular exercise.

Suppling the hindquarters

Although we do these elementary exercises separately, remember that they are interrelated in their action on the horse. As you advance in saddle training, you will be better able to see how they fit together to supple the whole horse and to improve his agility and balance.

Up to now, we have worked only with the forehand; the colt must also learn how to respond to the rider's leg and heel, to move his hindquarters in response to pressure on or behind the girth. Since a horse will move away from pressure, we use this principle in teaching him to move his hindquarters. This is a lateral suppling exercise.

To begin, stand at the near side facing the horse, and hold the reins in your left hand. Hold a short crop in your right hand (or you can use your fingers or fist—gently). You will ask the horse to move his hindquarters to the left. Tap him intermittently behind the girth where you will give the aids with your leg when you are in the saddle. If he doesn't move, you may have to tap at first on his thigh and move forward to the girth area. Reward his slightest step in the right direction by immediately ceasing the exercise and praising him; then try again.

Remember, as always, the importance of forward movement: In moving his hindquarters to the left, the horse's near hind leg should cross *in front of* the other—it should not step behind the off hind leg. If you have any trouble with this, begin by leading the horse forward a step before asking him to move his hindquarters.

Reverse the whole process when asking the horse to move his hindquarters left; stand on the off side. Do extra work on the side on which the horse seems stiffer, but don't overdo. Develop both sides equally.

Suppling at a walk, from the ground

If your colt is too young to ride, or seems especially stiff on one side, or needs more ground work before he seems safe to ride, this suppling while moving forward may be the exercise he needs. Also, it is excellent preparation for driving. On the other hand, if you are having problems maintaining the forward impetus, and the colt is old enough to ride, you may have more luck giving the exercise from the saddle. If the horse will move forward readily for you as you walk at his shoulder, this exercise will give you a training advantage since it teaches response to the bit as well as suppling.

Stand at the near side of your horse, at or just behind his shoulder. Hold one rein in each hand in approximately the same position as when you are riding (your right hand will reach across the withers). Say "W-a-l-k" and encourage the horse to move forward. He may not understand at first, because you are in a different position from what he is used to. It is helpful to have an assistant to help him move forward until he understands (the assistant may stand in the longeing position with a longe whip to start him out, or may lead him).

As the colt walks, finger the reins lightly (in the same way you did in earlier exercises) to encourage him to flex at the poll and relax his jaw. Always cease the action and praise him when he does well.

When he walks freely and yields to the reins as explained above, begin working the reins separately to ask him to turn left and right. Make it easy for both of you: Head him first toward a wall or fence. As you approach, it becomes obvious to him that he will have to turn or stop. Use a direct rein to turn him left (going forward with your indirect, or right, rein in order to follow the movement of his head). He will learn to yield to direct pressure on the bit—in this case, turning left—and at the same time feel the indirect rein on the right side of his neck (this will later help in teaching him to neck-rein). You'll find this ground training to be a great help when you begin riding, as he will already have a somewhat knowledgeable mouth.

Practice turning both left and right. Use both reins together lightly (and say "Whoa!") to teach him to halt. Whenever it seems helpful, make use of a barrier to make the command obvious and thus minimize problems.

This suppling while walking will teach the colt to respond to the hackamore as well as to the bit. In fact, you may teach the colt to respond to rein pressure with the hackamore before he even has a bit in his mouth.

Principles to remember in using suppling exercises:

• Maintain the inclination toward forward movement.
• Release pressure when the horse yields.
• Proceed gradually: It takes time to develop muscles and improve suppleness.
• Aim for flexion with relaxation.
• Invite the horse to accept the bit and to take contact with it.
• Praise generously.

LONG-REINING AND DRIVING

What is the purpose of long-reining?

Long-reining, like longeing, is a means of working the horse from the ground. However, it uses two long reins instead of one and does not limit work to a circular pattern.

Long-reining's greatest advantage over longeing is the increased amount of control it gives to the trainer. When the reins are attached to the bit, they exert control on both sides of the horse's mouth, and also contain the hindquarters. Horses that may have difficulty in bending correctly while longeing usually learn quickly with long reins.

Long-reining teaches the horse to respond to the bit as he will learn to do under a rider—he learns to obey the action of the reins in turning and halting. This is a step in the gradual process of "making the horse's mouth": first, carrying the bit while longeing; second, introduction to its action by suppling exercises; third, learning to obey its action and to accept contact while long-reining (driving); and fourth, gradual and ultimate refinement under saddle.

Long-reining again reinforces voice commands and develops the colt's confidence. He learns to accept the lines or ropes touching him around the body, and the outside rein working against the hock encourages him to bring his hindquarters under him, rather than to throw them to the outside as he turns.

Transition from longeing—working alone

Begin by longeing the horse to start him in his lesson routine and to make sure his mood is a good one for introducing the new experience. If the colt has had sufficient experience with the snaffle bit during longeing and the suppling exercises, you may begin by attaching the reins (two longe lines will do) directly to the bit. However, it may be safer, at least for a few lessons, to attach the reins to the bosal of the hackamore or to the longeing cavesson (whichever you are using). Make the transition to the snaffle when you feel he is ready. Attach the side reins as you did for longeing.

When ready to begin long-reining, longe the horse to the left, with the longe line attached to the bosal of the hackamore or to the near ring of the snaffle bit. Halt the horse, go to his off side, and attach the second longe line to the bosal or to the off ring of the snaffle. Run this outside line through a dee ring on the surcingle or through the stirrup (run the stirrups up on an English saddle; tie them together under the belly with a Western saddle). Then set the bight of the line up on the saddle so that you can take it properly from the near side.

Return to the longeing position and use a fairly short line (perhaps twelve feet). You'll hold the first line as you did in longeing (straight from the bit to your left hand). The second line (running from the off side of bit or bosal through the stirrup or dee ring) will come across the saddle to your right hand.

As you say "W-a-l-k," flip the second line very slightly so that it slides over the horse's croup and rests against the outside of his leg just above the hock. Some youngsters may jump a little when they first feel the line against their leg, but this shouldn't worry you, as you have full control with the first longe line. Talk quietly to reassure the colt, repeating the command to walk, and he will have no alternative but to settle quietly to walking in the circle to the left. Have him halt; if he is calm at the walk, have him trot. To reverse, you will have to go to him and rearrange the lines (now the right rein will come directly to your right hand, and the left will lead through the dee ring or stirrup and around the body).

Continue to use the lines in this way until the colt is thoroughly calm

Beginning adjustment of the long lines with the near line running straight from hand to bit. The off line is run through the stirrup.

and works willingly in both directions. You have a great deal of control with the inside line going straight to his head and the outside line encircling his hindquarters.

As he walks calmly in a circle, gradually step toward his hindquarters until you are walking more nearly behind him though still to the inside. This transition may take a few sessions.

Longeing with two lines can be a great aid for horses with special problems in bending and flexibility or with problems of control. In this case, since you may well have your hands full with the two lines, a knowledgeable assistant can aid you by using the longe whip. Much can be accomplished by a good team of trainers.

Transition from longeing—using two assistants

If you are inexperienced in driving and feel unsure about attempting this transition alone, this method is a simple and safe way to initiate the new training. Although it may seem overcautious, those of us who have driven horses know that mistakes and fearful experiences at this stage of training can set up barriers to later training that are almost impossible to overcome. Experienced trainers may find the method helpful when working with nervous horses, problem horses, and horses afraid of ropes. This system has a further advantage of minimizing the problem of a horse's natural tendency to turn and face you.

You will need two assistants who are calm, receptive, and willing, and it will be a great help if they are also knowledgeable.

Tack up the horse with English (stirrups down) or Western saddle, and tie the stirrups together. Leave a halter on under bridle or hackamore, and adjust the side reins as you have for longeing (or tie them and place them around behind the cantle, exerting no pressure on the bit). Attach the driving lines directly to the bit (or the heel knot of the bosal). Use of two longe lines is safer at first than using lines made specifically for driving because they are longer and allow you to position yourself farther from the hindquarters.

Assistant A will stand at the head on the off side. Throughout the exercise, his duty will be to steady, guide, and reassure the colt, at first using a lead rope attached to the halter. If all goes well, he may later detach the lead and steady the horse as necessary with his hand on the bridle rein.

Assistant B will manage the outside driving line until you are ready to take both lines. This negates the possibility of the colt getting tangled in the lines if he should become excited or upset. B will stand on the off side beside the horse's hip (not too close) and hold the off driving rein, which has been passed through the stirrup.

You will stand in the longeing position (prepared to longe to the left) holding the near driving line just as you do in longeing. The line goes directly to bit or bosal; it does *not* pass through the stirrup. Say "W-a-l-k" and have the horse longe as usual to the left. Assistants A and B will be walking beside him on the outside.

As the colt circles, B will allow the outside driving line to gently touch the right side of the hindquarters at different heights, especially lower on the leg where it will fall naturally when you drive from behind. After several circles left, change direction (changing the reins so that the outside line is through the stirrup, the inside line direct to the hand, and of course both assistants on the outside). Repeat the exercise, again letting the outside line gently touch the colt about the hindquarters. If there are no problems, B may step back so that the colt may feel the outside line constantly against his leg (both directions).

From your longeing position, you will step back also, gradually assuming more of a driving position. Soon you and B will be walking together behind the colt, at which time you may take both lines (have B continue to walk along so that he may take the outside line back if trouble occurs and move it away from the colt's leg).

A will continue walking at the horse's head to help on turns, halts, and general reassurance. If all is quiet, B may go along where most needed —either at the head or alongside—and eventually move away altogether. Finally, A also may leave.

If any trouble arises, move the colt forward. Be quick and try to anticipate any problems, but there shouldn't be many with this system. Of course, talk to the colt as you go along, stay calm, and be generous in your praise.

Elementary driving (long-reining or long-lining)

Work in the usual corral or enclosure. As you'll find that this is great exercise for you, too, begin at a walk, and certainly go no faster than a slow trot.

The next step is to pass the inside line through the inside dee ring or stirrup iron—when taking a circle to the left, run the left line through the left stirrup. Now both lines run through the stirrups or dees before coming to your hands.

Start the horse in a circle, using the usual command. As he walks, gradually step toward his hindquarters as before, but now you can begin walking directly behind him. At this point you may begin to turn right and left, and go straight ahead, without making a circle. Use pressure on the right or left line to indicate turns (this is direct reining). Take advantage of natural barriers to help the colt make the turns until he understands what is expected of him.

To halt, first say "Whoa" and then put equal pressure on both lines. Gradually reverse the signals and finally dispense with the word command. Be sure to give the pressure lightly and release—repeat if necessary at first. Always release immediately as the horse begins to stop. The long lines should help to make the horse's mouth, not deaden it.

If at first the colt is nervous about having you walk directly behind him, step a little to the inside so that he can see where you are. Switch sides as you turn right and left, and gradually move back behind him.

If the colt is flighty or has trouble making turns, you may save time and trouble by having an assistant help you. His only job would be to walk beside the horse and steady him by holding the hackamore or bridle if necessary. The assistant should not touch the driving reins, as that would interfere with your communication with the horse.

Remember your goals and work to improve the colt's responsiveness to these new rein aids. He should learn to stop immediately when signaled by lines alone (as he learned to do on the "Whoa" command), he should learn to turn left and right by bending his whole spinal column rather than just his neck, and he should gain confidence in moving forward freely. Now he's "out there by himself" and finds that he can move forward without fear of whatever may be following behind.

Plan your driving routine to include work on straight lines and on curves (corners, circles, or serpentines). He should learn to move quietly away from and toward the rail on long, shallow curves. The lines, containing the hindquarters, will help the colt to keep his body straight on the straight stretches, and to bend his spine on the curves. Work toward improving both straightness and bending.

Urge the colt forward with your voice, or carry a longeing whip or buggy whip along with one line. Do not slap the colt on the rump or sides with the driving lines. This is considered very poor technique and interrupts your contact with the colt's mouth.

Use the lines delicately and try to establish a flow of communication in which the horse takes up the lines by relaxing his jaw and moving his tongue against the bit. You can't force this or insist upon it—you can only

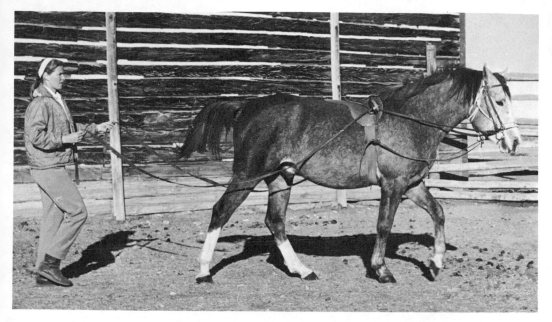

When the colt has accepted the feel of the long lines, begin walking directly behind him. Use the direct rein as lightly as possible to signal him in making turns, and concentrate on your goal of developing responsiveness (Courtesy E. F. Prince and Arabian Horse News)

invite the horse to take the initiative. If you achieve it at this stage, your training is going magnificently!

Driving in Harness

Training a horse to drive, whether hitched to a cart, buggy, or other vehicle, will increase his versatility and add to your pleasure. A colt may pull a light weight long before he is ready to carry a rider. The driving experience will add to his confidence, ability, calmness, and handiness, and he will also improve in flexibility and balance. Working within the shafts will improve straightness. He will develop both joints and muscles, and lengthen his attention span. Driving can also teach the youngster to make transitions smoothly from one gait to another. It will encourage him to move forward boldly and freely. Also important, it will provide the exercise that is vital to good horse management, especially if the colt is restricted in his environment.

If you are training a prospective roping horse and do not wish to longe him, driving will give the extra ground training he needs.

So, how does one go about introducing driving?

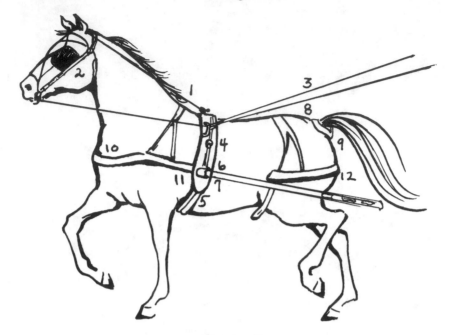

Parts of Driving Harness

1. overcheck
2. blinders
3. lines
4. saddle
5. belly band or girth
6. tug
7. wrap strap
8. back strap
9. crupper
10. breast collar
11. trace
12. breeching

THE HARNESS

The first problem, of course, is the harness. Your best introduction to fastening the harness is to have someone show you how it goes. If this isn't possible, you'll have to proceed from directions. Be sure that the harness is strong and in good condition—as always, tack should be in top-notch condition when used for training.

There are many varieties of harness, but in general all use either breastplate (breast collar) or collar for the horse to push against. Most lightweight harness uses a breastplate, so that is what we will consider here. (The principles are the same, however, when using a collar and heavy harness.) The traces run from breastplate to cart or whiffletree and are what pull the cart. In some fine harness and racing outfits, the traces run from shaft to saddle; these rigs use a thimble on the tip of the shaft, instead of breeching, to hold back the cart when going downhill.

The saddle or backpad fits on the horse's back by means of a girth, just like a surcingle. It has rings or terrets on the top for the lines to pass

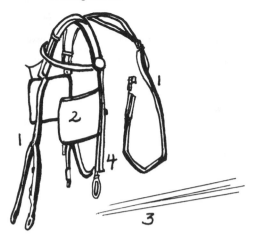

Parts of Driving Bridle
1. *overcheck*   3. *lines*
2. *blinkers*   4. *(boxed) cheeks*
In double-bit bridle, bridoon is fixed to overcheck. In training, sometimes a running martingale is used (adjusted under breast collar).

through, and loops or straps on the side—these tugs, holders, or lugs hold up the shafts. Another strap on the girth, called a tiedown, safety girth, or wrap strap, holds the shafts down.

The crupper runs from the saddle to fit around the tail. The checkrein runs from the saddle up the horse's neck to the bridle.

THE CART

There are all sorts of sulkies, roadsters, buggies, and driving rigs. What you use may depend on what you have or what is easiest for you to obtain. Without going into detail on these, let's consider just the most basic points.

Buggies are four-wheeled vehicles that do not turn as easily as a two-wheeled cart, nor do they pull as lightly. Backing, especially, is open to problems, as the four-wheeled vehicles tend to jackknife. Generally it is best for a colt to learn first with a two-wheeled cart, and to stay with this vehicle until he is stable and settled in harness.

There are two basic types of two-wheeled cart usable for training: first, the light cart, ranging from sulky to large-wheeled road cart; and second, the heavier breaking cart. The breaking cart has longer shafts than an ordinary driving cart so that the horse cannot hit the cart easily with his heels. It may have extensions coming out the back to prevent its being tipped over backward, or it may have a step attached low at the back, serving the same function and also allowing the trainer to step on easily. With the step, the trainer may add his weight just for a moment, stepping off again quickly if the colt becomes frightened. Some breaking carts also have brakes.

Breaking carts are fine to use if they are not too heavy. Some are cumbersome and do more to discourage or frighten the colt than to train him.

A light cart should be perfectly safe if you proceed step-by-step and do not rush your training. Whatever you use, make sure that it is strong and in good condition and that the wheels turn easily with a minimum of noise.

INTRODUCING THE HARNESS

Your first problem is to fit the harness to the horse and to let him become accustomed to it. Begin at the crosstie—a familiar place where the colt is used to a lot of handling and fiddling. Decide on a routine that will be most comfortable for you to stick to; some trainers put the bridle on first, then breastplate, saddle, and crupper. Others prefer to put the saddle on first (sometimes using a pad or towel underneath to prevent any soreness on the tender back), with the crupper, then breastplate and bridle.

Let's say we start with the bridle. The checkrein (one overhead rein or two side checks) will probably be attached to the bridle, but don't worry about fastening it yet. Side checks offer more maneuverability laterally than does the overcheck. Some horses tilt their head sideways to evade the overcheck. In fact, fastening the check rein or side reins will be the last thing you do. The driving lines will be added later.

Driving bridles usually have blinders; you may introduce these now or later. Most trainers train without blinders and introduce them in the finishing stages. By then, the colt has become used to seeing things behind him and is not so apt to spook. Although some pleasure drivers don't use blinders at all, it is generally considered safer to have them. The blinders should be rigid and should fit at least an inch from the eye. Have someone help you when you first try on blinders so that you don't hit the eye by accident. Make sure that they are properly adjusted.

Put on the breastplate. Make sure that the traces are folded up and tied—you don't want them dangling. The breastplate should be high enough so as not to interfere with the colt's shoulder movement, but low enough so as not to press on his windpipe. It is kept in place by a neckstrap. In fitting collars, keep the following in mind: The collar must be the right size, neither pinching nor rocking back and forth, and it must be well and evenly stuffed. It should be long enough to let you put your hand be-

tween it and the horse's breast, and between his neck and the top of the collar. It should rest evenly against each shoulder and, if pushed to one side, should let a finger pass between it and the shoulder for its full length. Hames fit against some collars, and have the traces attached to them.

Put on the saddle with the girth set farther back than for riding and fasten the girth loosely. Then place the crupper under the tail (you may find it easier and less bothersome to put the crupper on first). Raise the tail a little at a time before placing the crupper. This may be a new experience, frightening to some colts, but if you've been handling and combing his tail all along, he should accept it fairly quickly. You know how to work slowly and reassuringly with him, praising him when he accepts the new equipment. The crupper's purpose is to keep the saddle in position; it

Judy Wilder of Loveland, Colorado, demonstrates working the colt in the driving harness before adding breeching or weight. All loose ends are tied up.

should be smoothly lined and well padded. Make sure that the crupper is not fastened too tightly to the backpad. It should allow three fingers to pass between it and the croup. When the crupper is properly adjusted and the colt has accepted it, tighten the girth—it doesn't have to be as tight as a girth for riding.

If the colt seems nervous about any of this, go ahead and lead him now, making sure that the traces, tugs, tiedowns, and assorted loose straps are all tied in place as well as possible. Run the driving lines through the terrets and snap them into the bit rings; drive the colt until he is comfortable in the equipment.

At this point, you may begin accustoming the horse to the idea of pulling weight—that is, of pushing into the breastcollar. Untie the traces and run them back, letting an assistant hold them. As you drive, the assistant will put mild pressure on the traces, gradually increasing his resistance as the colt understands that he is to pull against it. When going around corners, there should be more resistance on the outside trace to simulate the action of the cart.

When he is ready to accept the next step, put on the breeching (pronounced britching). Some driving is done without breeching, but if you go up and down hills, or on a very smooth surface, or at any speed, you will need it to keep the cart from running up on the colt. The strap (sometimes two) over the rump adjusts the height to keep it from riding either too high or too low on his thighs. If the breeching is too tight, it will interfere with his leg movement—it should be comfortably snug, allowing the width of your hand between it and the horse. Again, tie up any loose ends.

Fasten the checkrein or reins to the saddle—loosely, at first—or simply tie without fastening. It is not necessary to use the overcheck in early training; care should be taken to adjust it correctly if you do use it. As the horse is standing and holding his head and neck in a normal position, the overcheck rein should clear his crest by about four inches when lifted clear. The overcheck is used only to keep the horse from overbending; it is not intended to restrict his normal head and neck movement.

Lead the colt in full harness, and when he is ready, drive him on foot as you have done before, including longeing at walk and trot with the two lines.

When unharnessing, work in the reverse order, first unfastening the breeching, and tying up loose ends as you go. When removed properly, the harness should make a very neat and compact bundle.

INTRODUCING THE CART

When the colt is accustomed to the harness, the next step is to accustom him to pulling weight. This can be done by introducing the cart immediately, or by some other method.

It used to be common to introduce horses to heavy weights by having them first pull two poles that dragged on the ground. These were slender, about twelve feet long, with a crosspole tied on to keep the ends about six feet apart. Although the poles will accustom a horse to pulling weight and to the feel of the shafts against his sides, they are awkward and may do more harm than good for a well-trained colt.

If the colt seems nervous or flighty and not yet ready to hitch to a cart, we prefer to repeat the exercise where the assistant pulls on the traces (as outlined above) and then graduate to a singletree arrangement instead of the poles. This can be used without breeching. The singletree (whiffletree or whippletree) is laid on the ground directly behind the horse, and the traces are attached to it (see illustration). A sandbag can

The process of introducing the cart, as demonstrated by Dave Gardner at the Arabian Horse Fair in Reno, Nevada, 1976.

One method of introducing weight is to attach a singletree to the traces and tie a sandbag to the center of the tree. Dragging the sandbag accustoms the colt to the sound and feel of weight without the problems of pulling a cart.

Working the colt in long lines while helpers pull the cart behind him to ac-custom him to its sound.

be tied to the center of the tree so that it drags on the ground. The horse becomes accustomed to the sound and feel of the weight and to the traces touching him low on the legs. The weight can be adjusted and increased gradually, which is especially valuable if the horse seems disturbed about pulling into a weight. This way he can become used to it before the added concern of shafts is introduced.

When you feel that the colt is ready for the cart, select a large enclosed area to work in. The colt must have room to make wide, gradual turns so that the shafts won't press too hard against his shoulders.

First lead him to the cart and let him smell and investigate it. If you have an experienced driving horse, hitch him up so that the colt can see and hear the cart in action. If not, have an assistant pull it around. When the colt accepts this, lead him forward while the assistant pulls the cart behind him. It may take several sessions before the colt will walk calmly—some horses are particularly nervous about noise behind them.

When the colt is calm and you feel he is ready, bring up the cart behind him. Try to have two assistants to help for the first few times—it will make the whole project much safer and easier. The colt should be wearing his halter under the bridle, the breastplate, backpad, and crupper, and breeching if you are using it.

Keep the shafts up in the air as you approach the colt so that you don't poke him with them if he moves suddenly. When almost in place, lower the shafts and run them through the tugs, but don't tie them. Your

Bringing the cart up with shafts high.

The shafts are run through the tugs and fastened. The trainer checks thoroughly before the next step is taken.

When ready, the trainer again drives the colt with long lines while one assistant leads and others walk beside the cart (note the arrangement of the lines).

assistants can hold them in place as you lead the colt forward with "W-a-l-k" and "Whoa!" (use a lead rope attached to the halter). If the colt should panic, the assistants can release the shafts and the colt will be unharmed. When he finally realizes that the cart won't hurt him, the cart can be hitched.

Run back the traces and attach them to the cart. Check to make sure that they are even—it's very important to have the cart follow squarely. Fasten the breeching and tiedowns, attach the driving lines, and adjust the checkrein.

Have an assistant lead while you hold the driving lines and walk behind the cart (if the cart is heavy, ask another assistant to help by pushing the cart or by walking at the tugs and helping to pull). Make only wide turns, as the pressure of the shafts can be frightening to the colt. Practice

Turning so that the colt feels the shafts. The assistant's hand on the cart helps relieve some of the pressure against the colt.

Working at a trot, still with all assistants at hand.

walking and halting, and insist that he stand still at the halt—this will be vitally important when you begin getting in and out of the cart.

Don't overdo on these first sessions. Five or ten minutes are plenty. Undo everything and tie up the loose ends, then back the cart until you can raise the shafts and push the cart away from the colt.

DRIVING SAFELY

Driving can be a delightful country pastime, beyond making your horse more steady, reliable, and versatile. But it can be dangerous if safety precautions are not observed or if basic training has been skimped. Just because your colt behaves well the first time you hitch him up doesn't assure that he won't bolt on the third hitching. Don't rush your training.

And it bears repeating that equipment *must* be in good condition— not just "Oh well, it looks okay—let's try it," but "I know it's good because I've inspected it, tested it and cared for it." Nothing will ruin a potential driving horse quicker than having an important part of harness or vehicle break at the wrong moment. Besides, it could kill you.

One thing often overlooked is your cart's balance. If the cart is balanced properly, you'll notice a gentle up-and-down movement of the shafts at the tugs when the horse trots. If there is too much weight in front, the shafts will bear weight on the horse; if too heavy behind, the shafts will bear upward and prevent a direct pull. Some carts can be adjusted by sliding the seat forward or back. Make sure your cart isn't severely overweighted one way or the other by adjusting the load or adding weight either in front or in back.

Work within a large ring or enclosure until you are very sure of the colt's reliability. Walk behind the cart at first and drive the colt in both directions and in figure eights. Always make your turns wide and gradual. When you have him halt, encourage him to stand squarely and quietly. It would help to have your assistant at hand in case of trouble, but you should be able to manage this alone.

When the colt is working well and calmly, it is time to mount the vehicle. Ask your assistant to lead the colt. If possible, step into the cart (or sit in it) as he is walking calmly—the colt will be less likely to balk at the added weight if he is already moving. If this is not feasible, or if you feel the colt may be overly startled, have him halt and then get into the cart. With one assistant leading, ask a second assistant to push gently behind the cart as you say "Walk," in order to ease the load at first.

Sit on the ends of your driving lines rather than allow them to drop over the side of the cart—they could get caught in the wheel spokes.

After the colt accepts the added weight and will walk out calmly without the aid of assistants, you may begin to trot. Again ask an assistant to

Gradually adding weight to the cart, the trainer is able to step out immediately if there is trouble, and the assistants remain close by until the colt is steady. Note that the lines are in the cart, not dragging behind, where they could tangle in a wheel.

lead for your first few trotting attempts. Work at a slow trot for a short distance and come back down to a walk.

When teaching to back (from a halt), ask the horse to step forward before asking him to back. An assistant might be helpful at first. Sufficient ground work with the voice command "Back" should condition the horse adequately.

As the colt gains in confidence and reliability, drive without assistants (although it would still be helpful to have their aid in hitching and unhitching), but stay within your large enclosure. Work at walk, slow trot, and at a faster trot, trying for smooth transitions and sensitive response.

PROBLEMS WHILE DRIVING

Remember to slow down for corners and be sure to give room enough for the vehicle to clear the sides of the enclosure. If the colt should begin skipping—trotting in front while cantering behind—you're making the turns too tight. Later the horse will learn to lean over into the shafts on sharp turns while you maintain forward impulsion with voice and whip.

Many colts tend to overbend when being driven, because of the leverage that driving causes. In this case, keep the forward movement and light hands. If the habit persists, use an overcheck (make sure it is adjusted correctly).

One problem that may occur when driving is that the horse may flick his tail over a line. If you try to pull it loose, you will either pull him into a turn or encourage him to clamp down his tail and make matters worse. Instead, urge him on and loosen the line—his tail should come up and free the line. If it does not, stop him and lift the tail off of the line.

On steep inclines, especially when going down, get out of the cart and walk until the colt is used to the weight of the cart pushing against the breeching.

What should you do if, in spite of careful training and precautions, you have a runaway?

Some trainers advocate use of an emergency rein or safety rope—a line that runs through the ring of the bit on the near side, over the poll, and snaps into the ring on the off side. The driver may hold this line and use it only in case of emergency. However, this is only a training device, and the possibility exists that a runaway could occur when the emergency rein is not attached.

To avoid catastrophes before you even get started, always check your harness and bridle for proper adjustment before mounting. Hold the lines firmly when you mount the vehicle—don't get in if someone else is holding the lines.

If a runaway occurs when you are driving, and the colt does not respond to regular pressure on the lines and the command, "Whoa," remember to seesaw the lines—put pressure first on one line, then on the other. This will be far more effective than a steady pull that the colt can set his teeth against.

Try to anticipate special situations and prepare for them under controlled conditions. If you plan to drive at night, in heavy traffic, under lights, or what have you, make sure you introduce the situation when the colt is on the longe line or at least under extra control—perhaps with an assistant walking at his head to hold the bridle and talk calmly to him. Sometimes on his first few drives in the open, a youngster will be steadied by the company of a calm, mature horse under saddle. Think ahead to avoid problems.

If you plan to stop and visit somewhere with an inexperienced horse, leave his halter on under the bridle and take a lead rope; do not tie him by the lines. If you are going to be out of sight, or plan to be any more than a few minutes, unhitch the cart from the horse, push it away from him, and block the wheels.

WHAT ABOUT THE DRIVER?

Driving is an art in itself, and the best way to learn it is to have qualified instruction. This is harder to find, however, than qualified instruction in riding. And experts, when you can find them, tend to be specialized.

If you discover that you are especially interested in driving, you may decide to develop your colt into a roadster or fine harness horse and enter him in shows, or you may wish to develop a racer. Each of these special

Besides the enjoyment of pleasure driving with cart or buggy, driving your horse may open up whole new fields of activity. (Courtesy Wyoming Travel Commission)

interests has definite and precise requirements for types of harness and vehicle, shoeing, appointments, methods, gaits, action, and style. Consult the current *American Horse Shows Association Rule Book* for details, and, if possible, find an expert to instruct you. Go to shows and observe; take notes on every detail.

For basic training and pleasure purposes, however, you can enjoy driving even without expert instruction when you remember the main principles of using the reins in riding. Use your lines in the same way, developing a sensitive communication with your horse. However, when driving, the lines are your primary means of communication—you don't have legs or back to help. You will want to maintain firm, elastic contact, and through it, to cultivate responsiveness, impulsion, and calm confidence. Here are some suggestions to help you enjoy driving.

Sit in the cart as you would in a saddle—straight and erect but not stiff, head up, and looking forward. Watch your horse. Sit well back and brace your feet comfortably. The driver usually sits on the right side. Beginners would do well to hold a line in each hand and keep them rather short. Experienced drivers often hold the lines in the left hand, using the right only to adjust the length and to help in turning. The whip, if you use one, is held in the right hand, away from the passenger. (A buggy whip, like a training whip, has a long stock and a short lash.) The whip is to encourage impulsion if necessary. It should be used *in front of* the saddle, usually with a stroking motion against the shoulder, rather than a flick. To use it on the quarters may induce the colt to kick. Use voice and whip rather than slap the reins.

Keep your hands close together, your forearms parallel to the ground —this way you are in the best position for control, and you are able to adjust the lines quickly, if necessary. Further, the position is comfortable over a period of time. Don't try to imitate flashy positions just because you've seen them used in shows—you are training and enjoying your horse, not competing in a style class.

When you first get into the cart and are ready to start out, take up the lines as you would with a saddle horse, gently establishing communication with the colt's mouth. This will alert him for your next signal. You will find that the horse becomes extremely sensitive to the feel of the lines; therefore it helps to keep a steady hand if you wish to achieve smooth forward progress and flowing transitions.

Plan to drive in a manner that will increase your horse's confidence, steadiness, and reliability. Your main concern should be to drive carefully, safely, and sensitively. This is what makes driving a pleasure.

CHAPTER 4

TRAINING TO RIDE

Training the young horse to saddle is not an isolated training method. The ground training that you have accomplished by now—longeing, suppling, driving—continues, and saddle training becomes another element in the overall training program. Together, the different elements work to give the colt a well-grounded, basic education that contributes to his confidence, versatility, and reliability.

Before you introduce the youngster to the saddle, he should be practiced and steady on the longe line, stopping readily on "Whoa," walking forward freely, reversing smoothly, and trotting on command. The saddle training will be incorporated into the training period, usually after longeing. During another training period in the same day, the colt may be given driving and suppling lessons. Work should progress concomitantly in each phase of training—the colt should become more adept in reining, for instance, as the result of increased proficiency in longeing, in driving, in responding to suppling exercises, and under saddle.

By ground-training your horse each day before saddle-training him, you will have an idea of how co-operative he will be that day and you'll be better able to plan the saddle-training period. Moreover, the prior exercise and handling will make the colt more settled and steady.

A Fifteen-day Introduction to Saddle Training

An experienced trainer will know almost instinctively when to begin and how to progress with saddle training. But until a trainer has many horses under his belt, so to speak, he has far more questions than answers. Too often the big question turns out to be: What went wrong?

Usually the answer lies in rushing the training—expecting too much too soon. Often this results in a horse that has become unmanageable or that unseats his rider or that plans and manages the lessons himself because the trainer isn't sure how to insist on discipline without being unreasonable. Sometimes a novice trainer thinks he is being firm and sensible when he is actually being unintentionally cruel and demanding.

Saddle training can proceed safely and gently for both rider and horse. A trainer need not be able to ride a wildcat with a twisted tail in order to saddle-train a horse—indeed, it may be just as well if he can't. Then he will be more willing to proceed gradually and gently, measuring his success by small gains and lack of mistakes rather than by hours or minutes.

The fifteen-day training plan we're outlining here can serve as a guide until experience helps you to rearrange the program. As you know so well, every horse is different, and therefore the plan can be *only* a guide —you'll have to adapt it to your own situation as you go along. But for the most part, this *sequence* of events gets you firmly in the saddle without the development of problems such as bucking or rearing or balking, and it gets you there safely. If your horse does have the kind of problem you feel you can't handle, you'll know about it before you place yourself in a precarious or dangerous position; and in this case, you'll be able to seek professional help before the horse is set in his ways of wrongdoing.

By all means, have an assistant help you if at all possible; but don't give up if you must sometimes work alone. We've trained many horses alone without undue difficulty, and we'll include suggestions on how to go about it.

TACK

The tack you use to begin saddle training will of course tie in with how far you have progressed with the colt's ground training. Let's say that the horse has been carrying a bit, but that he is receiving direction from the hackamore. This is a good combination in which to begin saddle training, whether you plan to ride English or Western.

Bits were discussed in Part I, Chapter 2; if you have any question about them, please refer back. (Another discussion of bits, focusing on their action, is in Part II, Chapter 5.)

We like to start our horses with the felt saddle pad that we have used so much for longeing and other ground training. The colt finds this to be light, comfortable, and familiar. Its main advantage, however, is for the rider: Its construction allows the rider to have maximum contact with the horse. Leg and back aids are more easily taught because pressures are more easily transmitted (Western saddles are particularly difficult to use for this because of the stiff stirrup leathers). The felt pad is safer, too, in the beginning stages of saddle training—there is no horn nor strap to become caught in, and the safety stirrups will release if you have serious difficulties.

Whatever you use, though, be sure that the colt is thoroughly familiar with the tack from being longed in it at both walk and trot.

FIRST DAY

In the early stages, saddle training will always follow a period of ground training. Let's say you have just finished a fifteen- or twenty-minute longeing session. The hackamore reins were tied to the girth, and the longe line was attached to the hackamore heel knot so that the colt has felt pressure from your tug when you asked him to halt. The stirrups were allowed to hang so that he has become used to the feel of them bumping against him.

Now detach the longe and untie the reins from the girth. Recheck the girth for snugness (it is difficult to check the tightness of the girth on a saddle that has no tree; if you are unsure, it will help to use a double-thick blanket under the saddle pad).

Lead the colt, using the hackamore reins, and repeat the "Walk" and "Whoa" routine briefly. Work within a corral or enclosure, even if you have been longeing him in the open. If he seems calm and responsive, face the near side of the colt, take the hackamore reins up around his neck, and grasp them in your left hand along with a lock of mane as though you were going to mount (holding a lock of mane along with the reins prevents an uneven pressure on bosal or bit as you mount). With your right hand, pull down several times on the stirrup leather, gradually putting more and more weight on the stirrup.

After doing this several times on the near side, repeat the exercise from the off side; remember that you'll want your horse to stand for mounting from either side.

You may also wish to put your arm across the saddle pad, pressing down on the colt's back. Again, increase pressure gradually.

Praise the colt generously for his quiet acceptance of these shenanigans, and lead him back to the barn.

SECOND AND THIRD DAYS

After longeing and other ground work, repeat the first day's saddle-training exercises.

If the colt seems calm and willing, go on with the next step. Ask your assistant to hold the colt from the off side (with right hand on the reins near bit or bosal) and to pull down on the off stirrup (to keep the saddle from turning). Put your left foot into the stirrup and swing up into an upright position (standing in the stirrup). Your movements should be fluid

In the following series of photos, trainer Leslie Turner is assisted by Margaret Smith. Leslie prefers to use a web halter instead of hackamore or bit for preliminary training with this colt. He has been longed and long-reined, and is now ready for the new experience of being ridden. For safety, Margaret should be standing more to the side, rather than directly in front of the colt. The exercise is repeated on the other side.

and easy. Balance for a few seconds in this position, talking quietly to the colt and praising him generously. Then, with your weight on your hands, remove your left foot from the stirrup and drop quietly to the ground.

Again, walk, stop, and repeat this exercise from both sides of the colt. It may take several repeats before the colt accepts this new situation—at first it may startle him. You want him to stand quietly under your weight. Speak softly and reassuringly to him and reward him often. Don't go on to the next step until the colt stands quietly for you.

The horse must learn to stand still for mounting. It is dangerous and unpleasant to have a horse move off when your foot first touches the stirrup. But keep in mind that you must first teach the youngster that he need not be afraid of something on his back before you can teach him to stand still willingly. This is contrary to his nature and instincts—a mountain lion on the colt's back might mean death unless he could buck it off. That's why we don't hesitate to move off the youngster's back quickly in these early lessons—when he learns that the weight and motion will not hurt him and are not stuck to him permanently, he'll be prepared to hold still.

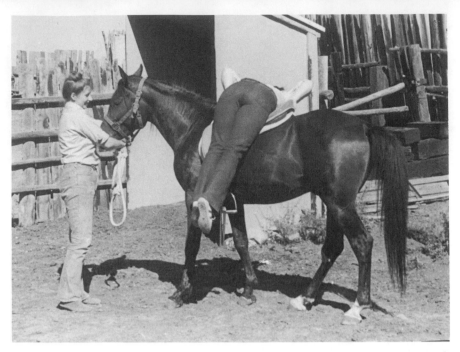

Leslie leans across the saddle to let the colt become accustomed to the weight and movement.

Then the lesson may be enforced. We have found this method to be the safest and to virtually eliminate the chance of the colt's bucking—he has no need to.

If you have no assistant, be especially careful to check the girth before putting your foot into the stirrup. Try to put much of your weight into your left hand (resting on the neck and holding the mane) to relieve sideways pressure on the saddle. If the colt wants to move forward, lead him up to the corral fence or wall before you try again. If he jumps around or is frightened, you can come down easily without scaring him. Reassure him with your voice until he understands that there is nothing to fear. Be sure you don't stick the toe of your boot into his ribs. Reward generously and do not rush.

FOURTH, FIFTH, AND SIXTH DAYS

Begin each day with ground training and repeat earlier saddle-training exercises. The next step in saddle training is to sit on the colt side-saddle.

Why side-saddle? Because it's safer for the rider at this stage, and because it provides a gentler and more gradual transition for the colt. If the colt becomes frightened, the rider can slip off easily, without becoming entangled and without going head over heels. The colt finds that he doesn't

Sitting on the colt side-saddle—if there are problems, Leslie can slip down without frightening him.

have to fight, that there is really nothing to be frightened of, and usually accepts this new exercise within the first few times. When, on the other hand, a rider mounts the youngster astride, he is there to stay (we hope) —if the colt becomes frightened, legs tighten around him and his reaction is more likely to buck or fight the rider. This can be avoided by beginning side-saddle.

With this step it makes a big difference whether or not you have an assistant. Let's consider first how to proceed if you do have help—of course, an assistant will make this stage both quicker and safer. He will act as a dumb jockey while you give direction from the longeing position.

Repeat earlier lessons, having your assistant stand in the stirrup while you hold the horse and keep the saddle from turning. If the colt seems ready, the assistant will turn in the stirrup and sit side-saddle on the colt, removing his foot from the stirrup as he does so. If there are problems, the assistant can slip off easily, landing on his feet beside the colt. Repeat until the youngster accepts the weight. Praise him generously.

When the colt is steady, you may lead him forward at a walk, repeating "Walk" and "Whoa" as usual. Snap on the longe line and step back into the longeing position; longe him at a walk in both directions, stopping frequently. Avoid letting the colt make sharp turns because it will be difficult for the rider to keep his balance in the side-saddle position. Make the lesson brief and reward generously.

In succeeding lessons, the rider can begin taking control of the colt. He won't be able to give leg aids in the side-saddle position, but he will be able to give cues with voice and reins—which is what the colt is used to. Eventually the longe line may be detached and all direction may be given by the rider.

Now, what if you have no assistant and must go it alone?

Lead the colt up to a feed rack or other rail about level with the stirrup. Stand on the rail in a natural mounting position and talk to the youngster. Lean over his neck, pat his rump, stroke his neck on the off side. Put your left hand (holding the reins) on the pommel area of the saddle and your right hand on the cantle; push down intermittently. When he accepts all this monkey business calmly (and it may take several sessions), you're ready to try sitting on him side-saddle, with both feet out of the stirrups. You can balance with the balls of your feet on the rail; if the colt rebels or moves away from you, you can quickly and easily move back onto the rail without scaring him.

Toward the sixth day, if you are feeling courageous and the colt is behaving well, mount him side-saddle and give him the command to walk. After a few steps forward, stop him, using voice and reins. Slip off his back and reward him. Repeat, and be satisfied with only a few steps, as many colts are hesitant about moving forward under your weight.

Remember that a youngster must develop muscles to carry weight, and keep these early lessons brief. If you overdo and make his back and loin muscles sore, you'll cause him real pain the next time you mount—probably with disastrous results.

SEVENTH, EIGHTH, AND NINTH DAYS

If all has been going well, it's now time to mount the colt astride. Since he is used to your weight both in the stirrups and in the saddle, this transition should be easily accomplished. It would help to have an assistant to steady the colt as you mount, and perhaps to help start him walking if he is hesitant to do so; otherwise, an assistant is no longer needed.

Be especially careful in mounting for the first few times. Don't let your left toe dig into the tender girth area or elbow as you swing on, and don't drag your right leg over the colt's rump. Sit gently into the saddle, speak quietly to the youngster, and then dismount. You can dismount either English style (weight on hands, feet out of the stirrups, and drop to the ground with knees bent) or Western style (keeping left foot in the stirrup until the right foot has reached the ground). We prefer the English method for these early lessons, but use whichever method works better for you.

When you can mount and dismount without worrying the colt, then proceed with the "Walk" and "Whoa" routine. Do not stay on the colt's

Mounted astride—and no problems.

Margaret leads the colt while Leslie talks to him and pats his neck.

This colt, mounted astride on the seventh day, moves forward under control of the rider, while the assistant stands in longeing position to give the colt confidence. The longe line is held but not attached. The colt is working in a hackamore. (*Courtesy E. F. Prince and* Arabian Horse News)

back for more than three to five minutes at a time, as he will tire easily. Very young animals can actually become low in the back if forced to carry too much weight for long periods in their early training.

If you have trouble getting the colt to move forward, turn his head (this will affect his balance enough so that he will probably have to take a step), repeat the walk command, and press your legs against him. Do *not* kick. At this point in training, a kick might set off a buck or other undesirable action. We believe—and experience bears this out—that if the colt doesn't get the idea of bucking in the early stages of training, he probably never will. So let's do everything we can to keep bad habits from forming. Praise any step the youngster takes, thereby encouraging him to walk on.

TENTH TO FIFTEENTH DAYS

When the colt accepts your weight calmly, encourage him to walk on. Give the command "W-a-l-k," and at the same time give equal pressure with both legs against the girth area. This asks the colt to walk forward in a straight line. Use unequal pressure only in turning. Encourage the horse

The youngster must learn to travel straight and to walk on freely with good stride and rhythm.

to move on in a clean, free walk—this will take time, but you should hold it in mind right from the beginning.

On "Whoa!" give equal, intermittent pressure on the reins until the colt obeys—that is, pull lightly, then slack. (At this stage, you are not riding with much contact—that will come later.) Dispense with the word command when the colt understands and obeys the physical direction. However, remember the safety factor of the command, "'Whoa!" If he should shy or react violently to something, say "Whoa!" sharply. He should obey automatically.

When the colt moves forward, begin working on turns. If you have done your ground work thoroughly (especially the suppling and driving exercises), the colt will be used to giving with his head and neck in response to rein pressure and will turn readily. Exercises for suppling the hindquarters will have taught the colt a rudimentary response to pressure behind the girth. With this introduction, then, direction from the saddle will not be unfamiliar to him except for the added weight and use of weight aids.

To turn left, then, move the left rein down toward your knee, several inches from the colt's neck (you are holding a rein in each hand, English fashion). This action of the rein is called an open rein in English, plow rein in Western. Keeping the rein low approximates the rein action with which he is already familiar, and encourages the proper carriage of his head. As the colt moves his head in response to pressure on the left rein, follow this movement with the right rein; that is, the right rein moves forward to follow the longer curve of the colt's neck. Allow the rein to touch the neck, thereby preparing the youngster to respond to neck-reining. At the same time, your left leg, against the girth, will deepen in the stirrup, your right leg will press behind the girth, and your weight will sit more heavily on the left seat bone. All of this is somewhat exaggerated at first, until the colt recognizes and responds to the aids. Later you will give the aids more subtly. Avoid overexaggerating your weight, however, to the point of throwing the youngster off balance.

To turn, then:

•Move the inside rein down and away from the neck,
•Follow with the outside rein,
•Deepen your inside leg against the girth,
•Displace your weight to the inside seat bone,
•Press behind the girth with your outside leg.

Encourage the colt to turn with his whole body, rounding his spine evenly from poll to tail, rather than turning only his neck and throwing his haunches out. Keep your turns shallow at first, closing them gradually as he learns to bend his spine correctly. Avoid souring the youngster by making too many turns, and watch closely for signs of weariness or restlessness. His ears will give you an idea of how he feels and whether he is listening to you. Keep the riding lessons short.

If you use your leg and weight aids consistently, you will be able to depend less on the reins. Later, the colt will turn in response to leg pressure and weight displacement alone.

In these early riding lessons, practice turns and straightaways by using a variety of simple exercises. These keep the colt interested during the brief sessions, while he is still quite limited in his accomplishments.

Figure-eights. Start the youngster working on large eights, cutting down the size later as he improves in suppleness and balance.

Using a wall. Walk your horse along a solid wall or fence, keeping six feet or more from the barrier. Let the wall serve as a guide to improve straightness. Then turn the horse into the wall, using all aids correctly. This method encourages him to turn his whole body. As he responds you may sharpen the turns by narrowing the distance between horse and wall.

Serpentines. Wind back and forth across the ring, turning in half circles to make a snakelike trail. Emphasize your weight shift toward the inside of the turn in the early stages of training, but don't overbalance the colt. Serpentines help teach the colt to respond properly to leg and weight aids. Vary the serpentines by riding the long way across your training area, turning at the ends. This gives relief from continual bending and helps the colt to improve in straightness.

Remember that one of the most difficult things for a horse to learn is to travel straight. You must work at it. In eagerness to teach a horse to rein well, it is easy to overlook this important phase of training.

Later Lessons

Since so much depends on the individual horse, along with varying external conditions, it is difficult to time later lessons accurately. When the colt learns one lesson to your satisfaction, go on to the next. However, continue reinforcing former exercises until they become automatic, and the accumulated knowledge is demonstrated by improved performance.

Remember the importance of consistency in training. You can't expect a youngster to learn quickly if your signals are fuzzy, unsure, or inconsistent. Good riding is important. Exaggerate your signals at first to make them clear to the colt, using your weight, legs, hands, and voice in co-ordination, but work to refine them once they are understood.

Refer again to the sections on suppling and developing responsiveness in Part II, Chapter 3, and apply the suggestions to saddle training. Be continually aware of how you can best communicate with this particular colt, and be active in praising desirable behavior.

Saddle training, progressing now in conjunction with ground work, is aimed toward developing responsiveness to the aids—that is, a soft mouth and sensitive understanding of leg and weight aids, as well as improving suppleness, balance, and calm.

HACKAMORE AND BRIDLE CONTROL—TRANSITION

As mentioned at the beginning of this chapter, we will assume that your colt is carrying a bit but is receiving direction from the hackamore. So far, no pressure has been put on the colt's mouth through the bit. It's now time for a gradual transition from hackamore to bit.

Many trainers, especially of English style, omit hackamore training. Some prefer to go straight to a snaffle; others avoid the hackamore because they are unfamiliar with it and with its uses. Chapter 3 in Part II prepares the colt for either hackamore or bridle training; if you are already using the snaffle bit, you may continue doing so and skip this section. On the other hand, you may wish to consider using the hackamore now if you have not tried it before.

Attach the bridle reins if they are not already attached to the bit. During the ground part of your lesson, work with the reins as described in that Chapter 3 in the section on exercises—first with the hackamore reins, then with the bridle reins. Begin the riding part of your lesson as usual and use the hackamore reins. Let the bridle reins lie on the colt's neck at first. How you make the transition will depend on how skilled you are with the reins. There are several different ways to hold them.

If you are adept at holding four reins, as with a Weymouth or Pelham bridle, you can work both hackamore and bridle together. This is probably the best system, since the transition can be made so gradually that the colt hardly notices it. Hold all four reins (a hackamore rein and a bridle rein in each hand), with the bridle reins adjusted very loosely at first. Gradually take up the bridle reins until equal pressure is given on both bit and bosal. Then work with the bridle reins alone.

If this seems like too big a handful of reins, let the bridle reins lie on the colt's neck while you work with the hackamore. Knot the hackamore reins and let them lie on the neck when you are ready to use the bridle. Put a little pressure on the bit for a few turns and straightaways, and then go back to the hackamore. Avoid tiring the youngster, or trying to do too much too soon.

If your colt responds well to leg and weight aids on his turns and if he begins to understand the rudiments of neck reining, you may hold the hackamore reins in one hand, bridle reins in the other. This method, once you are used to it, allows you to exert pressure to any degree on either bit or bosal, using them separately or together.

Use the method that works best for you and produces the best results in the colt. Gradually you may dispense with the hackamore for ring work; however, on his first few trail rides or when working with other horses (where a youngster might shy or act up), tacking up with both hackamore and bridle is a good safety measure.

NECK REINING

Western trainers like to "put a good rein" on a horse, and English trainers, too, find that it is often a pleasure and a convenience to have a horse that neck-reins well. Your colt should understand leg and weight aids, and should be able to bend his body fairly well in response to them, before you begin neck reining.

We use an unorthodox (as far as the show ring is concerned) method of holding the reins when teaching the colt to neck-rein. Usually this

One way of making the transition from hackamore control to bridle control is to hold the reins in this way. Control may be gradually transferred to the bit, but in case of trouble, the rider may rely instantly on the hackamore. For this method to be most effective, the youngster should respond to leg aids and have at least a rudimentary understanding of neck reining. The rider's boots are loose as a safety precaution in this early stage of training.

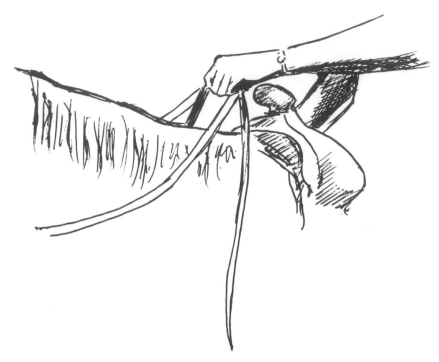

Holding the reins for training the colt to neck-rein.

Problems with neck reining occur when the horse noses to the outside (first photo) or otherwise positions his head unnaturally. Using the reins correctly will help to keep his head positioned properly (second photo).

method helps the youngster to grasp the concept a little more quickly. Both reins are held in one hand (usually the left), but they cross over one another and the bight of the reins falls on either side of the neck. Your hand has considerable control of both reins, and the method prevents the youngster from nosing to the outside or otherwise positioning his head unnaturally (a habit that a colt seems to fall into easily and that is difficult to break). When directing the colt to the left, move your hand a few inches left, holding it horizontally and keeping it low. This will give a good feel of the rein on the right side of the neck, and there will be enough pressure on the left side of the snaffle (through the left rein) to keep the head positioned properly.

When reining to the right, you may find it helpful at first to take your right hand and give a slight bit of pressure on the right rein, thereby aiding the forehand to make the turn.

If you are well co-ordinated, you can shift the reins from one hand to the other as you make the turns. Use whatever method seems most comfortable and effective so long as the colt's nose is pointing correctly, and so long as you are co-ordinating all your aids. You may incorporate a few minutes of neck reining into each lesson, both at a walk and later at a jog.

STABILIZING THE GAITS

It takes patience, time, and effort to settle a horse in his gaits—to indicate the gait you desire and have the horse stay in it willingly until he receives other directions. It is difficult also to teach a horse to walk straight on without wobbling or drifting from side to side. Stabilizing the gaits is an important and necessary part of training the young horse.

The walk. The walk is probably the most important and most neglected gait. A horse with a fast, flat-footed, evenly cadenced walk is a joy to ride. The unschooled horse tends to walk in fits and starts and has a difficult time walking in a straight line.

Use your legs to keep the youngster walking forward and straight. This will require a lot of work at first; you must continually correct or anticipate and prevent his weavings and hesitations. Of course, you must use your reins too, moving your fingers quietly to restrain when the colt tries to break into a trot. Beginning trainers often give too much emphasis to the hands at this stage, and this is a mistake. To keep a light mouth, avoid overuse of the reins and unnecessary nervousness in the hands. Keep your horse straight and moving forward by using your legs.

You will not be asking for collection at this early stage in training. Your main concern now is to encourage the youngster to move forward freely. He should be enthusiastic but relaxed. Don't let him lag or jig. It will be a great help to ride him in the company of horses well trained in the walk.

The trot. At first there will be no need to differentiate between a slow, collected trot or a faster, more extended trot. Find the colt's most energetic, natural trot and concentrate on developing his balance, cadence, and muscular development on the straightaways and shallow turns. Until free, energetic forward movement has been established, it's usually a mistake to work on either collection or extension.

When the colt seems ready, you may begin to encourage collection by pushing him up on the bit—that is, use your fingers as you do in the suppling exercises to invite the colt to flex at poll and jaw and take up the bit, and use your legs to encourage him to bring his hind legs under him. Ask this gradually of the youngster, rewarding him with a return to the free trot or free walk as he begins to respond. Work in large circles as well as in straight lines.

Gradually you will make a definite distinction between the trots. You will develop a slow, collected trot (sitting) as well as a faster, more extended trot (posting). Push him into the faster trot, encouraging long strides but don't tire him by keeping the fast trot too long—again, work up gradually. Do not ask for collection here, as you wish to encourage free natural action. When you are able to ride your colt outside the enclosure, the more extended trot can be perfected on long, smooth stretches of open meadowland. This exercise will develop muscles, broaden the youngster's chest and hindquarters, and help him work in straight lines, as well as help in stabilizing the trot.

If you plan to concentrate on Western riding, you will want to develop the jog—a slow trot that is smooth and relaxed with a little collection. Practice the jog on the trail when accompanied by a well-trained Western horse, but don't neglect the other trots in your ring work. The practice the colt receives now in developing collection and extension will help him later in reining and overall handiness.

The canter and lope. When the colt is stable and unexcited at walk and trot, you may start him at the canter. This training often works best when co-ordinated with your longe work. Introduce the canter on the longe as explained in Part II, Chapter 2. The colt should be well balanced and well co-ordinated at the canter on the longe before he carries any weight.

If you have an assistant who is a good rider, have him ride the colt as he is longed. The assistant will begin to give the aids for taking the canter on the proper lead: He will direct the nose a little to the inside, sit deeper on the inside seat bone while the inside leg presses on the girth and the outside leg gives pressure behind the girth. If the youngster doesn't take the cues readily, use voice and longe whip as before. When this seems to be going fairly well, dispense with the longe line but continue to stand in

At a canter, the young horse should be encouraged to move out at a comfortable speed, in an easy and forward-moving manner, with control but without excitement.

the longeing position to clarify the cues if need be. You can then mount and try the canter without an assistant.

We have found this method to be excellent because it eliminates confusion and the tendency to excite—both of which can be problems in teaching the canter. And the colt learns his leads very quickly.

If you are teaching the canter without the transition from the longe line, don't worry at first about leads. For the first few days, canter short distances in straight lines. To start the colt into a canter, put him into an energetic trot, collect him slightly, then urge equally with both legs and at the same time release with your fingers, thereby releasing his head and allowing him to move into the new gait. (In later training you will start from the walk.) Let him canter or lope a short distance, praising him as you go. Expect the canter to be fast, but don't allow him to run. Use your voice to calm him—let him know you are pleased when he moves correctly.

When you are progressing well in straight lines, begin working him in medium-sized circles, asking for a particular lead. The size of the circle is important at this stage and depends upon the individual horse—he must be able to balance himself well on it. The circle should be large enough to encourage him into a canter, but small enough so that he will be inclined to take the correct lead. Begin from the trot and give the aids to canter:

- Collect the colt slightly,
- Give slight pressure on the inside rein,
- Sit deeper on the inside seat bone (weight more on inside seat bone, deeper on inside stirrup),
- Press with inside leg on the girth, and
- Press with outside leg behind the girth.

If the youngster fails to move into a canter, you may need a training whip or willow stick to tap him as you give the other aids. Give the aids as you move into a corner of the arena or enclosure. You may have to try several times before he takes the canter, but this is unlikely, since he has already responded for several days on the straightaways. Stop him if he takes a wrong lead and try again. When he takes the correct lead, urge him on and praise him. Of course, avoid overdoing at first.

Cantering on the trail is excellent for promoting a smooth, stable gait. If your colt tends toward overexuberance and wants to gallop rather than work in a controlled canter or lope, ride him on long, uphill slopes or in smaller, restricted areas. Uphill grades will tend to slow him (unless they are too steep—youngsters will almost buck up a steep hill), and the necessity of turning will encourage him to slow down to keep his balance. The inexperienced colt will be less apt to stumble when going in a straight line up an incline.

For now, you are working for a smooth, easy, controlled canter, one that is balanced, supple, and in the correct lead. Later you will begin working on collection. Later still, you may wish to introduce the flying change of lead, but this should not be started too soon. Rushing into this training produces all sorts of problems, including crosscantering (one lead in front, the other behind), poor head position, and confusion of aids. The flying change requires the horse to collect well, to be balanced and flexible, to take either lead with ease, and to be stable in the correct lead. This is more advanced work and should not be attempted too early.

If the canter is going well and you wish to work on perfecting it, you may begin working on large or medium-sized figure-eights—with a simple change of lead. Take a few steps walking or trotting on a straight line before cueing for the other lead. Do not overdo this exercise or tire the young horse.

TRAINING OUTSIDE THE CORRAL OR IN THE OPEN

Before riding the colt outside the corral or arena, you should feel confident in his ability to remain quiet at the faster gaits. We usually lead the young horse around the immediate environs of the ring or corral at first, then ride him in figures in the vicinity of the corral, gradually going farther on each ride. For the first few rides beyond the corral area, it will help to be accompanied by a good rider on a mature, well-trained horse. That horse will set the pace for the youngster (fast walk, calm trot, or lope) as well as set a calm, quiet example in case of problems (blowing papers, sonic boom, etc). Of course, the colt must also learn to go out on his own.

A good program is to divide your lessons into three parts. First longe or drive the colt (or any other ground work), then work on improving his gaits, turns, and halts in the arena, and for the last part of the lesson, ride him outside the corral. This method of planning the lessons will keep him interested and help him progress in three different areas of training at one time. Your chances of having trouble outside the arena are lessened, since you will have taken the edge off in the arena training. The colt also will finish his lesson on a positive note, as trail riding is relaxing and interesting for him.

PRODUCING

A PLEASURABLE MOUNT

The Pleasure Horse—English and Western

We generally think of a pleasure horse as a mount used for relaxed recreational riding, whose merits may be demonstrated and judged in a pleasure class at a horse show. Let's take another look.

Basic training aims at making a horse supple, obedient, willing, and versatile. In other words, no matter what his future specialty may turn out to be, the basic training of a saddle horse should be aimed at producing a pleasurable mount. The attainment of the status of "pleasure horse" should be the first step in the training of any young horse.

With this in mind, then, let's redefine a pleasure horse to be "a horse that is a pleasure to ride, to associate with, and to own."

Exactly what are we looking for in a pleasure horse, and how can we attain these goals? (Remember that occasionally it may be worthwhile when selecting a horse for a particular purpose, to overlook certain faults because the horse has other qualities that make him especially suitable for his specialty. You may be willing to put up with a sour disposition if the horse is such a good jumper that he's worth the extra time and inconvenience involved. Usually, however, this kind of horse should be handled only by professionals who are capable of dealing with his deficiencies.)

For the most part, then, you want your youngster to have the following qualities, all of which will help now to make him a pleasure to ride and own, and all of which will serve as a basic foundation for progressive training in the future.

Of prime importance is his disposition: He should have good manners, be trustworthy to work around in stable and pasture, and be generally friendly and well disposed toward humans. The training and handling he's received up to now should have made him willing and obedient. He should be mentally steady—a sensible horse free of such habits as cribbing, weaving, or barn sourness. Bad habits such as kicking, charging, or rearing have no place in the pleasure animal. He should be naturally healthy and athletic, free of any unsoundness or other problems such as azoturia. He should be of good conformation for his breed, with smooth, ground-covering gaits. This doesn't mean that he has to be a blue-ribbon

Training can be—and should be—pleasant for the horse as well as the trainer. Good training develops a happy personality as well as a solid basic education. Both Fred Collier and his Morgan gelding Thor seem happy after the day's lesson.

winner in a halter class, but it does mean that he should be of a basically sound, quality construction that predisposes toward a long life of usefulness and quality performance. Finally, the pleasure horse should be *able* to do the things you plan to ask him to do; he should, in other words, be suitable. You can't expect a draft horse to race with Thoroughbreds.

Now, let's say that our horse has all these qualities, that he's suitable, sound, and sensible, with a pleasing disposition and good basic education. To progress further, the trainer must be able to produce an experienced, well-trained saddle animal *without disturbing the happy, pleasing ways of this horse*. The trainer must be careful not to spoil him by impatience, cutting corners in training, or letting inexperienced riders work him before his training has been stabilized. The trainer must not rob him of his sensitivity, perhaps by using the wrong bit or using his aids roughly. He must be wise enough not to ask more than the horse can give, considering his conformation and present level of training which could cause unnecessary problems. This horse comes to us with a good foundation. Let's build on this foundation to produce a pleasurable mount for either English or Western riding.

RESPONSIVENESS IN THE PLEASURE HORSE

A pleasure horse should have an educated mouth. He should understand gradations of pressure and be able to co-ordinate these pressures with the other aids. He should be learning what it means when we resist with our hands, yet encourage forward motion with pressure or vibration of our legs. The true pleasure horse should respond to light contact and refined aids.

To obtain this light response, a trainer should use only as much aid pressure as is necessary. You don't shout when you only need to whisper. If a trainer gives more pressure than is necessary, he sets up a reaction in the horse that must be countered by an equally strong or stronger counteraid. This confuses any horse, whether experienced or not. Too much of this overaided riding frustrates the horse and results in the development of undesirable responses. For example: A horse has been trained correctly, using dressage principles, to halt and back (see "Backing" farther on in this chapter). An untrained rider mounts the horse, runs him around a minute, then tries to get him to back by pulling back on the reins, shooting his legs forward, and leaning back on the cantle. The horse is confused. Should he rear? Throw up his head? Do nothing? His reaction will depend on his personality and volatility. The rider, not receiving the response he expected, is annoyed. He spurs the horse forward, then raps his mouth even harder. What will the poor horse do now? He has been confused and chastised; any confidence he may have had now dwindles rapidly.

This may be an extreme example, but we see some kinds of overaiding frequently, even in shows. It seems reasonable that this is one of the main reasons why there are so many problem horses. They actually don't know what is expected of them. There are not many people, either, who could stay sane under the same circumstances.

The greatest source of overaiding and misguided training is in use of the bit. The young or inexperienced horse will resist mouth pressures that

Amateur riders and trainers often think that reins and bit are of paramount importance in controlling a horse, whereas they are actually means of communicating more subtly and efficiently. To prove that reins and bit are not even necessary for basic communication, horseman Allen G. Richardson of Fort Collins, Colorado, trains horses to work without them. This mare, still not completely trained, wears a light bosal and safety line attached to saddle, but these remain untouched as a student demonstrates. She gives aids only through the legs and seat.

are too severe, which of course is why we have taught him *gradually* to respond. The trainer must understand the action of various bits on the horse's mouth in order to use them correctly.

MORE ABOUT BITS

We've discussed use of the snaffle as an introductory and training bit, particularly thick, heavy snaffles such as the German D bit (see Part I, Chapter 2, and Part II, Chapter 2). There should be no rush to graduate from the snaffle, since many months, even years, can be spent happily with it. For training, it is the most valuable and widely used bit available.

Why is the snaffle so good and when should there be a change to a different bit?

The snaffle is used by most trainers for several reasons, one of which is its mild action. One of our goals in training is lightness—sensitive response. The snaffle is best able to induce and maintain this softness in the horse's mouth. The snaffle is also the best bit through which the rider may maintain a steady contact with the horse's mouth. Often, even during advanced training in a double bridle, the trainer will return periodically to a mild snaffle bit to refresh the horse and soften his mouth.

One often hears that the action of the snaffle raises the head, and the action of the curb positions the head. One hears, "I can't control my horse with a snaffle—his nose is always up in the air." Sometimes a horse will open his mouth with the snaffle, or stick out his tongue, or work his tongue over the bit.

Some of these problems reflect more on the rider's use of the bit than on the bit itself. Progressive, intelligent, step-by-step training and development of the horse are essential. Some of the problems can be prevented or corrected by use of a dropped noseband in conjunction with the snaffle bit. Proper fit of both bit and noseband is of paramount importance. (Twisted snaffles, gag snaffles, and other specialized bits may be useful corrective bits in the hands of an experienced, knowledgeable trainer, but they have no place in training the youngster, and we do not recommend using them.)

One more advantage of the snaffle bit is that it requires the trainer to make the horse's mouth in the correct way, using his legs to induce forward impulsion and inviting the horse to respond with flexion and collection. When using a curb bit too early there is danger that the *attitude* of collection can be obtained by reaction to the more severe bit—in effect, the force is backward instead of forward. This basic fault lays the foundation for a host of difficulties including overbending, evasions, and loss of forward impulsion.

Let's consider here the comparative action of snaffle and curb bits. We know that the snaffle puts pressure on the corners of the horse's mouth and also on the bars. The curb works on the lever principle, hence its more severe action. The curb strap or chain works in conjunction with the shanks of the bit to put pressure both against the bars and under the chin (in some curb bits also against the tongue or against the roof of the mouth). Usually the severity of the bit is in proportion to the length of the shanks and the tightness of the curb strap. Proper fit is an absolute necessity for proper action and performance. The curb's stronger action gives more control. Its type of action encourages flexion but may impede impulsion if not handled properly.

For some riding—notably hunting, jumping, and racing—the snaffle continues throughout the horse's career to be the most desirable and most widely used bit. In other forms of riding, the horse generally graduates to a different type of bit—at best to attain the finest possible communication between horse and rider; at worst, a more severe bit only substitutes for good horsemanship. Horses have different preferences and physical needs (the bars of the mouth may be fleshy or lean, or the horse may react more or less sensitively to a curb strap), and these, too, influence the kind of bit

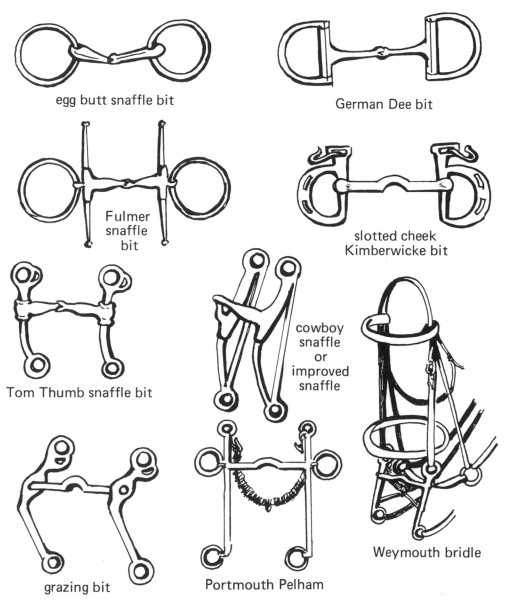

egg butt snaffle bit

German Dee bit

Fulmer snaffle bit

slotted cheek Kimberwicke bit

Tom Thumb snaffle bit

cowboy snaffle or improved snaffle

grazing bit

Portmouth Pelham

Weymouth bridle

to be used. A rider's ability, his goals, and the extent to which he wishes to perfect his riding skill also add to the considerations of which bit to select.

In English riding, the double bridle (also called Weymouth or full bridle) offers the most highly refined type of communication. The double bridle is exactly that—two separate headstalls with separate bits, each bit having its own set of reins. The thin snaffle (or bridoon) is placed above the curb bit. Through sensitive and expert use of the four reins, a complete range of intercommunication can be achieved between horse and rider. Most proponents of classical equitation use either the snaffle or double bridle, often changing from one to the other as the occasion warrants.

The double bridle, however, must be introduced gently to the horse, both because of its potentially sharper action and because it "fills" the colt's mouth. Expert riders can make the transition without losing impulsion, but in general it is easier on both horse and rider to use an intermediate bit, one that gently introduces the action of the curb. The Pelham is popular for this purpose, and often becomes the preferred bit for the English pleasure horse.

The Pelham is a one-piece bit with rings for both snaffle and curb reins. The shanks are relatively short, resulting in mild leverage on the curb. Although lacking the full range of communication possible with the double bridle, the Pelham is quite satisfactory for many forms of riding.

Another popular transitional bit for English riding is the Kimberwicke. It is a versatile bit often used in training and for pleasure riding. The Kimberwicke may have curb or snaffle mouthpiece and may be used with or without a curb strap.

Most bits come in many different models, varying in width and thickness of mouthpiece; length of shank; jointed or solid mouthpiece; bar or size of port, and other features. This great variety may make choice difficult when selecting a bit, but it does mean that somewhere there's a right bit for almost every horse, even if it may take some patience and experimentation to find it. We know of a horse that absolutely refused to work in every bit and hackamore in the book until a snaffle-mouth Pelham was tried—it proved to be the right bit for that horse.

For Western riding, the snaffle is still the ideal training bit. Training with a hackamore is also especially useful to prepare the horse for a Western curb bit. Again, the youngster should work well and be thoroughly experienced in hackamore and snaffle before the curb is introduced.

The Western horse performs with less contact than the English horse. (Most horses will react responsively in both types of riding when properly trained. Many enjoy the variety of style, as the change keeps them fresh and soft in the mouth; others definitely prefer one style over the other—which may be mainly a reflection of the rider's skill.) The Western horse, using a Western curb bit, receives his direction for turning through leg and weight aids and through neck reining—not through the bit. This is why the Western horse must have thorough training in snaffle, hackamore, or both, before going into the curb. The curb directs the horse in collection, flexion, and straight movements such as transitions, halting, and backing. The bits range from fairly mild to very severe, and for proper use require, at the least, experienced hands and at the best, highly skilled hands.

We prefer the grazing type of bit (with moderate, backward-flared shanks). Generally these bits have a low port, and their overall effect is less severe than the straighter-shank, higher-port bits. Another relatively mild bit is the swivel dee cheek reining bit, popularly known as the cowboy snaffle. This comes in a variety of models, some with rein rings only at the end of the shanks. The most versatile cowboy snaffle has large dee rings at the mouth and smaller rings at the end of the shanks; it can be used with four reins (like the Pelham) and makes a good transitional bit to either the one-piece Western curb or the double bridle. The Tom Thumb bit, with short shanks and snaffle mouthpiece, makes another mild but effective transitional bit.

The Western horse should respond quickly, quietly, and willingly. He should work enthusiastically on a light rein—without resort to gimmicks, tiedowns, and excessive hardware. Properly trained, he should have a soft mouth and be ridden with light hands. The milder the equipment used, the softer his mouth will be, if this equipment is used properly. Many gymkhana and roping horses sour when their routine is overpracticed, and many learn to evade the bit because of hands made hard by the excitement of the moment. These horses benefit greatly by relaxed ring work in a snaffle bit—a total change that improves suppleness, flexion, obedience, balance, and interest.

Bits and bridles must fit properly. Use the right width bit for the horse: If too narrow, it will pinch; if too wide, it will move in the mouth and bruise the corners. The bit should fit into the corners of the mouth without

When the bridle is well fitted, the bit fits into the corners of the mouth. As a rule, the curb chain is properly adjusted when you can place three fingers easily between it and the jaw.

wrinkling the lips (with some bits, one or two wrinkles in the corners is permissible), and it should not be so low that it touches the teeth. The curb chain or strap should lie flat against the chin; it should be adjusted so as to come into action when the straight shanks of the bit are drawn back, making an angle of forty-five degrees with the mouth (make proper allowance for curved shanks). A cavesson noseband should lie halfway between the cheekbone and the corners of the mouth; it should allow two fingers between noseband and nose. The dropped noseband fits over the snaffle bit and should not be so tight that it prevents the horse from flexing his jaw; the front should be above the nostrils; the back fits in the chin groove. The browband should not touch the ears or interfere with the hang of the headstall. The throatlatch should allow three fingers easily. All pieces should lie flat and smooth against the horse's head.

Elementary Dressage for Obedience, Suppleness, and Balance

Although the ultimate goal of a pleasure horse may be trail riding or some other pleasure-oriented purpose, he must prepare for this work in the riding arena. Performance and practice of basic exercises help the horse to become more responsive, better balanced, and supple in a shorter time. Boredom can kill progress, however. Although the basic maneuvers need plenty of practice, variety is needed to maintain interest in both horse and rider.

These basic exercises can be arranged in a variety of patterns to form routines of increasing complexity. We begin with simple figures and work gradually into the more difficult exercises, demanding more of the colt as his ability improves. These exercises and routines are, in fact, elementary dressage. They are suitable and beneficial for any horse, English or Western, and are as helpful in retraining the spoiled horse as they are in properly training the youngster.

Although true dressage patterns must conform to official requirements of size and geographical location within the ring, that is not our concern at this time. It is the type and form of the exercise that improves the horse, and these can be adapted to whatever conditions you have and the stage of your horse's training.

If you don't have a large, rectangular riding arena, lay one out on level ground with cones, stones, or poles—anything to mark a suitable area. If possible, lay the area out to be 60 by 120 feet; come as close to these measurements as your situation allows. In order to perform the routines correctly, the center of the ring or arena should be clear of any obstacles.

Begin, as always, with the simple exercises and routines and work up gradually to those that are more difficult. All of these should be worked at a walk before trotting through them. Precision is the goal of continually improving obedience.

FIGURES AND EXERCISES

Corners and straightaways. In riding around the ring (traveling the perimeter of the arena along the wall), you will be traveling along straight lines and around curves. Ride parallel to the straight sides, and make shallow turns around the corners. Always ride in both directions. Traveling on the track around the whole arena is called "going large."

Remember that your main concern in the early stages of training is to encourage free forward movement. Encourage the youngster to move straight on the straightaways and to bend his entire body on the curves. Practice halts along with other work unless the colt finds the halt so attractive that it interferes with his free forward movement; in this case, discontinue practicing the halt (other than necessary, of course) until later.

Reverses can be made in either direction: toward the center (normal reverse) or toward the wall (half turn in reverse). The reverse is really the execution of a half volte (small circle), followed by a diagonal line back to the track. Keep the turns shallow in the early stages of training. If you use too much rein, or try to turn too sharply, you will bend only the horse's head and neck rather than his whole body, and you will create resistance in the colt.

Form the habit of looking around your curves with your head up. This automatically puts your weight on the inside seat bone. Looking where you intend to go—whether describing a circle or following a jump course—is a subtle aid that helps your horse interpret your desires. It is one of the tiny but important factors that make precision possible.

When reversing to the wall, begin with a diagonal line toward the center, moving into a half circle large enough to allow a shallow turn. Turning into the wall encourages the colt to keep his head low and to bend his whole body through the turn. It is also a good retraining exercise for horses that tend to raise their heads on turns.

Change of hand (change of rein). You may also change direction through the diagonal or through the center of the arena. By traveling across the center (parallel to the short sides, parallel to the long sides, or diagonally), you will be working on a straightaway with no wall to aid in straightening the horse, and so will be able to gauge his improvement in straightness.

Voltes (small circles) help to improve reining and proper bending. The official dressage volte has a diameter of twenty feet or six meters. But for now, make them large enough to keep the turn shallow. It is more important for the colt to bend properly on a shallow arc than to try for too

Training Figures and Exercises

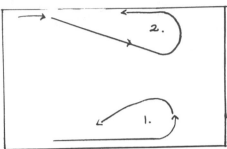

shallow corners and straight
lines—ride in both directions

reverses—normal, 1., and half
turn in reverse, 2. (in both
directions)

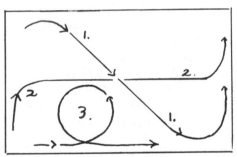

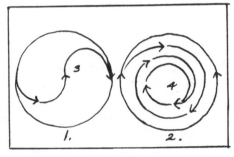

change of hand (rein) 1.; across
the diagonal, 1.; change of hand
through the center of the arena,
2.; large volte, 3.

large circles using half the arena
1. and 2., changing direction
through the circle (practicing in
both directions), 3.; spiraling, 4.

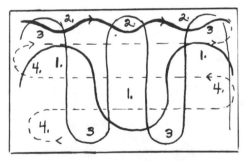

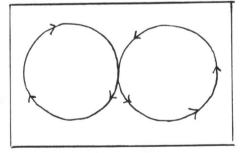

serpentine of 3 half circles 1.;
broken line 2.; alternate straight
line and turn 3.; serpentine long
way of the arena, 4.

figure eight

small a volte (one that the youngster cannot execute without overbending his neck or swinging his haunches out). Look ahead around the circle you wish to describe. The horse may tend to slow down coming out of the circle back onto the rail (he may do the same when reversing); anticipate and prevent this with gentle, encouraging aids to move forward (alternately push with seat bones and squeeze with lower legs). Practice voltes both ways of the ring, in corners as well as along the sides. Work for a *round* figure—not easy!

Circles and changes through the circle. Large circles using half the arena are especially good in the early stages of training because of the shallow, undemanding turn. Nevertheless, they are not easy to ride correctly. If your arena is laid out in the correct proportions, half of the arena will form an exact square. When you ride the circle, you should approach the rail at the exact center of each side (always leave enough room for another rider to ride along the rail if you are not riding alone). Ride with an even bend, practicing in both directions and at both ends of the arena. Work for precision in the correct execution of each figure.

You may change direction through the circle, forming half of a figure-eight (a good transitional exercise).

Spiraling is a variation of the circle. It is begun by riding a circle, gradually working in to a small circle and then working out again to the full circle. The figure is not easy to do correctly—precision, even cadence, and proper bending are important. The young horse will not be able to work into a small circle until he improves in suppleness—more lateral flexion can be asked later as the horse progresses. Vary the spiraling exercise with work on straight lines.

Serpentines and broken lines. The serpentine may be executed in a variety of forms, with a change of rein on each turn to re-establish the proper position and proper bend of the horse. The horse may be ridden straight for one or more strides between each alternate turn. The serpentine may be three half circles across half of the arena, three or more half circles across the whole arena, or it may be ridden the long way of the arena, turning at the short ends.

Broken lines are a series of shallow curves and may be performed along the long wall or down the center line.

Care should be taken to aid the horse to bend properly when riding the curves—this is an exercise in the rider's precision in giving the aids and must be approached with care and thought. Always look ahead and think ahead into the turns.

Figure-eights are excellent reining exercises, especially at the trot. The size of the eight must be kept large at first, perhaps using the entire arena for the two full circles, and may be varied later with smaller eights as the horse progresses in his suppleness and ability. Work for precision in execution, keeping an even gait whether at walk or trot. Ride the figure as two circles, with one or two straight strides in the center. When trotting and posting, change diagonals in the center.

ARENA TRAINING ROUTINES

How can you best use the figures and exercises to benefit the young horse? It's usually helpful, especially to the novice trainer, to have a plan of organization worked out in progressive training routines. These routines may be incorporated into the saddle-training part of each training session (following ground work). They will have to be adapted for each horse, and each routine repeated or reviewed until the horse is capable of progressing to the next. Use of planned routines eliminates boredom for both horse and rider, and provides a purpose and goal for each day's training session rather than permitting aimless round-and-round riding.

With practice, you will be able to plan your own routines, fitting them to the individual horse according to his needs, problems, and abilities. Don't leave these to guesswork; take the time to write them out, both to act as a training guide and to serve as an up-to-date record of your progress.

Routine 1.
a. Walk; go large (following track around whole arena), both directions.
b. Continue large; reverse occasionally, both to the center and into the wall (make turns large and shallow enough to keep proper bend in young horse).
c. Circle one end of arena, ride straight line down the center, circle other end of arena.
d. Repeat, circling in opposite direction, end on straight line down center.

After each training session, stop to dismount in a different place so that the youngster won't come to anticipate a "quitting spot."

Routine 2.
a. Walk large in both directions.
b. Continue large; reverse both ways.
c. Volte in each corner, both ways of ring (keep voltes large until colt can perform them in the proper size.
d. Walk large; change rein through the diagonal.
e. Volte on long sides of arena.
f. Repeat change of rein and voltes, opposite direction.
g. Walk broken line down center (series of shallow curves). If not very successful, try it along long sides with guidance of wall.

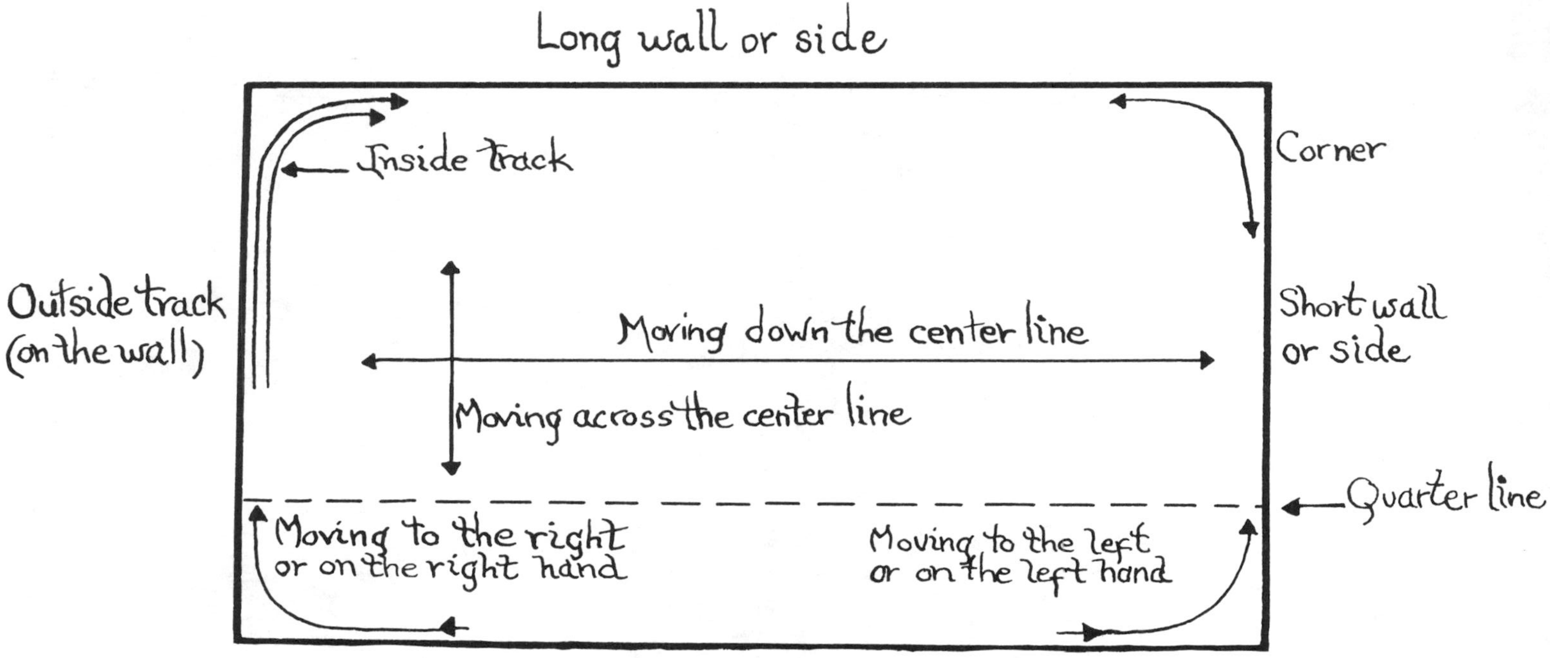

Riding Arena

Labels on diagram:

- Long wall or side
- Corner
- Short wall or side
- Quarter line
- Inside track
- Moving down the center line
- Moving across the center line
- Moving to the left or on the left hand
- Moving to the right or on the right hand
- Outside track (on the wall)

Routine 3.

    a. Walk through Routines 1 and 2, perhaps changing order of figures. Intersperse curves and straightaways.

    b. Introduce trot for a few steps on long side of arena. Reverse, repeat.

    c. Walk through curved figures, intersperse straight trots on long wall (a few more steps each time, little contact, much praise).

    d. Walk large, circle both directions, halting occasionally.

Routine 4.

    a. Review Routines 1 and 2.

    b. Trot one half of arena, walk one half, halt.

    c. Walk a serpentine (make shallow turns).

    d. Trot three fourths of arena; walk through volte; reverse.

    e. Repeat b. through d. in opposite direction.

    f. End session with walks down center line and several halts.

Routine 5.

    a. Review Routines 1 through 4; be sure to ride each figure in both directions.

    b. Walk large; change rein by trotting through diagonals.

    c. Go large; practice transitions in both directions: Walk, trot, walk, halt, walk, etc., varying distance between each.

    d. Circle both ends of arena (large figure-eight) at walk; then trot.

    e. Circle both ends at walk, changing through the circle.

    f. Walk large around track; halt occasionally, varying length of time at each halt; dismount.

    g. Drop reins, begin teaching colt to stand (see "Intermediate Longeing" in Part II, Chapter 2); repeat at least once during lesson from now on, and repeat after finish of each lesson.

Work through these routines, varying them as you wish, until the youngster is stable in his trot. At that point, begin differentiating the trots, working for a slightly collected slow trot (sitting) and a free, faster, posting trot. The posting trot should be done only on straightaways, diagonals, and very shallow corners.

Routine 6.

    a. Review parts of previous routines.

    b. Go large; slow trot once around left; walk one half around; reverse; slow trot once around right. (Work gradually on increasing contact and on the pushing aids of seat and legs.)

    c. Walk through a serpentine the long way of the arena.

    d. Go large; posting trot once around left (make the corners very shallow); change rein at walk; posting trot once around right.

    e. Finish lessons as in Routine 5, e., f., and g.

Routine 7.

    a. Review earlier routines at walk; follow each figure with same figure at sitting trot. Do each figure in both directions, including reverses.

    b. Go large; posting trot long sides of arena; sitting trot short sides; work on perfecting transitions.

    c. Circular figures at walk.

    d. Slow trot short sides of arena; change through diagonals at posting trot.

    e. Go large; work on transitions: walk, slow trot, posting trot, and halt both ways.

    f. Walk circular figures and straightaways to finish.

It is likely that up to now you have been working in an arena or ring near your corrals, perhaps an indoor arena. At this point, if you have not done so earlier (depending upon the horse's stability), you will want to move outside or into another area and review the earlier lessons. On these days, it would be wise to do your ground training in this new area before riding. Generally, the colt's work will tend to be rough, since there are new things to see and his attention will be diverted. Don't be discouraged at this seeming regression, but if he tends to become overly upset or unmanageable, return to the more enclosed area until he is more stable. He'll soon work well in the new area, and eventually he will be able to tend to business no matter what his surroundings.

When the horse is working well at walk, slow trot, and posting trot, you may add the canter to your routine. Most work at the canter can be considered advanced and will be discussed later, in the material on advanced training. For now you will work merely for balance, correct leads, and a stable rhythm. Starting the horse in the canter was discussed in Chapter 4 under "Stabilizing the gaits: The canter and lope." If the youngster doesn't yet take his leads well, you may canter him across the ring on the diagonal, without making any demands at first for a specific lead.

Routine 8.

    a. Review Routine 7, a. through c.

    b. Begin canter on large circle on lead favored by colt; go full circle if possible, or only half or less until colt is balanced and able to do more. Repeat in opposite direction. (Praise generously every effort made by the youngster—if you understand that he may be fearful and unsure of his balance, or may be confused by the new exercise, you will be more patient. Use the word command "Can-ter" to help the colt understand.)

    c. Walk through several circular figures and straightaways.

d. Try canter again, going large partway around—gradually work up to once around. Walk, reverse, and canter in opposite direction.
e. Finish with more circular figures and straightaways at walk and sitting trot.

If you have not done so earlier, now is a good time to end lessons with a relaxed ten minutes or so outside of the arena. This gives your training sessions the three components we mentioned in Part II, Chapter 4 (under "Training outside the corral or in the open")—ground work, arena or ring training, and trail riding.

If your colt has trouble with the canter, you may try incorporating one or more of the following exercises into your training routines. They will help the horse to become more balanced and rhythmical at the canter.

Exercises to help obtain the correct lead:

a. Volte at a walk (or trot through a larger circle) in a corner. As you come out of the volte, your horse should be bent correctly. Give aids and voice commands (help with crop, if necessary) for canter just as you come out of the volte.
b. Reverse toward the wall, give aids for canter as you come out of the reverse.
c. When in the open, ask for canter as you are going uphill and around a rock formation or group of trees.
d. Review canter on the longe.

Exercises to help maintain the correct lead and to help slow down the canter:

a. Canter in circles within a barrier.
b. Spiral from large circle in toward center and back out. Take care not to go too small.
c. Canter for longer periods as horse becomes stronger and his attention span lengthens. Use restraining aids if necessary, gradually take up more contact, use seat, legs, and weight to obtain some collection. Let the colt extend a little, ask again for a little collection. Keep the youngster from becoming bored or tired.

We do not advocate changing direction at the canter, or asking for the counter-canter, until the youngster is well-balanced, supple, and completely stable in his leads. Flying changes will be discussed in the material on advanced training; for now, all changes of lead should be simple.

Getting the Most from Exercises and Routines

WHAT TO WORK ON

The exercises and routines in themselves will do little for the horse unless they are ridden correctly. Let's consider again briefly what to work on, and what pitfalls to watch for and avoid.

Your first concern at this stage is free forward movement in all gaits. If your colt tends to be sluggish and unresponsive, you'll have a lot of work to do right here. Avoid banging his sides incessantly with your legs; it will only make his sides numb and increase his unresponsiveness. Instead, use a long whip or willow stick. Ask with your leg and then reinforce with the whip—this should help him to become more sensitive and responsive to your wishes. Most important, put some spice into your training program: Use cavalletti (Part II, Chapter 6), go on trail rides, and incorporate a variety of training exercises; ride with friends, in different locations, and under varying conditions; work stock if you can find some—ask a neighbor if you could herd his sheep, cattle, even chickens occasionally. Keep the colt alert and interested. He should *want* to move forward enthusiastically.

Work also to obtain regularity and stability in the gaits—even tempo and cadence expressed in confident, enthusiastic strides. Balance, impulsion, suppleness, obedience, muscular development, and overall handsomeness should improve gradually in response to athletic training.

In performing curves and circular figures, the hind legs should follow exactly the tracks of the forefeet. The hindquarters should swing neither to the outside nor to the inside. If you have difficulties with this, you may be making your curves too sharp; don't expect the youngster to bend beyond his ability. Increase work with suppling exercises and ride long curves at walk and trot to strengthen and exercise muscles along the back and sides. Don't neglect work on the longe.

On straightaways, work for straightness by constant subtle correction through leg, weight, and rein. Watch that the youngster doesn't carry his neck crooked to the inside, or that he doesn't lean out toward the wall as though for support, causing his hindquarters to swing in.

Plan your training routines to vary the work period by interspersing halts, free walks (see below), straightaways, curves, trots, and walks. As the colt improves in balance, suppleness, and regularity of gaits, you may begin to ask for a little collection—that is, you will encourage him to flex neck, poll, and jaw, encourage him to move his hindquarters farther under him, encourage animation of gait (not speed). This should be followed by exercises in extension—encouraging the horse to stretch out and lengthen his stride. Balance may be improved by working on transitions, both within a gait (such as slow trot with partial collection to extended trot with light contact), and from one gait to another, as well as by simply increasing or decreasing the speed of any gait.

COLLECTION VS. EXTENSION, CONTACT VS. FREE REIN

In collection the horse is shortened, made more compact as a result of increased impulsion combined with restraint. The horse steps farther under himself with his hind legs, bends the joints in his hind legs more, and takes more of his weight on his hindquarters. The result of this process is to elevate the forehand, animate the action, and improve the horse's capability to react in instantaneous response to the aids.

Contact is necessary to collection. Contact is the process of feeling the horse's mouth through the reins. Ideally, rather than restricting with the reins to make contact, the rider takes up the reins, and the horse flexes his jaw and moves his tongue to accept contact with the bit. This occurs because the rider invites the horse to step into the bit by using his legs and back (weight through the seat bones) to initiate impulsion. If the rider were to restrict with his hands while giving with his seat (leaning forward, thereby allowing no influence of the seat bones), the desired result of shortening the horse could not occur.

Contact is also an ingredient of extension, in which the horse is invited to lengthen himself—that is, to stretch out in longer strides. In an extended horse, the energy of impulsion is transferred forward rather than upward. This has nothing to do with speed. Again, it is the result of the co-ordinated effort of our whole body in communication with the whole horse.

When there is no steady contact with the horse's mouth (he is guided only by a long rein), the horse is said to be on a free rein. This can occur at any gait. When on a free rein, the horse is not working, but relaxing. Since he is not in contact with his rider—not collected—he will not be ready to respond immediately, with ease. He will not be able to react in harmony with his rider, to perform a pirouette or a rollback or even a transition in gait without first gathering himself. He may respond rapidly, however, to a snatching up of the rein, perhaps for a turn or stop. This jerky movement of the rider is reflected in a jerky movement of the horse. The sudden pressure will make him wary of the bit, and he'll react quickly to protect his mouth. We see a lot of this in pleasure riding, especially in Western tack—the rider is unaware that he should be using a light rein

Compare mild collection at the trot with extension. Contact is important in both cases, but the profile of the horse in collection is more compact: His neck is more arched, his weight more on the hindquarters. In extension he lengthens, stretches out.

On a free rein, the horse relaxes, lowers his head, and moves forward freely.

rather than a free rein. Western riding involves light contact, not lack of contact, and must be accompanied by light, sensitive hands to achieve proper performance.

The purpose of the free rein is to relax the horse after working, or to reward him for proper execution of an exercise. He should not be ridden all the time on a free rein. A pleasure horse should accept the bit and obey the aids.

BACKING (THE REIN-BACK)

Backing is often considered to be part of a horse's most basic and elementary training. Why have we left it out until now?

There are three main reasons why we don't like to begin backing too soon. Let's consider them separately.

The first reason is physical. When backing properly, the horse moves his diagonal legs together (as at the trot), stepping back in a straight line. In order to do this, he must bend the joints of his hind legs more deeply than he is used to doing. To require this of a youngster who is not yet sufficiently developed is to put more strain on joints and muscles than he is ready for. Even when he is more physically developed, the exercise should be introduced gradually to prevent sore muscles and increased mental resistance to backing. This is one reason why so many horses dislike backing —when the training is rushed, backing can cause considerable discomfort for them.

The second is that when done correctly, backing is the result of im-

When performing the rein-back correctly, the horse moves his diagonal legs together. Backing should be the result of impulsion plus collection—not of a backward pull on the reins.

pulsion plus collection—the youngster simply isn't ready for this until somewhat advanced in his training. To ask his horse to back, the expert rider uses his legs and hands to collect the horse and put him on the bit. Continuing to apply leg pressure, he asks the horse to move out. But just as the horse is about to take a step, the rider increases rein resistance so that the horse steps backward instead of forward. The result is that the horse is collected, has already increased the bend in the joints of his hind legs, and thus is ready to step back cleanly and well (rather than dragging back a leg at a time). Leg and rein pressures are reapplied as necessary to move the horse back. The legs keep the horse straight. Properly done, the rein-back is a demonstration of suppleness and obedience.

Third, our main concern in the young horse is to encourage him to move forward freely. Too early an emphasis on backing may interfere with this in two ways. He may find that he can halt or back to evade the aids and simply avoid doing what he's supposed to. Occasionally a horse will develop the vice of backing uncontrollably—an extremely dangerous habit for both horse and rider, and one that is very difficult to correct.

The other way that early introduction to backing may interfere with forward movement is in response to the bit. You can't teach a youngster to back as explained above until he is prepared for it both mentally and physically; instead, you will have to use a different method, involving backward pulls on the reins. These signals are very similar to those given for the suppling exercises (Part II, Chapter 3)—so similar, in fact, that they are easily confused by the youngster. The result may be that instead of learning to flex at the jaw and poll in answer to rein pressure or vibrations, the youngster simply backs up.

With all these considerations in mind, then, it is usually best to wait until the horse is well along in his training before teaching him to back. Even with Western horses, where backing—sometimes at speed and for long distances—is important for trail and reining contests and for roping work, it is well to wait until the horse has developed enough so that backing does not strain either his mental or physical capabilities.

Unfortunately, this is not always possible. Sometimes it is necessary for the horse to learn to back quite early. Care must be taken not to overdo, thereby straining muscles. Take advantage of natural situations to help teach the horse to back: If he goes into a straight stall or a trailer, he must back out. Say "Back!" firmly as he backs out, and, if you can, encourage the movement by light tugs of the lead rope toward his chest, or by pressing intermittently against his chest with your fingers. He will come to recognize these signals, and this will aid in your training.

Driving horses often must learn to back early, and using long lines to help train the horse to back is often a good way to go about it. The lines keep the horse backing straight. Have an assistant help you by standing at the colt's head. Make sure the horse is standing square. Then say "Back!" and wait for him to take a step back. Repeat, and have your assistant press against the colt's chest with his fingers or with a whip held horizontally. When the colt takes the least step backward, praise him enthusiastically and ask him to move forward again. Repeat the exercise and go on to other things. The colt will probably not be able to back properly for some time —that is, be able to move his diagonal legs together, backward step by step, cleanly and without hesitation.

You may also teach backing from the ground alone. Stand at the colt's head, grasp both hackamore or bridle reins near bosal or bit, and give gentle, intermittent tugs toward his chest, repeating the command, "Back!" Wait for him to take a step, and try again. Press whip or fingers against his chest as above. Try to be clear in your own differentiation of the command to back and the elementary suppling exercises. Keep backing lessons to a minimum. If the youngster becomes confused or develops a hesitation to move forward, discontinue backing for several weeks.

A good way to teach a partially trained horse to back is to proceed from the saddle as does the expert, applying impulsion with the legs and resistance with the hands. Have an assistant stand in front of the horse to tap with a whip handle against the chest, or to press with his fingers as you say "Back!" Although the colt may not be ready to understand the aids alone, with this assistance the meaning becomes clear. Have the assistant help for several lessons; then ride the horse up to the assistant, halt, and ask the horse to back while the assistant stands still. Gradually halt farther from the assistant and then work without him. With this method, the youngster can learn to back correctly, with a minimum of confusion, by proper use of the aids and maintenance of straightness and forward impulsion.

In summary, then, when training a horse to back, remember the following:

•Free forward movement is essential and must be maintained.
•After backing—whether one step or ten, depending on the degree of training—always move the horse forward again.
•When backing correctly, the horse steps back with his diagonal legs working together, hitting the ground at the same time.
•Correct backing requires suppleness and muscular development because of the strong bend required in the joints of the hindquarters.
•Work slowly. Backing is a difficult exercise for the horse and must be taught gradually in order to avoid sore muscles, confusion, and sourness.
•Keep the horse straight when backing, by using your legs. Backing him between rails laid on the ground can be an aid.
•When backing correctly, the horse steps back because of forward impulsion. He is *pushed* into backing, not pulled into it.
•Praise generously and keep backing lessons short.

The rein-back will be discussed further in the section on advanced training.

ALL-AROUND USEFULNESS

Any horse may profitably spend several years developing his pleasure-horse status. This is a general basic education that should include a wide variety of experience and should aim for continual improvement in precision, suppleness, balance, and willingness. By the time the horse has spent three or more years in general pleasure riding and general stock work (around the age of six), his training and his mental and physical develop-

One of the best means of educating your horse is to give him a wide variety of experience. (Courtesy Wyoming Travel Commission)

ment should have matured to the point where he is ready to specialize, if that is your intention. At this point, his advanced training may begin.

During this basic-training period, you will probably discover, at least in part, his special aptitudes and interests. He will do better at some things than at others. His conformation and temperament will also have a bearing on the tasks for which he is best suited. If you wish to specialize in any equestrian endeavor, the success of your training and performance will depend largely on the horse's suitability for and interest in that endeavor. We have an old mare who loathes ring work. Her feet drag, her ears droop, she may even feign lameness. It's a major project to get her into a slow trot. But show her a cow and a job to do, and her whole carriage changes. She's alert, works off her haunches, is always ready to take off in a lope to do the job for which she was trained and that she enjoys. She's a top cowhorse and at her age we'd sure have a time trying to turn her into a hunter or dressage horse.

Of course, through early grounding in a basic education, most horses can be more versatile. A horse is a great mimic and adapter. A true pleasure horse adapts his wishes to ours. Depending on his limits of conformation and temperament, he is influenced by our interests. If he senses that we are enjoying ourselves, he'll pitch right in and help. This willing generosity is characteristic of a horse trained with love and understanding. Gymkhana horses (those that have been trained for games rather than bullied into them) are good examples of this and often seem to be enjoy-ing themselves. Polo ponies have been known to hit the ball with their hooves in an effort to participate more fully.

You don't have to have a goal in mind the minute you first greet your new foal. You can discover his potential through everyday training—through his gradual development as a pleasure horse.

Fitting the horse to your goal is more difficult. If you have a specific interest and goal in mind—one that requires a high degree of specialized skill—it is wise to choose your horse with care. Find a mature horse that already has a good basic education and whose aptitudes point in the direc-tion you desire. If you wished to raise a certain foal to be a cutting horse, and then discovered that as a four-year-old he cares not one whit for cattle and cannot work independently, you've spent a lot of time and money in the wrong direction. You'd best sell him and find a horse with cutting po-tential. The experienced horseman will come closer to picking a suitable animal, but the novice horseman should be prepared either to compromise his goal and keep the horse, or to sell him and find a horse that will con-form better to his desires. When you plan to buy a horse with a specific goal in mind, ask the advice of a well-recommended horseman—it would save you time, money, and disappointment.

Overall, however, versatility is the keynote for most horses. Many horses are capable of developing a high degree of skill in several different areas—three-day eventers are skilled in dressage, jumping, and cross-country racing. The true pleasure horse should be a pleasure to ride—whether in the arena, over a low jump course, in some show and contest classes, for stock work, or on the trail.

CHAPTER 6

CAVALLETTI

AND JUMPING

To "make haste slowly" is the sensible way to prepare a horse for jumping. As with all other steps in horsemanship, jump training must proceed logically from a basic foundation. The use of cavalletti helps a horse to acquire the basic skills and athletic ability that will prepare him for jumping.

Cavalletti are a series of parallel rails or low obstacles properly placed for the individual horse at a walk, trot, or canter. The word is Italian (cavalletto for a single obstacle), and the idea was initiated by the forward-seat proponent, Captain Federico Caprilli, who revolutionized the method of jumping in the early 1900s, although it took a quarter of a century for his method to be universally accepted. Caprilli observed that horses use their necks to balance in jumping, and that the style of jumping, then, in which the rider sat upright hindered the horse in using his neck and back. When the rider moved forward to remain over the horse's center of gravity, the horse was freed to make a smoother, more natural jump. Caprilli encouraged his horses and riders to go over obstacles of different heights in this manner, and his method of natural schooling proved its worth in the jumping world.

Elementary Work

HOW DO CAVALLETTI HELP THE HORSE?

As with most training aids, cavalletti must be used correctly or they do more harm than good. Here are some of the benefits that accrue from using cavalletti properly.

Cavalletti capture and maintain the horse's attention. He must watch the ground and mind where he places each foot. They force him to remain alert, leaving him less open to distraction. Consequently he improves in sure-footedness, balance, and handiness.

Use of cavalletti requires the horse to remain alert, develops his muscles, and improves his rhythm and co-ordination.

Use of cavalletti requires the horse to undergo disciplined exercise, using and developing the correct muscles. He must lift his legs higher, arch his back, and stretch his neck, thereby easing stiffness, both loosening and toughening muscles, and improving suppleness and flexibility. By engaging his hindquarters, he increases impulsion. This exercise develops the heart, increases circulation, develops stamina, and aids overall condition—factors that are especially important when training a horse for endurance riding or three-day eventing.

Cavalletti work regulates and improves rhythm and cadence during the walk and trot. It increases animation and improves carriage, suppleness, and balance.

It improves co-ordination and agility by teaching the horse to judge distances and to shorten and lengthen his stride.

Use of cavalletti teaches the horse to relax and to accept obstacles in varied placement. He settles down and learns to take the obstacles in rhythm and without excitement. This calmness is reflected in improved obedience.

Cavalletti work may present a pleasant change of pace that increases the horse's interest, builds his confidence, and inspires his willingness.

Use of cavalletti can help the trainer in evaluating his horse. By observing him over cavalletti, either free in the school or on a longe line, you will learn if he is quiet and willing. His resistances can give you a clue to his character and temperament. How intelligent is he? The animal that learns by one misjudgment is more intelligent than the one that repeatedly misjudges the same obstacles in the same place.

Proper use of cavalletti helps to make the horse a better athlete. It can also help the rider to develop his balance, timing, and judgment, and so enable him to do a better job of training his horse for jumping.

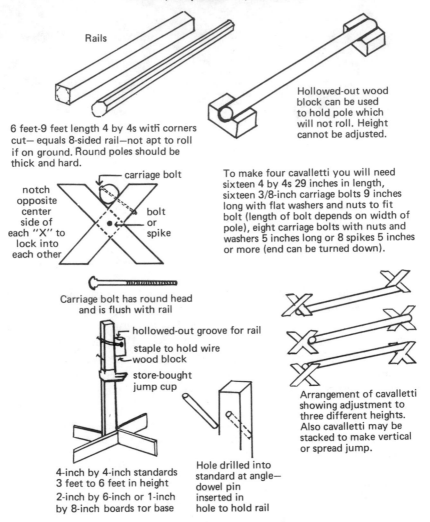

Rails

6 feet-9 feet length 4 by 4s with corners cut— equals 8-sided rail—not apt to roll if on ground. Round poles should be thick and hard.

Hollowed-out wood block can be used to hold pole which will not roll. Height cannot be adjusted.

carriage bolt

notch opposite center side of each "X" to lock into each other

bolt or spike

To make four cavalletti you will need sixteen 4 by 4s 29 inches in length, sixteen 3/8-inch carriage bolts 9 inches long with flat washers and nuts to fit bolt (length of bolt depends on width of pole), eight carriage bolts with nuts and washers 5 inches long or 8 spikes 5 inches or more (end can be turned down).

Carriage bolt has round head and is flush with rail

hollowed-out groove for rail

staple to hold wire
wood block

store-bought jump cup

Arrangement of cavalletti showing adjustment to three different heights. Also cavalletti may be stacked to make vertical or spread jump.

4-inch by 4-inch standards 3 feet to 6 feet in height

2-inch by 6-inch or 1-inch by 8-inch boards for base

Hole drilled into standard at angle— dowel pin inserted in hole to hold rail

HAZARDS IN USING CAVALLETTI

Correct placement of the cavalletti is essential. If they are improperly positioned, they will interfere with or discourage a horse's natural rhythm; cause a false, cramped position; and perhaps even result in injury.

Injuries—mental as well as physical—also result when cavalletti work is overdone. This should be a change-of-pace exercise and should be enjoyed by both horse and trainer. Don't make it a chore for your horse. Some trainers work with cavalletti no more than twice a week.

Be careful in laying poles on the ground; they may roll if stepped on, which can be especially injurious to fetlocks and pasterns.

PROPER PLACEMENT OF CAVALLETTI

Correct placement of cavalletti depends upon the individual horse—his size, conformation, and stride; the gait he is performing; the degree of his training. Even his disposition or the ability of his rider may have a bearing on how cavalletti should be spaced.

It doesn't mean, however, that with all these variables, you need to hire a mathematician with a micrometer to arrange your cavalletti. With care and common sense, and with the willingness to change the spacing as different situations warrant, you can arrange them properly to derive full benefit from their use.

Although details will be given on placement throughout the chapter, let's consider here the principle behind this placement and how it affects the horse's way of going.

By spacing cavalletti equally, you determine the horse's rhythm. It is important, in early training, to keep the space between cavalletti exactly the same. You wish to encourage free forward movement at first, while developing rhythm, cadence, and co-ordination, and this can only be done if the spacing is regular.

The horse should print the ground exactly in the middle of each space. If he steps closer to the upcoming rail, the space is too narrow: he will come closer and closer to succeeding rails until he must step on one or jump over two at once. On the other hand, if his step lands farther from the upcoming rail, the space is too wide; in this case, he will step farther and farther from the rails until he will have to jump the last one or step inside it.

Your first concern will be to have your horse step over a cavalletto without altering his pace or stride. As you add rails, up to a series of four, you will want him to continue through them in good rhythm. Therefore, to begin with, you must space the cavalletti to suit his stride. Later, by spacing them farther apart, you will induce him to lengthen his stride and to use himself more fully.

How can you arrange the cavelletti to suit your horse? Simply by observing his footprints on the ground and arranging the rails exactly between them. Measure the distance to be sure it is equal between all rails.

Most likely, the measured distance for your horse will fall within the range we suggest for various exercises. If it is off by more than a few inches, consider your horse (Is he a small pony, an average horse, a leggy, long-striding Thoroughbred?) and remeasure if necessary. Cavalletti will be spaced wider for the trot than for the walk.

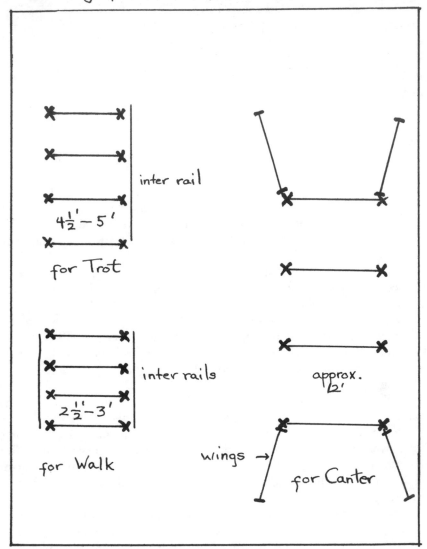

WORKING FREE IN THE SCHOOL AND WORKING ON THE LONGE

Longeing over poles and cavalletti was introduced in Part II, Chapter 2. Cavalletti work on the longe should not be attempted until longe work is well stabilized. Generally, this means that the horse is well along in its saddle training.

Working free in the school or arena may begin earlier, if the area is

Sample arrangement of Cavalletti and introductory jumping while working free. Use variations; start simple arrangements as 1. and 2. and with progress add more challenge: 3. and 4.

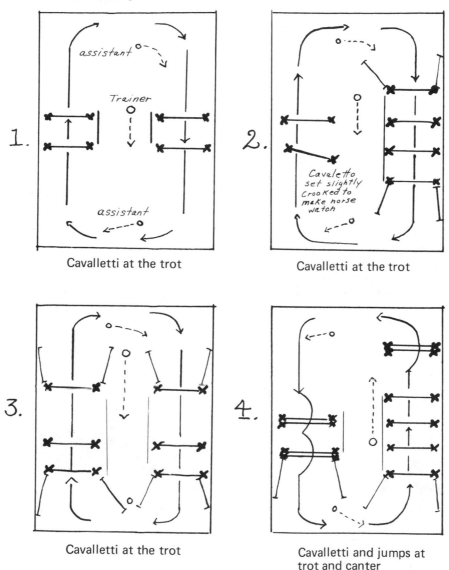

1. Cavalletti at the trot

2. Cavalletti at the trot

3. Cavalletti at the trot

4. Cavalletti and jumps at trot and canter

large enough, since the young horse can better learn to balance himself without a rider. Problems occur, however, if the circle or turns are too small or tight; a green horse is unable to flex well laterally, and he must not be asked to bend more than his conformation or training allows.

Cavalletti work on the longe, or free in a small arena, should not be over-done; work on the circle reduces impulsion, whereas work on the straightaway tends to increase impulsion.

A jumping lane is a great help when schooling free over cavalletti or jumps; X-type cavalletti can be used to construct a temporary jumping lane. When schooling free, you will need to position several assistants around the arena to maintain control of the horse and to keep him from running out.

Whether free or on the longe, begin by introducing one cavalletto; add one obstacle at a time, gradually working up to four. Although most cavalletti work should be done at a good working trot, use the walk to introduce new obstacles and as a relaxing exercise. It may be wise to lead the horse at halter when first beginning cavalletti work until the structures are familiar to him. When a strange object suddenly appears in his usual work arena, it is more frightening and exciting to him than when it appears in a strange place.

The working trot forces the horse to use and develop the correct muscles. Try to regulate and improve rhythm and cadence when the horse is familiar with the work and has overcome any hesitance. Cantering over cavalletti—especially free in the school—is usually too exciting for the youngster and tends to use too much energy.

When first introduced to a cavalletto on the longe, an inexperienced horse is inclined to overjump the obstacle. This horse is in good position, taking the jump straight and at the center.

One if your main goals in this kind of cavalletti work is to develop your horse's neck and back preparatory to training for jumping. He should stretch his neck forward and downward when taking the obstacle, and arch his back. To achieve this, his head should not be restricted, except that he should not be able to touch his nose to the ground. Tack up with saddle and bridle as suggested in the afore-mentioned Chapter 2. You may attach the longe line in one of several ways—to the longeing cavesson, to the hackamore, or to the snaffle bit. Three ways of attaching the longe line to the bit are discussed under "Adjusting tack" in that chapter.

RIDING THE CAVALLETTI AT A WALK

Introduce cavalletti work at a walk. Begin with one cavalletto and add others one at a time until you have four, placed 2½ to 3 feet apart. They should not be over 8 inches high; we prefer the height to be about 6 inches.

Since you wish to encourage the horse to move freely, drop his nose and relax the muscles in his back, you must keep your hands low and let your upper body give with the movement of the horse. Keep him straight and headed for the center of each cavalletto. Work for evenness and regularity of the pace, and use your aids judiciously to maintain cadence and impulsion.

Walking over cavalletti—work for evenness and regularity of pace.

Riding cavalletti at an energetic trot. The horse should step exactly in the center of the space between cavalletti, as shown with right forelegs and hind legs. However, he will be stepping short in the next space. The spacing was shortened before the horse went through again. Lengthening of stride can be encouraged by widening the space slightly, after the horse has mastered his natural spacing, but to overdo would be self-defeating.

RIDING THE CAVALLETTI AT A TROT

When riding over cavalletti, the trot is the most beneficial gait for both horse and rider. The horse begins to develop the bascule (desirable arching of his back when passing over an obstacle) at this gait, and the rider begins to feel it and to develop his own timing, balance, and influence on the horse. In order that the bascule can be felt by the rider and encouraged in the horse, the cavalletti must be placed correctly for the trot (generally 4½ to 5 feet apart), with a height of 6 to 8 inches. The lower the horse extends himself in the forward, downward movement, the greater the bascule. Conversely, when he raises his head, he stiffens his back and tends to lose his balance. (Do not confuse this with the slight movement in which his head comes up before the cavalletti as he is attempting to see the obstacle.)

When the horse accepts the obstacles calmly and his balance is stabilized, work up to riding the cavalletti at a brisk, energetic trot. Be sure to ride into them straight and directly at the center. Maintain light contact without undue restraint. Encourage a cadenced trot with gradual lengthening of stride, but do not attempt an extended trot; the energetic, working trot is most beneficial in developing muscles while maintaining balance and impulsion.

For variety, you may remove one of the cavalletti and place it at the end, at the regular measured distance. This will double the distance between two poles and allow the horse to take one nonjumping stride.

Be sure to praise the horse generously and avoid tiring him.

RIDING THE CAVALLETTI AT A CANTER

Although riding the cavalletti at a canter is beneficial for the beginning jumper, many experts advise against riding them at a canter for the dressage horse. In dressage, the forehand is encouraged to move forward with the impulsion from the hindquarters, while the jumper is projected upward by this impulsion.

Since riding the cavalletti at a canter tends to excite the horse, it should not be introduced too early. Indeed, since most benefit accrues from working at a trot to develop the bascule, working at a canter may be of little additional help if the horse doesn't proceed calmly and correctly. He should not be allowed to rush, or to let speed, rather than impulsion, propel him over the obstacle.

Cavalletti must be much more widely spaced for the canter, which will appear to be a series of small jumps. Note that the cavalletti are set at their highest position to encourage the horses to respect the obstacle and take it correctly.

One foot, four inches is a good height for most horses; if it is lower, he may not show proper respect for the obstacle and merely increase the speed of his trot instead of taking the canter.

Begin with one cavalletto, and add them one at a time until there are three. Measure the horse's stride at a canter to space the cavalletti correctly; the space between them will probably be in the neighborhood of twelve feet.

As cavalletti work progresses in preparation for jumping, think of the jump as a longer, higher canter stride. This will help you visualize the values of using cavalletti to develop the jumping horse. Before actually taking a fence, he will already have developed confidence, balance, and muscular control. The transition to jumping will be gradual, avoiding the tendency to rush obstacles or otherwise approach them with loss of control.

ARRANGING SETS OF CAVALLETTI WITHIN THE ARENA

Where should you place them within the arena?

• They may be placed in various positions on the track.
• They may be set up inside the track. This is usually a convenient arrangement because it is relatively permanent—you need not move them out whenever using the track for other exercises.
• They may be erected on the center line, offering you more opportunity to change rein down the center.
• They may be erected on the diagonal. This gives you the advantage of a longer straightaway, but it is often difficult to keep the horse from wandering, and it is difficult, as well, to place them exactly on the diagonal.

Several of these arrangements may sometimes be used in conjunction, and it is often helpful to place two sets side by side, one for walking and one for trotting.

JUMPING TRAINING

It is important to pay as much attention to the mental aspect of training as to the mechanical and physical process of taking a jump. Horses don't naturally make educated jumps, judge height and distance instinctively, nor do they often deliberately jump an object if they can go around it. It is as important to develop a horse's interest and willingness to jump as it is to develop his physical ability to do so properly.

Arrangements of Cavalletti Within the Arena (for Riding)

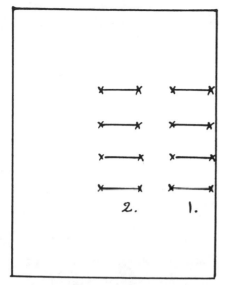

Cavalletti set on the track 1
Cavalletti set on center line 2

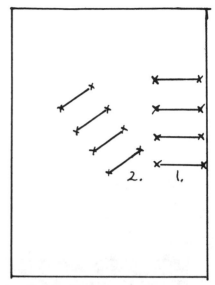

Cavalletti for trotting on the track 1.
Cavalletti placed on the diagonal 2

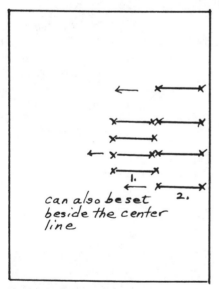

Cavalletti set side-by-side:
arranged for walking (inside track) 1.
and for trotting (on the track) 2

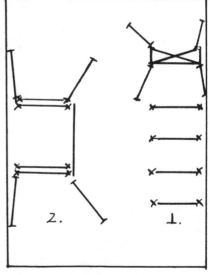

Cavalletti (set for trot) combined
with cross pole jump 1.
Cavalletti set for jumping 2

Some horses are willing to jump, even though untrained, but they usually jump twice as high as necessary, and pop the obstacle besides (stop or hesitate directly before the jump and then give a mighty—and jerky— leap). By gradually introducing obstacles and new situations, the trainer induces judgment, confidence, and muscular development. Generally, this takes the form of cavalletti work, from which the transition to jumping is made easily and naturally.

When your horse is taking the cavalletti calmly and in rhythm, having developed confidence, balance, and suppleness, you may begin adding one jump at the end of the cavalletti course. Place the jump ten to twelve feet from the last cavalletto (double the spacing on your trotting cavalletti course). Use a crosspole jump at first, rather than a straight fence, to encourage the horse to jump in the center, which is the lowest point. Measure the height of a jump at its center, and from the top of the pole—not at the jump-cup height.

When introducing the jump at the canter, avoid allowing the horse to become excited and thereby rush the jump. Calmness and rhythm are essential. Leave a double space before the jump at first.

Trot through the cavalletti and take the jump in good rhythm, continuing on in a canter if need be. Jumping from a trot teaches the horse to avoid rushing and to use himself correctly, developing muscles, co-ordination, and bascule.

Keep the horse straight. Approach the jump in line over the cavalletti and keep him straight for at least ten feet afterward (always arrange your course so that it doesn't run too close to a corner). It is very easy for the horse to develop the bad habit of turning after the jump, and this is difficult to break. Although in advanced jumping, you'll want the horse to become handy (able to turn in either direction in little space), for now you'll want to encourage straightness. Remember, too, that impulsion is encouraged on the straightaway.

For the canter, a good placement is four or five cavalletti about 12 feet apart, with the jump 24 feet from the last cavalletto. For variation and to help the horse make some of his own decisions on placement, remove one or two cavalletti—perhaps the second and the fourth when there are five cavalletti.

If you have questions about the mechanics of jumping, the proper way to ride the jump, what tack to use, how to correct vices such as refusing, rushing, and running out, or about kinds of jumps, please refer to the basic texts cited under "Recommended Reading."

SIGHT AND JUMPING

Your horse's sight affects his ability and mental attitude toward jumping. When you realize how the horse sees his environment, you will better understand that his vision has much to do with his response and his attitude toward jumping.

Because a horse's eyes are located on the sides of his head, he can see about three hundred degrees around him, but he has a blind spot directly in front of him and directly behind him. The blind spot in front covers from two to four feet, and severely limits the view he has of a jump in front of him. He will probably jump only if he has confidence in his rider and has been educated in jumping.

A horse can rotate his eyes forward, however, so that both eyes focus on the same object. When his ears prick forward attentively, he is probably focusing both eyes on a single object. This is the only time that he experiences depth perception. If a horse jumps with his head cocked, or frequently refuses to jump at all, he may have monocular vision (from only one eye) and simply does not have confidence in what he sees.

Considering both these aspects of a horse's vision, it's a wonder that he jumps at all. He may not be able to tell if a jump is one foot wide or three, or if there is an unknown depth on the other side. It explains, at least in part, why he is nervous in a new environment; new sights and sounds may cause mental fatigue and unpredictable behavior until he becomes familiar with the area, or becomes conditioned to accepting new surroundings (as in traveling a show circuit). It takes patience, praise, understanding, and a good basic education on the flat to develop the confidence that will produce a willing, relaxed hunter or jumper.

Another aspect of a horse's vision involves head carriage. His vision differs from ours in that we have a focusing lens to correct vision when the light doesn't fall directly on the retina. In a horse, the retina is farther away from the lens in the lower part of the eye: He controls placement of light by raising or lowering his head. To see objects close up, he lowers his head; to see at a distance, he rotates his eyes forward and raises his head, allowing light to fall in the lower part of the retina. This is why he must carry his head correctly when jumping; it is important not only for balance, but also to actually see. Ideally, he will approach the jump with head lowered and ears pricked (maximum vision of the object is achieved). During flight, he usually will have his ears toward the back, but on descent, again his ears prick and he looks down and forward.

If for some reason the horse does not follow this pattern, problems can't help but follow. Take, for example, a horse that rushes into his fences with his head up. If his rider punishes him by jabbing him in the mouth, his head rises even higher, and the problem is compounded. Severe punishment will make him lose confidence. Such a horse should be returned to the basics and a gradual retraining should take place.

Some horses will never be suited to serious jumping because of their mental attitude. An unhappy horse will lack attention and, since he carries his ears toward the back, will not be able to focus on objects ahead of him. (Ears and eyes are related: When ears are forward, attention and vision are focused forward; when back, attention and vision are on something else.)

In order to maintain attention and interest, obstacles and their placement should be changed periodically. Overdoing certain exercises or using the same jumping pattern too long can lead to boredom and mistakes. These, in turn, lead to frustration (for you both), punishment, and loss of confidence—a vicious circle. You, as trainer, must understand your horse and present your well-thought-out teaching techniques in an atmosphere of trust and mutual respect.

AFTER CAVALLETTI—WHAT?

When your horse calmly trots through the cavalletti and willingly takes the low (two-to-three-foot) jump at the end from both directions, it is time to introduce more interesting obstacles, both inside and outside the school.

A series of natural, low jumps along a wooded trail is ideal for a change-of-pace exercise. These may be logs, brush, ditches, or some similar obstacle. Be sure that the footing is safe and that there are no drop jumps or hazardous spots that could undermine his confidence. Your horse is more likely to accept a spread jump successfully when it is in a natural setting. We like to use this outdoor exercise as a reward after arena work on the flat. Not only will he tend to take the outdoor work more quietly, but also perform the indoor or arena work with more enthusiasm.

It should be time now to introduce the horse to scattered obstacles of varying sizes and shapes and to jump at a designated gait. At this stage, you are mainly concerned with control.

One arrangement could include a "box" or square of cavalletti turned to their maximum height (this should not be more than 18 inches). Allow an adequate approach from all directions. Introduce the horse to this placement of obstacles by walking him around and in between them, making sure he has time to look at them and to inspect them if he wishes. Repeat this at a trot. When he seems calm and responsive, ride into position and jump one of the forms. Circle in and out among the obstacles, jumping them from different angles. After this has been repeated a few times, walk him or take a short, on-the-flat trail ride and finish for the day. On successive days, vary the routine by jumping the square from various angles at the trot and canter.

Another arrangement, one that discourages a runout, is the Z shape. Again, use cavalletti turned to their maximum height, and place them in an arrangement that enables you to jump in either direction (with lead-up cavalletti if desired), and gives you the aid of a wing. Although wings are not used in most jump courses, there could be a temporary stage in your mount's training when they may help.

Since our aim is to encourage the horse to jump any obstacle at any time, we must add variety not only in kind of obstacle but also in gait and placement of obstacles. Try several small jumps in a series. Vary the length of the approach—sometimes long, sometimes short. The height of the jump, however, should be raised very gradually; at this stage it is more important to take low jumps well than to attempt high jumps and create problems. When your horse jumps 2'6" or 3', depending on his size and ability, jump only two or three times a week.

To encourage the horse to achieve the bascule and use his neck and head correctly, he should learn to take spread jumps. Begin with low spread jumps early in his training so that he will learn not only to use his back, but also to make a long arc over a jump rather than to pop over.

Multiple jumps, but preferably not more than three in sequence, help the horse to judge distance and also to collect and jump off his hocks.

When you begin jumping fences of 2'6" and more, it is a good idea to use a ground line (a pole on the ground six inches to a foot before the jump) to aid in depth perception. Generally, you'll find that your horse will jump solid-looking obstacles cleanly and in better form because they command his respect. Post and rail fences do not look as solid and formidable; your horse may collect more faults such as ticking or a knock-

Suggestions for Cavalletti and Jumping Arrangements

box or square

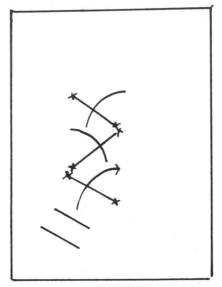

Z form can have
lead-in Cavalletti

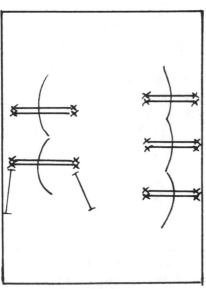

multiple jumps using
stacked Cavallettis.

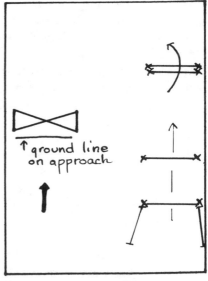

Canter over stocked Cavallettis
with jump 1.
Jump using ground line 2

down on this kind of obstacle. Give your horse experience with both kinds of jump.

HUNTER OR JUMPER?

If jumping appeals to you, you may wish to train your horse for competing in shows. In this case, you will be entering classes designated either for hunters or for jumpers. (In some areas of the country, you may be able to enjoy hunting in the field with a group or hunt club, but on the whole, this is pretty limited.) What are the differences between hunters and jumpers?

The hunter is judged on even paces, manners, jumping style, and soundness between fences as well as over them. Since the course for hunters should complement their style and way of moving, it is set on stride and without tricks. The fences should simulate natural obstacles such as you might find on a hunt: brush, post and rail, stone wall, and so on. The hunter should be calm, sensible, obedient, and safe, as well as sure-footed. In the hunt field, the challenge of changing terrain (which may sometimes be hazardous) along with the stimulation of other horses and riders, can add an ingredient of excitement that will quickly fault the overly excitable horse. The field hunter, then, must possess certain qualities that make him a pleasure to ride under special hunt conditions; in the show hunter, however, performing alone in the ring, these qualities will not be as readily apparent.

The jumper is judged solely on his ability to jump fences cleanly with a minimum of faults. He must achieve more height, speed, and variety of jumps than the hunter, no matter what his breed.

But whether you expect to turn out a hunter or jumper, he should have a good basic education. Before specializing and progressing to advanced schooling, you must prepare your mount, both mentally and physically, to enjoy jumping and to do it correctly through physical development and increasing capability. Only then will he be ready to train for the specialty you select.

DRESSAGE TRAINING FOR THE JUMPER?

Most of today's trainers agree that control on the flat is necessary for control over fences. Because dressage helps you to control every part of your horse, it is pertinent to all forms of equestrian activity. Since dressage training involves a mental as well as physical approach to schooling, it develops in the horse willing obedience, understanding, and rapport with his rider. Physically, dressage improves suppleness, flexibility, balance with forward impulsion, smoothness, and regularity at all gaits. The trained horse can extend and collect, bend and flex, and make smooth transitions in gait. In short, he is responsive and confident. The better he responds to the aids, the more happily and successfully he will jump.

Dressage need not be "art for art's sake." Its principles can be practiced by knowledgeable, sensitive horsemen in all forms of riding.

More Advanced Schooling

Aside from jumping higher fences and specializing in the hunt field or arena, advanced training involves negotiating combinations of jumps, perfecting style and form, accepting strange obstacles, and manipulating turns and courses.

COMBINATIONS

Ways of teaching your mount to negotiate combinations at the canter include varying the distances between jumps, varying the height, and alternating verticals with spreads. The idea of combinations won't be new to him because he has already jumped in and out of a cavalletti box, and also because you have arranged the poles in a variety of placings.

Begin with a low vertical fence. About thirty feet beyond it (depending on your horse's stride), erect a low spread jump. This should give him two free strides between jumps. When he takes this well, try some of the other combinations as shown below.

•Two inclined spreads with two strides between.
•Spread first, then vertical, with two strides between (you may have to increase the spacing by a foot or so, since the horse needs more room to jump a vertical and must place his take-off farther from the jump).
•Vertical first, then spread, with gradually increased height. Three feet six should be a maximum height at this stage, and three is sufficient for most horses.

Schooling with these double jumps will take several weeks. It's best to

Combinations – alternating verticals and spreads – varying distance and height

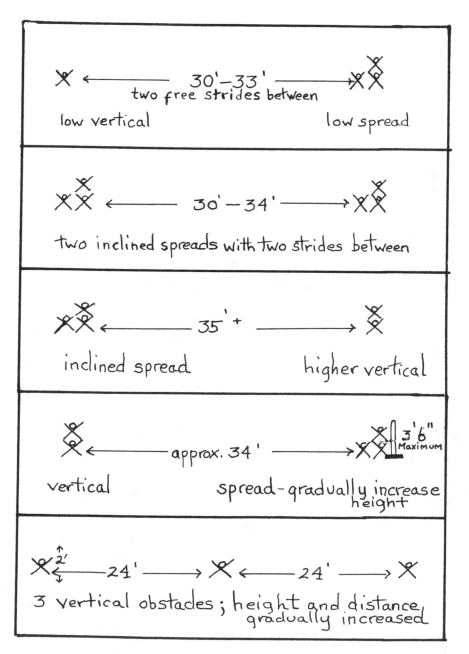

X ⟵————— 30'–33' —————⟶ XX
two free strides between

low vertical　　　　　　　　low spread

XX ⟵——— 30' – 34' ———⟶ XX
two inclined spreads with two strides between

XX ⟵——— 35' + ———⟶ X
inclined spread　　　　　higher vertical

X ⟵——— approx. 34' ———⟶ XX 3'6" Maximum
vertical　　　spread – gradually increase height

X 2' ——24'——⟶ X ⟵——24'——⟶ X
3 vertical obstacles; height and distance gradually increased

jump only two or three days a week, and some of the work during that time should be with cavalletti or jumping at a trot.

When the horse manages the double jumps freely and in good balance, you may introduce a third obstacle. Place the jumps an equal distance apart (about ten or eleven feet between), using a two-foot jump as the third obstacle. To begin with, use cavalletti for the first two jumps. Gradually build up the spread or height of the third obstacle, adjusting the spacing as necessary, and occasionally leaving out either the first or second jump.

PERFECTING STYLE AND FORM

It is always a temptation to jump a willing horse higher and for longer duration than we should. If basic work is neglected in favor of the jumping alone, your horse's style and form will suffer. He should be encouraged to jump cleanly with legs tucked, back arched, and head and neck properly stretched. Even if too much jumping weren't likely to sour your horse (though it probably would), he would start evasive tactics and develop bad habits such as refusing, running out, or losing respect for the obstacles. The sequence of your work should run something like this: work under saddle to perfect turns, stops, extension, collection, two-tracking; take some cavalletti and small jumps at the trot; and finally, jump at the canter. Only by gradually leading up to the higher jumps at the canter can the horse be properly in hand and work toward better style and form. A horse that jumps with good style and form will have a far better potential for the more difficult tasks asked of him.

ACCEPTING STRANGE OBSTACLES

Introduce new obstacles only after former ones have been accepted willingly and calmly. Design a variety of courses, using your imagination and many common ingredients. A post and rail fence is more interesting and looks more formidable, with bales of straw under it or with fifty-five-gallon drums or tires. Use your imagination to combine common materials into interesting jumps. Take care, however, that what you design is safe. The natural course that you have constructed in a field or along a trail will be especially helpful in increasing the confidence and enthusiasm of your horse. When introducing new obstacles, we are trying to "take the worry out of getting close." A worried horse will not jump freely and willingly. We must build his confidence by gradual training and generous praise.

When he accomplishes his lesson well, reward him by praise and cessation of work. Stop while he is still enthusiastic; don't wait until he's tired.

TURNS AND COURSES

If your ground work has been thorough and gradual, your horse will be learning to flex laterally and vertically as well as to extend and collect. At this point, he should have no difficulty with the turns and other problems found in performing a jump course.

Use your leg aids to help your horse adjust his stride. As you use them progressively stronger, you increase impulsion and lengthen his stride. When you resist with your hands against the movement of his neck, you will shorten his stride, and if done properly, help to improve his balance. Three to four strides before the fence, you can adjust your horse's stride to prepare for the take-off. Learn to co-ordinate your aids so that you maintain both contact and impulsion, without loss of balance. If you should lose contact, you will also lose impulsion, causing him to become unbalanced, with a good chance of his failing to clear the obstacle. Because of the many obstacles involved in a course, the ability to lengthen and shorten stride is very important.

To take a jump downhill, approach slowly with a short stride and take off well back from the jump. This will place you near the base of the far side and reduce the drop on landing. To jump uphill the reverse is true. Approach at higher speed with a longer stride and take off near the base of the obstacle.

Since the approach is the most important part of the jump and the success of the entire jump may be gauged from it, this area of training warrants study and practice. In courses where timing is important, the ability to turn without extra strides can "correct" a poor approach. For instance, if you can see, while still several strides away, that your horse will be taking off too close to the jump, then approach it at an oblique angle so that your take-off is farther back.

To start your horse negotiating low obstacles from different angles, set two cavalletti at their highest point. Run the course in figure-eights and other combinations so that you come into the jump sometimes straight, sometimes obliquely, or obliquely from a turn. The high cavalletti (from 10 to 16 inches) encourages the horse to jump because the height is not enough to warrant a refusal, but is still low enough for optimum control. This will help your horse judge distance and improve in agility, as well as regulating your approach to the obstacle.

After mastering the above, make combinations with nonjumping strides between, but allow enough room to take the jumps at an oblique

Cavalletti and Jump Arrangements Including Turns and Circles at Trot and Canter

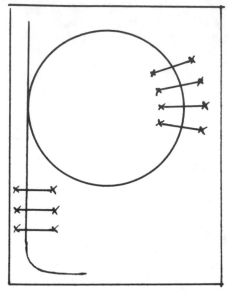

Simple arrangement of straight cavalletti and cavalletti set on a circle

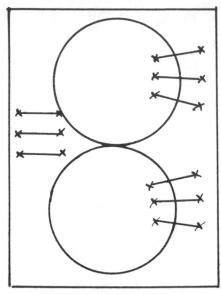

Figure 8 alternating with cavalletti on track

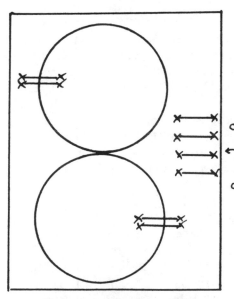

Starting on low obstacles from different angles. Set two cavalletti at their highest point. Run course in figure eights and other combinations—jumping sometimes straight— sometimes obliquely.

cavalletti set for trot or canter

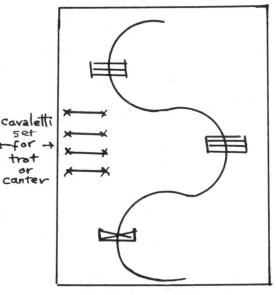

Serpentine with jumps; cavalletti on track for variety.

angle or to make turns in both directions. When you reach this stage in jumping, your horse should also be accomplished in advanced work on the flat, such as the flying change of leg (see Part III, Chapter 2). The flying change should be perfected, as this will help on every major change of direction.

HINTS TO IMPROVE YOUR JUMPING

1. If your horse has problems with balance or straightness at the canter, give him more practice in approaching and taking jumps at the trot. Lead up to the jump with well-spaced cavalletti.

2. Using the word "Hup" just before take-off encourages the horse, makes him more willing and alert, and aids the placing of point of take-off.

3. Unless you are an expert at using a whip, it is usually better not to use one at all. In jumping, you should be in contact with your horse's mouth, following the movement of the jump. Wielding a whip involves both moving your arm back and displacing your weight left or right; your balance is disturbed, and this in turn unbalances a green horse. If you must use a whip, take both reins in one hand and use the whip with the other hand directly behind your leg (on the horse's stiff or refusing side), at the same time leg aids are given. Thus, eventually, you will progress to more leg, less whip.

4. As much as possible, keep your horse from worrying and fretting. Punishment should be minimal, as he should not associate punishment with obstacles. Keep from tiring or boring him with too much cavalletti work or jumping.

5. Be patient with your progress. It is better that he jump well over a low fence than erratically at a greater height.

6. Investigate any disobediences. Perhaps the jumps are too high, the cavalletti not spaced correctly, the lesson too long, the horse not feeling up to par, the equipment wrong or poorly adjusted.

7. Ride one fence at a time—but look ahead and set up for the next jump. To look down or in the wrong direction throws off your balance and rhythm and interferes with your horse's performance.

8. High jumps are usually taken at a collected canter; long, spread jumps at a faster, more extended pace. Give your horse freedom to stretch his neck.

9. Give him a chance to think for himself. He should develop his judgment.

10. Find out his strengths and weaknesses and consider how best to

work with him. Make sure his health, strength, conformation, and stamina are in accord with your training program. Frustration and mistakes occur when a horse is asked to do more than he is capable of doing. He must understand, as well as have the conformation and stamina to perform.

11. Make a daily lesson plan. Be flexible but try to accomplish something specific each day.

CHAPTER 7

BASIC TRAIL TRAINING

It is curious that a horse will allow us to uproot him from his natural, nomadic environment and wholly change his way of life. That he not only survives this change but even flourishes is exciting.

Trail riding comes closer to finding him in a natural environment than many other forms of riding. Perhaps this is why most horses seem to enjoy it so much. Their vision, digestive and skeletal system, hearing, and nervous reactions evolved to make them adept in dealing with this environment.

To understand a horse's physical and psychological makeup helps us in training him for the trail. It is our responsibility to consider his nomadic heritage when caring for him and training him, and through this understanding to gain his co-operation and interest.

Trail Psychology

GENERAL CONSIDERATIONS

Because a horse is more apt to be influenced by natural stimuli when on the trail than when in the arena, he is more prone to react in a primitive manner. We must train him to control some of these reactions, but we may take advantage of other reactions to increase our safety and enjoyment of the ride. Let's consider how a horse's physical and mental makeup affects training him for the trail.

Because a horse is gregarious, he enjoys moving along with other horses. And because of his mimic qualities, he'll be influenced by his companions' behavior. We can take advantage of both these characteristics when training a green horse for the trail. With one or more experienced, fast-walking horses as his companions, he can be encouraged to move out briskly and enjoy the new scenery. The steady, experienced horses will not

When training a youngster (or a high-spirited, excitable horse) for the trail, let him accompany calm, experienced horses that will set him a good example. (Courtesy Wyoming Travel Commission)

be upset by unusual objects, or by sudden movements of jackrabbits or other animals; their calm acceptance of these phenomena sets a good example for the youngster. If a companion horse were to spook at every bird twitter, the youngster would soon be in the same deplorable condition. Make sure that your companion horses are reliable when training a green horse for the trail.

A horse can find his way home. He seems instinctively to know the right direction in which to go, but this is usually cross-country as the crow flies (although some horses and mules will backtrack rather than short-cut). If you do get lost and must depend on your horse to bring you home, remember that gates and bridges may not be on his route. You'll have to keep your wits about you and make the most of your intelligence plus his instincts.

Because a horse is sensitive to sound and smell, he will be aware of approaching horses, wild game, coyotes, and other animals before you will. The wise trail rider will be alert to his horse's signals. If leading a pack string or a group of dudes, you'll want to take advantage of the warning to keep everything together and under control, for it could be calamitous to have a bear in the path send dudes, pack horses, and whatall in ten directions at once. The horse is also aware of ground vibration and has an innate suspicion of dangerous footing. If there is any question, it is often wise to trust his judgment.

Remember how a horse sees his world—his eyes view a wide panorama with a different picture on each side. And although he can see long distances with his head up, he cannot distinguish objects clearly. Just because you passed a piece of fluttering plastic without incident on the way out doesn't mean your horse will be as unconcerned on the return trip. It may look entirely different to him. Watch his ears and anticipate reactions before they occur. Prepare yourself for possible reactions to strange objects or movements, but use your voice and aids to soothe your mount, to encourage him, and to keep him as calm as possible.

Of course, what we're really talking about here is overcoming the horse's fear—one of his strongest emotions. As fear and flight combined to save the wild horse from enemies of all kinds, this is still the horse's most primitive reaction to sudden movement, or strange sounds or objects. His innate desire to escape danger can put the rider in a precarious position. How can we best deal with this problem?

There are two things that combine to produce generous, reliable performance in a horse, whether he is show-jumping in the Olympics or moving along a wilderness trail. These are confidence and experience. Experience, of course, can only be gained by doing, and it is this that puts the final polish on any horse's performance. Confidence, then, is especially important until the shine of experience can bear its own weight in the horse's training.

We've talked a lot about confidence in earlier chapters. When applying this to trail training, we must add a dimension—the confidence becomes mutual. We find that we must have confidence in the horse's instincts to avoid pushing him into situations that he knows are dangerous, while at the same time we build his confidence in us to the point where he will confidently accept our overriding of his judgment, if necessary. In order not to spoil his confidence in us, we must avoid testing him beyond his readiness. We develop his confidence slowly, building on a rock-sure foundation of basic ground training and ring work until good behavior habits are well set and a mutual bond has been established. At that point, experience and confidence build on each other. Keep conditions as controlled as possible until the youngster is ready to encounter surprises.

One thing more. Although trail riding should be relaxing and rewarding for both horse and rider, do not be lulled into carelessness. It may be

To let your horse poke along while you dream in the saddle doesn't help his trail training. Keep alert, and keep your horse responsive.

tempting, on a beautiful spring day, to let your horse poke along, picking his own way through the buttercups, plucking at grass, and scratching his head on his pastern, while you dreamily watch cloud shadows drifting across the hills. The good riding habits you were so conscientious about promoting in the arena should be sustained on the trail. Encourage your horse to walk out briskly, take gradual contact on the bit, extend his trot on command, keep steady gaits—in short, to be as responsive on the trail as he is in the ring. This means that you must be alert. You must continually *ride* your horse.

CONSIDERING THE INDIVIDUAL MOUNT

Consider your own horse's temperament. How will be behave on the trail?

If your horse is particularly spirited, nervous, or high-strung, you'll need extra work in the arena before you introduce him to the great outdoors. This kind of animal rarely makes a good endurance horse because he expends too much energy in jittery movements and is unable to pace himself. Still, he can be made pleasurable. Take your time in establishing the bond of confidence along with good behavioral habits and ready response. He'll need restraint and constant reassurance, and probably a lot more experience before he can be considered reliable.

The lazy horse will need perking up and stimulating in order to sustain his interest. You'll be able to take him out on the trail earlier in his training, not only because his quieter temperament will be less likely to become startled and upset, but also because you'll need larger open areas in which to push him into free and energetic gaits.

In any case, whether your horse is high-strung, lazy, or somewhere in between (as most horses are), you should have controlled rides. Plan your distance and route ahead of time to avoid taxing the animal's stamina. Since this early trail training will be accomplished in conjunction with regular ground training and ring work, it will be easy to overdo if your lessons are haphazard.

When you first begin riding away from the ring and corrals, choose areas familiar to the horse, or that you know are relatively free of distractions such as barking dogs, traffic, or strange horses. Gradually extend the scope of these daily excursions, introducing strange sights and sounds when you think he is ready to accept them with relative equanimity. Encourage steady gaits, whether on the flat or up- and downhill, and duplicate on the trail the good habits you practice in the arena.

Whenever possible, your rides should be laid out on a circular route, rather than returning over the same course on which you set out. Along with providing more variety and interest, this discourages the tendency to rush home.

Encountering Obstacles

In these days of extensive traveling with horses, your trail horse must be able to traverse many kinds of terrain, not just what he is familiar with in his own area.

As different areas of the country offer varied trail problems, it's helpful to have your horse experience as many of these as possible. Open country, as is found in much of the West, generally holds fewer distractions, although jackrabbits seem to materialize right out of the sagebrush, and gophers pop in and out of holes with a suddenness that sometimes startles even an experienced horse. Since the horse can see for long distances, the movement of a distant band of antelope or deer, even a Jeep, may capture his attention.

Eastern trails and back roads often wind through dense and shadowy forests. Because you're likely to meet anything and everything on these routes, including game, hikers, and trail bikes, be sure your horse can handle these problems before exposing him to them. Suburban bridle paths, also, are often used for more than hacking. Even carefully regulated bridle paths are disrupted by youthful "cowboys" whose only concept of riding is to gallop wildly while screaming like television Indians or ta-da-ing a cavalry charge.

Experience, of course, is the best teacher, and as experience and confidence work together, the horse will become steadier under these conditions. Still, it is your responsibility to approach the type of terrain or special obstacle with the knowledge of how best to traverse it. Safety for you and your horse should always be a prime consideration. (For more on trail riding, see Chapter VIII in *Basic Horsemanship: English and Western.*)

OPENING AND CLOSING GATES

The rider of a good trail horse should not have to dismount to open or close a gate. His horse should help him to perform the task while mounted. In order to pass through the gate smoothly, the rider must keep control of it at all times. This means that one hand must be on the gate from beginning to end.

Before a horse will be able to open and close gates, he'll have to know how to side-pass, to pivot on the forehand, and to back well, although he may not have to use all of these moves on any one gate. These are all discussed in Part III on advanced training. Do not attempt to open and close gates until your horse is responsive and knowledgeable in these maneuvers—it will be asking too much and may lead to special gate problems that are difficult to overcome.

Preliminary gate training. A horse should be familiar with gates before he is actually asked to open and close them. Ride him through all kinds of gates in the company of an experienced horse so that he is not disturbed by watching them swing, by squeaky hinges, or by noisy metal panels that rattle in the wind.

Opening a gate by pivoting. In trail classes in horse shows, most gate latches are about forty-eight inches from the ground—a convenient height to reach from your horse. It would be nice if all gates were that convenient, but they're not. Some have difficult latch arrangements in strange locations. Some, on sagging gateposts, must be lifted and carried around by sheer muscle power. Some wire gates are almost impossible to open without a mechanical helper, and in any case, wire gates should not be handled from horseback. A pole, board, or metal gate, properly hung and properly latched, is ideal to practice on.

There are several variables to consider when passing through a gate—whether it opens to your right or your left, whether you will be able to pass through by backing or pivoting, whether it opens toward you or away from you.

Let's say the gate is hung on the right as you face it, with the latch on your left. The gate opens out away from you. Approach the gate and stop parallel to it, with the horse's head about even with the latch (the horse's off side is next to the gate). The reins should be in your left hand. Open the latch with your right hand (you may need to move the horse forward a few steps) and slide your hand to the top of the gate. Now you may have to back a few steps. Ask your horse to sidestep toward the gate, thereby pushing it open. Keep constant control of the gate with your right hand so that it doesn't bang the horse or get away from you. Eventually, you will want to open the gate only far enough for your horse to pass through. The horse's body should always block the open gateway so that no other livestock can get through, unless, of course, you are opening the gate for a group of riders. But for now, open the gate wide enough to give your horse room. Until he understands the maneuver, he may feel uncertain about bumping gateposts or about squeezing through what appears to be a narrow opening. Then pivot the horse around the end of the gate, using your right leg actively behind the girth. *Your right hand should stay on the gate.* This will take practice. You and your horse must develop the precision to work together accurately. When the horse is again parallel to the gate, having pivoted 180 degrees (his head now facing the hinges), sidestep to the right to close and latch it.

Stop parallel to the gate and open the latch, then back a few steps to be in the best position to proceed.

Ask the horse to sidestep and push the gate open.

Your right hand should keep control of the gate at all times.

Your horse must pivot around the end of the gate while you maintain control of it with your right hand.

Sidestepping to close the gate.

Much of your success in opening and closing gates will depend on taking the time to position your horse properly. By moving forward or backward a few steps, you will improve your position to make it easier for you to work the latch, and easier for your horse to clear the gatepost. If you find yourself leaning excessively to hang onto the gate, or your horse swinging his head or bumping his hindquarters, you need to practice for that extra precision to make the whole operation appear effortless.

If the gate opens inward (and is hung on the right as before), approach it in the same way, but sidestep to the left to open it. Pivot around the end of the gate as before and sidestep to close it. In this case you will be pulling the gate toward you throughout the operation instead of always pushing it away from you.

If the gate is hung on your left, with the latch on the right, take the reins in your right hand and keep the gate on your left.

Opening a gate by backing. In some cases it works better to back through a gate. This may be due to an unusual positioning of the gate: perhaps in a corner or at a junction of several gates. Some horses prefer backing through to pivoting. The horse should be responsive to leg aids and should be able to back well through a series of turns (as arranged by rails or barrels—see the section on trail classes in Part IV, Chapter 1).

If the gate is again hung on the right, latch to the left, approach the gate with your reins in your right hand and keep your left side next to the gate. Back up to unlatch it, slide your hand to the top of the gate, and move forward enough so that the horse's hindquarters will clear the gatepost. Sidestep left, opening the gate enough for the horse to back through, and keep him backing right on around the end of the gate so that he is again parallel to it. Sidestep left again to close it.

Gate training. When training a horse to work with gates, give him plenty of room to maneuver. Work slowly but consistently until he is experienced in several kinds of gates. Let him learn how to handle one kind of gate (opening outward, latch on left) before trying him on another (opening inward), but don't spend time perfecting his performance on the first before going on to the second. He should remain responsive to your aids, but it is your job not to confuse him.

Begin gate training on a quiet day. High winds can make gates difficult to handle—too much clatter, or a gate that is pushed too strongly against a green horse (due to wind) may spook him and make him gate-shy. Then you'll have a problem even getting him close to one.

After the horse understands the basic operation of going through a gate, vary the way you do it. Open the gate wide, giving your horse practice in pushing and pulling it while sidestepping. Allow actual contact with the gate so that when the wind does come up someday, this contact won't disturb him. Work also on precision and economy—getting through the gate with the fewest number of steps, opening it as little as necessary.

It is your responsibility to consider the gate before approaching it, to decide upon the best way to go through it, and to give your horse clear instructions on how to do it. Think about it.

WATER

Horses that live with water as a natural part of their environment have no fear of it. They are used to wading through ponds, puddles, or wet pastures, and they cross streams and irrigation ditches as a matter of course. We have had horses come from the dry land area of eastern Colorado, however, and others that have been stabled during their young life, and to them, water is a frightening thing.

In Part II, Chapter 2 we discussed longeing a horse through puddles and during rain to condition him mentally to splashing and to getting his feet wet. Although this in itself is often not enough to prepare the youngster for crossing water under saddle, it does help.

When conditioning the young horse to cross water on the trail, ride him with experienced trail horses. The fact that he wants to be with the others horses will act as incentive to cross, and seeing the others move quietly and safely along will help to overcome his fear or mental block.

Start with shallow, quiet streams—preferably those that are clear, with good footing that the horse can see. Work up gradually to broader, deeper streams, especially if they are fast and noisy. Be prepared for the youngster to bunch up and jump across, or to rush or lunge through if the stream is too broad to jump. It is easy to become unseated if you are not prepared.

Never dismount and attempt to lead your horse across a wide stream. He could jump on top of you. If necessary, let an experienced horseman on a steady horse lead you across while you stay mounted.

In warm weather, it is tempting for some horses to roll in the middle of a shallow stream. Usually such a horse will warn his rider by stopping to paw the water or by stopping and humping up his back. In either case, push him forward immediately, or you'll both be in the drink—especially embarrassing if you are with a group.

Swimming horses. Deep, swift water is a special problem that should not be attempted until the horse is steady and fairly experienced. Even then, it is dangerous for both horse and rider, and is best avoided. The occasion may sometime present itself, however, when crossing deep water is unavoidable. Most horses swim well if they must, though some are less proficient. In deep water, a horse with rider is topheavy and can easily turn over. Or if a rider were to pull back on the reins, the horse could go over backward, drowning both himself and his rider. What are some of the important things to consider when going into deep water?

Deep, swift water can offer a problem. The experienced horse will usually pick a good route if given his head—let the youngster follow a length or two behind him. Avoid crossing very deep water that requires swimming until the horse is experienced and calm in a variety of situations. (Courtesy Wyoming Travel Commission)

First, loosen your cinches a little so that the horse has more room to breathe and to allow for any shrinkage when the cinch becomes wet. Some cinches can really bind up on a horse and make swimming difficult or impossible.

Rein your horse upstream a little to compensate for the current. If the water is deep but the horse can still walk on the riverbed, you may put your feet up in front of the saddle in hopes of staying dry.

If there is even the remotest possibility of having to swim, be sure you have open reins. Unbuckle English snaffle or curb reins, or if necesary, cut them with a knife. A horse could easily get tangled in closed reins, and they could pull him under.

If you don't know whether or not your horse is a strong swimmer, you might want to try staying in the saddle. Many horses can pack a rider while swimming if they are not interfered with—that is, if you allow them complete freedom of the head. A horse must stretch out his neck to swim, and it doesn't take much to pull his nose under.

Do not attempt to rein your horse in deep water; he won't be able to feel a neck rein, and a direct rein could pull his nose under. Instead, if it's necessary, guide him by splashing water by his head on one side or the other.

If a young horse should panic when his feet come off the bottom and he must start swimming, or if you find that your horse is not a strong swimmer, slip off him gently either to the upstream side (and hold onto mane or horn), or better yet, behind him and hold onto his tail (get a good hold before you slip off!). This will encourage him to swim out and will improve his chances of doing so. Don't get downstream of the horse— he will be pushed into you by force of the current and may try to get on top of you.

If crossing deep water with a group of horses, stay well spaced out so that a panicky horse won't be able to climb onto the horse in front of him.

If a horse becomes frightened and goes over on his side, he may give up and not try to swim. If this happens, hold onto his tail, do a lot of kicking and splashing, and splash water at his head. This may encourage him to straighten up and swim out.

We hope you won't need any of these deep-water suggestions!

CROSSING BRIDGES

Bridges, especially those over rushing water or high bridges over traffic, can present a problem. Wooden bridges make a hollow, thudding sound under a horse's feet, and most other bridges also have a different sound to them. This can be very frightening to an inexperienced youngster.

To some extent, crossing bridges can be prepared for ahead of time. If your barn or stable has a wooden plank floor, the youngster will be familiar with the sound of his feet on the wood. This alone will be a big advantage. You can also simulate a bridge by nailing together several heavy planks into one solid unit. Leave this "bridge" in his corral or pasture for several days; tromp around on it yourself several times to make a racket; then lead him back and forth across it.

When ready to try an actual bridge, try to find a small one, such as a six- or eight-plank bridge across an irrigation ditch. In any case, be sure first that the bridge is safe—not in danger of swaying or collapsing, and with solid, firm footing (you don't want the youngster's leg to go through a rotten board the first time out). Lead your colt up to the bridge and give him time to smell it, look around, and listen to the water, or whatever. Then have an assistant lead or ride your trusty, experienced companion horse across. If the youngster will follow right along, fine. If not, lead the companion horse all the way across, bring him back, and try again.

This time, be prepared to use some persuasion if it should be necessary. Have a knowledgeable assistant help by urging the youngster from behind. Or carry a longe whip in your left hand as you lead him with your right (be sure to stay at his left shoulder, not in front of him). Use the whip only in the event he definitely rebels; swing it around behind you so that it gently touches his hind legs. Be ready to go right along with him if he jumps forward.

Once you begin bridge training—especially if the horse is reluctant to cross them—take advantage of every bridge you can find and cross them frequently. Make the experience so familiar that it ceases to hold any worries for the youngster. Although you probably can't anticipate and train for every situation you will ever encounter (such as, perhaps, the unavoidable necessity of crossing a busy highway bridge over a railroad track), the more experience the horse has under his cinch, and the more confidence he has in his rider, the easier it will be to convince him to cross.

LOW JUMPING

Any good trail horse should willingly jump low natural obstacles such as fallen trees, irrigation ditches, or clumps of brush. These obtacles will be easier for him than constructed ring jumps, but he will still have to learn how to judge distances and heights. Although experience must be the main teacher, you can help your horse to judge distance and height in half the time by use of cavalletti and a variety of low jumps in the arena.

Chapter 6 in Part II covered the subjects of cavalletti and jumping in detail, and we hope you will consider these carefully before attempting to jump your horse.

Early jump training—both with cavalletti and very low jumps—can be done in Western tack if this is all you have. Do use a snaffle bit, however, at least until your own position is secure. It doesn't take many jabs in the mouth to sour a horse on jumping.

When jumping in a Western saddle, you will not be able to assume the proper jumping position. This should make little difference if the jump is low; you may rise in your stirrups, leaning forward slightly, or you may sit the jump. Be sure to allow the horse enough freedom of his head so that he does not come up against the bit.

When you and your horse are progressing satisfactorily together over cavalletti and low obstacles, use your imagination to conjure up interesting, natural-looking jumps. Try bales of straw, low brush jumps, and dead logs (singly or a few piled together). If possible, construct a jump course out in a field or along a woodland path. Arrange it so that your horse can see the obstacles clearly and so that he has a good approach to them. Place some close together, others farther apart. This kind of arrangement will make an interesting, as well as an educational, ride.

TRAFFIC

Traffic cannot be taken for granted. A horse is no match for any kind of vehicle; and there is no guarantee that a frightened, inexperienced horse won't jump in front of a car instead of away from it. Always undertake highway crossings with care—don't try to beat a car or other vehicle, but wait until all is clear. If there is a possibility that the road surface may be slippery, dismount and lead your horse across.

Riding in the borrow pits bordering Western highways can be harrowing. You must be continually alert to avoid the never-ending procession of broken beer bottles, cans, wires, miscellaneous car parts, old shoes, raggy shirts flapping against a barbed-wire fence, plastic sheeting, decaying carcasses (jackrabbits, deer, dogs, cats, porcupines, skunks, and other unfortunates), and so on. Passing motorists sometimes honk their horns, wave out the window, and otherwise distract your horse, and semis and motorcycles can be terrifyingly loud. Be aware of any possibility, and avoid guiding your horse into situations that may get you both in trouble. As he gains experience and confidence, he'll become more seasoned, more able to cope with traumatic adventures.

Of course, the easiest, simplest, and probably the best way to familiarize your horse with traffic of any kind (or trains or low-flying planes or any other local hazard) is to pasture him next to it, preferably with a stable, imperturbable companion horse. It takes only a short time for him to get used to trucks, motorcycles, sirens, and flashing red lights, or rumbling locomotives when they go by frequently, especially if his equine friend remains totally undisturbed.

If the pasture is fenced with barbed wire, or if it contains hazards that might be injurious if he should run into them, stay with him for a while, longeing him or soothing him, until he sees what he has to contend with. Avoid problems by prevention whenever possible.

STRANGE ANIMALS AND FRIGHTENING OBJECTS

Again, the value of pasturing your horse with quiet friends near the source of the problem cannot be overstated. The youngster then makes his own adjustments in his own time, aided by the example of the other horses, and once he has drawn his own conclusions about the harmlessness of the animal or object, he seems to retain these conclusions permanently.

One thing that terrified even our experienced horses on first sight was

Deep snow and drifts can present another problem for the young trail horse. If possible, give him some experience over familiar ground before exposing him to the situation in strange territory. (Courtesy Wyoming Travel Commission)

a gentle, innocuous burro. Perhaps it was those outlandish ears. But corraled nearby, they soon lost even their interest in her.

Horses that run in large pastures are generally unconcerned about coons, skunks, or porcupines (an inquisitive youngster will often learn about these animals from close up and may come in smelling like a skunk or with a nose full of quills). But these and similar animals may terrify a barn-raised horse.

It would be wonderful if you could prepare ahead for every eventuality, but of course this is impossible. You'll no sooner think you've done it than someone will turn up in front of your horse with a pet kangaroo or a cobra in a basket. So what can you do?

It takes patience, time, and understanding to encourage the youngster to come close to an object he fears. We've considered this earlier, when we stressed the development of confidence and experience, and also the advisability of having a calm, experienced horse to lead the way.

You should have confidence in your ability to ride up to an obstacle or to pass it. If you don't and if the object is unavoidable, you may do better to dismount and lead your horse. Be sure to position yourself safely and to stay alert so that he cannot jump or step on you.

Until a horse is experienced and reliable for most trail encounters, it is wise to always carry a strong, long lead rope with you on every outing. If trouble occurs, you may dismount and clip the lead into the snaffle. With a long lead you may have a better chance of holding him from running off, and you can encourage him to longe near the offending problem. As you calm and soothe him with your voice, and as he has the opportunity to observe that the object won't hurt him, he'll become less frightened. Then you may lead him closer and eventually ride him near and around it.

Ground Tying, Hobbling, Staking Out

If you're out on the trail for any length of time, especially for overnight, you'll have other things to do than sit forever in the saddle. When you leave your horse—for a minute or for hours—it's nice to have him around when you get back. There are several methods of ensuring his sticking around, if he is fully trained to the method. These include ground tying, picketing, staking out, and hobbling. You may prefer one method over another as a rule, and you may find that one method works with one horse where another method won't.

GROUND TYING

Ground tying is meant to keep a horse in one place only for a short time, and its effectiveness depends entirely on the horse's training and on his willingness to co-operate. If he decides otherwise, that's the end of it. Please refer to Part I, Chapter 2, for preliminary training methods ("teaching the horse to stand and to ground-tie"). This is a good way to begin training for hobbling and picketing also.

To improve training for ground tying, plan to do something near your horse while he is standing—perhaps hammer on a piece of wood, unwind or fold up bale wires, open a gate. Keep a close eye on your horse without appearing to do so, and correct him immediately if he offers to move. This training will also help for trail classes, because usually the horse must stand ground tied or hobbled while you accomplish a specific task (for information on training for these classes, see Part IV, Chapter 1 on showing).

As your horse understands and becomes more stable, begin subjecting

Make ground tying a habit with your horse, but don't expect him to stand for long periods. Never ground-tie a horse with closed reins.

him to noisier, more frightening conditions while he is standing. But prepare for them first by leading him, longeing him, or riding him in similar circumstances. Don't start up a chain saw next to a horse that has never heard one before and expect him to stay ground tied. Even such activities as putting on a slicker, rattling a sack of cans, folding a sheet of plastic on a windy day—all of which may well be part of a pack trip—should be prepared for before asking the horse to stand ground tied during them. Cover as many situations as you can think of, and the horse will be better prepared for the unexpected.

In short, make ground tying a habit with your horse. But do not hope to satisfy your ego by straining his patience, taking undue advantage of his willingness, or letting other people try to scare him (just so that you can prove he'll stay there). Once his steadiness is broken, he will probably never return to his original trustworthiness.

HOBBLING AND SIDELINING

Hobbling is often a convenient method of restricting your horse's wanderings, but it has more drawbacks than some of the other methods.

Hobbles restrain movement by tying together the front pasterns—usually, depending upon the horse, with about six to twelve inches between them. With hobbles, a horse may move around to find good grazing and get to water, but theoretically he can't move fast enough to travel very far.

The fact is, however, that many horses learn to travel very well with hobbles, especially downhill. It can be embarrassing and frustrating to walk miles after your horse, especially if you're not sure which direction he finally settled on during the night. If this does happen, your guess will probably be pretty good that he's gone downhill.

Sidelining is a more effective restraint for most horses. In this method, the fore and hind feet on the same side are tied together. When the horse travels, he tends to move in a large circle, with the tied legs to the inside.

With both these methods, a major problem is that pasterns may become rubbed and sore. Care must be taken with all kinds of hobbles, whether commercial or homemade, to prevent them from causing soreness. Keep leather hobbles soft by lubricating and oiling them regularly. Sheepskin lining will help if you use hobbles often. Nylon and cotton rope hobbles must be checked frequently and washed if necessary to keep mud from drying on them and making them stiff and rough. An emergency set of hobbles may be made from a burlap feed sack (if you can find such a thing anymore). Cut open both ends of the sack and roll it up on itself to form a ring. Put this around one pastern, then twist the ring several times and slip it over the other pastern.

To train a horse to hobbles or sidelines, remember that he has a natural and fundamental fear of having his feet restricted, his means of flight limited. Of course, if he has had a good basic education, he will be used to having his feet handled, and this new restriction should not be too disturbing for him.

To begin, choose an area of level, soft ground, away from fences, rocks, and other projections or sharp objects. At first adjust the hobbles so that there is plenty of space between them and there is little restriction. Stand away from the horse and let him work out the problem, but stay nearby and watch him carefully. He may fight and throw himself while learning to adjust to the restriction. You should be out of the way but ready to come to the rescue immediately. Most horses learn quickly, and in subsequent lessons you may gradually close the hobbles to the desired adjustment. Never leave a horse alone before he is thoroughly familiar with hobbles or sidelines. In the event of trouble, he could injure himself. Your proximity in itself will reassure him, and of course you'll talk quietly and calmly to him.

Hobbling and sidelining, like ground tying, are meant to be a temporary restraint, although perhaps for several hours rather than several minutes. For longer periods, staking out is more satisfactory.

To Stake or Hobble a Horse

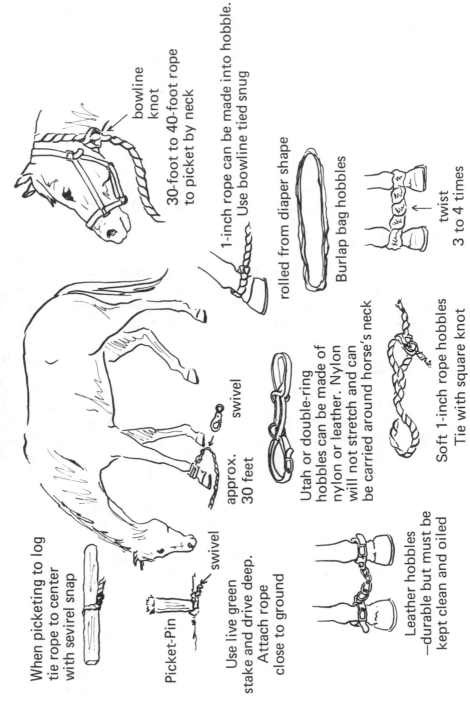

bowline knot

30-foot to 40-foot rope to picket by neck

1-inch rope can be made into hobble. Use bowline tied snug

rolled from diaper shape

Burlap bag hobbles

twist 3 to 4 times

swivel

approx. 30 feet

Utah or double-ring hobbles can be made of nylon or leather. Nylon will not stretch and can be carried around horse's neck

Soft 1-inch rope hobbles Tie with square knot

When picketing to log tie rope to center with swivel snap

Picket-Pin   swivel

Use live green stake and drive deep. Attach rope close to ground

Leather hobbles —durable but must be kept clean and oiled

STAKING OUT AND PICKETING

Staking out or picketing is usually the better and safer method of restraining horses on the trail. It works well at home, too: If fenced grazing is limited or unavailable, the horse may be staked out to take advantage of unfenced grazing.

Use of a picket line on large trail rides and pack trips is a good way to tether many horses for feeding, but it does not allow grazing. A horse should be calm, steady, and thoroughly halterbroken before joining other horses on a picket line.

A horse may be staked out by either the halter or a front foot. Picketing by the foot is preferred because the horse is less apt to become seriously injured and because he is less likely to become tangled in the rope. Generally, however it's best to teach the horse to picket with the halter first and then switch to a foot rope. In either case, if the colt has introductory training with hobbles, he is less likely to become upset or panicky if he gets tangled in the rope.

Use a strong, thick cotton rope for training to avoid rope burns. Attach it to the halter, and let the horse drag it in a corral or other enclosed area. When he first steps on it and it holds his head down, he may be frightened; but he'll soon learn to maneuver his feet around it. Do not tie the horse until he is used to seeing a rope behind him; if he were to spook and run, he could be badly injured when he hit the end of the line.

Occasionally, whether due to a bad experience or some native fear, a horse will be afraid of a dragging rope, even if use of a lead rope, or work on a longe line, doesn't bother him. Perhaps a dragging rope looks too much like a snake. If you have this problem, you may try accustoming the horse to the rope by rubbing him with it, letting it dangle around his legs and over his back, as you soothe him with your voice. (An older horse that has not been thoroughly gentled may need to be restrained with Scotch hobbles while he is sacked out and then gentled with the rope—see Part V, "Corrective Training and Special Problems.")

Another way to handle this problem is to let the horse begin by dragging a short piece of rope, perhaps only a foot long. Lengthen the rope gradually, by tying on other short pieces, until he accepts the rope and is no longer bothered by it. Then substitute the training rope.

Some horses will learn to handle a dragging rope in a single session; most will need several lessons. A fearful horse may need to work up gradually over several weeks' time to dragging a rope. When the horse is no longer bothered or spooked by any aspect of dragging the rope, he's ready for picketing.

There are several ways to go about this next step. You may tie the horse securely to a post, still in an enclosed area, to let him work out the problems of entanglement that are bound to ensure. Stay nearby in case he really gets wound up or becomes cast, but for the most part, let him work it out. Use a post instead of a picket stake until the horse is knowledgeable —horses have been known to kill themselves by falling on the stake. Do not begin with a full-length picket rope.

Another method is to tie the horse to a movable object, such as a heavy log or tractor tire. This should be heavy enough so that the horse can't run off with it or even move it easily—but if he should get tangled or became frightened and try to run, the fact that it is not stationary may lessen or prevent injury. If a large log is used, tie the rope around the middle instead of at one end: It will be less apt to move with the horse and scare him. A movable picket should be placed in a grassy field that is free of rocks, sticks, and other objects that might hurt the horse or become tangled in his rope.

As soon as the horse accepts halter picketing with equanimity, train him to a foot rope. Buckle a leather strap around his pastern; it should have a large dee ring attached so that you can tie the rope to it or attach a swivel snap. The strap should be kept clean, soft, and pliable. It may be lined with sheepskin for softness, but should be inspected frequently for irritating burs, foxtail, or other foreign matter. Again, let the horse drag the foot rope around the corral in order to get used to it, before tying him. Proceed as you did with the halter rope, keeping a close eye on him until you are sure he is steady and experienced with the picket line.

CONSIDERATIONS WHEN PICKETING A HORSE

Use a rope about twenty-five to thirty feet long. It is better to check on the horse and change his position every few hours than to try to get too much mileage from a long rope.

Attach the rope with at least one swivel snap or chain—better yet, one at each end. If the rope gets too twisted, it will curl up like a telephone cord and make unending trouble.

To avoid having the picket rope coil around pasterns or other objects, you may slip a length of garden hose over the rope. This will hold it straight. The horse should be familiar with the sight of the hose before picketing him with it.

Be sure to use a safe stake—one with a wide, flat top—and drive it down close to the ground. Because there is no upward pull on the picket line, the stake will remain firm and in place.

When first staking out a horse, set him in the midst of luxuriant feed on soft, unobstructed ground. If you anticipate problems, let him go hungry for several hours ahead of time so that his attention will be on grazing.

Staking by a front foot is safer and easier for the horse, once he understands the idea of picketing. He will be less likely to become tangled in the line (the rope stays on the ground rather than lifting and shifting position each time he raises his head, as with a halter rope), he won't get a foot caught in the halter when scratching his ear (same reason for not leaving a halter on when turning a horse out to pasture), and he'll be less apt to injure himself seriously.

Be on hand during early lessons, to prevent mishaps. Begin by staking the horse out for half an hour; gradually work up to several hours, but check on him often. Time spent now to ensure the success of this training will be well rewarded later when on camping trips and trail rides.

Stock Work

Working with stock can be an excellent training aid for the young horse. His interest remains high, and he is usually predisposed to ready acceptance of your aids because he can see the reason for following a cow or turning a calf. Stock work, both beginning and advanced, is covered in Part III, Chapter 3, "Advanced Western Training."

Working with stock can be an excellent training aid for the young horse.
(*Courtesy Wyoming Travel Commission*)

All-around Usefulness

Training a horse for the trail means, as much as anything, to make him a generally useful, all-around handy horse. His education, while not necessarily deep in any one field, must be broad enough to cover the multitude of situations in which you and he may find yourselves. He must be as calm in his willingness to stand and wait for you, while you gather firewood, as he is energetic in his willingness to carry you across the rushing creek and on up the mountain trail. He should allow gates, ropes, and poles to bump against him, he should gently allow a lamb or calf to ride on his back, he should be quick enough to turn a cow, or bold enough to pass a kennel of excited Great Danes. He should willingly drag in firewood or a calf, or sometimes help pull a vehicle out of the mud. He should carry double if necessary, or pack in a carcass. He should bear all sorts of miserable, unusual, and unpredictable weather with equanimity.

Trail training is really an extension of training a horse to be a pleasurable mount; it is a higher degree in his course of basic education. Let's consider some of the most important aspects of this general training.

SLICKERS, HATS, AND BLANKETS

A good trail horse will allow his rider to put on, or take off, a jacket, slicker, or poncho while in the saddle. He won't fall apart if your hat blows off in the wind, if you wave happily to a low-flying airplane, or if you shake the dust out of your serape. But usually this takes training. Some horses come unglued if you so much as raise your hand to scratch your ear, and this doesn't make for a pleasant relationship.

You began the proper training at the crosstie when you showed the colt a saddle pad or blanket, rubbed him over with it, put it on his back, and so forth. Now when your horse is at the crosstie, while grooming him for a ride, introduce the slicker in the same way. Let him look at it, smell it, and feel it over his back, neck, sides. When he is saddled, take him outside and repeat. Flap it around him. Mount up, if he seems calm, and move it around him from above. Have someone hold him while you put the slicker on, take it off, and so on. This may take one lesson or several, and can be repeated with ropes, blankets, sheets of plastic, anything you can think of. If possible introduce the object in a nonfrightening way, let the horse investigate it, and then gently prove that there's nothing to be afraid of as it moves.

Some horses, however, seem naturally more concerned about flapping objects, or about movements taking place over their heads, which flash,

A horse that will remain calm in Arabian costume in a noisy parade on a windy day will probably be ready for anything. Many horses, like this stallion, seem to enjoy the pageantry and excitement without becoming overly excited themselves.

after all, in and out of their vision. They should be thoroughly sacked out until their fear is overcome (see Part V, "Corrective Training and Special Problems"). If your horse seems especially frightened when you first introduce the object at the crosstie, you may be ahead to leave it for now and give him sacking training. If you haven't done this before, you may wish to get the help of a knowledgeable horseman for your first experience.

Don't skimp on this training if you intend your horse to be a pleasant companion for trail riding, showing, or any activity beyond a quiet lap around your indoor arena.

OFF-SIDE MOUNTING AND RIDING DOUBLE

A versatile pleasure horse—and especially an all-around trail horse—should have training that will make him prepared and reliable for those special situations that are likely to occur sometime during his career.

When riding on a narrow mountain trail, it is best not to dismount (or, if you are already leading your horse, not to mount) until you have reached a place where the horse may turn around easily. Of course, there may be times when mounting or dismounting in such a place is unavoidable. In this case, always mount or dismount on the uphill side. This is an important safety measure; to unbalance your horse in such a place could pull him over on top of you.

Since it is not always possible to turn your horse around on this kind of trail, he should be trained to allow you to mount or dismount from either side. There are other cases, too, where off-side mounting may be useful, such as when ponying another horse, or dragging something large, or when there's trouble at a gate or along a fence.

In our early training methods, we have tried to emphasize working from both sides of the horse, so that there should be no problem at this stage in mounting or dismounting from the off side. If you wish to review, please see the section "A Fifteen-day Introduction to Saddle Training" in Part II, Chapter 4, "Training to Ride."

Riding double is a practice that should be avoided for the most part, as it puts too much weight on the horse's loins and kidney area. At anything faster than a walk, the second rider will bump up and down, making the horse uncomfortable or even injuring him. Even so, riding double for short periods will not be harmful. If it is necessary to carry a second rider for a long distance, be sure not to push your horse out of a walk. If possible, have the lighter rider behind the saddle. There may come a time when you need to help someone—perhaps a hiker with a sprained ankle—and the fact that your horse permits riding double will add one more jewel to his crown.

The horse should be mature before you attempt this—at least four years old, but preferably five or six. Starting too early will add to the stress on his back, possibly induce him to buck, and thus start a bad habit. He should be experienced in trail training, and should be used to a rider mounting and dismounting from either side, leaning across his back, sliding over his croup, and so on. A horse that is used for gymkhana, vaulting, or other gymnastics on horseback will offer no objection to a second rider.

When first beginning, pick a small (and preferably good) rider and have him mount slowly from a fence or other height. There will be less of a sudden weight change this way, and no leaping or scrambling that might scare the horse before he understands what you are trying to do.

As always, introduce the new experience as gently as possible to avoid developing mental blocks or problems. By showing this respect and consideration for your horse, you set the stage for him to reciprocate in kind, even if he does think humans are a little nuts.

TRAINING TO DRAG OBJECTS

It is particularly useful for a trail horse to be able to drag objects on the end of a rope. Around a camp, it seems that something is always needed: firewood, a bale of hay or straw, a log to serve as a row of seats. Begin by training your horse to picket, as outlined earlier in this chapter. The effort will not be wasted, and it serves as good preliminary training. The horse must first learn that a dragging rope is harmless before you can expect to proceed in this training.

Carry this rope training further. Make the horse thoroughly familiar with the rope no matter where it appears—on the ground, between his legs, over his back, or swinging through the air (be sensible and avoid hitting him with it, especially on the head). He should stand calm and relaxed while you rub the rope around him or throw it out on the ground in front of him.

When he accepts this, mount him and repeat the rope training. Let your lariat rope dangle around him, quietly throw it out a way, draw it back in, and recoil it in your hand. Build a loop, swing it quietly first to the side, then closer to his head. Do all of this on both sides. Let the colt become accustomed to seeing the rope moving around him, away from him, toward him.

Although some horses take naturally to ropes, most seem to remain wary of them. The above paragraph may not sound like much, but it may mean several weeks' work. Proceed gradually, as always, allowing the horse to accept one step before going on to the next. Rushing this type of training may produce fears that are compounded instead of alleviated as time goes on. Taking the time to build a firm groundwork will pay off later in reliability.

When the horse stands calmly as the rope moves around him, throw the rope out ahead of him, then turn and walk slowly, letting the rope drag behind him. Do this on both sides so that it rubs on either side of his rump. Be careful in turning that it doesn't get under his tail.

For the next step, dismount and stretch the rope out in front of the horse. Tie several light sticks at the end. Go back toward your horse and pull in the sticks so that he can watch. Show him the bundle and let him smell it if he is worried about it. Then stretch the rope out again, mount up, and pull in the sticks so that he can see them. This may take one lesson or several, depending again upon the nature of the horse. When he accepts it, cue him to back and actually pull the sticks for several feet. Then gradually turn and move forward, dragging them. Work from both sides.

Do not dally the rope or tie it to the horn at this stage. You want to be able to release the rope instantly. As the horse learns to drag the sticks without problem, you may gradually substitute heavier objects and begin dallying the rope (take a turn or two around the horn). It is never a good idea to tie the rope around the horn. You or your mount could become entangled in the rope, and once under tension, the knot would be difficult or impossible to untie. A dally done correctly is as effective as tying the rope, and it is easily released.

Teaching the horse to drag firewood. Do not dally the rope around the horn until the horse is steady and unafraid of objects following him.

Keep your horse quiet and steady when dragging firewood or other objects. He should move straight and evenly, without prancing, jigging, or shifting sideways. For more about dragging objects, especially oddball things, see the section "Training for a trail horse class" in Part IV, Chapter 1, "Training to Show."

PONYING

It's often necessary, on a trail ride, to lead an inexperienced or balky horse from a trained horse, usually across water or around a frightening object. This is called ponying. In training a young horse, ponying him for his first few times on the trail is often a good way to begin. Sometimes, too, it may be necessary to pony a horse when his inexperienced rider is unable to handle a certain situation.

Before training a horse to lead, or pony, a second horse, be sure that he has a good basic education and is sensible and steady. He should be adequately rope trained, should neck-rein well, and should be used to performing in close proximity to other horses, such as in a parade or drill team. His manners should be impeccable—no kicking or biting, whatever the provocation.

When you feel he is ready to begin this new training, choose with care the horse that he will first be working with. This second horse should be sensible, gentle, and tractable, and he should also be congenial with your mount. They should know each other and be friendly. Ponying a horse to whom your horse holds an aversion might make him timid or unruly, in either case making him unsuitable for this kind of work.

When beginning, work in a large enclosed area. Hold the lead rope in your hand until you have observed the reaction of both horses. Wear gloves, or at least a glove on the hand that holds the rope. The lead line should be long enough to give you leeway if the led horse becomes recalcitrant, but not so long that you and the led horse could become entangled. If you normally hold the reins in your left hand, hold the lead rope in your right and try to keep the horse's head near your right knee. He should be positioned back far enough so that he can't easily kick your mount (the pony horse).

Begin leading at a walk, on a straightaway. Give word commands to help the led horse know what to expect, and minimize jerking on the lead rope. Halt, walk again, and then begin taking turns in both directions. If all goes well, try it at a jog.

If there are no problems as you hold the lead rope, you may dally it with one wrap around the horn. Keep your fingers together and out of the dally—if you wrap one finger up in the rope and one of the horses shies or sets back, your finger will be the first casualty. Cowboys have lost fingers this way when roping wild stock.

Teach your horse to pony from either side—the trail is likely to present situations where it is safer or more desirable for the led horse to be on one side rather than the other.

Your horse should also be willing to let the led horse fall behind and follow in his footsteps, as would be necessary on a narrow trail. Your rope should be long enough to allow this, but don't try it until both horses are steady in their part of the job.

When your horse is accustomed to leading in an enclosed area, try progressively longer trail rides with the tractable companion. Then give your mount practice in leading other horses, first in the enclosed area and then on the trail. Avoid pairing him with a horse that he particularly dislikes, however. There should be another horse that can handle the job in that case.

PACKING GEAR, GAME, AND LIVE ANIMALS

Whether you plan to go on a pack trip or just carry a bucket from one place to another, your horse will be a more valuable and more pleasurable mount if he tolerates loads and strange objects on or around him. Any all-around trail horse should willingly carry gear and domestic livestock (lambs, calves, dogs, cats) on, or in front of, his saddle; this should be an integral part of his trail training.

If you plan to use your mount as a pack horse part of the time (or if you plan to train a horse or mule strictly for packing), he'll need more specialized training. Along with the problems of carrying loads over all kinds of terrain, he will have to become accustomed to the smell of wild game, hides, and carcasses. And he'll have to learn about tailing.

Training your trail horse to carry gear and domestic stock. Let's first consider training your trail horse or stock horse to carry those oddball things you're likely to come up with some time during the course of his career. He should first have a solid basic education as outlined earlier, and he should be trained to picket, to drag things, and to pony as explained above. Whether or not he is used as a stock horse, he should have as much experience as possible in working with, near, or around livestock, barking dogs, and other horses.

If you have brought him this far in his basic education, you'll know whether he is sensible and steady (and he should be by now!) or whether he is somewhat of a security risk. Some horses are simply too nervous, flighty, or high-strung to make good trail prospects. You may be able to enjoy riding them on pleasure trail rides, probably not on endurance or competitive trails rides), as long as you maintain full control and are not hampered by carrying extraneous material on your saddle or by leading another horse. They are not good prospects for packing.

So let's assume that your horse is sensible and calm, and that you and he have established your brand of mutual respect and confidence. Training at this point is an extension of that confidence.

Somewhere along the line, whether as a youngster or later, you have given your horse some experience in sacking out. Whether with a sack, saddle blanket, slicker, or rope, you have rubbed the object over and around him and perhaps flapped or swung it near him so that he has learned that it won't hurt him. Now is the time to extend this training to all kinds of objects.

Let the horse live with you, whether on the trail or around home; let him watch as you saw or chop wood, take out the garbage and rattle it around a bit, and so on. Haul out your camping gear, bang around some pots and pans, let him look at them. Mount up, let someone hand you a pan, carry it around, and go hand it back again. Tie several together so that they rattle against each other and do the same thing. Then tie the pans onto the saddle. Walk and jog a little. Gradually introduce as much variety of objects, noise, and motion as you can think of.

Your horse may need very little training along these lines, or he may need a lot. Do what is needed and don't rush it, or your horse may be set back in training or develop a permanent mental block at the sight or sound of some objects. Remember, if he is a sensible horse, he's alert, observant, and probably cautious. Build his confidence; don't destroy it.

The same goes with livestock. If he has a cat friend, perhaps you can hold the cat in the saddle and get things started that way. Some horses and cats naturally take to each other; the cat will curl up on the horse's back in the barn. But take all precautions to avoid having a cat hang on by sinking in her claws! If a small calf or lamb is available, introduce the animal gradually and work up to carrying it around for a minute or two. Probably your horse will never *need* this training; but if it is at some time necessary to carry a calf, you'll be happy if he has been trained to do so.

Training a pack horse.

When training a saddle horse to pack, begin with the same education outlined above. Having a horse that is versatile in both saddle and packing can be a great joy to campers. Backpackers and campers can take more gear and stay longer if they lead a pack horse in with them. When they make camp, the horse is there to help them enjoy wilderness trail riding, or he may help pack out game. Hiking in with provisions may be even more of a pleasure when you know that when the provisions are gone, the horse is there to carry you home.

If you are training a horse solely for packing, you may skip the saddle part of his training, but do work with him driving. The pack saddle uses breast collar and breeching similar to the driving harness. Even so, it never hurts to give the pack horse an elementary saddle education: You never know when a saddle horse may go lame and you have no choice but to press your pack horse into service. It used to be that the rank horses that didn't work out under saddle went into the pack string. But now you have the leeway to choose and train your pack animals with the same care you give to a saddle horse.

A good pack horse should be gentle, sensible, and steady; he should move along freely and should be sure-footed. For the best pack horse type, his conformation should include tough feet, relatively short pasterns, good straight legs, well-developed hindquarters, a short, strong back, prominent withers (to keep the pack in place), deep chest, and a strong neck.

What special training does a pack horse need? Extend his ground-tie training a notch by teaching him to stop and stand the minute his lead rope drops. Perhaps he does this already. If not, reinforce his education by hobbling him and then running his lead rope through a ground ring and attaching it to his hobbles. The ground ring may be one of those screw-type stakes with a ring on top, or you may find a protruding root, or fasten a chain to a stationary object and run the lead rope under the chain. Tell him to stand and back away and leave him. If his earlier training was thorough, this should reinforce it and there should be no problem. Do keep a close eye on him, however, in case trouble does occur. Teaching the horse to stay where he is when the lead rope drops will be invaluable to you if your pack string ever separates due to a hitch coming untied.

Extend your sacking training to include hides of various kinds,

Horses must be trained to accept carrying game or hides. (Courtesy Wyoming Travel Commission)

antlers, and meat. You may have to tie and Scotch hobble the horse to get him used to hides. Remember that a horse is naturally afraid of a wild animal on his back and digging in claws; as we mentioned in the first chapter, this fear is behind the horse's instinct to buck and dislodge from his back anything that he considers fearful. Take your time and do a thorough job of teaching your horse, gently, patiently, and considerately, that he has nothing to fear from hides and carcasses.

Follow the training as indicated under ponying, but as soon as possible, lengthen the lead and let your pack horse follow directly behind your lead horse. Take him on narrow forest trails, if possible, so that he can learn to follow over obstacles and around trees, exactly where the lead horse goes. He must learn that he can't take shortcuts. A pack horse should lead easily with the rope held in your hand. There should be no

The Tail Hitch

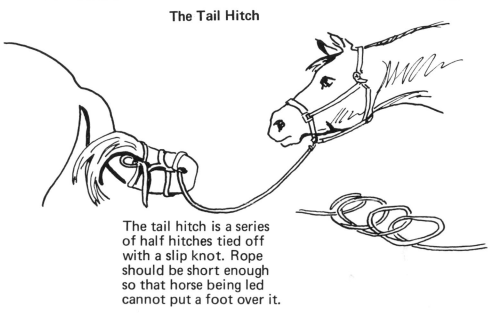

The tail hitch is a series
of half hitches tied off
with a slip knot. Rope
should be short enough
so that horse being led
cannot put a foot over it.

need to dally it except if you occasionally need both hands free. *Never tie the lead rope to the horn!*

A pack horse must also learn to tail—that is, one horse's lead rope is tied to the tail of the horse ahead of him. A horse will of course have to learn to let his tail be used in this way. Handle the tail more when you groom him, gently pulling it back and to the sides, and eventually putting some weight into pulling it. Tie a lead rope into his tail using a quick-release tail knot, and gradually begin pulling on it. Begin tailing in a large enclosed area with horses that are experienced in leading and that will have no inclination to kick or fuss. Use a hitch that will break away if trouble occurs. Change places with the horses so that they both have experience in tailing (of course, your lead mount will also be steady and experienced). If all goes well in the corral, take the horses out for practice on the trail. Have another rider follow behind the last horse so that he can help in case of trouble.

Even if your prospective pack horse is trained to saddle, he will need special training for packing. He will have to learn how to manuever around trees and over obstacles with a pack that may add considerable bulk on either side. Pack saddles usually have breast collar and breeching to keep the load from shifting forward or back, and most have double cinches. Whether using panniers or cargo slings, the load must be equally distributed on either side. As a pack horse will carry 100 to 150 pounds, the limit per side would be 75 pounds. To be absolutely accurate, use scales, at least until you are able to judge weight. Packs must always be well organized, properly placed, and well balanced. The burden should be carried on top of the sides of the rib cage so that the horse can move and breathe easily. If the pack sways or weaves, a sore back and a sore kidney area will result. Take care, however, not to make the pack topheavy.

When training your horses to pack, load them lightly with items that will not be hurt if the horse bangs them into trees and rocks. Partial sacks of feed, or partial (or light) bales of hay, arranged in good balance, would make good training loads. Mantee (wrap in tarps) any kind of feed that might tempt a horse to nibble, or that needs protection from moisture.

On the pack trip.

The intricacies of packing and outfitting are beyond our scope here, but there are several excellent books available on horse packing (please see "Recommended Reading" at the end of the book). These explain various slings and hitches, and indicate which are best for various kinds of cargo. They also illustrate the different kinds of pack saddles and their uses and give details on how to pack game.

In training your horses for pack trips, here are a few suggestions:

•Let your novice pack horse experience his first pack trip free of any load. Let him just go along "for the ride." The experience he gains in following another horse, in tailing, in becoming accustomed to the sights and sounds, and in managing his own footing without the complications of a load will make him steadier for the next trip.

•Keep blankets and pads clean and wrinkle-free. Keep cinches clean and adjusted far enough forward. The front cinch should be tight; the back cinch (used to keep the pack from slipping) should be snug but not tight enough to interfere with breathing.

•Know your knots and hitches, keep a load balanced, and double-check your packs. If you have a load fall apart on an inexperienced horse, you may ruin him as a pack animal. Arrange your pack so that it is quiet; items that rattle or bang can either be wrapped or carried in with grain.

•Although experienced pack strings may tail four horses behind the leader, it is safer and it saves a lot of trouble if a rider leads only one or two horses. Extra riders should be spread out through the pack string to keep an eye on trouble spots.

•In bad areas—a steep, narrow spot on a trail, a bridge, passing a frightening object—lead each pack horse through individually. Although it may take a few minutes to untie and retie the tailing hitches, it could save you hours of rounding up horses, redoing packs, and

A good pack animal may never need to be led or tailed at all—he will willingly follow the other horses. (Courtesy Wyoming Travel Commission)

picking up scattered cargo if trouble occurs.

•Sometimes pack horses may be driven or hazed across bad spots, but there are regulations against hazing pack animals in some areas. Check to be sure before doing this.

•Pack your breakable or valuable cargo on your best, most experienced horses. Grain, hay, and other nonbreakables may go to the novices. Experienced horses may take a heavier load than novices.

•If you are leading one or more pack horses, keep your mind on your job. Don't let the lead rope get under your mount's tail when turning corners. If you must stop for a while, keep alert to see that your pack animals don't take a notion to lie down and roll.

•Use common sense, think ahead, don't take shortcuts, and always be safety-conscious.

TRAINING THE DUDE HORSE

A dude horse must be sensible, sound, and imperturbable. Usually he is an older, thoroughly experienced trail or stock horse. Since he is likely to be ridden by children or adults, timid or bold, rank beginners or experienced riders, he must be able to tolerate all kinds of monkey business and remain a safe mount. Young horses have not gained enough experience (nor developed that ho-hum attitude) to make them completely trustworthy.

Really, a dude horse is more a matter of selection than of specific training. Look for the horse that has as many as possible of the following qualities and then round out his education where he needs it.

A dude horse should be sound and sure-footed, not prone to stumble. He should be attractive. Usually, a dude string has horses of different sizes to accommodate the variety of riders.

The dude horse should have good manners, be friendly and well disposed toward people (including children), and be inclined toward a quiet, dutiful nature. A dude ranch is no place for spooky, cranky, or unreliable horses.

However, the dude horse should not be a clod. He should move along willingly, without undue urging, either to follow the horse ahead of him or to move out on his own.

He should stand quietly while being mounted or dismounted, and he should allow his rider free movement—that is, he should tolerate the rider waving his arms, removing or putting on clothing, losing his funny sunhat, hanging cockeyed in the saddle, touching him all around his body, and so on.

He should tolerate floppy jackets, ponchos, canteens, and cameras tied to his saddle.

Although the dude horse should be responsive and willing, it is usually best if he has not had training as a reining horse or other advanced or trick training that would make him react quickly to any unintentional cue of the beginning rider. Such traits would be dangerous for inexperienced riders not accustomed to the speedy movements of the handy reining horse.

Young horses destined to become dude horses are generally trained as all-around ranch horses with emphasis on trail experience. During the dude season, they are ridden on trail rides by dude wranglers or other experienced ranch personnel, providing a kind of on-the-job training that seasons and prepares them for their future vocation. They are ridden for several years or for as long as may be necessary until they are deemed reliable.

Part III

---◆---

BASIC ADVANCED
TRAINING

CHAPTER 1

ADVANCED GROUND TRAINING

Advanced work usually means specialization. There are few specialties, however, that are not based on a good training foundation. And there is a core of advanced training that may still be considered basic to many differing areas of specialization. Work on two tracks, for example—shoulder-in, leg-yielding, half-pass, and similar exercises—requires more than elementary knowledge and development, yet it is fundamental education for the trail horse (in opening gates, for instance) as well as for the dressage horse.

What we are looking for here, then, is the development of proficiency in more advanced techniques and in more refined communication, which together form the basis for specialized training. There are many books listed under "Recommended Reading" that deal specifically with advanced work—to produce a reliable hunter, cutting horse, show jumper, dressage horse—and we recommend that you study them if your horse is ready for advanced specialization. This section on advanced training should serve as an introduction to more intensive study in your selected specialty, as well as provide an overview of basic advanced work.

At What Point Can Advanced Training Begin?

First, what do we require of a horse with a good basic education? He should move forward freely and rhythmically, in a relaxed manner, when performing all three gaits. Within reason, he should be able to travel with his spine parallel to the track he is describing, whether circular or in a straight line. He should willingly accept the bit and obey the aids of his rider. He must be sound in mind and body, keen, disciplined, sensitive, and stable both in the arena and on the trail (or in the field), alone or in company. His manners should be impeccable, free of vices such as cribbing, weaving, kicking, rearing, and so on. In short, he should be a pleasure to work with on the ground and in the saddle.

At this point, then, when your horse seems stable in his basic education, you may begin advanced training. However, there are no hard-and-fast rules to follow saying, "This horse is finished with basic education, and this horse is not." Although he may be well along in some areas, in others he probably needs more work and experience. You must be the judge and realistically evaluate your horse's physical and mental development as well as his education.

One of the most important things to consider in advanced training is your own ability. Are you capable and experienced enough to give your horse specialized training, or had you both better go out for lessons? If you have never ridden a cutting horse, do you think you could professionally train one? If your desire is strong enough, and you go about educating yourself in this field through clinics, apprenticeship, attending a cutting school, reading, and gaining daily experience, then the answer could be "Yes." Even so, if you are not properly prepared and trained, your shortcomings will reflect in the training of your horse.

Advanced training involves ground training as well as specialized work under saddle. What do we hope to gain from advanced longeing and long reining? First, we wish to make our basic good start even better. The qualities we are trying to produce in a good horse can be sharpened and accentuated by advanced ground training to make a really great horse.

Advanced Longeing or Long-Reining

We like to think of advanced longeing as long-reining—the use of two reins, sometimes in driving position (when the trainer stands behind the horse) and sometimes in longeing position (when the horse moves around the trainer). Advanced longeing must involve two reins so that the trainer can influence the hindquarters to a greater extent than when using only one rein (as described in Part II, Chapter 2). Long-reining gives the trainer the opportunity to see just what his horse is doing and thereby enables him to give the most efficient aids when in the saddle. And, by first performing introductory exercises without having to carry weight, the horse is better prepared for the lesson under saddle.

Why is long-reining not called driving? Although the initial position of horse and trainer may be identical, we like to think of the motive for each process as contributing to its definition. In driving, our motive is to direct the horse from a buggy or cart; in long-reining, the conveyance is not a factor. In long-reining, we strive to build and supple muscles, to improve acceptance of the bit, to perfect dressage movements (especially in the areas of collection, extension, and lateral movements), and to establish an even stronger mental rapport. Long-reining can also be used to correct the problem horse—one that refuses to go forward, that exhibits no impulsion or lacks interest, that resorts to hollow-back or choppy, rhythmless gaits, or that may have developed a bad attitude.

Introductory work in long-reining was discussed in Part II, Chapter 3. For this chapter, you should already be able to drive your horse with two reins attached to a snaffle bit, and he should be familiar with the touch of

Using the long reins in longeing position. Each rein is run through a stirrup, both of which are let down. The stirrups are often tied together to prevent so much play; however, the trainer may prefer or require the special effect of this method.

Using the long reins in driving position. Note that a simple halter is used on the young horse, indicating his experience and reliability at his present level. This would probably not be advisable in the open, but may be preferable within the training corral.

the reins on his hindquarters. He should, in fact, accept the bit, go forward freely, stop and stand quietly, turn easily, and keep a steady gait.

Tack

The long reins (single, not joined) should be about twenty-four feet long and be made of light, strong material. We prefer leather in this windy climate, but many trainers prefer heavy webbing or nylon. At any rate, if you put your reins through the rings on a surcingle, they should slide easily—round nylon is especially good this way.

Use a well-padded surcingle, with rings and dees set in high, medium, and low positions so that the lines may be adjusted. Or, if you expect to ride your horse immediately after long-reining, you probably would wish to use your English saddle instead of a surcingle.

An ordinary snaffle bridle is most often used; the riding reins may be removed or they may be fastened to the surcingle or saddle. Do not allow the reins to slop around on the neck, as the buckle, being heavy, will weight the reins to either one side or the other, thus interfering with direction.

A long whip is a must, and most longeing whips, usually Fiberglas, are acceptable.

Handling the Long Reins

There are various methods of arranging the long reins:

• Danish: The reins go from the trainer's hands through the terrets on top of the driving pad to the bit or cavesson.
• English: The reins go from the trainer's hands through the tied stirrup irons directly to the bit. If the irons are too low, the horse will tend to overbend; however, this might be helpful for a horse that car-

Danish: from trainer's hands through terrets to bit or cavesson

English: from hands through tied stirrup irons directly to the bit

French: reins low through rings of surcingle to collar and to bit

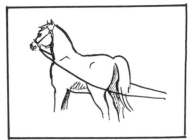

Viennese: from hands to bit; trainer directly behind horse

Methods of arranging the long lines.

ries his head too high. The English method is used primarily on young horses.

•French: The French use a collar as well as a surcingle, and the reins pass low through the rings of the surcingle up through the rings on the collar and then to the bit.

•Viennese: The reins go directly from the trainer to the bit, and usually the trainer stands directly in back of the horse's quarters. The horse is already highly schooled under saddle.

As mentioned earlier, from the point of safety, the reins should never be run through rings or stirrup irons until the horse is used to their touch on his hindquarters and will perform calmly. If he should become frightened, you can start to longe him if the inside rein goes directly to the bit. Another safety factor to consider is the area in which you work. An enclosed outdoor or indoor arena is best, as disturbing influences should be kept to a minimum. An enclosed area also helps to keep an animal from evading the trainer's control.

The Aids

In long-reining, your position in relation to the horse is important, and acts as an aid. The closer you are to your horse, the more control you exert. Ten to fifteen feet is usual and will vary depending upon the movement and the level of training. When you stand a little behind the horse's inside hip, you encourage forward movement. As in longeing, stepping toward the horse's forehand restricts forward movement.

The advantage of long-reining is that you have control of the hindquarters and therefore can insist that they follow the forehand. With your position behind the horse and toward the inside, your outside rein restrains the haunches from escaping outward. It helps the horse to bend correctly in the direction of movement.

Use your reins in rhythm, keeping a light contact; neither let them become slack nor give a dead pull. The inside rein (while turning) provides flexion, whereas the outside rein maintains contact, balancing and resisting if your horse tends to overflex.

Your whip is carried either behind you (in the right hand if you are right-handed), or, as we prefer, resting across your left forearm. You are then able to immediately raise or move your whip without losing contact, which can happen if you are fumbling around getting your whip into working position.

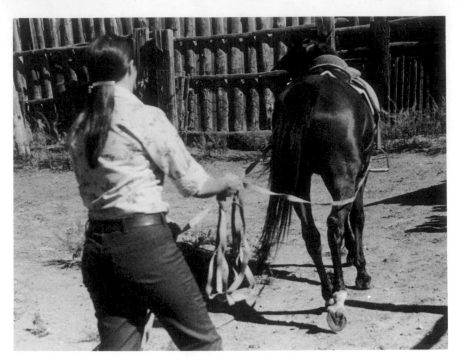

Proper use of long reins helps the horse to bend correctly in the direction of movement.

Beginning Exercises

Because it is as important for a horse to travel straight as it is for him to bend properly on the curves, your first exercise in long-reining should be to travel the track around a rectangular arena. This gives you the opportunity to go straight on the sides and curve at the corners. At this advanced stage of training, you should become very precise. Make sure your gait is even and rhythmical. You probably will have more problems going straight than turning the corners; however, make sure your horse goes into his corners correctly and does not cut in or swing outside. Take each corner on the track the same as every other; in other words, concentrate not only on being precise, but also on being uniform.

Work on both hands (in both directions). Rarely does a horse work equally well in both directions, and by now, you know the direction in which your horse will need more work.

Work also in large circles, and when these are executed properly, graduate to serpentines. Again, a smooth performance with symmetrical figures is your goal. In working your serpentine with long reins, the horse passes in front of you. The curves on your serpentine should be large and shallow enough to allow you to keep a flowing rhythm; sharp curves will hinder your horse from moving freely and calmly.

Using a rectangular arena allows the horse practice on both curves and straight-aways. On the long side, he may be encouraged to stretch out and move straight.

Corners may be used for reverses and serpentines to encourage proper bending (in this case, the turn is a little too sharp, but illustrates the horse's ability to flex).

Long-reining can assist you in obtaining straight, well-balanced halts. Encourage your horse to move up into the bit, stop, and stand quietly without ranging his haunches in or out.

Half-halts

Half-halts are important in advanced work, both on long reins and in riding. The movement helps to supple the horse, to engage the hind-quarters, and to encourage impulsion. By rebalancing the horse, it prepares him for any movement and is therefore necessary for smooth transitions.

Ask for the halt as the horse moves rhythmically forward. As his weight becomes rebalanced toward the haunches, by your restraining rein, immediately (but smoothly) open and close your fingers on the reins and encourage forward movement. Performing half-halts around corners helps the horse that tends to range his haunches to the outside of the curve.

Backing (the Rein-back)

Backing can be readily taught on long lines because you have more control of the haunches. The horse should halt correctly and be stable in the forward movements before this is attempted (see "Backing" in Part II, Chapter 5). You will find that working parallel to the wall of the school will help to keep him straight in the early phases.

Work to make the backing exercise rhythmical. Open and close your fingers on the reins in rhythm with the horse's forehand after the halt. Do not ease your contact after the halt. There should be no pulling back, as then you destroy the forward impulsion that you generated at the beginning of the exercise.

As an exercise, we ask the horse to go forward, halt momentarily, back up three or four steps, go forward three or four steps, halt or half-halt, and continue on at walk or trot. Work for smooth transitions, rhythm, balance, and straightness.

Collection and Extension

Collection and extension were discussed briefly in Part II, Chapter 5, where we emphasized the importance of this longitudinal shortening and lengthening of the horse's body in the performance of a well-rounded education. This is especially true of a horse specializing in jumping, dressage, cutting, or other individual activity. How does long-reining help prepare him for collection and extension under saddle?

An experienced trainer, working with a trained animal, makes long reining look easy, whether in collection, extension, or a good working trot. Mary Rose, F.B.II.S., of Martinsburg, West Virginia, and Denver, Colorado, has the horse working in good balance and rhythm. Incidentally, while the experienced trainer may prefer to let the ends of the long reins trail behind, it is not recommended for beginners. (Sodergreen Horsemanship School Clinic)

In early work, whether longeing, long-reining, or riding, we purposely kept our circles large in order not to strain the green horse beyond his minimal ability to bend and flex. In more advanced work, traveling a smaller circle increases the engagement of the hind legs, as the hindquarters work well under the body and the center of gravity moves toward the rear. The long reins are helpful when asking for an increased bend in the spine, as they restrain the hindquarters from escaping to the outside— an evasion often used to resist the requested increase in bending. Under saddle, it is more difficult to keep this escape under control, but with long reins you can drive forward with whip and voice and at the same time control this escape with your outside rein. You can see the entire horse and know immediately whether your method and timing are correct.

When working your horse on circular figures, make the circle smaller by degrees. Too small a circle would require more collection than your horse is capable of and thus lead to frustration and loss of confidence, as well as to the loss of his calm and relaxed way of moving. Even the most advanced animal should not be asked to make a circle so small that his hind feet cannot follow the hoofprints of his forefeet. Do not ask for something physically impossible.

In your quest for collection, do not overdo. Extension is just as important, and as always, extension and collection should be worked together. Any work on small circles should be balanced by work on large circles and on straightaways. As practice in extension and collection progresses, you will see a distinct improvement in balance and rhythm, as well as in longitudinal flexibility.

Your position, while asking for collection on the smaller circle, is somewhat farther behind the horse and to the inside. Your whip is carried so that it is evident and can immediately be used to encourage impulsion. By this stage in training, you will of course know your horse well, whether to use your whip lightly behind him, or to use it gently below the hocks. You should notice not only a longitudinal shortening of your horse, with the center of gravity closer to the hindquarters, but also a higher action both in the forehand and hindquarters. In extension, the stride will lengthen, as the horse lengthens longitudinally.

Lateral Movements

Lateral movements against the wall are usually easiest to accomplish with long reins. Begin with a shoulder-out exercise (described in the following chapter), using your rein against the hindquarters to encourage the lateral movement. Stress forward motion in the lateral movements, as it is easy for your horse to evade by stepping backward.

Shoulder-out and shoulder-in can be accomplished by working just behind the horse's inside hind leg. The outside rein works in rhythm with the horse's shoulder and encourages forward and sideward movement. The inside rein maintains flexion. Remember that in shoulder-in and shoulder-out the horse looks away from the direction of movement. In most other figures, such as the travers, renvers, and half pass, the horse looks toward the direction of movement.

Any transition from one lateral movement to another should be accomplished smoothly; therefore it should not be attempted until the horse is properly prepared and suppled.

Lateral movements may be taught with long reins. Here Mary Rose uses a longe whip in conjunction with the reins to encourage the half pass.

High-school movements such as flying change, passage, piaffe, pirouette, and levade can be taught on long reins. However, such advanced exercises should be attempted only by a very experienced handler and horse. Refer to our section on recommended reading.

Long-reining is an art. To see your horse progress and to feel the rapport that long-reining provides are real pleasures.

ADVANCED ENGLISH TRAINING

Building on Elementary Dressage

Most advanced English training involves dressage methods and movements. In Part II, Chapter 5, we suggested elementary movements and routines to produce a pleasurable mount. Now, on a more advanced level, we'll build on this same kind of training, make transitions into more precise work, and ask more of the horse both physically and mentally. Higher levels of dressage are considered to be an art form.

Although it may be necessary or helpful for the jumper to execute some dressage movements skillfully, other movements are less important and are even controversial. Included among these are movements that involve extreme collection, such as the piaffe, levade, or pirouette. Many trainers feel that, for the hunter, attainment of extreme collection is not only unnecessary but may actually be detrimental.

We feel that horses with a well-rounded education should be capable of some degree of collection in every activity. Suppleness, balance, flexibility, and what we call "catty action" require working off the hocks; and this means shortening the body in order to perform any movement immediately.

Some specialized activities requiring advanced English techniques are jumping, cross-country, dressage, polo, English show classes, and English gymkhana or contest events (found mainly in the Eastern United States). There are many excellent books relating to these specialities, and some are included in our list on recommended reading.

TACK

Bits and bridles were discussed earlier. The snaffle bridle is used even at advanced levels. The double bridle is required in the higher dressage tests such as the third and fourth levels, the Prix St. Georges, and the Kur. Contact with the horse becomes more refined and subtle. In international dressage competition, the double bridle is the only one accepted. The only restrictive device allowed is the dropped noseband, and although martingales and running reins are used in training, they are not permitted in competition. The above devices cannot take the place of good basic education, but they sometimes do help in retraining. Their use and correct adjustment should be attempted only by advanced horsemen.

A dressage saddle is built so that the rider can use a longer stirrup (although he sometimes uses no stirrups) and can thereby maintain a more refined and subtle contact with his whole leg. It has a deep, well-padded seat and is styled so that the rider can use his back to influence his horse's movements. The saddle flaps are usually unpadded, and the shape allows for the longer leg position. It is a well-balanced saddle and is usually more expensive than other variations of the English saddle.

In cross-country and jumping, the rider assumes a more forward position. The saddle he uses reflects the difference in style of riding by giving more support and security for the seat and leg position: The flaps are positioned farther forward and have padded knee rolls. Cruppers and breast collars are often used to help keep the saddle in place, and martingales are also sometimes used. These riders often use the snaffle bridle, which may have a cross-over noseband or dropped noseband to keep the horse's mouth closed and the bit in place.

Three-day-event horses compete in dressage, cross-country, and stadium jumping. The trainer working an event horse would probably find a good all-purpose saddle most useful if he were unable to afford two English saddles. Ideally, most eventers have both styles with bridles suitable both to the event and to the level of progress. Close attention must be paid to correct fitting of all tack.

Training aids (artificial aids) widely in use are the whip and spurs. Whips are not allowed in the dressage arena, but spurs are optional, and most riders use them. Both whip and spurs are considered to be extensions of the human body (since the leg, heel, and hands cannot give aids beyond their reach without destroying the contact with the mouth and sides of the horse). Spurs and whip are used only behind the girth, sometimes in punishment for disobedience to a leg aid or at other times to encourage impulsion. Just carrying a whip can encourage some horses to perform more satisfactorily. Long willow or hazel switches make excellent whips; in fact, they are traditionally used at the Spanish Riding School in Vienna.

Kinds of English Saddles

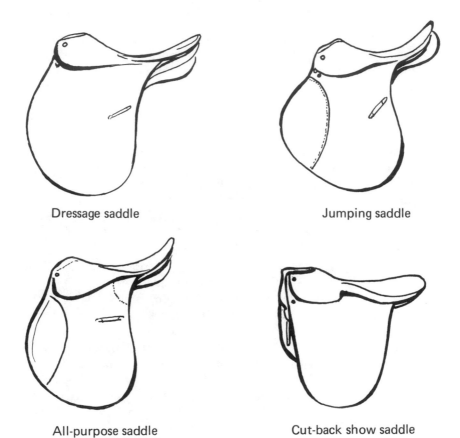

Dressage saddle   Jumping saddle

All-purpose saddle   Cut-back show saddle

EXTENSION AND COLLECTION
IN THE VARIOUS GAITS

Earlier, we mentioned that we first ask a horse to extend, then gradually to respond to contact, and eventually to make the transition to various degrees of collection. Long-reining and ground driving are helpful in initiating collection. It is important to remember the dressage principles behind the theory of collection—that impulsion and the overall shortening of the horse come from the drive of the hindquarters to the forehand.

To be sure of the proper development of suppleness that results in the ability to collect, we ask for collection only when the horse is moving. This

Incorrect collection may result in a "broken neck"—that is, one that bends sharply at the wrong place, rather than flexing uniformly with the poll as the highest point.

helps to produce a flexible, supple animal. At many horse shows, we have observed stalled horses with their heads "tied up" (with the reins) to cinch or saddle horn. They stand in this unnatural position to "set their heads." This static, immobile method may well pull the head to a vertical position, but can result in rigidity and loss of lateral flexibility, as well as produce an overbent and incorrect head set. Artificial aids, such as tight draw reins, can also contribute to poor head position.

Correctly collected, the horse's head will approach the vertical with the poll as the highest point. Incorrect collection will result in a "broken neck"; development of the muscles along the spine from poll to croup are neglected, and this forced head and neck position results in an unpleasing picture as well as an unpleasant ride.

Collection must be obtained gradually as a result of developing muscles, co-ordination, and impulsion. Since no two horses are built alike, you must recognize the limitations of your particular horse's conformation. Problems in conformation, such as short, heavy neck, hollow back, or croup higher than withers, must be considered when planning a training program. In our previous basic elementary work, we used exercises to help the horse develop balance and muscling in his neck and back; now he should be ready for more collection. We must further train and strengthen the hindquarters to carry more weight, thus raising the forehand and allowing shorter, higher strides. Collection involves the whole horse, not just the forehand.

The best gait at which to initiate some degree of collection is the trot. Because the horse's rhythm and balance are best at the trot, the rider can most easily feel the increased impulsion he creates. The horse should first be limbered up by his usual longeing or long-reining and by riding circles and straight lines at a good, light posting trot. The time involved in this loosening up will depend on the individual horse. When he seems responsive and limber (not tired!), start pushing with your back (while sitting the trot), squeezing with your legs, and resisting increased speed with your hands. Maintain this for several paces, then release. As collection is achieved, increase for longer periods and ask for more collection, but reward frequently. If he begins to toss his head or swing it from side to side, or if he jigs, rears, or makes other evasive movements, you are probably asking for too much too soon. Be content with a little, as this exercise truly taxes a horse's physique. The best places to practice this are on the long and short sides of the arena moving on the straightaway. Later you can try collection on corners, but because this involves bending, it also involves more strain.

Halts and half-halts keep your horse alert, impelled, and responsive, especially when asked for from a collected trot. When they are performed correctly, you can really feel the lightening of the forehand and the engagement of the hocks. The halt should be followed by a period of immobility (four to six seconds). Be sure that *you* remain absolutely quiet—any change in your weight distribution or movement of leg or hand can cause movement in the horse and set up an unpleasant habit. Immediately after this halt, ask for a trot; you will appreciate the definite feeling of drive that the horse gives with his hindquarters. We often use this exercise in a group drill, as both horses and riders like the exhilarating change of pace. The correct use of the half-halt also aids in this feeling, although it is more difficult to teach in a group situation.

After gaining some success on the straightaway, work to obtain lateral and vertical flexion on large curves. The corners of the school are fine for this, if not executed too sharply, because the walls serve as guides to aid precision. Because the chief difficulty you encounter will usually be loss of rhythm, stronger back and leg aids should be given in anticipation of this problem. Usually this interruption occurs as you come out of the curve.

Serpentines (three half circles using the center line) not only help in both lateral and vertical flexion, but the fact that the horse must be straight for one length before each change of direction also helps in the transition from curve to straightaway. Take care that your half circles are large enough for his physique and muscular development, since again there will be a loss of rhythm and a tendency for the haunches to range to the outside. Since, in the serpentine, you cannot use the walls as a guide, it will be more difficult to make good, true, uniform half circles. Circles and figure-eights also help develop lateral suppleness.

Longitudinal suppleness is developed by increasing and decreasing speed within a gait and by changing from one gait to another. Such transitional exercises help the horse to engage his hind legs simultaneously, opening and closing the key joints of the quarters (sacroiliac and coxofemoral). These transitions also help him to respond to leg and rein aids. As he improves, he becomes more supple, rhythmical, and responsive to the aids. Make sure your aids are gentle, but also precise and clear.

In extended paces, we are looking for the driving action of the hind legs, where in collection we want the lifting action. Since the driving action is restricted by corners and circles, it is best initiated in open country on long, straight stretches over smooth, good ground. As the horse extends, he will take a longer, lower shape, moving freely and in rhythm. We often hear the instruction, "Do not let him run!" If he is "running," he is trotting without rhythm, and this is valueless. We want good length of stride *and* rhythm. Post to the extended trot, taking positive contact but not encouraging lugging.

The extended gaits are fully as important as the collected gaits. Smooth transitions between gaits and within gaits should be practiced.

THE HALF-HALT

To improve collection and vertical flexion, the half-halt is an excellent exercise. It also supples the horse and rearranges his weight, putting him "on the aids." This momentary hesitation, performed correctly, shifts the horse's weight to his hindquarters so that he can strike off into any movement or gait with impulsion and good head carriage. The half-halt helps to steady the overbold horse and to correct the head carriage of horses that carry head and neck to one side.

He must first be stable and proficient at the halt, standing squarely

Dominique Barbier, B.H.S.I., gently helps the young horse in lateral flexion as they curve in a small circle. (Sodergreen Horsemanship School Clinic)

Although extension, like collection, is best taught at a trot, it applies to the other gaits as well. Extension involves a driving action of the hind legs, which is somewhat restricted by corners and curves. This horse is beginning to extend as he moves through the corner.

and relaxed, but alert and willing to hold his stance for the length of time you desire. Actually, the half-halt is a hesitation: The rider asks the horse to halt, thus collecting him; but before he comes to a complete stop, he asks him to move out. Although the aids are almost imperceptible when performed correctly, the movement has the effect of "putting it all together"; it alerts the horse and tells him something new is to be asked of him.

To ask for the half-halt, fix your hands and brace your back while squeezing with your legs. The moment the horse hesitates, but before he can halt, give and follow with your hands while your legs keep the forward momentum. In other words, the driving controls (legs and back) hold and outweigh the restraining ones (hands). As the horse becomes more sensitive and responds more readily, your aids can become more refined. Timing is very important in this exercise, and success depends on well-synchronized, effective aids co-ordinating with the movements of the horse. Half-halts help the horse to keep his rhythm, aid satisfactory transitions from one pace to another, and are especially valuable when coming down from a potentially faster gait to a slower one (trot to walk). In lateral work, half-halts are valuable to prepare for lateral flexing; a series of half-halts (using the diagonal aids of inside leg and outside rein) keeps the horse from "falling out" on the corners.

REIN-BACK OR BACKING

The rein-back or reinforced halt is an exercise that will improve collection and vertical flexion. It is also useful for horses that are insensitive to the legs. The rein-back must be thought of as a forward movement. We push the horse forward by squeezing our legs and bracing our back, asking for impulsion; yet our hands remain fixed, although a squeezing action (similar to pressing a sponge) induces the horse to lower his head and accept the bit. With each step back, the rider relaxes his aids and then resumes them immediately to ask for another step. Performing this exercise correctly requires that the horse move his diagonal legs simultaneously in a two-beat gait. The horse should move back straight in the track; aim for a rhythmic movement, regulating each step back without hesitation or rushing. After the desired number of steps has been accomplished, immediately relax the aids (use a following hand) and encourage the horse to move forward in the same rhythm in which the rein-back was performed. Remember that impulsion should be asked for through the back and seat, while the horse is encouraged to accept the bit. If he throws his head or otherwise resists with head and neck or lack of calmness, gently ask for obedience with your hands by opening and closing the fingers. Pulling back or keeping the hands in a rigid position will exaggerate the problem and, in all probability, will confuse the horse. Again, do not demand too much too soon, as this is a difficult and unnatural exercise for the horse. This exercise should be interspersed with free forward movement. If much resistance is encountered, it would be wise to review your training program. The rein-back can only be accomplished successfully if the horse has learned to accept his aids; it is an advanced exercise.

Two-track Exercises

Up to this stage in training, all exercises have been on one track— that is, the hind footsteps follow in the tracks of the forefeet. As the horse progresses, he becomes more supple and flexible until he is physically and mentally able to bend and flex in such a way that he can travel on two tracks: forehand on one track, hindquarters on another. Our book *Basic Horsemanship* explains two-tracking, discusses how to ride the movements correctly, and includes some diagrams of two-track exercises. Here we are concerned with the use of two-track exercises in training.

One important note for the rider/trainer to understand in performing two-track exercises is that they must be ridden while sitting deep in the saddle and very squarely balanced. There should not be a significant shift in weight.

LEG YIELDING

Leg yielding is currently a controversial exercise within the dressage community, but whether or not it has merit in itself, we do find it helpful as a transitional training aid and as a suppling exercise.

We think of leg yielding as an exercise to supple the horse before he is physically capable of performing the shoulder-in. Leg yielding is not a substitute for the half pass, but rather a helpful transition to the shoulder-in, travers, and other two-track exercises. The horse learns to move away from your leg; his head is slightly bent at the poll, but he is almost straight along his spine. Most important, he learns to accept the bit. Leg yielding requires that the trainer use his leg aids sufficiently, while co-ordinating the use of his hands in such a way that the horse proceeds willingly and in rhythm, with obedience to the aids. One of the best patterns used to teach leg yielding is the V-form (see diagram) away from the long side of the arena. After the corner, make a half-halt, bending the horse slightly to the left. Pressure should be increased with your left leg behind the girth. The inside leg position will depend on the horse—whether he drags his haunches (use inside leg behind the girth) or whether he resists (use inside leg on the girth). The outside rein leads the horse away from the long side, while the outside leg keeps him straight and keeps his haunches from escaping. It is important for the rider to keep his weight over the middle of the horse (do not collapse the inside hip).

A few steps at a time are sufficient so that he will not lose his forward impulsion. The horse should be kept parallel to the long side of the arena, with his shoulders leading slightly.

SHOULDER-IN

This is one of the few suppling exercises that require the horse to look away from his direction of travel. As in all exercises, the preparatory work before the actual execution of the movement is important; in this case we are introducing more collection and we wish to encourage freer movement of the shoulders, willing obedience to the aids, and improvement of the gaits.

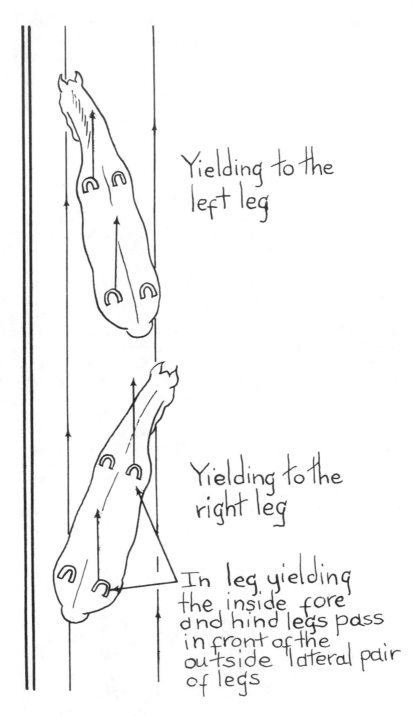

Yielding to the left leg

Yielding to the right leg

In leg yielding the inside fore and hind legs pass in front of the outside lateral pair of legs

Yielding to the left and right leg.

LEG-YIELDING EXERCISES

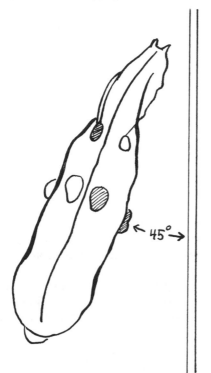

← 45° →

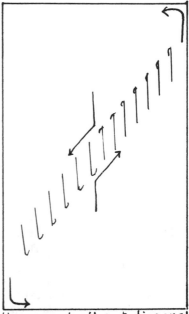

Use of center line & diagonal
for leg yielding exercise

Right Leg Yielding progressing left

Shorten right rein; shift
weight to right seat bone.
Both legs slightly behind girth;
Drive horse forward rhythmically
with right leg. Hold angle with
left leg. Left rein has more
tension because of right leg
drive.

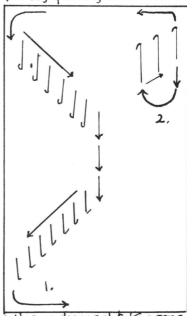

2.

1.

1. Use of diagonal & ½ arena
2. Exercise on corner

Again, a few steps at a time are sufficient. When the movement is executed after a corner or volte, it is usually more successful, since the lateral bend of the horse's body is already achieved. This lateral bend must be maintained as forward movement is initiated.

(When speaking of "inside" or "outside" in this movement, during a right shoulder-in, you are tracking to the right, and the right shoulder is considered to be the inside one.)

When moving to the left in the shoulder-in, we use the left rein as a guiding rein that holds the correct bend of the neck and forehand toward the left. The right rein and the left leg (which acts slightly forward of normal) not only hold the bend of the horse but also give the necessary impulsion. The right leg acts slightly behind its normal place to keep the haunches on the track, to keep the off-hind leg engaged, and to keep the forward motion.

Try not to use the left rein too strongly, since the horse will overbend his neck and lose the desired even curve from poll to tail. Your right rein (when moving to the left, as above) resists any excessive bend in the neck to the left.

When you and your horse understand the aids and mechanics of this exercise, try to perform it at a medium collected trot. Two or three strides in rhythm are enough at first. Your upper body should be kept upright, with your weight balanced and square, since shifting of weight will collapse your hip and defeat your goal. When tracking to the right, take care that you look straight up the track, not down at your horse's left shoulder.

Sometimes work "in hand" is helpful in giving him the idea of this exercise. For a left shoulder-in, stand on his near side, hold the reins in your left hand, close to the bit under his chin, and by using your right fingers or fist to push impulsively in the girth area, move him up the track, keeping his forehand inside of the track.

Remount and try the exercise again. Start with a large volte in the corner to initiate the correct bend, then use your legs to push him forward up the track while still maintaining the bend with the left leg. If he drifts slightly toward the center, which is natural at this stage, try again, giving more resistance with your right rein.

Intersperse the exercise with free forward movement at a medium posting trot. Be sure to practice the shoulder-in in both directions.

TURN ON THE FOREHAND
(PIVOT AROUND THE FOREHAND)

In order to execute a successful turn on the forehand, your horse must yield readily to leg aids as well as respond to rein effects. This exer-

Turn on the forehand. Note that the right hind leg is passing correctly in front of the left hind leg.

cise can be initiated from the halt or from the walk. In either direction, the active aid will be given by the rein and leg next to the wall.

Proceed at a rhythmical walk with the wall on your right side. Halt the horse and, still trying to keep the rhythm of the walk, squeeze the right rein and use the right leg behind the girth to move the haunches to the left (lateral aids). The left rein restrains the horse from overbending his neck to the right; the left leg on the girth steadies him and helps restrain the forehand. Your hands should be sensitive and not used too strongly. After the 180-degree turn, walk on and proceed in the opposite direction. A good halt will help to produce a good turn on the forehand, since the horse will be well balanced and in the proper position to succeed. Be sure to work in both directions equally.

When successful at the halt, try to initiate the exercise from the walk; or a half-halt will help set your horse in balance. A full turn (360 degrees) can eventually be undertaken. Work to maintain rhythm.

There may be problems such as backing up or moving forward. Use your leg aids strongly when your horse backs, and restrain with your hands when he tends to move forward. Work slowly, reinforce your leg

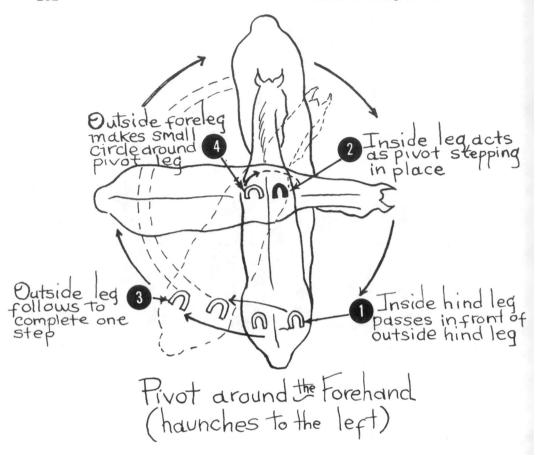

Outside foreleg makes small circle around pivot leg ④

② Inside leg acts as pivot stepping in place

Outside leg follows to complete one step ③

① Inside hind leg passes in front of outside hind leg

Pivot around the Forehand
(haunches to the left)

aids gently with the whip if necessary, and reward generously when your horse responds.

TURN ON THE HAUNCHES
(PIVOT AROUND THE HAUNCHES)

In this exercise, the forehand turns around the haunches. There are two schools of thought in executing the movement properly. In one, the inside hind leg steps in place; in the other, the inside hind leg describes a small circle. In either case, the rhythm of the walk should be maintained, with each foot stepping in proper sequence.

The turn on the haunches should be initiated from a walk; it can

Turn on the haunches to the left.

begin with the half turn and proceed to the full turn. The exercise eventually evolves into a pirouette when performed at the canter.

To begin, when tracking left, execute a good half-halt along the wall. The left rein acts as a leading rein; the right rein bears on the neck, restraining from a tendency to overbend or to walk forward, as well as helping to move the shoulders to the left. Your legs initiate action from the horse. The right leg on the girth or slightly behind the girth controls the haunches and keeps them from swinging out. The left leg stays slightly forward of normal and becomes active if your horse tends to step backward. If he steps backward, your forward impulsion has been lost, perhaps because rein aids were too strong.

1 Left foreleg passes in front of right pivot leg

3 Right or inside foreleg follows to complete the step

4 Left or outside hind leg makes a small circle around pivot leg

2 Inside hind leg acts as pivot stepping in place

Pivot around the Haunches
(forehand to the right)

In this exercise, your seat is very important. Sit square, look in the direction you wish to go, and do not lean forward. When leaning forward, you lose the influence of your seat bones; they should exert pressure downward and toward the direction of motion to influence the movement of the horse's haunches. Again, your rein aids and leg aids must be adequate as well as co-ordinated. In this movement, both you and the horse look toward the direction of movement.

HALF PASS
(LATERAL MARCH OR TRAVERSAL)

While the shoulder-in promotes flexibility mainly in the shoulders, the half pass causes the horse to lower his hindquarters and thus improves his balance and promotes greater mobility in those hindquarters. At the same time, it improves elasticity in the shoulders. It is also a useful lesson in obedience. The half pass can be executed at walk, trot, and canter, and should be developed in that order.

The half pass is usually executed on the diagonal of the arena. It differs from the shoulder-in in that the horse has his head slightly bent at

The half pass. Note that the horse's head is bent slightly at the poll in the direction he is going, while the rest of his body is straight. He is just returning to the track and will now proceed straight.

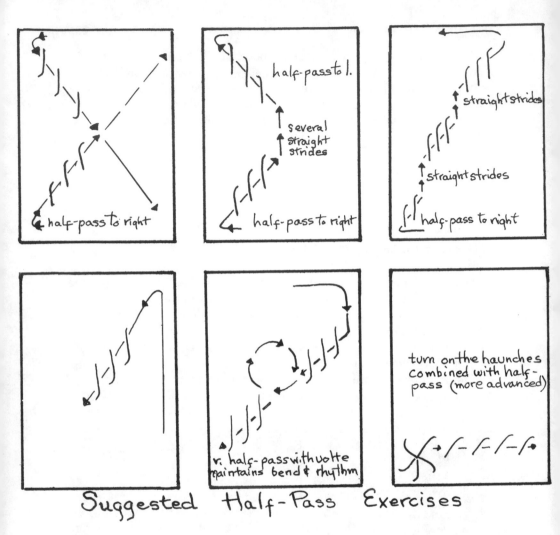

Suggested Half-Pass Exercises

In the diagrams:
- half-pass to right
- half-pass to l.
- several straight strides
- half-pass to right
- straight strides
- straight strides
- half-pass to right
- v. half-pass with volte maintains bend & rhythm
- turn on the haunches combined with half-pass (more advanced)

the poll in the direction toward which he is going, with the rest of his spine held straight. Use diagonal aids to initiate and maintain the half pass. For half pass to the right, use your right rein to lead and to induce a lateral bend of the neck to the right. Use your left leg actively behind the girth to move the quarters to the right. Your weight will be slightly on your right seat bone. The diagonal regulating and supporting aids are your left rein pushing the base of the neck to the right and holding the correct bend to the neck, and the right leg used on the girth to keep impulsion. When performing this movement and most lateral movements, the shoulders of the horse should precede the haunches. The horse can put too much weight on his leading shoulder (right shoulder when moving right), and this can result in loss of balance. When this happen, move the horse straight forward, asking for more impulsion, and then again ask for the half pass.

The Counter-canter and Flying Change

COUNTER-CANTER (COUNTER-LEAD OR FALSE CANTER)

Before undertaking the counter-canter, your horse should be stable in his leads, take them willingly from walk or trot, accept light contact (not lean on your hands), perform regular circles as small as twenty yards in diameter, and be well balanced. This exercise is excellent for promoting suppleness and willing obedience. We suggest that you do not start work on the counter-canter and the flying change of lead in the same lesson or series of lessons; working on both at the same time would be very confusing to your horse. This exercise, however, is excellent preparation for the change of leg in the air.

The counter-canter (as in the shoulder-in) is one of the few exercises that require the horse to look away from his direction of movement. He must be flexed toward his leading leg, which in the counter-canter is the outside foreleg. Your aids should stay constant for the lead, as any change in weight or aid will initiate change of lead. In other words, clearly maintain the aids for the desired lead.

To initiate the counter-canter, you may ask for the wrong lead on the long side of the arena, but break back into a trot before you come to a corner. Or prepare your horse for the counter-canter by taking the correct lead while starting down the long side, work toward the center, and then move back again to the track.

A third method, which requires more experience, is to start your canter on the long side, take the correct lead, continue on the short side, and change rein, still on the same lead. Make your turn at the counter-canter on the opposite short side as large and shallow as possible.

Finally, you can attempt the serpentine (begin with very shallow turns, working toward more defined curves) without changing your lead; the horse will alternately be cantering true and cantering false. If your horse should disunite, bring him gently back to a walk and strike off again on the desired lead.

FLYING CHANGE OF LEG

Although this is a perfectly natural movement for the horse, it is difficult for the rider to obtain because of the timing involved and because

Patterns to Initiate the Counter-Canter

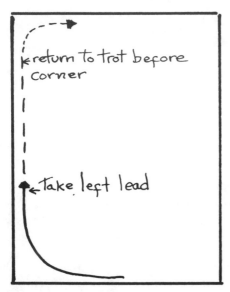

1. Ask for wrong lead (left) on long side of arena

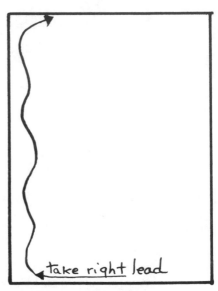

2. Take correct lead (right); work toward center and back.

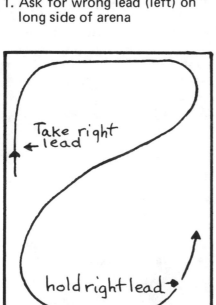

3. Start canter on long side right lead; change rein and maintain right lead

4. Ride shallow serpentine without changing lead

of the interference of the rein aids. To perform a successful change of leg, your horse must be able to collect on an easy rein, as he needs to stretch his head and neck to some extent. Prepare for the flying change by changing direction and walking several paces between the changes.

Since timing is so important in this exercise, give your horse some warning before asking for the execution of the movement; generally, you will ask for a slight increase in speed or impulsion before asking for a flying change.

Canter with adequate speed (deceleration makes the change difficult) and keep plenty of impulsion. To be correct, the exercise must be performed very smoothly.

An excellent exercise to teach the flying change and counter-canter is to work in a large circle, asking for lead changes every ten to twelve strides—alternately cantering true then false. This exercise can be varied by going a predesignated number of strides walking, then so many strides right canter, so many walking, so many left canter, and walking. The walk will help keep the horse calm, which is necessary in this exercise.

Changing leg at every third or second stride, and finally at every other stride, is very difficult; it requires precision in timing and refinement in understanding between horse and rider. Any interference with the aids or loss of impulsion destroys the exercise. Although Olympic competition asks for many precise, consecutive changes, this is unnecessary for general training, and perhaps not even desirable, since confusion can result if the trainer is not thoroughly experienced.

CHAPTER 3

ADVANCED WESTERN TRAINING

Many Western maneuvers are similar to, or even identical with, their English counterparts. Although terminology may differ, the action is essentially the same. And as a method of demonstrating these maneuvers, Western reining patterns are on a parallel with English dressage tests. The overall goals of the Western trainer are little different from those of the English trainer. Both are looking for a well-balanced, supple, experienced, alert, responsive, and pleasurable mount.

In this chapter, we will concentrate on producing an all-round horse capable of specialization in any Western field. If your horse is an experienced trail horse, a handy ranch horse, one capable of performing well in a Western pleasure class, and also able to perform creditably in reining and stock events, he should be considered a fine all-round Western mount. Because responsiveness is inherent in all of these activities, we'll concentrate on the elements and exercises that go into making a reining horse—a horse wholly responsive to the requests of his rider.

As in the performance of the advanced English maneuvers, your horse must be capable, both mentally and physically, of performing the requirements of the advanced Western horse. Is his conformation adequate (leg problems or other unsoundnesses)? Has he the maturity and strength (length of attention span, tendency to sour)? Is his physical condition up to par (infestation of worms, poor nutrition)? He should be mature; it takes time to stabilize the early basic lessons, even five or more years. No basic lesson should be skipped or skimped just so that you can rush into advanced work. Since advanced training is based on the stepping-stones of earlier lessons, so training must be progressive and cumulative to produce a satisfactory final product.

Tack

WESTERN BITS

A finished Western horse should perform equally well in snaffle, hackamore, or curb. Many trainers, both English and Western, often put their finished horses back into the snaffle during exercise sessions. Versatile show horses (performing in both Western and English classes) must perform in a Western curb as well as in a double bridle or Pelham. As the double bridle is used in advanced English riding, the Western curb should be used for advanced Western riding to promote refined rein aids.

Some of the best Western reinsmen are the California hackamore and spade bit artists. Instead of controlling the horse's head through mouth pressure, the Spanish method (which came to us through Mexico) controls the horse through the hackamore. The hackamore horse is started in a thick, heavy bosal (noseband) and graduates to lighter, smaller bosals, sometimes progressing through five different bosals as he is polished over several years' time into a refined reining horse. The authentic bosal has a rawhide core that can be fitted to the horse, both over his nose and under his jaw. It does not have a steel cable core, as do some modern types; these are apt to sore a horse's underjaw. True hackamore control is not by pain.

The hackamore is not used like a bit; its action is quite different and requires knowledgeable handling for more advanced training. To oversimplify the correct use of the hackamore, we can say that the primary action is a low, wide pull on one rein only. However, this should always be a pull-release action; a steady pull on a hackamore can make the horse hard because he'll learn to lean into it. One of the first basic maneuvers is the double, or doubling, which reverses the horse suddenly and teaches him respect for the hackamore. For excellent instruction in hackamore training, see the books by Dave Jones listed under "Recommended Reading."

If the horse is to be bitted, the Californian uses the spade bit, which is thought of by many to be cruel and inhumane—and indeed can be when improperly used. In experienced hands, however, it is just the opposite; the spade bit has been scientifically designed to operate sensitively in a sensitive mouth. California reinsmen often use the snaffle as a transitional bit between the hackamore and the spade bit. They are very careful to preserve the sensitivity of the mouth.

The spade bit contains copper (sometimes in the cricket; other times in part of the mouthpiece), which helps to keep the mouth moist; and this in turn keeps it light. The cricket is sometimes called a pacifier; it has a calming effect as the horse plays with it. The controversial part of the bit, of course, is the spade mouthpiece, which can be from 2 inches to 4½ inches high. The reasoning behind the height of the spade is to keep the horse from getting his tongue over the bit. There are two kinds of spade bits: the loose jaw and the solid jaw. Because some trainers claim that the loose jaw bit has a tendency to pinch, many prefer the solid bit. The loose-jaw proponents claim that since a horse's mouth is flexible, so should be his bit. The choice is an individual matter. We think that the most interesting and important fact about the spade bit is that it actually helps the horse to adopt the proper head carriage. The bit is heavy and scientifically balanced; the angle of the bit (when properly fitted) is such that the horse is comfortable when his head is positioned properly. It may be uncomfortable if he carries his head too high or too low. The horse should never be pulled or rough-reined in a spade; sloppy reining results in the bit twisting and the spade hitting the roof of the mouth and causing pain. Spins, stops, backs, and other advanced maneuvers are taught with hackamore or snaffle. Only a knowledgeable horseman, trained many years in its use, should use the spade bit; but the horsemen that excel in the California style are truly artists.

The hackamore, with the transition to snaffle-bit control, was discussed in Part II, Chapter 4. For more advanced work, the horse should be introduced to the ordinary Western curb. To make the transition from snaffle to curb, we like to use a transitional bit, the cowboy snaffle. The bit has a snaffle mouthpiece with which the horse is familiar, but has shanks and curb strap which are new to him. Its mild leverage introduces the curb action without changing the mouthpiece. When this action has been accepted, a mild curb bit (low or no port), generally of grazing type, can be used. For a horse very sensitive to the curb strap, it would be wise to use a strap at least one-half inch wide and adjust it so that when the rein is taut, the curb barely touches. As he gets used to the pressure, the curb strap can gradually be adjusted to its normal position (room for three fingers when the bit hangs naturally in the mouth with no pressure on the reins). Another transitional bit is the Kimberwicke (see also Part II, Chapter 5).

USE OF THE CURB BIT

The horse should be taught his maneuvers in hackamore or snaffle. He should respond well to rein, weight, and leg or heel (with or without spurs) before the transition to curb bit is made. The use of the curb helps to refine these aids, to make them nearly imperceptible to the viewer. Response should attend the barest touch of the curb rein. As explained in Part II, Chapter 5, the curb directs the horse in collection, flexion, transitions, halting, backing, and head position. It does not govern direction. The horse receives all lateral direction through leg and weight aids in conjunction with neck reining. If it seems that more control is necessary to teach a certain maneuver than hackamore or snaffle provides, the trainer may have success with a Pelham or double bridle. Do not use a curb until the horse is properly prepared.

To keep his mouth sensitive and flexible, handle your reins as if you were squeezing a sponge. Steady, hard pulling results in star-gazing or overbending. You are working now for lightness, and this is impossible to achieve with implacable hands and by throwing around body weight. Because the horn of the Western saddle necessitates that the rein hand be held slightly higher than with the English saddle, the slight backward curve of the shank helps alleviate the increased leverage of this hand position.

The bit is an aid, a means of communication, and in advanced work you communicate with your mount by the merest whisper—not an Indian war whoop. We see too much jerking and violent pulling in Western riding, especially in shows where youngsters are attempting to replace training with bullying in hopes of forcing the horse to perform maneuvers for which he has not been properly prepared. If the horse is unmanageable in a snaffle because of inadequate training and poor horsemanship, he will be no better in a curb, and, in fact, will quickly resort to head tossing and other evasions to lessen the pain in his mouth. If you have trouble with the curb, and suspect it may be caused by rushing the training or impatience to make the transition to the curb bit, go back immediately to snaffle or hackamore, or try a transitional bit. If you need to remind your horse to respond to your whispers, a reminder with the crop or bat is a far more effective and better method of correction than pulling on the reins.

No matter what bit you are using, be sure that it and the bridle are fitted properly. Don't neglect your horse's comfort; sometimes bit guards and curb chain guards are necessary. Take the time to thoroughly check and fit your training equipment, and also find out which bit is right for your horse.

SADDLES

As with your bit and bridle, your saddle should not only fit you and your horse but also be correct for the job. Use a roping saddle for roping; a parade saddle for parades; and an all-around saddle for pleasure and light work.

For training, we like an all-purpose Western saddle (moderate swells and medium cantle). Look especially for three important features. First, the saddle should fit our modern breeds well; it should be wide enough in the gullet to allow for the wider withers and shorter back. Too low a gullet is the prime cause of fistula of the withers. While mounted, you should be able to pass three fingers between gullet and withers.

Also important, the saddle should allow the rider to sit over the horse's center of gravity. A saddle seat that slopes down to the cantle keeps your weight too far back. This will interfere directly with training for several maneuvers (see the section on the sliding stop); a level seat is much preferred for training.

Finally, the stirrups should be hung farther forward than on the older-type stock saddle, and should be free-swinging. This enables the trainer to make full use of his weight and leg aids.

Stock Work

Although we think of stock work as the main province of the Western horse, most Western horses probably will never see a cow. They are pleasure horses, and, while they may often perform in stock-horse classes in shows, their life remains far removed from the actual routine of a working cowhorse. But where the stock horse is used, he is indispensable. Although trail bikes, all-terrain vehicles, four-by-fours, and snow machines may have relieved horses from some of the heavy packing (such as carrying salt, hay, and fence wire to areas inaccessible to regular vehicles), they're poor substitutes when it comes to driving and cutting out cattle and sheep.

Many large cattle outfits raise their own cowhorses, while others buy young horses and train them. Smaller ranches which may need only two to four working cowhorses, generally prefer to buy already trained animals. The quality of horse stock on cattle ranches has improved considerably in recent years, with many ranchers rating "cow sense" high in a horse's pedigree. A horse may be trained to rein, halt, spin, and roll back, but either he has what it takes to work cattle or he doesn't. A good cowhorse saves his owner time and money. It is up to the cattleman or his trainer to give his prospective cowhorses a thorough basic education, along with giving them time to grow and mature.

A well-trained ranch horse should be able to hold a cow, cut out a calf, allow the calf to be roped, and help hold or drag the calf, even if he's not up to specializing in rodeo cutting or roping. Such skills use, to some extent, the more advanced maneuvers performed by the reining horse and the rodeo stock horse—sliding stops, rollbacks, spins, and so on. In many cases, these may be performed naturally by the horse; they are natural movements used as necessary by the horse that understands his job in handling stock. However, it is also useful to be able to direct the horse into these maneuvers, increasing his versatility and responsiveness.

Let's begin here at the beginning, by introducing the young horse to basic ranch work, since this, with his other basic training, serves as a foundation for more advanced skills.

BASIC RANCH WORK

Ranching is a seasonal operation, and ranch horses often alternate months of no work at all (when they remain out on pasture, perhaps with no human contact whatsoever) with days or weeks of intensive activity. Generally, this activity takes one of two forms: moving the stock and working the stock. Moving stock often involves two- or three-day trail rides, driving the herds to or from summer pastures; roundups, in which small bunches of cattle are collected and moved to a central location to build the herd for trailing or shipping home; or shorter drives that move the stock to different pastures or sections on the ranch. Working the stock involves branding, splitting the herds, herd-holding, penning, shipping, and so on.

The young horse may find a job in both operations that will enhance his basic education, but he won't be ready for specialized cutting or roping work for some time. As soon as the young horse is reliable in his basic saddle training outside the arena, he will be able to join short drives—not to be depended upon as a worker, but as a youngster going along to watch, so to speak, and to learn the ropes. Long drives should be avoided until he has worked up to them in maturity and education.

The young horse can help during cattle drives and roundups when no specialized skills are required. The experience he gains will settle him and be a great aid in his later training. (Courtesy Wyoming Travel Commission)

Let the youngster follow behind a lagging member of the herd, or if one is wandering out to the side, help him to follow it closely and work it back toward the herd. Stay with one animal for a few minutes, then turn the horse away, pat and praise him, and select another one to follow. In this way, the youngster can learn the nature of cattle—how they think and move—and he will learn to anticipate their actions.

This is an excellent way to reaffirm your training in responsiveness to rein and leg. The horse actually sees the reason for your aids and will usually co-operate wholeheartedly.

Stock work of this kind is excellent basic training for any young horse, if the rider knows what he is doing. If you don't have cattle of your own, perhaps you could help some knowledgeable ranching neighbors move a herd to summer pasture. By watching closely and asking for pointers, you (and your horse) will pick up hints on how best to move a herd, when to push and when not to crowd, how to handle strays, or plan a route, or move traffic through a herd on the highway. During these maneuvers, you'll probably find out whether your horse has cow sense. This training-by-doing is the best kind of training there is, especially if you can work in the company of quiet, experienced cowhorses.

BEGINNINGS IN DEVELOPING A CUTTING OR ROPING HORSE

A young horse should develop his general education for several years before beginning specific training for roping or cutting. It is rare that a horse does both of these jobs equally well; almost always, he will be better suited to one than to the other. It is to your advantage to find the job to which he is best suited and to support it by thorough basic training and physical maturation, rather than to push him before he is ready.

If you are definitely developing a stockhorse, however, there are several things you can work on and be alert to. Work with ropes, as outlined in Part II, Chapter 7, including teaching the horse to drag objects. Other trail training will be beneficial.

If you have the opportunity to work a calf or cow in a corral or arena, try out the youngster, depending on his degree of training. Don't force. He should rein well and be responsive to the aids before you begin working him alone with stock. You may single out a calf and rate it, following at the exact distance you favor for roping. Don't let your horse run it down, or get too far behind. If the colt takes to this and likes the idea, he'll probably make a roping horse. But take your time and don't rush into concentrated training. You are discovering his potential, not exploiting it. Keep up the general cow work along with regular ring training.

If you're hoping to develop a cutting-horse prospect, try working in a medium-sized corral with a small, quiet herd. Cut out a gentle-looking cow and follow her, pushing her into a corner. Don't crowd her, but try to hold her there. Praise the youngster so that he understands it's good to hold the cow. Back up and let her walk along the fence; then get ahead of her and turn her back. Again, this requires good response to the aids and should not be rushed. The educated cutting horse will act on the cow's move, not force the move. If your horse seems to understand that he can block the animal, then back up and wait, he's probably cutting-horse material. If he wants to rush in and move after the cow, he's probably better suited to roping.

ADVANCING IN STOCK WORK

Continue to develop the youngster through general ring training, trail training, and stock training. When he is physically mature, demonstrates good cow sense, and is thoroughly responsive and stable in his basic education, he is ready for more advanced Western skills leading to specialization in roping or cutting, or simply developing into a top-notch ranch horse. He should learn to perform sliding stops, a straight back (backing), rollbacks, spins, pivots, and lead changes, as explained below under "Reining Work." These skills may be applied to cutting and roping. Producing a finished cutting or roping horse, however, is a highly specialized endeavor best undertaken by experienced trainers. Please refer to the appropriate books in our list of "Recommended Reading." Rodeo cutting and roping will be discussed further in Part IV, Chapter 1.

Reining Work

The reining contest is a test of advanced Western training, comparable to the dressage test in English training. Both, when properly executed, demonstrate an advanced degree of responsiveness, willingness, and harmonious understanding between horse and rider. Horses competent in reining and stock events are comparable to English three-day-event horses.

THE REINING HORSE

What should the reining horse be able to do? He should be finished in the various gaits: walk, jog-trot, lope, and gallop/run. He should perform stops, backing, flying changes, pivots, and rollbacks. These maneuvers, and all transitions, should be accomplished smoothly, with grace, balance, and agility. When combined, they form a reining pattern. There are several official patterns, offering variety in order and in difficulty of the exercises.

A "pattern horse" learns one pattern by heart, looks well in that one, but has difficulty if asked to perform another. As with the English dressage horse that learns a test, anticipation of each maneuver can ruin a performance. Thus it's necessary to work on the various components of the reining pattern and to vary their order.

In Part II, Chapter 5, we worked on the Western gaits and mentioned ways to improve them. The reining horse must be stable and finished in all gaits, and his transitions, whether from gait to gait, or within a gait (changing from extended to collected lope, for example), should be smooth and flowing. For contest work, you should know how to rate your horse in his gaits so that he looks his best: Maybe he appears better if his jog-trot is slower and more collected; or maybe his lope is too fast and shows him to disadvantage. He should be absolutely stable in his leads. Any resistances, such as tail-wringing, star-gazing, charging, head-tossing, fighting, traveling sideways, or holding his mouth open, are indications of rushed training, overwork, or some other fault. Evaluate your program and correct the problem before continuing any advanced work.

SPEED IN THE REINING HORSE

It often seems that speed is the primary attribute and goal of the reining horse. Contest judges sometimes contribute to this notion by rewarding speed too highly, ignoring poor horsemanship, improperly executed maneuvers, even abuse of the horse. Such judges do incalculable damage, because they prove to a whole ringside of possible future competitors that training and horsemanship play poor seconds to speed.

Speed comes last. It is a result of perfection in training. When a horse thoroughly understands an exercise, when he has been physically developed to be able to perform it properly, and when he and his rider have attained a compatible and workable understanding through the aids (and through that subtle, undefinable quality of reading each other's intentions), *then* speed is a natural result. It is the last thing to develop in any exercise.

In teaching some maneuvers, such as the flying change and the rollback, increased speed, asked for at the proper time, will make the maneuver more easily accomplished and better understood. There is a difference between increased acceleration at a given point in the execution of a movement, and general racing madly about. Overall, the movements are taught slowly; as in English dressage movements, they are taught at a walk before progressing to a trot, a trot before progressing to a canter or a lope. Such teaching makes more use of the English half-halt and similar Western "dwell" than it does of bursts of speed.

A reining horse is not developed in a month, or even a year. If you're in a rush to enter reining contests, buy a fully trained horse. Otherwise, plan to *develop* your horse, mentally and physically, over three, four, five years, to his peak of ability—with speed the last and crowning glory.

THE SLIDING STOP

The Western horse should be able to perform a sliding stop. This means that his hind legs slide forward under his body as he appears almost to sit down. To do this properly, his back becomes rounded and his head and neck balance the slide by staying down, not throwing up in the air. The length of the slide depends on ground surface, shoeing, the speed at which he is going, his degree of training, his rider, and his own ability. A horse may slide to a stop at a slow speed. It has been demonstrated by many trainers that a horse can do a beautiful sliding stop with no use of the reins—even without wearing a bridle or hackamore at all.

When teaching and practicing the sliding stop, select an area that is soft (such as level, plowed ground) and free of bumps, mud, and slick spots. The horse should be properly shod, and should wear skid boots, since bruising or injury will be a psychological, as well as a physical, barrier to good performance. Don't sour him on too much work at this exercise.

Begin teaching the stop from a walk. Always give the horse a warning before the actual cue to stop. Since he knows the word command "Whoa," you can say this immediately before you ask for a stop. Begin giving this command in conjunction with the cue you plan to use—perhaps a lift of the reins, or, as ropers do, resting the left hand on the neck (preparing for rapid dismount).

Lightly lifting the reins while using your seat bones in downward pressure, both in rhythm with the gallop, lifts the forehand, tucks the hindquarters under him, and so enables him to make his No. 11 on the ground. Be consistent in your use of the cue.

Ask for the stop itself by applying slight pressure (and release) on the reins, using your seat bones in a downward pressure, and at the same time squeezing lightly with your legs. You are trying to get the horse to gather his legs under him. Let's consider this for a moment. As the horse learns to slide his hind legs forward in response to your squeezing with your legs, his back humps slightly and his hindquarters lower. The use of your seat bones in downward pressure, as part of your cue to stop, will be effective only if the saddle you are using allows you to sit well forward in a balanced ride, as on a dressage horse. However, too much pressure, or worse, too much weight behind the center of gravity (as is the case with many Western saddles), will hinder your horse. In this case, rise in the

Using the hackamore when teaching the sliding stop minimizes the development of problems with mouth and head. Jeff Lacy, a Dave Jones apprentice, rides the youngster calmly into a nice slide. Note that he is pulling on one rein—never on both at the same time. His left hand is ready to bring the nose down if necessary. (Courtesy Dave Jones)

This is an excellent sliding stop—the rider is quiet and forward in the saddle, and the horse is well collected with rounded back, flexed neck and poll, mouth closed, and head down. Ken Serco is using a Dave Jones Western Pelham bit on Baron, a Colombian Paso. (Courtesy Dave Jones)

saddle as you squeeze with your legs, to keep your weight well forward and allow him to round his back.

Using the same cues, progress through the trot, lope, and finally the gallop. As your horse accepts the warning cue you have selected, you'll be able to dispense with the voice command. Stop at various places, rather than always in the same spot.

If your horse has trouble recovering his balance after the stop, immediately back him a few steps. But use this sparingly. Keep your weight even, so that your stop is square. His forehand must be light; otherwise he bounces to a stop on his forefeet—uncomfortable and undesirable. Problems, such as open mouth or nose pointed to the sky, are caused by lack of basic work at the slower gaits, or by a heavy-handed rider.

BACKING

Please refer to the rein-back in the previous chapter. The principles involved in the Western method of backing are the same as in the English. Backing requires refinement of the aids and perfection in execution when in the advanced stages. In advanced work, your horse should back equally well in snaffle or curb, and he should perform his backing exercise with rhythm, impulsion, overall straightness, and willingness.

As in the sliding stop, the rider's weight placement can have a great effect on the horse's ability to back properly. If your saddle does not allow you to sit forward and use your seat bones as a weight aid, your weight will be a hindrance, causing the horse to swing his haunches with each backward step. If this is the case, rise out of the saddle to put your weight forward and free the horse to get his legs under him.

The advanced Western horse should willingly back for longer distances, and with more speed than is required of the English horse. Do not hurry the training, however, or make your work periods for this exercise too long in hopes of forcing speed. Instead, work gradually, asking for only two or three backs per session. As these improve in execution, you may begin to speed up the forward walk before the backing exercise; this may become progressively faster in order to build impulsion for a speedier back. However, do not sacrifice straightness or rhythm for speed. Again, speed is the last touch to put on a finished horse.

If you have problems obtaining enough impulsion for the faster back, try performing some trot-halt, trot-halt exercises as in advanced English training before initiating the backing exercise. Half-halts and other collecting exercises are beneficial as well.

CIRCLES AND CHANGES OF LEAD

The large and small circles used in reining patterns allow the horse to demonstrate his ability to lope smoothly on the correct lead at various speeds and to make the flying change of lead. The advanced horse should be able to make the smaller circle at a slow, even lope, and a larger circle at a fast lope. He should be very stable in his leads, as well as in the speed of the lope. Make sure that his lope is united and that his body flexes to the direction and curve of the circle. To check yourself on whether your horse is making a good circle, ride in soft, untracked dirt or after a new snow, and check his hoofprints.

When practicing, start with large circles and make them progressively smaller, always bending the horse to conform to the circle. The spiraling in-and-out exercise (Part III, Chapter 2) helps the horse that tends to lope too fast, and aids in developing precision. Give and take lightly with your hands; keep some degree of collection, and don't let him string out on a loose rein. When he is making round, consistent circles, you may begin the change of lead.

Begin simply and gradually, as explained in the previous chapter for "Flying change of leg." Since he is advanced in his training, do a drop-to-trot change rather than a walk. He should know his cues well for each lead, so that the few trotting steps you take will give him time to adjust to the next cue and collect himself to take the opposite lead. Before trying tight circles and figure-eights, it is better to make your curves large and shallow. Large, open serpentines are a good variation. Changing leads (simple) out in a pasture, where the contour of the land will often help him, makes more sense to your horse and is certainly more enjoyable than endless ring work leading to boredom. Take advantage of juniper bushes, trees, rocks, and other natural objects to lope around and work into an informal pattern.

A more advanced exercise is to perform a series of transitions: walk, lope, trot, walk, halt, walk, lope; or walk, lope, walk, lope. Some collection should be asked in order to make the transitions smooth. Keep each gait until it is cadenced and balanced before making the transition. At first, this may take many strides; eventually, a well-trained and well-collected horse may make a transition within only a few strides. These exercises must be used with discretion, as they tend to excite a horse. This, of course, can work to your benefit if your horse is inclined to be too quiet or lazy.

When, while describing a figure-eight, he changes his leads correctly and consistently after a few trotting steps, gradually decrease these steps until he finally makes a flying change. Factors important to the success of this maneuver are the timing of your cues, your weight aids, and the extent of his collection. At the point where he must perform his flying change, reverse your aids just as the horse begins his stride. Use a little more speed in your lope, try not to interfere with his head, and don't throw your weight violently. If your ground work has been thorough, he will probably respond the first time. A horse that tends to be lazy, or one that will not collect, often disunites; he changes in front but not behind. If this should happen, sting him with a willow switch when you cue him to change in order to wake him up. Be free with praise when he succeeds.

PIVOTS (QUARTER TURNS OR OFFSETS)

Pivots, spins, and rollbacks are all performed with the horse's weight on his hindquarters. Actually, the pivot is one quarter of a spin. Your

Pivots and spins require essentially the same aids. Here Ken Serco is spinning a Paso colt. The horse is looking slightly toward the direction of movement, without yawing or tossing. Whether English or Western, lightness is a quality that is developed with good training and is a goal to work for. (Courtesy Dave Jones)

horse's forehand is lifted and turned 90 degrees to the right or to the left. His forehand should not touch the ground until he turns the full 90. The pivot should look like one movement, not a series of hops. If he pivots to the left, he uses the right forefoot to push off, and, of course, vice versa pivoting to the right.

In training your mount to pivot, ask for a little at a time, not the whole 90 degrees at once. Work in hackamore or snaffle; he should not perform with his mouth open or throw his head. As he learns the movement, increase the distance, making sure that the mechanics of the movement are correct. If you pressure your horse too hard, you can produce a wring-tail. Be sure to settle him before you start the pivot, and don't allow him to move forward or backward.

Use the same aids as described below under the spin. As he learns to pivot, he can be worked gradually into a spin. If you have trouble, it may help him to feel the movement if you gallop him parallel to a wall or fence, do a sliding stop, and then lift and place him away from the fence. In this way, his weight will be placed correctly on his hindquarters, and the momentum of the gallop helps him to turn. Your weight should be placed toward the direction of the turn, with your outside leg applying pressure behind the girth.

SPINS OR 360S

A spin demonstrates a horse's ability to make rapid turns, theoretically to cut off or turn back a cow or calf. The horse should be able to spin 90 degrees, 180 degrees, or the full circle.

Most trainers use both hands on the reins with either a snaffle bit or hackamore when training reining horses. When training for spins, the direction of the head is important: The horse must look toward the direction of movement. Two hands on the reins will insure his head position. Training to turn with only one hand (neck-reining with a curb bit) tends to make him follow his ear, with his nose pointing in the other direction.

The horse spins with his near or inside hind foot fairly stationary, while the other feet push the horse around. Shift your weight slightly toward the direction of movement, your inside leg moving slightly toward the rear, and your outside leg and heel pressing against the horse's side. All your aids should work in harmony. To spin left: Place your weight slightly to the left, use your left leg a little behind the girth to weight the horse's pivot leg (left hind), use your right leg and heel on the girth, pushing and encouraging the forehand to move left. The left rein is the direct rein and places his head toward the left. The right rein keeps his neck from turning too much. It helps to start your spin from a collected standing position—be sure he is not strung out.

Start slowly, a step at a time, and reward generously. Gradually encourage him to go the 360 slowly. Don't ask for speed yet. The cues and timing must be accomplished first. In order to stop your horse at 180 or 90, release the pressure of your right leg and left rein. To make this exact takes practice and correct timing. Work in both directions equally.

If the mechanics of your spin are correct and your horse does not demonstrate a wringing tail (too much, too fast), or sour ears (definite resistance—take him back to the basics), then it's time to speed things up. Start your horse in a circle at the trot, decrease the size of your circle so that he is almost turning on himself, and give the cues for the spin. The forward impulsion of the faster gait will help to push him around in a well-balanced spin. After executing these successfully, try to lope in a decreasing circle, and again give your spin cues. With this exercise, as with most advanced movements, it is important to remember that two or three times a week are sufficient. Try an occasional spin in a pasture or out on the trail. Don't sour him.

ROLLBACKS

The rollback is also called a rollback over the hocks, and a set-and-turn. The horse gallops straight in one direction, slides to a stop, swings 180 degrees in a single motion, and gallops back on the opposite lead. He should land running on the correct lead for the direction of the turn. The rollback is not correct if the horse makes a small circle with his hind feet. He must first make a good stop; his weight must be on his hindquarters so that he is in a balanced position to whirl a full 180 degrees and proceed in the opposite direction.

When starting to train for the rollback, you will find that working along a wall or fence helps to set him up for proper turns, and guides him straight in gallop and stop. It is easier to teach the rollback to an energetic horse than to a sluggish one. Top reining horses are not lazy.

Begin teaching the rollback from a walk, using a hackamore or snaffle. Walk along the fence, between four to six feet from it, and halt properly, using your legs to put the horse's hind legs well under him. Stand, or "dwell," just long enough to be sure the horse is properly positioned and balanced. Then swing him abruptly over his hocks (toward the fence), and use both your legs and a bat or whip on his rump to bring him out running. It will be natural for him to land running on the correct lead.

Work in both directions, avoid overdoing, and praise the horse lavishly when he performs correctly. As he begins to understand the movement, increase the speed of your approach. Performing a good gallop and stop puts the horse in good position. As in jumping, the approach is all-important. For the rollback, the approach includes the "dwell." The horse must have his hind legs under him, his forefeet ready to lift, if the rollback

Dave Jones describes a very hard and fast rollback or set-and-turn: "The aids are vigorously applied, for this is natural with very fast work. The colt is sliding and will be pulled to the left. Spurs are applied for collection (the rowels are dull blanks)."

"The colt is turning hard and fast. The reins are thrown away and the rider gets into time with the colt."

"The colt has completed a 180-degree turn and is jumping out. The fast work has frightened him, and the rider will now circle until the colt slows and calms down. Left spur and left rein will bring him into a left circle." (Courtesy Dave Jones)

is to be made correctly. Try not to rush your rollback, as this can result in rearing, yawing mouth, and wrong leads.

Avoid making all your rollbacks in the same spot, since your horse will come to anticipate your aids. Of course, on the perimeter of the show arena you will have markers that you are required to use as guides, but as in English dressage, your horse must respond to your aids, not anticipate them: His timing and your aids may not coincide.

REINING PATTERNS

The most often used pattern for a reining horse seems to be Pattern No. 1 in the *Official Handbook* of the American Quarter Horse Association. There are five patterns in all, and any contestant in the reining event should find out and learn the pattern called for in his chosen show, and keep current with the rules. As in dressage tests, the reining patterns grow progressively more difficult—that is, reining pattern No. 5 asks for double spins and for specific leads and circles to show the superior training and experience of the advanced reining horse.

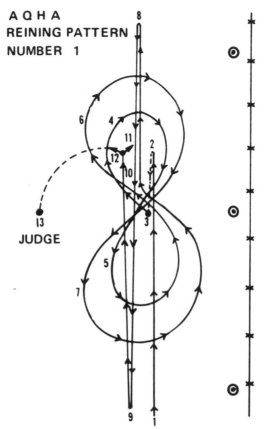

AQHA
REINING PATTERN
NUMBER 1

JUDGE

◉ MANDATORY MARKER
ALONG FENCE OR WALL

AQHA reining pattern No. 1. The arena or plot should be approximately 50 by 150 feet in size. The judge shall indicate with markers on arena fence or wall the length of the pattern; markers within the area of the pattern will not be used. Ride pattern as follows:

1 to 2. *Run with speed, past center marker.*

2. *Stop and back up to center of pattern.*

3. *Settle horse for approximately 10 seconds. Start lope to the right. Figure-eight should be made inside the end markers.*

4 and 5. *Ride small figure-eight at slow lope.*

6 and 7. *Ride a larger figure-eight at a faster lope.*

8. *Left roll back over hocks (should be made past far end marker).*

9. *Right roll back over hocks (should be made past near end marker).*

10. *Stop (should be made past center marker), let horse settle, and in approximate area of stop, do the pivots.*

11. *Pivot, right or left, no more than 90 degrees.*

12. *Pivot opposite direction, no more than 180 degrees.*

13. *Walk to judge and stop for inspection until dismissed.*

(*From* Official Handbook of the American Quarter Horse Association, *1977*)

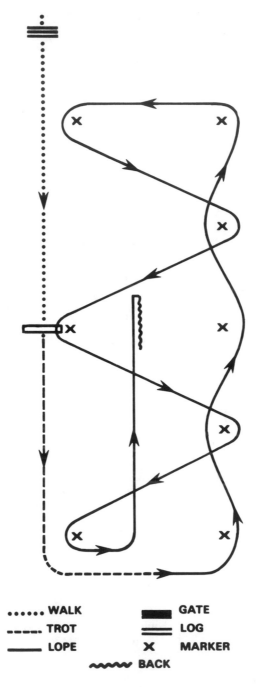

•••••• WALK	▬▬ GATE
▬ ▬ ▬ TROT	≡ LOG
──── LOPE	✕ MARKER
∿∿∿ BACK	

Western Riding Pattern. (*From* Official Handbook of the American Quarter Horse Association, *1977*)

Almost all Western riding requires good stops and turns, and a horse that is handy in basic maneuvers can be a real pleasure to ride. When you first start putting all your basic maneuvers together into the reining pattern, work for a smooth performance and stress correct execution of each maneuver. You may begin to increase speed gradually, when the entire performance is smooth and correct. Avoid too much repetition and give him a change of pace often.

WESTERN RIDING PATTERN

One reason for mentioning this show event here is that it makes a pleasant change-of-pace exercise in training your horse in a combination of pleasure, working, and trail-type maneuvers. In the AQHA and in the AHSA rule books for the Paint Horse Division, it states, "This contest is neither a stunt nor a race. It is a competition in the performance and characteristics of a good, sensible, well-mannered, free and easy-moving ranch horse that can get a man around on the usual ranch chores, over the trails, or give a quiet, comfortable, and pleasant ride in open country, through and over obstacles." Setting up a similar pattern (see diagram), or even designing your own, would make an excellent training exercise. This type of course can prove the handiness and versatility of your horse, and most horses and riders enjoy the novelty.

Part IV

———◆———

COMPETITION

CHAPTER 1

TRAINING TO SHOW

Showing is a demonstration of achievement—the result of your preparation, knowledge, and experience. You should have confidence in your horse's ability and willingness to perform correctly, and in your own ability as a rider or handler because of the training you have given him at home, and because of the opportunities you have made for yourself and your horse to gain experience in working away from home.

If your horse is not yet able to perform an exercise at home, he will not suddenly blossom into full-blown excellence at a show. On the other hand, the fact that he performs well at home is no sign that he will reproduce this performance at his first or even second show. Why? What will he encounter at a show that will affect his behavior?

Taking a horse to his first show may be similar to dropping you or me in the midst of a foreign country. The sights, noises, smells, and confusion inherent in showing will excite even a usually calm, sensible animal. From the moment he is unloaded from his trailer and led to his assigned stall, all will be interesting and unsettling. His whole way of life will be changed. It is not surprising, then, that he will react to this extraordinary disruption and take several days to settle down to the new routine. Most horses require several experiences with shows before they will accept, within a day or two, the new conditions and confusions.

Experience, then, as well as training, is important for top performance in the show ring. The wise showman will give his novice horse plenty of opportunity to become accustomed to traveling, strange conditions, different horses, people, and confusion, before expecting attentive, calm, and skilled performance at a show.

And he will remember, also, that showing is a demonstration of competence—the show ring is too late for training or for gaining an animal's confidence. The winning show horse learned his lessons and his trust at home.

On the Show Grounds

Most horses are trailered or trucked to the show grounds. A show horse should accept this mode of travel with equanimity and willingly enter or leave a trailer at any time. It can be frustrating and dangerous to people and horses alike to have a horse fight trailering. Information on trailer training may be found at the end of this chapter.

The tack you use when not in the show ring should be strong, serviceable, and of proper fit. If your horse were to act up on the way to his stall after unloading and break or slip his halter, disaster could result not only to him but also to some other horse or person. Use tried-and-true tack, not just something pretty that you bought yesterday.

Your horse's health and safety are your responsibility. Confinement to a stall may be a different experience for him. You must see that his feed and exercise are geared to this confinement, so that colic, stocking up, and other health problems do not occur. Check to make sure he is drinking adequately, and blanket him if it is colder or damper than he is used to.

Changes in altitude and climate are reflected in your horse's actions. He should arrive at the show in time to become acclimated. Horses moved from low to high altitudes tend to be nervous, and will become short-winded more easily. There is not quite such a problem for horses moved from high altitudes to low, but they can develop coughs if it is damp, or feel logy because the atmosphere is heavier. Excessive heat or cold can affect performance as well.

Most important in a show animal is his ability to get along with others —in short, good manners. These begin at home. If you've allowed your horse to become a spoiled brat, do everyone a favor and don't take him to a show. Even during his first show season, he should remain mannerly (and always manageable!) while stalled among strange horses and while moving about through confusion, noise, and strange sights. If his temperament is usually calm, he often is too interested to become upset. If he is high-strung, you must find the opportunity to introduce him to a variety of sights and sounds before expecting much of him at a show.

A young stallion may be a problem, especially if stalled next to another stallion or to a mare in season. In this case, it would be wise to bring along a tarp, wallboard, or four-by-eight-foot piece of burlap or canvas to hang on the partitions next to the disturbing influence, especially if there are spaces between the boards. He will calm down if he is unable to see his neighbor. It may be good judgment to affix a webbed stall guard also, if the stall gate is low. Fixing a crosstie in his stall will facilitate grooming and saddling, especially if he is nervous, or if you have no one to help you groom or tack up.

If you are fortunate enough to have a fair grounds in your community, you can familiarize your horse with these new surroundings before entering a show. Pick a weekend when you expect some activity there. You can observe his reactions and he can find out a bit of what will be expected of him.

If possible, come a day or two early to his first show. Lead him up and down between the barns, around the ring, and especially in front of the stands. If there will be live music, especially a loud band, be sure that he has a chance to become accustomed to it. At many show grounds in the West, chutes form one wall of the ring. Pay special attention to this area, especially if stock is milling around in or behind the chutes. Once he becomes afraid of a certain section of the ring, it is difficult to allay this fear; during his performance class, he will invariably "blow up" or shy at that spot.

If all is proceeding well up to this point, ride him in the ring or show arena. Preferably, start when there are only a few horses working—a good workout early in the morning is very beneficial and the horse won't feel overwhelmed. As it gets later, more horses will appear, and he will take them in stride. Be especially careful around show buggies. If your colt is not used to seeing driving horses, these can send him up into the grandstands on first sight and sound. Another bugaboo is the grounds crew with those spooky-looking hoses, jets of water, tractors dragging harrows or discs, and trailers carting barrels and jumps, straw, or other articles.

Of couse, because the point of bringing him to the show is to exhibit him at halter or under saddle, you will want to practice for the classes you have entered. In practice sessions, work your horse in both directions in the ring. This can be a problem, since it often happens that everyone works to the left indefinitely. During a recent show, one gentleman solved this problem nicely when he shouted, "All pretty girls reverse!" What action!

It is also easy to keep your horse practicing one thing too long. As in your basic home training, vary the exercises and plan the practice session. You and your horse should practice with the clothes and gear you intend to use in the specific class. If you intend to enter a Western pleasure class, be sure that your horse is used to chaps, rope, spurs, and two cinches (if your saddle is double-rigged). This could be an embarrassing oversight.

If classes are to be held at night, he will have to become accustomed to lights and spotlight patterns on the ground. And if he's not used to working indoors, this too can be unsettling, as it gives many horses a feeling of claustrophobia, as well as magnifying sounds and confusion.

Arriving several days early should help alleviate all these problems, as the horse has time to settle down in his new surroundings.

Training Your Horse to Show at Halter

Showing horses at halter (or in hand) becomes extremely competitive in the large, sanctioned shows. No longer do the ill-groomed, poor-quality, bad-mannered, or "rough" horses parade the ring—rather the horses are of such excellence that very few points separate the ribbon winners from the remainder of the class. If you plan to show a halter horse for either advertising or pleasure, you must elevate your total picture and performance (horse and handler) to be superior.

How do we try to achieve perfection in this area? First, your horse should definitely conform to the type accepted for the breed. He should be sound and in "show condition" (exhibiting the best of grooming, exercise, and nutrition), with the natural quality and presence of a top halter horse. The training of this paragon can help him go to the top—or to the bottom —of the line. Your choice of tack, your appearance, and the performance made by both you and your horse should also be taken into account in order to make a total visual image of beauty. You as the handler should neither detract from your horse (your grooming and attire inappropriate or shabby), nor attract away from your horse (gaudy or unusual clothes). Rather your attire should harmoniously blend into the general picture.

Another important aspect of your performance is your attitude and courtesy toward other contestants. Your horse reflects your attitude. Show him proudly with a brisk, alert walk, a free, natural, straight trot, and a show stance that shows grace, presence, and pride. Remember that the judge is looking for winners, not losers. He is judging what he sees in the ring at that moment, not what may be potentially a winner. If you use a whip, it should be thought of as an aid, to attract the attention of your horse or as an extension of your arm. Crowding other contestants, inattention to your ring steward, indiscriminate use of your whip in the area of other contestants, allowing your horse to longe and run into others, or permitting yourself to look irritated or angry—all are considered bad manners and certainly detract from your horse.

YOUR ATTIRE

Avoid the gaudy, overdressed look; instead, dress with simplicity, good fit, and neatness.

The Kentucky-type show suit in a neutral or dark color is suitable and becoming to both men and women. Your hair style should be tidy (ladies, a hair net), and make sure that your number is not obscured. Western attire is also acceptable, but again, it should be attractive and in neutral colors. Sometimes, choosing a color co-ordinated with the browband of your horse can be effective.

When choosing your kind of dress, consider whether your horse is the English type or Western. Your clothes can co-ordinate: English for the tall, animated, English-type horse; Western for Western breed or type. Standard dress when showing an English-type horse is an English saddle-suit, tailored shirt, tie, and jodhpur boots; derby and vest are optional. You may also use the vest (without derby) instead of the jacket. For Western attire, you may choose a Western suit or Western-cut shirt, Western dress slacks, and Western boots. Hat and tie are optional. Avoid the too-casual appearance of blue jeans. Such things as gloves and suitable hat finish an outfit and make you look more professional.

Wear footwear and clothing that are appropriate and that permit free motion. Trying to run the length of the arena in pants that are too tight and in boots that pinch will detract from the performance of your horse. If you do not have the conformation (and wind!) to show a horse at halter, do admit it (if only to yourself). Find a professional showman who will show for you in the arena. This, however, does not mean that you cannot train your horse to perform at halter.

TACK AND ACCESSORIES

Your choice of tack should depend on several factors—the age of your horse, the size and shape of his head, his breed, color, and sex, and your finances.

From foal age to about two years old, your horse should not be shown with a bit. Since the young horse has a small head, his halter should be fine and strong. The mature mare is usually shown with normal show halter (without bit); she may have the chain from the halter shank arranged through the halter for additional control. The mature stallion may be shown with a bit and curb strap or chain. All halters should be equipped with a throatlatch. In fact, it is required for most shows. Some show halters include a close-fitting, buckled curb strap under the jaw.

Small, very fine, well-modeled heads should have fine, well-fitted show halters. The larger breeds and big-boned horses should be shown in wider, heavier halters. The choice in leather show halters is usually black (flat or patent leather), or several shades of brown (dark oil finish). Black seems more attractive on black horses, while brown seems better on chestnuts. Gray horses look well in either. Browbands are not necessary, but can add color and keep the headstall from slipping. Halters may be plain, either flat leather or rolled, or can be enhanced with silver on the browband, or silver trim on the cheekpieces. The fit and style of the halter are more important than the price. You wish to enhance the appearance of the head, not detract from it.

How should the halter fit? It should look neither too small nor too large. The browband must be long enough so that the ears and crown piece are not crowded, but should not be so large that it bulges away from the forehead. The cheekpieces should be adjusted so that the nosepiece is about 1½ inches below the cheekbone (the adjustment of the cheekpieces can be behind the ears or on the cheekpiece itself). This adjustment can be changed for the individual horse: The noseband may be raised or lowered to improve the appearance of his head. The throatlatch should allow for maximum movement, but be snug enough to look neat.

Look at your horse's head and halter as a whole picture, and try to make it as pleasing as possible. Try adjustments, as well as several halters, and make your own comparison. Contoured halters help make an attractive picture.

In fitting the stallion bridle (with bit), take care that the cheekpieces do not overly draw up the corners of the mouth. Nor should they be so long that the bit hangs below the corners of the mouth. Follow the rules of fitting the snaffle bridle. There is no rule that says you must have a bit in a stallion's mouth. If he is well mannered and easy to control, he may wear a standard show halter.

Your halter lead should complement your halter. If the halter is oiled, rolled leather, so should be your lead. Some have ferrules, others are plain. Most show leads are from seven to eight feet long and may have a fine-link lead shank chain (twenty-four to thirty inches) attached. A halter lead with a stopper at the end gives more security. Some leads for stallions are split to fit on each side of the bit and can give a neat, finished appearance when using the stallion show halter. Leads that buckle to the halter, rather than snap, give better security. (We make our snap leads more secure by wrapping fine wire around snap and halter.)

The halter whip is about forty-eight inches long, usually black with a snapper. Some have a steel-lined center, covered with black thread, and may be nickel-capped or have a rubber handle. Some are made with flexible Fiberglas center. Dressage whips can also be used and have the added nonslip button head.

Because valuable show halters are much more subject to damage when traveling than while being worn in shows, they should be protected en route with a special halter bag or some other protective device.

Let your horse use the halter and other show equipment often enough in training sessions so that he becomes familiar with it, and so that it is comfortable to wear.

PERFORMANCE OF THE HALTER HORSE

What do we look for? Above all, the ideal halter horse should have manners, especially no tendency to kick, bite, or rear. He should walk willingly, briskly, and straight, with his handler positioned by his left shoulder, not crowding or attempting to pass in front or lag behind. His ears should be pricked, and he should move forward freely without attempting to shy or shorten his stride.

When asked for a show stance, he should respond immediately, and hold this stance (square or stretched, depending on breed) while you gain his attention. He should not creep forward. When again asked to walk and turn, he should perform smoothly, with his hindquarters tracking correctly.

When requested to trot, he should stride out straight and evenly, staying parallel to his handler, but with several feet between. Again, he should not crowd, lag, or run ahead. Most important, he should not longe around his handler. This shows poor manners and showmanship, and develops a bad habit. In some breeds, such as the American Saddlebred and Arabian, the trot is of great importance, and much time and training should go into this aspect of the performance.

While in the line-up, either side by side with other horses, or head to tail, as in most final line-ups, he should stand quietly but look wide awake. His attention should be on his handler and not on the other horses. If the class is very large, your animal should not be asked to show every minute; he can relax, but should immediately respond if the judge works the line or shows an interest in him.

CONDITION OF THE HALTER HORSE

The halter horse should be at his peak of physical perfection. Rather than padded with lard, as is sometimes thought to be proper to show well at halter, he should be in top physical shape. His muscles should be developed and hard, his coat shiny, his manner alert and willing. This can't be accomplished with a can of coat spray the day before the show. It's the result of a balanced and nutritious diet combined with good grooming and a regimen of well-planned exercise—beginning months before the show.

TRAINING TO SHOW AT HALTER

Many months before your horse's first show, you should designate a time for the in-hand training—usually after longeing and before riding or driving. The edge will be off him and yet he will not be tired mentally or physically. Train in tack similar to what you will use in the show ring, or use his show tack. Just as a dog learns to distinguish his obedience from his conformation tack, so can a horse. This conditions him mentally for the task. Possibly he already leads well; if not, general retraining is in order. You should have a flat area with good footing and adequate room to move with minimal outside interference, at least at first.

We use two leads in the initial training sessions (not using the stallion halter). One is attached to the cavesson, while the other has a chain on one end that passes through the side halter rings, providing a curb chain effect. This is used to reinforce the message that you convey with the normal lead—that is, you ask for a halt by gently tugging on the normal lead; if the horse does not respond, you give a sharp tug on the chain lead. This

One lead is arranged with a chain passing through the halter ring on the left side, under the jaw, and attached to the right halter ring. This lead enables the trainer to reinforce a command given with the normal lead. However, the arrangement can be severe and should be used with care on a youngster; overuse or too-rough use can make him head-shy and frightened of human contact. (Photo by Sandy Whittaker)

will be startling and may be painful, causing him to toss his head or even rear. But it makes the point that obedience is expected. He will probably respond to the normal lead when next asked to slow down or to halt. The chain lead can be used to correct charging forward, biting, or other bad habits, such as longeing around you. Make sure that the placement and type of chain is such that it will tighten and release easily; otherwise it will not be a training aid. Avoid tugging the chain lead too roughly or too often, and be especially careful with young animals. If you frighten the horse, or cause him pain that he does not understand, you will lose his confidence and create far more problems than you were hoping to correct. Incidentally, if he should rear, your normal lead shank can pull him down before he goes over backward. Thus the use of two lead shanks can be a safety factor as well as a training aid.

After adjusting your halter and leads satisfactorily, take your whip (longeing or long whip without a snapper) and stroke the horse gently. He should respect the whip and move away from a definite whip aid; however, he should not fear it. If he is afraid of the whip, you must work him without one until you have his confidence and he has learned he has nothing to fear, either from you or a whip.

His first lesson should consist of leading in long, straight lines, preferably close to a long wall or fence. This will help keep him straight. You will be on his near side. Hold the normal lead in your right hand, at shoulder height; don't drag his head down or raise it to an unnatural position. The whip should be in your left hand, along with the chain lead. Only in case of misbehavior will you use the chain. Walk him briskly, using the whip below his hocks if necessary. Your horse should appear alert and calm, not jazzed up and frightened about what may happen next.

When he walks confidently in straight lines and will stop with a minimum of pressure on the normal lead, walk him down an imaginary center line. Because you will not have the wall for a guide, take care that he doesn't turn toward you with his forehand and away with his hindquarters. Nor should you allow your use of the whip to encourage him in this. Use only as much aid as you need, and place your whip correctly. Return to the wall if he does this two-tracking. It is not desirable and can become a habit that will restrict his gait, make for an all-over unpleasant picture, and prevent the judge from accurately determining his action or conformation.

If you have a problem with your horse walking or trotting ahead of you, use the whip as a barrier. You can either bring the butt of the whip around in front of his chest, or if more positive action must be taken, snap the end of it strongly against his chest. It is important that you don't pick at your horse when punishing him—give him one or two good cracks and leave him alone. He should not be afraid of you or the whip, but should respect and respond to your aids immediately. You are now creating desirable habits.

When you are satisfied with his walk and halt, near a fence and away from one, you may start perfecting his trot. He should neither pull ahead of you nor get overly excited. Trot near a fence and in the middle of a large area. Try to stay as far away from your horse as possible; he should trot parallel to you, four to six feet away. This positioning gives the judge maximum chance to see his action.

Work for an even, balanced, straight, free trot. He will need lots of practice and you will need lots of wind. If your own knee action is exaggerated (high), your horse will tend to mimic you. When you have given him a good basic education in leading at the walk, the trot should follow easily. If you do have problems, however, ask a helper to reinforce the trot by running directly behind the horse, encouraging impulsion straight forward; this will assist in the initial stages, and is especially helpful if the use of the whip tends to make the horse trot sideways.

During this work with walking, trotting, and halting, you can begin on the show stance. Most breed halter horses are expected to stand squarely on all four feet. To be square, his cannon bones should be perpendicular to the ground. Make sure he doesn't spraddle or hold his legs too close together. Encourage him to stand absolutely motionless, but look animated —not easy! Undoubtedly you have been longeing your horse and he knows that when the whip or your arm is raised, this means halt. Building on this training concept, you can halt your horse and move directly in front of him with your hand or whip raised. If he walks or creeps forward, take a step toward him and say, "Whoa—stand!" Soon he will learn that he must stay in place until you return to his shoulder and cue him forward. You should be able to position yourself eight feet in front of him and expect him to stay in place. (See Part II, Chapter 2, for preliminary training in teaching to stand.)

When he learns this concept, you may begin positioning his feet, neck, and head. You should first position the hind feet. You may do this from his head: With the leads in your left hand, move his head away from the foot you wish to move. If you wish to move the right hind foot back, turn the horse's head to the left, down, and back. To move the front feet, again with the leads in your left hand, move the head away from the foot you wish to move, and bring the head up. You will pull the head forward to move forward, or push the head back to move back. The head and neck must be correctly positioned to successfully move one leg at a time. This will take practice.

Some breeds are expected to "park," or to stand in a stretched position. Begin with a square stance and encourage the horse to move his forelegs forward a little at a time, by tapping him on the back of the leg or urging gently with your foot, while you stand at his head. Care should be taken not to overdo this stretching, which can look unsightly and be uncomfortable for the horse. Do not expect him to stand stretched for more than a few seconds at first, increasing the time gradually.

When you can position the legs squarely, move in front of him and ask him to prick his ears and stretch his neck. The extent of the stretch you'll ask for depends on the breed. Some stretching of the neck will enhance the throatlatch and show off the head. However, this too can be overdone: You don't want him to look like an animated anteater. To help him stretch his neck, make medium contact with the halter, giving and taking. When his neck comes forward, reward him with your voice. You can also encourage him to stretch toward you by enticing him with a piece of apple or horse cake.

When positioning your horse, pick a spot in the arena where his hindquarters are slightly lower than the forehand. Even in so-called level arenas, there will be uneven areas. When the hindquarters are higher than the withers, the horse can look ewe-necked and low-backed. Some success can be gained in pricking the ears by tapping now and then lightly near the throatlatch with your whip (always keep the whip away from the eyes). Also, you can run your whip back and forth across the lead shank, similar to strumming on a violin. This can not only be a graceful movement on your part but also gain his attention.

When you feel he is ready, you can practice at halter in different environments—among other halter horses, or if possible, van to a show

Good showmanship can be quiet and graceful. Work with your horse enough to show him well, confident that together you present a pleasing picture. Debbie Hogan and Dalia (Gleannoch Farms) at the Estes Park All-Arabian Show.

grounds and work in an empty arena. Even taking him to a friend's stable will be excellent training. When he becomes steady in his habits, work him two or three times a week. If he starts to act bored, reduce your training sessions or work only on problem areas.

Training to Show in Performance Classes

CLASSES SUITABLE FOR THE YOUNG HORSE

In your colt's first season at the show, you should choose your classes wisely—that is, place him in classes that will not be too large, and in classes with requirements he has been trained to fulfill. Unless the show is fairly small, you may be wise to steer clear of open classes ("open to all horses of any age, size, or sex, irrespective of the ribbons previously won and in which there is no qualification for the rider or driver"—*AHSA Rule Book*). Enter the right animal for the right event—you should have the right type of horse for the class. Be content with a few classes for your first show. Don't overtax his physical and mental capacity.

Maiden, novice, and limit classes are generally smaller, and the horses shown in them are less experienced. In general, maiden classes are restricted to horses that have not won a first ribbon in that particular division; novice classes are restricted to horses that have not won three ribbons; and limit classes, six ribbons.

Because there are exceptions and a variety of rules involved, it's vital for any potential showman to obtain the appropriate rule book and study it carefully. Breed shows, performance divisions, and local shows all have a variety of limit classes, such as junior and senior horses (four years old and younger, and five and older), green hunter (in first or second year of showing), or jaquima class (not more than five years old, never ridden in bridle other than a snaffle bit); and there are a variety of weight, age, or height specifications. Rules are generally the same from year to year, but often have changes in some details; occasionally major revisions are made. Don't guess—go by the rule book.

Consult your premium list to see what rules will be followed (AHSA, AQHA, or other). Class specifications should be clearly defined in the premium list for that particular show. Many of these classes may be appropriate for the inexperienced show animal.

In the show ring, good manners mean willing obedience and attention to the work at hand. When training for showing, keep good manners in mind as your primary goal. No matter how well trained your horse may be otherwise, if his manners are not satisfactory, he should not appear in the show ring at all.

Proper attire can be expensive. Choose your outfit with several purposes in mind—it should look well on you, should complement your horse, and if expense is a factor, should be easily convertible to do double duty. Judy Wilder's basic outfit becomes English by changing chaps, vest, and Western hat and boots for jacket, derby, and jodhpur boots.

Western Classes

TACK AND ATTIRE

Tack and attire for your Western classes should be chosen to conform with the rules, to enhance the appearance of you and your horse, to fit and be most comfortable, and overall to create a pleasing, harmonious appear-

Judy Wilder's basic outfit of pants, shirt, and tie is made Western with the addition of hat, vest, and chaps. Such versatility contributes to speed in changing outfits for classes that follow each other closely but require different attire.

ance. A saddle too big or two small for either you or your horse detracts from your overall picture; or a saddle that is uncomfortable, or wrong for your conformation, will inhibit your performance. Since Western Pleasure classes, especially, are so popular today, competition is tough. Give yourself and your horse a chance by taking the time to create a co-ordinated, pleasing picture that will create a favorable reaction in the judge—at least he won't rule you out from the start.

Your attire should fit well and be neat and clean. Wear Western boots, pants or new Levi's, chaps, long-sleeved shirt, tie or pin, and of course a Western hat. Spurs are optional. Although gloves, vest, and chaps may be optional, your whole appearance is more professional when you wear them. Leather gloves and chaps help you to ride better, since leather on leather sticks. Most Western showmen prefer well-fitting shotgun-type chaps to the batwing type, as they give the rider a neater look, stick to the saddle better, and do not cover up the horse or flap in the wind.

Show tack and attire may be expensive, and the temptation is to save it to use only in shows. Try, instead, to choose both your tack and attire with an eye to easy cleaning and dual purpose. When properly cared for, top-quality workmanship and serviceable goods will see plenty of wear before looking shabby. Use them enough while training so that you and your horse are thoroughly comfortable performing in them. Certainly they should be clean, polished, and showworthy to appear in the ring.

PERFORMANCE

Although you have already been practicing your Western performance at home, there are some things that only a show will bring to the fore. If possible, work with other horses at home, and do as much as you can to simulate a show situation. Briefly, here are a few show problems or situations to consider and keep in mind.

Be sure to warm up your horse adequately before entering your class. This helps him proceed quietly and gives you time to adjust your tack. Avoid crowding at the in-gate. Enter the ring counterclockwise at a brisk walk, and immediately begin your performance. Although it may appear that the judge is just waiting for the entire class to enter, he is more likely already picking out performers that he thinks worthy of consideration. This is also a good time to find a spot for yourself where the judge can readily see you. Being in the midst of a mob, or cutting a small circle around the judge, does not show you to advantage. There are times when you can hold back a bit to get in position or plan your spot as you come into the judge's view.

When you are asked to jog or jog-trot, relax as much as possible, as contracting muscles (maybe you are nervous!) tend to make you bounce.

Another hint is to tie up or eliminate anything that will flap or bounce. This would include long saddle strings, string ties, jackets with fringe, even your hair style. Your rope should be neatly coiled in small loops, rather than large, floppy ones. This can be especially important if you know that your horse is rough at the trot. In a Pleasure class, you should look relaxed and comfortable. Your horse should be a pleasure: Look as though you enjoy the ride.

Do not forget that the judge can ask for the lope from either the walk or the jog-trot. In classes where the hand gallop is asked for, be sure there is a distinct difference in speed between lope and hand gallop. However, both must be controlled, cadenced, and regulated—that is, "in hand." If you are asked to go from hand gallop to walk, come smoothly to the walk with no trotting steps. If the halt is asked from the hand gallop, it should be a sliding stop as stated for stock classes, and you should stay motionless until asked to move. Be aware of these possibilities and practice them at home.

In the line-up, keep parallel to the horses adjacent to you, be alert, and keep your horse standing squarely and at attention. Leave room for the judge to walk around you—be sure your number is in evidence, and try to look relaxed and pleasant (this may need more practice at home than anything your horse does!). You will usually be asked to back your horse, sometimes individually, sometimes in large classes as a group. Here is one place where good training, expressed in a properly performed back as explained earlier, stands out especially well. If the judge wishes an additional workout, the numbers will be called from the line-up. The judge does not have to ask for every gait, but what he does ask for must be performed in both directions of the ring. You should be ready and attentive. Take a long approach to the rail so that you can be in the desired gait, speed, and balance before you perform in front of the judge. He will expect a more finished performance when you are working on the rail with a smaller number of horses. If you win a ribbon, move briskly to receive it and be courteous. "Thank you" are valuable words. A horse that has never received a ribbon will sometimes shy or balk. If possible, practice having someone hand you similar items at home while you are mounted. Above all, don't interfere with other horses and riders, be friendly and courteous, and follow instructions.

STOCK HORSE CLASSES

Stock Horse classes exemplify the most advanced form of Western training, the basis for which is an agile, willing, and basically good Western pleasure horse. Sometimes a horse that has more pizazz than Western pleasure usually calls for will be necessary. Your judge is looking for free, smooth transitions with a minimum of obvious cuing. Your horse's halts and backs should be straight and smooth, and he should not have to be lifted into his pivots, or dwell for more than a fraction of a second in running his rollbacks. His performance should be both eager and agile. In the class, it is important to run your pattern at the speed that best shows off your horse. A slower, more even performance should count for more than a fast, rough performance. The ultimate is both very fast and smooth. As in any pattern class, know your rules and pattern, and follow directions.

Reining was discussed in the last chapter, and a reining pattern is illustrated there.

WORKING COW HORSE

The Working Cow Horse class requires a classic type of horsemanship —dressage Western style. Your horse should work in balance at high speed, roll back over his hocks, outrun, turn, and outmaneuver cattle. Because that is a tall order, he must be very responsive, well versed in his basic training, able to make sliding stops, and in addition know how to rate a cow or steer. Again, some of the best training you can provide is routine ranch work. The variety of the work, the necessity to do a job, and the experience gained in everyday work with stock are invaluable.

According to the *AHSA Rule Book,* when the horse is worked on cattle, one animal is turned into the arena upon the contestant's signal, and he works his horse as directed by the judge. "Precision, ease and speed with which the judge's instructions are carried out shall be considered in rating entries. The cow work is based on the same number of points as the rein work."

According to the *AQHA Rule Book,* both cow and rein work are mandatory.

CUTTING

Most riders interested in Cutting Horse classes belong to a cutting horse association and receive their publications. Unfortunately, training the cutting horse involves financial investment for cattle, a well-fenced arena, and perhaps hiring turn-back men and herd holders. Not the least of your investments will be time and patience. Unless you expect to train horses full time for cutting, it may be wise to buy a suitable horse already trained, or to send your horse to a professional cutting horse trainer or training school (trains both riders and horses). You too, should take lessons and make use of every opportunity to test your ability. A cutting horse trainer must have a thorough knowledge of cattle and their behavior.

Working Cowhorse Pattern

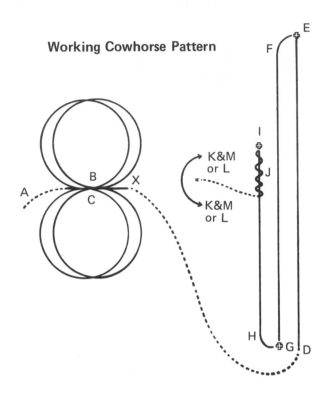

AQHA Working Cowhorse pattern. Ride pattern as follows:

A. Begin work to right,
B. First figure-eight
*C. Second figure-eight; then, after final lead change (before point marked X),
proceed to point D at walk or trot,*
D. begin run,
E. sliding stop,
F. turn away from rail and begin second run,
G. sliding stop,
H. turn away from rail and make short run,
I. sliding stop,
J. back up,
K. quarter turn to right or left,
L. half turn to opposite direction,
M. half turn to direction taken in K.

*Cattle work may be done immediately following each individual's pattern
work or immediately after completion of pattern work by all horses being
exhibited (at discretion of judge). The cattle-working procedure will be as
follows: A. One animal shall be turned into the arena and the contestant shall
hold the animal at one end of the arena long enough to indicate to the judge
that the horse is watching the cow. B. The cow then shall be allowed to run
down the side of the arena and the contestant shall attempt to turn the animal
at least twice each way against the fence. C. The cow then shall be taken to
center of the arena and circled once each way.*

(*From* Official Handbook of the American Quarter Horse Association, *1977*)

Cutting is strenuous exercise, requiring a horse in top physical shape with agility and instinct for working cattle. And he must be ridden by an expert rider—one with fast reflexes, who is alert and ready to take the stresses and strains of this type of competition.

A prospective cutting horse must have a good all-round education and adequate experience as a ranch horse. He must learn to do three things—separate an animal from the herd, drive it somewhere, and keep it from returning to the herd. As he progresses, his speed increases and more turn-back pressure is applied. Because cutting horse contests are becoming more popular, especially with the spectators, more shows are featuring this event.

ROPING

Essentials for the rodeo roping horse are maturity, the ability to stand quietly in the box, speed, a good sliding stop, and ability to work the calf. The calf roping horse is judged on manners in the box, scoring (the score is the distance allowed a calf in front of the chute before the roper may start after it), speed to the calf, rating the calf, making a good stop, working the rope, and manners while the roper returns to the horse after tying the calf.

Be sure to use proper, well-fitting equipment with plenty of padding during both training and contest work. The saddle should have two cinches. The sudden stresses received in roping work will sore a horse quickly if fit or padding is inadequate. A horse should have a thorough basic education with several years' experience in ranch work before training for roping.

Teach the horse to stand calmly in the box. Anticipating the start— whereby the horse frantically rears, jigs, breaks the barrier, or works himself into a nervous sweat—can become a difficult problem. Let him stand in the box to rest, and don't let him follow every calf. Avoid overcuing. If the horse knows what to do and is eager to start, a lift of the reins or a shift of weight is as effective as a great jab with the spurs, and he'll be less likely to work himself up in anticipation of the cue.

The horse should be unafraid of ropes: Give him plenty of preliminary training (Part II, Chapter 7), and drag long ropes as you proceed through the various gaits.

To train the horse to face and hold a calf, and for pointers on further roping work, consult books on Western training listed under "Recommended Reading."

Accepted and approved steer-roping events today include team tying, dally team roping, and tie-face roping. In the latter two events, the riders

A horse should be mature and have a thorough basic education before being trained for roping. Small, local rodeos can be less demanding than larger contests. Remember to train your horse during his first shows, and to avoid getting so carried away yourself that you push him into bad habits. (Courtesy Dave Jones)

stay mounted and the steer is not tied. In breakaway roping, often a girls' or youth-contest activity, the rope is tied to the saddle horn with a cotton string. The event is timed from the drop of the flag at the barrier to the break of the string when the calf is caught and pulls into the loop. This can be a nice event for the green roping horse, since he doesn't have to work the rope.

TRAINING FOR MOUNTED GAMES AND GYMKHANA EVENTS

Although mounted games and gymkhana events are now primarily offered for fun, many of them formerly had a practical application. The American Indian practiced the rescue race, as he knew that this skill might someday make the difference between life or death on the battlefield. The origins of the Pony Express race, cowhide drag, and ring spearing are also based in military or historical tradition.

A list of all the gymkhana events and games would be endless, since new ones are devised continually. Most of them, however, demand quick

The games horse should enjoy his work. It is easy to sour him if contest work is overemphasized. Give him variety and an all-around education. Star Deeds, owned by Dick Swanson, Ohio, Illinois, and ridden by Jean Donley. 2nd Stump Race, 27th National Appaloosa Show, Shelbyville, Tennessee. (Photo by Johnny Johnston. Courtesy Appaloosa Horse Club, Inc.)

starts, speed, sliding stops, obedience, agility, and calmness. Because barrel racing and pole bending have become the most common of all gymkhana events, and are considered big business in rodeos throughout the country, books, articles, and schools are available to teach both horse and rider. Professional barrel-racing horses do nothing but run barrels, and successful animals bring fabulous prices. Most games horses compete in a variety of events, however, as do their owners—the competition, excitement, and fun are more important than high winnings.

What kind of training does a horse need to compete successfully in these events? He *must* have a good basic education and the soundness, conformation, and endurance to bear the stress of speed, bodily control, and abrupt changes of direction. He should be old enough so that mentally as well as physically he is ready—we would say at least five years old.

Since safety is an important aspect of these games, the first prerequisite for your games horse is that he have excellent manners. Adrift in a scramble of equine and human bodies, he must be bold but have no tendency to kick, bite, or rear, no matter what the provocation. The immature horse simply does not have the experience to handle this type of situation.

The games horse should have a wide range of using experience behind him —with stock, on the trail, at shows, and in every conceivable situation. Your training should include plenty of work with other horses. Drill team experience would be excellent, both because it is controlled and because contact with other horses is inherent in the activity. He would become used to horses passing him, turning around him, flags being flown over him, different environments, and, also important, he would learn to control his speed while performing.

Your games horse should have thorough training for all-around usefulness. He will have to accept with equanimity objects you may have to carry around—poles, buckets, flags, brooms, ribbons. He should have no fear of obstacles in the arena such as wheelbarrows, tires, sacks, barrels, or cowhides. He should remain unconcerned amid flying slickers and hats, yelling and whistling crowds, bouncing balls (broompolo), and balloons. He should ground tie calmly while you and other contestants scurry hither and thither on foot, perhaps in outlandish attire, as during the costume race.

Another area of training involves mounting and dismounting under excitable conditions, as in the Pony Express race, or under unusual conditions, as in the tabletop caper (mounting from the top of a table). The rescue race requires mounting double—usually a scramble that may end with riders sliding sideways, or hanging on any old which way.

For the cowhide drag race, he must pull a person on a sack at speed —one of the more dangerous games, requiring steadiness in the horse. He should be thoroughly at home with ropes and accustomed to dragging objects of all kinds before practice at this game is attempted. Begin at a walk, of course, before asking for more speed. In the walk and lead race, the horse must lead well, whether at walk, trot, through obstacles, or over a bale of straw. For the trailer race, your horse must learn to enter any trailer (step-up or ramp), with or without a saddle.

These events require training at home—not only in the nature of acceptance, as outlined above, but also in that of performance. Since speed, sliding stops, flying changes, and quick turns are essential in most gymkhana events, training such as that given to the reining horse can be most valuable. Control is of primary importance. The games horse is expected to gallop at top speed, yet stop or turn on the dot. To do this, he must be light, supple, balanced, and responsive. Much of the training, if lightness and responsiveness are to be maintained, should be with hackamore or snaffle, rather than with curb bit. Don't sour the horse by overdoing practice for a specific event. Give him plenty of variety in his activity, including elementary dressage and relaxing trail work.

Last but not least, your horse must like these events. If he cannot enter into the fun and commotion happily, or if he lacks a competitive nature, he is not a good participant and it can be cruel to force him. Remember, he is an individual, too.

TRAINING FOR A TRAIL HORSE CLASS

The happy thing about training your horse for a Trail class is that it need not be just an end in itself. A horse capable of negotiating obstacles calmly, willingly, and with a relaxed alertness is a joy to own and ride any time or any place.

In this class, even more than many others, teamwork between you and your mount is required. Because he must trust you, take care not to betray his trust by punishing him unjustly, or by forcing him over an unsafe obstacle. The obstacles should be similar to, or the same as, what you would encounter in natural surroundings. Because of the great number of entrants in Trail classes today, most large shows have elimination events. The class is worked first in English or Western Pleasure, followed by the introduction of several obstacles, which are taken individually. The judge then picks the seven to ten best entrants, who will later perform before the audience. Classes are so large and competition so keen that this method of limiting class entrants is fair both to the competitors and to the audience. (Sitting through twenty Trail Horse trials can do things to one's posterior.)

Basic dressage training is very useful for the prospective Trail Horse. Most obstacles involve pivots on hindquarters or forehand, sidestepping, backing, the ability to collect, and low jumping—in other words, handiness, steadiness, balance, and responsiveness.

As important as dressage training is thorough trail training (Part II, Chapter 7). This is essential and will prepare your mount for most Trail class obstacles, including opening and closing gates (a popular feature of most trail classes), dragging objects, and familiarity with slickers, brooms, bridges, strange animals, and so on. Even so, Trail classes can present a variety of new problems, depending on the ingenuity of those designing the course. These will often include ways of getting through or around barrels, poles, tires, straw bales, or buckets by backing, sidestepping, straddling, jumping, or a combination of these. It's often best to train for these events by visualizing perfect execution of the activity, breaking this down to its simplest elements, and gradually perfecting and rebuilding those elements. One obstacle, for instance, is to back through parallel poles arranged in an L shape. First back your horse through a wide, straight set of poles. Set him up for the exercise by riding forward between the poles, stopping, and then backing out. If you encounter problems, arrange the poles so that you have a fence or wall as one side to help guide him. When he masters this, arrange them closer together. While working with the poles, also practice turning on the forehand. Combine the exercises when he is ready, turning ninety degrees on the forehand as he reaches the end of the straight poles. Finally, set the poles in the desired L

TRAIL HORSE CLASS Wyoming Arabian Horse Show – June, 1974

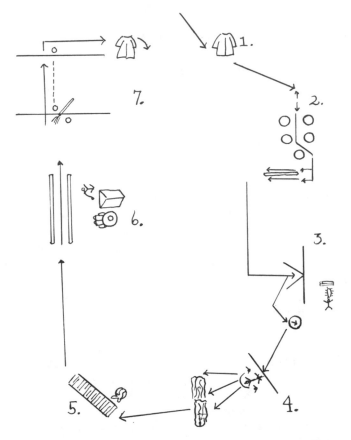

A sample Trail Horse class. Most classes include opening and closing gates; this one was designed by E. F. Prince for the 1974 Wyoming Arabian Horse Show to be different and interesting for both contestants and spectators. Directions:

1. Enter, turn left, and take slicker from attendant; put on while mounted; proceed through trail class, dropping it on the ground after obstacle No. 7.
2. Proceed to No. 2; back through barrels, going east of last barrel; sidestep to west for length of pole by straddling it.
3. Ride to No. 3; enter V of picket fence, remain stationary while wood is being cut by chain saw and while being handed piece of wood. Take wood and drop into barrel.
4. Proceed to white line, dismount on right side; lead horse (from either left or right) and run with him at the trot, jumping bale of straw. You may jump straw with horse or go out to side of straw. Remount.
5. Proceed over bridge (barrel on right has hide thrown over it).
6. Proceed between poles in front of goat and goatherder, while he raises up, stretches arms (with hat in hand), and returns to sitting position. Rider is at the walk, should not stop.
7. Ride to No. 7 and take broom from attendant (can be same person that hands raincoat at No. 1); rider hits ball with broom (no limits to hits) across the drawn lines; proceed at walk and drop slicker on ground before leaving the arena.

shape. If he has been properly schooled to leg commands, he will respond readily. Keep your weight even and look only to one side (the inside of an L shape). Turning your head back and forth will distribute your weight unevenly, making your aids or signals confusing to your horse.

You can negotiate five barrels in the same manner: first simplify the obstacle by allowing plenty of space between the barrels, and gradually make it narrower and thus more difficult.

Do not become impatient and make your horse unhappy, as he can develop a mental block toward the obstacle. You then have an increasingly difficult problem. Work a short time each day on several different obstacles as you practice ring work or trail riding.

Sidestepping is used when opening and closing gates, and for negotiating other obstacles. You may be asked to sidestep between poles, or to straddle a log and side pass along it. Start with a narrow pole or simply a line on the ground. Keep your mount's forehand fairly close to the pole. If he side passes willingly and without hesitation between steps, you will be assured more success than if you try to negotiate the pole too slowly. Again, keep your weight even and use your legs consistently. Gradually substitute larger poles and eventually a fair-sized log. We have also seen this obstacle arranged as a line of hay bales placed end to end.

Tires are a favorite trail obstacle, appearing in an infinite number of arrangements. Because a horse that has never seen a tire on the ground may consider it a great bugaboo, put some tires in his corral. Place them so that he must step over or through them to get to his grain. Some people use a large tractor tire for a hay manger. Begin riding around and through the tires when he is over his initial anxiety.

Stepping over a series of heavy poles, another favorite obstacle found in the Trail class, demonstrates your horse's ability to place his feet accurately. In training, longe him over poles at the walk and trot, forcing him to balance himself and to watch where he places his feet. The poles should be stout enough so that he has respect for them. When riding, lean forward over the obstacles, placing your weight over his center of balance. If your weight is carried too far back, his hind feet may drag or not clear the obstacle. Practice with cavalletti, as well as poles, aiming for rhythm and uniformity. When negotiating high or closely spaced obstacles, his gait should be slower and he should be more collected. Most judges will appreciate the horse that looks at the obstacles and willingly and smoothly performs, but they will mark down the horse that dashes through blindly, even though he may not touch the obstacle. You want a horse to consider his safety as well as yours.

A mailbox offers a variety of Trail class obstacles. You may be asked to dismount from the off side, leave your mount ground tied, take the mail from the box, mount again from the off side, and ride to the next obstacle. Or you might ride up to the box, open it, take your mail, close the box, and move on to continue the class. Your horse should stand patiently through the entire performance, and you should have practiced this sufficiently to know where to halt in respect to the box so that you can handily obtain the mail.

Other obstacles may involve passing frightening objects and animals, such as bicycles, baby buggies, an item of farm equipment, a smelly deer- or cowhide, a lawn mower, or a power saw in operation. Animals some- times used in these classes include chickens, goats, geese, pigs, sheep, bur- ros, and pet raccoons. The best training for these situations is simply exposure to them. Leading your horse through the animals at Fair Day, or repeatedly visiting nearby farm animals may give him the experience he needs. Similarly, using machinery near and eventually next to his corral will accustom him to the strange objects.

Still others may include a serpentine through upright poles, or tasks while on horseback. You may be asked to put on and take off a jacket or slicker, hit a ball with a broom, hoist a pail of water or sack of cans up and over the horse's back, lead your horse at a trot over a bale of hay, drag wood toward you, or pull it behind the horse.

When you believe that your horse is ready to perform satisfactorily in a Trail class, do not overdo your schooling, as he may become sour and sluggish. Refresh his memory on these exercises occasionally, while getting the bulk of your practice from a variety of ring work and trail rides over natural obstacles.

English Classes

TACK AND ATTIRE

As in Western classes, tack and attire should be chosen for several purposes—to conform with the rules, to fit and be comfortable, and to en- hance the appearance of both you and your horse so that there is an ap- pealing overall picture. Check the rule book governing your show classes to see what bits may be permissible. Generally, you'll use a light show-type bridle, and if you have a fine-headed animal, you should use a lightweight (usually three-eighths-inch) leather bridle.

More than in Western, the various English riding styles require different but co-ordinated saddle and attire. The rider using a cut-back show saddle will wear saddle-seat attire. All-purpose forward-seat and dressage saddles are usually ridden with hunt attire. However, you may ride the dressage saddle in Pleasure classes and Park classes. There are several girths acceptable for most classes, and these are made of leather, web, or string. For the young horse especially, the contoured leather girth with elastic at one buckle end is the most comfortable and most likely to avoid chafing.

The rule book will define the rules for dress; but generally, informal dress is worn for Pleasure classes, dark colors and saddle suits for more formal classes. If you can afford only one suit, it would be wise to choose a dark one, as it can be used in both Pleasure and formal. A soft hat is proper for pleasure, bowler or top hat for formal. Gloves are not required but do help your general appearance. Whips and spurs are optional. Hunt classes require breeches, hunting boots (high), and hunt cap.

Make sure your tack is clean and appropriate and that your attire fits well. Loose, floppy clothes or pants that are too short detract from an all-over pleasing appearance.

PERFORMANCE

Since you enter the ring counterclockwise at a normal trot, it helps to start the trot, and to obtain your correct diagonal, while still outside the gate. When you enter, your horse will already be balanced and cadenced. Because of lack of space and number of exhibitors, though, this is not always possible. Begin showing immediately as you enter, and keep alert and courteous, seeking your best position to show at greatest advantage.

Specific classes, such as park, hunt, and so on, have their own rules and styles, all requiring advanced training to conform to that style of riding. English Pleasure, however, like Western Pleasure, is a good basic class for the novice horse or novice exhibitor. While specialized performance is not required, there is vast opportunity for perfecting the basics.

For English Pleasure classes, the walk is brisk, flat-footed, and ground-covering. Don't hurry your horse, but do encourage free, willing movement. A good walk is considered one of the most difficult gaits to do well. Often it is ignored in training and used only to relax or rest the horse; not enough time is taken to train him in the walk.

In Pleasure classes, you are asked to extend your trot. While this means a faster trot, knowledgeable judges like to see real extension, with more action generated by the quarters. A horse all strung out and doing a racing trot does not look well. Because in this gait, especially, you will have to work harder to place yourself advantageously on the rail, try to look ahead and anticipate your most favorable spot. If someone is nosing his horse into your mount's rump, make a small circle and ease back to the rail. This can also help when you find your horse blocked by another. Take care that you don't lose form and cadence and let the gait degenerate into an off-beat trot. Your work at home should have determined just the correct speed for your horse at the faster show trot—one in which he moves freely easily, and smoothly. Pushing the horse too fast will result in an unbalanced, sprawling motion that looks forced instead of easy and ground-covering. If you are asked for the normal trot after the fast trot, gently give vibrations with your fingers and stiffen your spine (using your seat bones) to encourage the horse to slow. Doing it in this manner relaxes the horse at the poll so that he drops his nose and brings his legs under him, slowing smoothly and almost imperceptibly into his natural trot. Remember that all gaits in Pleasure classes should be ground-covering and pleasant—gaits you would use going cross-country.

The judge has the privilege of calling for a canter out of the trot or walk. It is more usual from the walk, but your training at home should prepare you for either. When being judged, your transitions count heavily; spend much time on them before coming to the show. The rule book states that the canter should be smooth, unhurried, collected, and straight on both leads. Do not rush into your canter. Here again, you do not want a strung-out, race-type gait. Mild collection and a balanced canter are looked for. You should not have to throw your weight to obtain a lead; subtle cues are all that should be necessary, and any turning of the horse's head should be toward the direction of movement. Cues may vary, however: In showing the American Saddlebred, the body is angled toward the rail. *Saddle Seat Equitation,* by Helen K. Crabtree (Garden City, N.Y.: Doubleday & Company, 1970), would help any rider showing this seat.

Though some shows ask for the hand gallop, the inexperienced show animal is usually not entered in such classes. The hand gallop is a definite gait, fourteen to sixteen miles per hour, depending on the horse's conformation. Your horse must be under control at all times. The hand gallop may be followed by a stop or walk, or even by the normal canter. These transitions should be practiced at home so that there will be no surprise if a different gait is substituted for the usual walk. Of course, the stop from a hand gallop takes more training; try to develop a smooth stop on the hindquarters.

In Jumping classes, it is even more imperative to know your horse, your class requirements, and to have prepared your animal for what you expect of him. In practice, vary your jump course rather than overdoing the size jumps you will find in the show. Cavalletti or longe work may be enough practice for two days before the show. Jumping can't be rushed. Have patience and do plenty of homework.

Your horse can acquire bad tricks at a show, because he will instinctively learn that you will not reprimand him in the show ring. Use your aids judiciously and prepare for trouble spots.

SIDE-SADDLE

In recent years, side-saddle classes have become popular with both exhibitors and audience. They are particularly colorful and crowd-pleasing events. In some classes, the rider may use her ingenuity in preparing her costume, whether medieval, Victorian, Old English, Old Spanish or Western, or modern English, but her entire appearance must be harmonious. Tack and ensemble should be co-ordinated to enhance the appearance of the horse.

When selecting tack for the side-saddle horse, carefully consider his conformation. (In fact, if you are able to select a mount especially for this purpose, you might give as much consideration to conformation as to manners and training. Choose a horse with well-defined withers; mutton-withered horses would have trouble keeping the saddle in place.) New side-saddles are costly; most riders must find an older saddle and refurbish it. Try to choose one with a broad tree if your horse has a broad back. A heavy pad should be used under the saddle to compensate for differences in shape of saddle and horse, and to keep the horse from becoming sore if his rider tends to slip off balance. In shows, however, no pad is used, except with a Western side-saddle.

There are several horn arrangements. Most common today, and the one considered safest, has two horns, both on the left side of the saddle: the leaping head curves downward over the left thigh, and the upper horn turns upward to hold the right leg comfortably. This is an extremely secure arrangement, because the knowledgeable rider, by squeezing her legs together against the horns, has an excellent grip, even superior to that of a cross-saddle. Except for situations of stress, however, she relies on balance, rather than grip, as does the cross-saddle rider. An older style of saddle has a third horn, which rises to the right side of the right knee, but this style is considered more dangerous and is not usually used today.

Beside the main girth, the balance strap is attached at the right rear of the cantle and buckles diagonally under the horse's barrel to the same location as the main girth. This should be adjusted tight enough to prevent the saddle from rocking. There is also an overgirth that keeps the right saddle flap from slapping up and down.

An acceptable bridle would be the one used by the English or Western Pleasure Horse (depending on style of saddle)—a fine, lightweight show bridle of the Weymouth type, or a neat Western curb show bridle.

In selecting and training a horse suitable for the side-saddle class, manners are of the utmost importance. Your mount must be an excellent Pleasure Horse, well behaved toward his rider, other horses, and his surroundings. He must stand perfectly still for mounting and dismounting, having no tendency to shy or kick. He should perform willingly, responding sensitively to the aids, and he should be both stable and smooth in his gaits. Overall, your training of the side-sadddle horse must be thorough and responsible. For this reason, the older, more experienced, and thoroughly steady animal is preferred to the young, flighty, unpredictable mount. The attributes of the side-saddle mount would be similar to those of the

This Western side-saddle with tooling and sueded skirt also has the English features of the leaping head or lower horn (sometimes missing from Western side-saddles) and breakaway stirrup iron designed to come apart in case of a fall. Ideally, there should be more padding in the underside of the saddle in the back to prevent the rider from having to "ride uphill."

finished Pleasure Horse; and the class is judged almost the same except for manners and elegance of attire.

Beyond this basic suitability, what further training does the side-saddle horse need? If he is not accustomed to draperies such as the skirt of the rider, or trappings of the medieval costume, it would be wise to longe him or lead him adequately before mounting. Also, he should become acquainted with the balance strap. Again, if he is longed briefly in the side-

Mrs. Anne Kimball of Roxbury, Connecticut, on Dune Swinger, a top ribbon winner in side-saddle classes. The correctness and style of the appointments and attire make an overall picture of charm and elegance. (Courtesy Charlotte Brailey Kneeland, Director of The International Side-Saddle Organization, Mount Holly, N.J.)

saddle, followed by being turned in hard circles in both directions, so that he can feel the strap, this will give you an indication of his intentions, and will probably be all the introduction he needs.

More important than these considerations is the advanced training of the horse to respond to the skilled rider—the rider, in fact, needs far more training than the horse if they are to present a correctly harmonious team. Because the rider is positioned on the near side, having in effect no right leg, this deficiency in giving leg aids must be corrected by other means. The whip may be used on the right side instead of the leg, and the rider may use the indirect rein of opposition to help place the haunches. She may also wish to use a spur on her left heel. While the horse must learn to respond to these aids, the side-saddle rider must learn to give them correctly from her new position. She must ride well balanced, her hips square to the front, most of her weight balanced on her right thigh where it crosses the horse's spine directly behind the withers. She sits in the center of the saddle, her spine exactly in the middle, erect, poised, and supple.

The side-saddle rider has a choice of sitting or posting to the trot. When riding a smooth horse, it may look better to sit; however, when riding a long-gaited or a rough-gaited animal (which would not make a top pleasure horse), posting would be more comfortable and make a more pleasing picture. In any case, care should be taken that the saddle does not rock, which would injure or sore the horse's back.

The classic instruction book on side-saddle riding, *Side-Saddle,* by Doreen Archer Houblon, is still the standard text on this style of riding. With the renewed interest today, *Side-Saddle News,* edited by Charlotte Brailey Kneeland, the founder and director of The International Side-Saddle Organization, keeps readers up to date on clinics, seminars, and all phases of side-saddle riding. With adequate training for both horse and rider, the side-saddle pleasure horse presents an artistic, graceful, and attractive picture, reviving an era of elegance and femininity.

DRIVING

In training for Driving classes, safety should be paramount. Don't attempt to show until your horse is stable and experienced enough to undertake this class. A few trial drives at a fair grounds or small show would be wise before any large competition. Watching other horses in harness helps too. Because a panicky horse can cause a disaster in a Driving class, be sure to put in plenty of driving time and gain a variety of well-controlled driving experiences.

The rule book specifies that a suitable two- or four-wheeled vehicle be used by the Pleasure Driving Horse. The type is optional to the show committee, but must be specified in the prize list. In Formal driving, a four-wheeled show vehicle must be used.

When considering Driving classes, it is important that you know whether to enter Formal or Pleasure. Formal classes require brilliance and animation, whereas the Pleasure Driving Horse should demonstrate good manners with a naturally free, easy, ground-covering action. As a parallel, the Pleasure Driving Horse is to the Formal Driving Horse as the English Pleasure Horse is to the park horse. Park or three-gaited action cannot be trained in—it's a matter of temperament and inborn natural action.

Your Pleasure Driving Horse should be just that—a pleasure to drive, and this should be apparent in the class. He should stand quietly, back willingly, and work happily in the company of other horses. Driving requires that you use good ring generalship. Plan ahead and use constant and careful adjustment on the rail. When reversing, change direction across the arena, and be very alert to the movements of the other fellow.

In Formal Driving, your whole performance should look finished. You should be the picture of pride and self-assurance that can come only from confidence in your horse's training, your own driving ability, and your use of proper equipment and attire. Your horse should hold his gait, stand quietly, and know how to back. Three strides are enough; but it is vital to back straight. When several buggies are lined up close together, crooked backing can cause a calamity. It is more difficult to back a four-wheeled vehicle than the two-wheeled pleasure cart. If your overcheck is too tight, it will be more difficult to back your horse, as he will be unable to round his back properly and get his legs under him.

4-H, FFA, and Other Youth Programs

For many years, 4-H and FFA programs have encouraged horse husbandry and improved horsemanship and horse care by our youth. These are excellent programs, which provide incentive, knowledge, and leadership. They usually insist on demonstration of achievement by participation in 4-H and FFA shows.

Unfortunately, however, not all the rules in 4-H are standardized by the states at the present time. Although there are basic similarities, on the whole, each state makes up its own manual. Even so, except for show ring technicalities, methods of training are not in conflict with those presented in this book, and safety is always emphasized.

It is possible to obtain horse publications prepared by the Federal and State Extension Services in co-operation with the National 4-H Service Commission and the AQHA for use in connection with the 4-H Horse Project. These publications are well written, concise, and contain a wealth of information on just about everything that involves the horse. Guidebooks help 4-H leaders to supervise individual projects, and the required record-keeping is a fine way for members to learn the everyday practical management of livestock. Many 4-H shows now do follow AHSA or AQHA rules.

Many breed organizations recognize the need to help our youth become horsemen and horsewomen. To this end, the promoters of these breeds gather material and formulate youth programs. Not only is this worthwhile for our young horsemen, but also these youngsters will go on to promote their specific breed. They will be knowledgeable not only in background of the breed but also in general management practices. Some breeds that sponsor youth programs are the Appaloosa Horse Club, The International Arabian Horse Association, the American Quarter Horse Association, and the American Morgan Horse Association.

Learning from Horse Shows

Both you and your horse can learn much from showing, especially if you are both novices. There are schooling shows as well as regular horse shows, and the former are excellent for the novice horse and horseman. Increase your knowledge and experience gradually; don't spoil everything by rushing. Enter only classes in which you feel confident that you and your horse are competent. If you have shown extensively, but this is the first show for the animal you have trained, the show is like a test—how well and how thoroughly have you done your homework?

The show ring provides you with a basis to work from. How does your horse compare with the others? If you came in poorly, work out the reason, analyze your faults, and determine what your winning opponents did (or didn't do) that made the difference. Use the experience as a standpoint from which to improve. Above all, don't take your loss out on your horse. Perhaps you were not prepared for that class, or perhaps *you* rode the class badly, possibly by interfering with your horse or not positioning yourself correctly.

Although winning a ribbon should not be your main goal in showing, still, don't kid yourself. If you enter a show, you hope to win—therefore prepare yourself and your horse to this end. Aim for the top—but take it gracefully and think constructively if you don't always make the winner's circle.

Eventing and Combined Training

In recent years, eventing and combined training have become increasingly popular as competitive, show-type contests. The Three-Day Event begins with dressage competition on the first day. On the second day, the same horse and rider compete in a cross-country speed and endurance contest including steeplechase and cross-country jumping, and on the third day, they compete in stadium jumping. At lower levels, the three phases (horse trials, one-day event, or three-phase event) may be held over one or two days.

Eventing requires and tests the versatility of horse and rider. Prerequisites are adequate conformation, maturity (physical and mental), and ability. The event horse is not a specialist, but he must be an outstanding all-round athlete. His basic training must be thorough and varied, and he should be properly conditioned for the stress involved. Give as much care to his mental attitude as to his physical capacity.

The dressage phase of the Three-Day Event demonstrates the thoroughness of his basic training. Although he will not give the finished performance of the specialist, he must be above average, and this phase of eventing should be given adequate time and training. Usually, the dressage tests asked for in the Three-Day Event are the more forward-riding exhibitions such as working trot and medium trot, with little collection or extension. The dressage tests are ridden in a double bridle, whereas the stadium jumping and cross-country competition make use of the snaffle. The horse should feel at home in both.

The show jumping and cross-country phases involve combination, water, and spread jumps. Adequate training in these obstacles is a necessity. Participation in drag hunting or cub hunting outings would help the young horse to gain cross-country experience. In any case, he will gain confidence if allowed to follow the lead of a mature, experienced horse over a relatively easy cross-country course.

While a calm, elegant, obedient way of going is necessary for the dressage phase, it takes a bold, courageous animal to complete the grueling cross-country phase. To promote all this in one horse is a difficult training task.

To train for the Three-Day Event requires that the trainer have an excellent basic position and lots of experience on the flat as well as in jumping events. The trainer must be sensitive to the needs and feelings of his mount as well as have the known-how to spot developing faults.

Training to Load in a Trailer

In our mobile society, horses travel almost as much as their owners. Certainly it saves time and frustration for a horse to enter a trailer willingly. Training the foal to load was discussed in Part II, Chapter 1. If a horse learns to lead willingly at an early age, he is usually set for life, barring any unusually frightening incidents, and this is certainly easiest on both horse and trainer.

Trailer training can usually proceed without difficulty, even with the older horse, when the trainer employs a sound basic investment of preparation, patience, and common sense. It is surprising that these three elements are so often bypassed when the results are so predictably disastrous. Within the bounds of preparation, patience, and common sense, a variety of different methods may be used, depending on the disposition of the individual horse. A professional trainer may have a method he prefers, but he'll be ready to try, or devise, a different method, or even a number of these, to suit the horse he's working with and to get him to load quietly.

Only after all these are exhausted will he resort to get-in-there-now-or-else techniques.

Occasionally it is necessary to load a horse without adequate time for training, as may occur if you buy a horse at a sale. He's got to be loaded *now*. Still, preparation, patience, and common sense will make the job easier. Let's look at some of the methods.

PREPARING THE TRAILER

If you take the time to prepare the trailer properly, you'll eliminate a host of potential problems and keep others to a minimum.

First, consider location: Where should it be parked? If possible, place the trailer in an enclosed area. If the horse should get away from you, at least he'll be easy to catch. If you plan to use the feed method of self-training (see below), the trailer should be parked in a feeding corral, out of the way and yet readily accessible, and placed both so that the horse can enter and exit without difficulty and so that he won't be hurt moving around the outside of it. As an aid to loading, the trailer may be parked at the door of a stall, the end of an alleyway, or by a gate or fence within your corral system. This may eliminate possible run-out to one side. Be sure the trailer is close enough to the barrier so that the horse can't run around it to freedom, or attempt to go through an opening and injure himself.

Be aware of other location problems. Place the trailer out of the wind, if possible, or at least so that wind doesn't make a howling or moaning noise in it. Such noises, rattling sounds made from wind blowing a chain or rope against the side, or movement of any kind occasioned by the wind, will discourage a horse immediately. Also, it may be wise to have the back of the trailer facing the sun, if possible. If the inside is well lighted, it will be less fearsome—more like a stall than the Black Hole of Calcutta. If you plan to load at night, make sure the lights work on the inside. Give yourself every advantage.

Second, make the trailer as solid and steady as you can. Block the wheel securely and make sure the hitch jack, if not hitched up to a vehicle, is well situated and stationary. With a step-up trailer, we take a railroad tie or similar heavy wood block, and place it as a step, half under the trailer and half out. The tighter it wedges in there, the better. We then cover the tie with dirt to make a solid ramp. The rewards of this arrangement make any extra time involved in its construction well worthwhile. For one thing, it looks safe to the horse and predisposes him to be agreeable. For another, it helps to deaden the hollow sound of the trailer, so that when he does step in, his own footsteps don't scare him out again. And most im-

Loading a foal in a trailer. First, block and prepare the trailer. Then have calm, knowledgeable assistants grasp hands behind the foal and gently push him in.

portant, it keeps his hind feet from slipping under the trailer, which can happen easily if his forehand is already in and he is pulling back against a rope, or if he is trying to back out. This can be a disastrous position because the horse can move neither forward nor back. Even if he does extricate himself, he will have skinned his cannon bones and probably frightened himself enough never to want to see a trailer again.

The third consideration in preparing the trailer is to inspect it for trouble spots. Use a nonslip rubber mat on the floor. Incidentally, the floor should be cleaned frequently and inspected for soundness, as wood flooring will rot out. Examine the inside for projections, screw ends, or other points that may cause injury. Small projections may be covered with tape. Check the upholstery and the edges of partitions; long, sharp edges can be covered with a split rubber hose. We attach permanent, adjustable ropes to the mangers rather than use the chain leads that come with some trailers; in case of emergency, a rope can be cut. "Panic snaps" (a safety snap that allows release when under tension) are excellent on manger leads. Tail chains should be covered with rubber hose or plastic. Keep them clean: Many horses lean back against them and can rub themselves raw if the chains are allowed to become rough or crusty. Use burlap sacks to wrap tail lights, license plates, and other dangerous projections on the outside back of the trailer.

Fourth, except for the loading door, close or fasten all doors, gates, partitions, and other movable parts. Tie up both tail chains out of the way so that they don't bump against the horse or make noises in the wind. Be sure the center partition is securely fastened. The feed door, escape door, and any other openings at the front of the trailer should be closed unless you intend to precede the horse and lead him in (only with a well-trained horse that you know well). If you must use a long rope to pull the horse in, and it must come through the feed door, at least close the door as far as possible so that it doesn't appear to be an opening. Some horses will enter the trailer and immediately stick their head out any opening, often scraping or injuring themselves. Others, forced into a trailer, hit the panic button and may try to escape by the unlikeliest means. We know of one case where a mare reared into her feed box, jamming her head and forelegs through the feed door. It took some doing to get her uncorked without serious injury!

Leave the loading gate or door open, either with someone to hold it, or else fixed so that it won't swing itself closed at a critical point; you should be able to close it quickly, however, when you're ready. Usually, if you're hauling just one horse, this will be the left door, as it's easier to keep track of the horse in the rear-view mirror when he's on the left side of the trailer. Leave the other gate closed but not latched, so that your helper may get in and out easily.

Finally, be prepared with extra rope, both long and short, preferably cotton to avoid burns. Place feed in the manger—good-quality hay and some of his favorite grain—both to serve as a reward for entering the trailer and to keep him occupied once he's there.

SELF-TRAINING TO LOAD IN A TRAILER

This involves gradual familiarization, which works especially well for young or inexperienced horses. Park the trailer in a small corral, taking all the preparatory steps mentioned above. Be sure the one door is fastened open securely. After a day or two, give the horse his grain on the tail gate or rear edge. At each meal, creep the feed forward. He'll soon put in his forefeet, and finally enter his whole length in order to get his feed. He actually trains himself and you needn't even be there; you can check his progress by the absence of his feed. When he enters the trailer willingly to eat grain in the manger, continue the gradual training; speak to him, enter the trailer on the other side, close and open doors. When he seems calm and ready, close his door and let him stand and eat while you bang on the outside of the trailer and accustom him to its sounds. Soon take him for a short drive.

For this method to be successful, the horse must come to the trailer free of associations; he will then make pleasant associations with the trailer as time progresses. A horse that has had unhappy experiences, however, probably won't get close enough to the trailer to even see the feed. We have witnessed scared, stubborn horses that would not go near a trailer even though they hadn't eaten for three days.

PATIENCE AND COMMON SENSE

There is not always time and opportunity for the self-training approach, even if it always worked. But before going on to other methods, keep several things in mind. Patience can be a prize even if you're in a hurry. If it takes you ten minutes to load a horse—nine while you and the horse stand there considering the problem, and one when he finally decides that you're calm and unconcerned, therefore the trailer has to be harmless, and therefore he walks right in—you're way ahead of the big project where six men with four ropes and a bullwhip manhandle the horse in (in ten minutes), and he's sweating, scraped up, and terrified, and really goes to pieces when it starts to move. There are times when it seems that chances of loading a horse easily are in inverse proportion to the number of people present. It also seems that nothing draws a crowd of "helpers" like leading a horse to an open trailer. They all know a method that "works every time," and all the fuss and shouting can work up a horse before the action even begins. You may well be better off alone. Best of all, you should have two calm, knowledgeable people who will keep quiet and do what you ask.

Don't try to rush a horse into a trailer. A sensible horse is cautious. He's not going to rush into what looks like a trap any more than you would. Give him time to look it over. If you know the horse and he knows and trusts you, chances are good that after his inspection he'll allow himself to be enticed in with grain. Some horses will load easily if there is a quiet horse already munching away in the trailer.

Remember the goal before you begin the job: The goal is to train the horse to load willingly. It seems all too easily replaced with the goal of getting the horse loaded or else. We know that if a halfhearted attempt is made to load a horse and he balks and we then give up, that it's going to be twice as hard to load him the next time. We also know that as trainers we build the horse's confidence and let each step grow out of the one before. Some horses require more patience than others, or more assurance. But it's equally important to know when to push a horse and take advantage of his hesitancy before it turns in the wrong direction. Insight and experience will have to help you make this decision.

Try all the easy ways first. After all, one of them might work. Prepare the trailer properly to give yourself the best possible chances for success, and let patience and common sense do most of the work.

METHODS OF TRAILER TRAINING

No matter which method you use to load a horse, once he is successfully loaded, make much of him, and let him eat his grain reward. Help him to back out, and load him again. If possible, do this several times, re-warding him each time, so that he will be assured of the harmlessness of the trailer. If you are unable to do this right away, be sure to follow through the next day, so that your lesson isn't lost. Repeat several times during the next few days, and take him for a short ride. Because the first sensation of motion sometimes scares the horse, we stand on the tail gate or walk beside the trailer at first to reassure him. Or, riding with a quiet, experienced horse may keep him calm until he's used to the motion. Until you are sure of his stability in loading and riding, take him for short drives often. He should eventually be as willing to enter a trailer as to enter his stall.

For the following methods of loading (methods 1 through 4), have two people help you, both of whom are knowledgeable, quiet, and willing to do as you direct. All three of you should wear gloves. Methods 5 and 6 may work well if you are alone.

1. One person should be inside the horse trailer, on the opposite side from where the horse will enter. His job will be to hold the halter rope when it is handed to him, and to entice the horse with grain. The other two people will be outside the trailer, one on either side of the horse. The person on the horse's near side (A) will hold two fifteen-foot halter ropes, each attached to the halter. One will be handed to the person inside (C); and A will continue to hold the other in case the horse backs out rapidly and attempts to run off. If he goes in easily, A will hold the rope until the tail chain is fastened, when the rope can be dropped (it can be removed when the manger tie is fastened). This rope must be long enough to hold until the horse is all the way into the trailer; if too short, A will have to let go and the horse might step on it and keep himself from loading.

2. Enticement alone doesn't always work. If the horse is known to be gentle, the two persons on the outside (A and B) may pick up one front foot and set it inside the trailer, then follow with the other forefoot; at this point, A and B may lock hands around his rump, and push and lift him in as C encourages with lead rope and grain. Most horses will not kick while you have them in this position; however, if your horse is panicky or very touchy, this may not be safe. The method usually works well for horses that are afraid of ropes, or for foals and small horses that can be literally picked up and pushed in.

3. This method involves the same three people in approximately the same positions. Attach two long cotton ropes to the outside rings of the trailer, one on each side of the entry door (use a knot you can pull loose in an instant). Arrange the ropes straight out on the ground so that the horse steps between them. Lead him forward between the ropes, hand the lead rope to C, and encourage him forward enough so that his head is inside the trailer. While C coaxes the horse, A and B quietly pick up the ropes (keep them above the hocks) and cross them behind the horse,

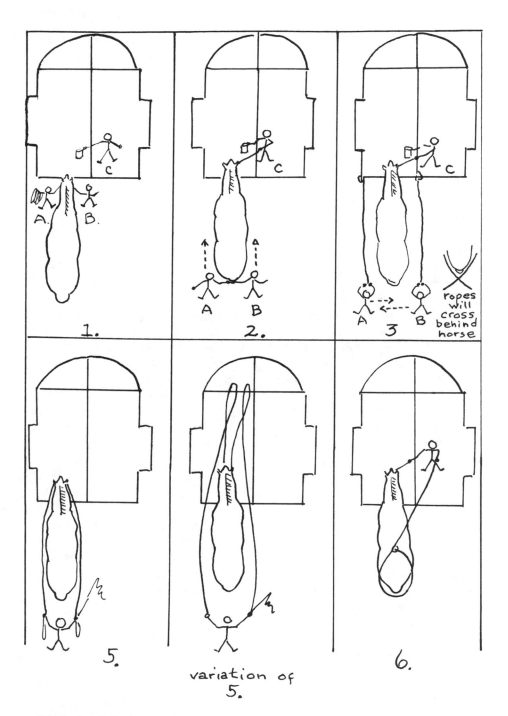

Methods of loading a horse into a trailer (numbers and letters correspond with text).

tightening the ropes around the rump. Sometimes just the feeling of the ropes will induce him to load; sometimes you must tighten the ropes and pull them intermittently. C may have to take a dally or two around an inside post—this should be done with care.

4. Sometimes a horse may be properly positioned to enter, as in the above methods, but can't be persuaded to go the final step. We've seen the extra boost accomplished by lightly touching him on the rump with an empty cardboard mailing tube, or with a broom. (When the business end of a broom was placed under the tail of one recalcitrant horse, he shot into the trailer as though intent on winning a race!)

5. We have found this method to be successful for horses that can be driven. Attach two long (twenty-five feet) cotton ropes, driving lines, or longe reins to the sides of the halter. You may prefer to put a driving bridle on the horse and attach the lines to the bit. If he is used to the whip, use one in its normal position and actually drive him into the trailer. Give him time to inspect it before asking him to enter. Then, if he seems hesitant, snap the whip and encourage him on. This is a one-man operation, except perhaps for a person to place the horse directly in line with the open door and speak encouragingly to him. One nice aspect of this method is that you can back the horse out easily when he is reluctant to leave, which happens sometimes on longer trips.

6. If you are alone, and driving isn't the answer, you might try using the come-along, as when training a foal to lead. Stand in the off side of the trailer and handle both the come-along and the halter rope. Use more pulling force on the rump rope, and only enough on the halter rope to keep him straight. You can vary this method by pulling on a rope attached to the back of the trailer and coming around the horse's rump, similar to method 3. Another variation is to stand on the near side beside your horse's shoulder. Your left hand leads the horse forward with the halter lead while your right hand holds and pulls the rump rope forward. It is important, when working alone, to know the horse you are attempting to load. You should be reasonably assured that one of these methods will work, or at least that the horse is steady enough that he won't become overly excited and panicky. It can be dangerous for both you and the horse to work alone, and should not be attempted unless you are experienced and sure of the situation.

UNLOADING

Sometimes a horse is reluctant to back out of the trailer. Even with someone pushing back on the halter rope from the feed door, he might not be persuaded to back out. He may even try to turn around. Do *not* attempt to scare him out from the front; he may rear up and hit his head, and in any case, he may be reluctant to enter again. Instead, attach a long rope to each side of his halter, as in driving, and pull intermittently from behind. Sometimes a rope around his chest pulled from behind will work.

If you are unloading from a ramp trailer, be sure to keep the tail chain fastened until the ramp is down; if the horse were to decide to fly back before you were ready, the ramp and horse would make mincemeat out of you. Also, when loading this type of trailer, always fasten the tail chain first, then the ramp. In this way, he cannot back up and run over you. If your step-up trailer is properly prepared with a railroad tie or block under the step end, the horse will have more confidence and be less likely to hurt himself when learning to back out.

FINAL CONSIDERATIONS

We use stout, strong, *short* manger ties with panic snaps; this discourages the horse from rearing into the manger. Tail chains (tail rubbers or butt chains) should be at the correct height for the horse. We do not use them for foals but tie them securely to the sides so they won't hit and scare the youngster. We discussed training a foal to load in Part II, Chapter 1. When traveling with foals, we attach a stout screen or board across the rear opening, so that if they should get loose and turn around, they can't jump out. When you travel with a mare and foal, remove the center partition if it is solid and do not tie the foal. He can then lie down or nurse. We have never witnessed a mare stepping on her foal. If you have a pipe partition in your trailer, this is even better, as the mare has something to brace against and the foal has the opportunity to nurse. Be sure there is adequate bedding and good footing.

When trailering a stallion or gelding, be sure to stop and unload occasionally so that your horse can urinate. Many times they are reluctant or unable to do so while in the trailer or when moving. This is extremely important: There can be permanent damage, or even death, if the male horse goes too long without urinating.

Use exceptionally strong tack for stallions. There are special stallion snaps for lead ropes, and you may obtain reinforced halters, or use two halters. When trailering another horse with a stallion, there should be a solid partition between the horses, both in the manger and all along the body of the trailer.

CHAPTER 2

TRAINING FOR COMPETITIVE AND ENDURANCE RIDING

Selecting Your Mount

The selection of your mount is an important consideration in distance riding. He must have the conformation, stamina, endurance, and willingness to travel for long distances under conditions of stress, or at least some pressure. Although veterans of distance rides offer different opinions concerning emphasis in their selection, they agree that the horse must have the agility, both mentally and physically, to do the job.

It's well to remember that selecting a mount is a one-sided operation. If the horse were able to choose his rider, would he select you? When you ride, train, and care for your horse in such a way that he would indeed choose you to be his rider, you are establishing a bond of mutual affection and respect that distance partners must have if they are to enjoy their work together. Make use of the horse's ability by helping him, not hindering him.

Although competitive trail riding does not require such rigorous training, nor involve the same level of stress as endurance riding, many of the same qualities should be found in both kinds of trail mount. What are some of the things to look for?

Since successful distance riding emphasizes moving over the ground smoothly and economically (using the least amount of energy necessary to produce the effect), we should select a horse with good conformation and balance, and then proceed to train him to use his potential. Versatility is important; he should be able and willing to take various conditions in stride, calmly crossing streams, jumping logs, and traveling over either deep sand or hard clay without nervous expenditure of his energy reserves.

GAITS

What gaits will he use most in distance riding? Most competitive trail rides are geared to about 5 miles per hour. Although this may seem slow (the normal walk is between 3 and 5½ mph), in reality it is not, when you

Competitive trail rides are timed so that the horse can walk on steep climbs and descents. On the flat or on rolling terrain, he must trot or canter. Regal Fire Mist, an eight-year-old Arab gelding, Ruth Waltenspiel up. (Photo by Paul Hughes. Courtesy Ruth Waltenspiel and North American Trail Ride Conference)

take into consideration streams, rocky stretches, mountainous terrain, and other obstacles. Because of the nature of the terrain in distance riding, the walk and trot are used almost exclusively. The canter or lope is used only on relatively short, flat stretches that are fairly soft and stable. In the mountains these are few and far between. Because your horse is not as well balanced at the canter, and because the concussion is greater on his forelegs, he will become tired and winded more quickly than when performing other gaits. For short stretches, however, a canter can be a welcome change.

The quality of the walk is very important in the distance horse. It may even be used as a yardstick in measuring his mental and physical potential. When selecting a mount for distance work, consider his walk carefully. Does he have a long, free stride? Or is his stride short and uneven? Do his hind legs track his forelegs or even overreach? Or do his hind feet "cut the daisies"?

You can measure a horse's attitude by his normal walk. Is he alert, watching where he is going? Or is he lazy or fretful? Constantly pushing him on or holding him back will sap your energy as well as his. You want a horse that has spirit but not a nervous or overly spirited, highly strung animal. The ideal mount will travel willingly at the pace you set, with or without company.

Does he forge, interfere, or demonstrate other structural malfunction in his gait? If so, he has some problem in conformation and could injure himself or his rider when under stress.

Because you will also cover a lot of ground at a trot, you should observe your prospect at his normal trot. This should be free and long-strided, in both fore and hind limbs. It should give the impression of great strength and demonstrate use of his hind legs for impulsion. A horse that is light on his feet is preferable to one that hits the ground with great concussion.

Although you may train your horse to be even-gaited at walk and trot, if he is straight-shouldered or muscle-bound, with short and choppy gaits, there is only so much you can do to improve him. Remember the hours, days, months, even years you plan to be associated with your horse. Is this prospect worthy in conformation, moving qualities, and temperament? If not, keep looking.

BACKGROUND

Consider his early years: Was he kept alone in a small area or was he allowed to run with other horses on a large pasture with hills, rocks, and water? As a rule, the horse that has had natural experience from the time he was foaled will be a better prospect. He will know how to get along with other horses, and he'll be familiar with rough terrain at all gaits. Buying a horse that was raised in corral or barn can bring up the question of whether he will be accident-prone. The pasture-raised horse will have proven himself one way or the other. A horse with natural, instinctive talent in handling himself and taking care of himself will generally be superior to a horse that must acquire this knowledge on top of his other training.

CONFORMATION AND SOUNDNESS

The legs and feet of a distance horse must be well-shaped and sound, free of any effects of concussion, such as side bones, ring bones, or splints. Such a horse should be free of any tendency to stumble, which may indicate poor balance. He should have weight-carrying qualities such as a short back and sturdy conformation, and he should have well-defined withers to hold the saddle in place.

Look for a long-muscled horse; avoid short, thick muscles. The thick-muscled, bull-dog type of animal will have a higher pulse and respiration because he must work harder, especially going downhill. Because lighter muscles have less trouble getting rid of the waste products caused by exertion, the conversion into energy is more efficient in the lighter horse.

BREED

Most distance riders favor one breed over others and prefer to select a horse within their favored breed. Many riders look for Arabian blood because, though such horses are relatively small and light, they are strong-boned with tremendous weight-carrying ability for their size. Some riders prefer more size.

Breed characteristics desirable in a distance horse include being short-coupled (indicative of being "easy keepers") but able to move freely with long strides, and heart and lung capacity for strenuous work. A well-proportioned head and neck aid in proper balance, and large nostrils and open throat allow good respiratory exchange. Large eyes, well set in an attractive head, are desirable because it is believed that a horse with small, poorly set eyes and roman nose often has disposition problems due to the frustration of not being able to see properly.

Breeds that have done well in distance work include Arabians, smaller Thoroughbreds, Morgans, Thoroughbred-type Quarter Horses, Moyle horses, part-Welsh ponies, Appaloosas, and some mules. Good, sound pleasure horses of any breed can and do compete successfully in competitive trail riding. For endurance riding such as the Tevis Cup, you must be more selective, and this comes down to evaluating the individual horse, regardless of breed.

SIZE AND AGE

Your prospective endurance horse must be big enough to carry your weight over the required distance. Generally, this turns out to be between 14 and 15.3 hands. If he is too small, his legs have to work twice as hard to cover the distance; because of this, it's hard to get him into a rhythmic speed he can maintain. A horse over 16 hands in size often has problems in rough country.

Most distance competitions require that entrants be at least five years old; those eight and nine are prime. Although some rides may permit four-year-olds, usually the distance is shorter and more time is allowed; such a ride would carry a junior classification. A horse should be mature before asking him to undergo the stress of a ride like the Tevis Cup competition.

SEX

As to sex, riders usually have their own preference, although again, it may come down to the individual horse. The gelding is, as a rule, more even-tempered, less subject to difficult days or easy distraction. Geldings are usually more dependable, and can be tied and ridden in company with other horses.

The stallion usually has that extra oomph or go-power (although some riders report that they fizzle out sooner), and will do well as long as he is not fretful or wasting his energy showing off to mares. He will need added attention to keep him from disturbing other horses: He must be double tied with two separate controls (perhaps with a halter and lead, and also with a neck rope); he requires special stabling at night; and there are often other special rules or restrictions for him. The stallion should be ridden and handled by a knowledgeable horseman or horsewoman who is experienced in handling stallions in general as well as this particular horse. The rules permit only adults to handle stallions.

Mares have their off days when in season, but some give no trouble, and, as long as they do an honest day's work and are willing, this should be no deterrent. Good manners are essential regardless of sex.

MENTAL QUALITIES

In selecting the distance horse, mental qualities are fully as important as physical characteristics. Although a horse may be perfectly suited for distance riding in conformation and soundness, he may be totally unsuitable because of temperament or disposition. A well-bred animal usually carries the edge for intelligence and competitiveness, and generally is more temperamentally fitted for great exertion over a period of time. A "hot" horse, however, burns out too fast; it is wise to seek the happy medium in temperament. He should be willing to go at the pace you set, be alert but also calm and sensible, and he should be handy, safe, and trustworthy. The distance horse should be gregarious in a kind way—that is, enjoy the company of both other horses and humans. Patience is a lovely quality in a horse.

FURTHER CONSIDERATIONS

In endurance competition, some vices and bad manners are allowed. In the competitive trail rides, however, this is not true. Ideally, your horse should stand quietly tied anywhere and should submit to any poking, squeezing, or feeling that the veterinarian might think necessary (including taking his temperature rectally). He should open his mouth, pick up his feet, walk and trot while being led on the halter, stand still while being mounted or dismounted, enter a trailer willingly, and be well-mannered around other horses.

Kicking, biting, rearing, charging, boring, and bolting have no place in the pleasure horse and should not be allowed in distance riding. Any horse with a vice that endangers other people or horses should not be on the trail with others. Shying may be frustrating, but a good horseman who knows his horse can usually anticipate the action and if not actually stop it, at least minimize it. Also, with experience and many miles under his cinch, the shying horse will wonder if the extra exertion is worth it.

Most important of all in selecting a distance horse is that you and your horse should like each other. It would be hard to associate with a horse you don't care for, considering all the hours of preparation that are necessary. And if you don't care for the horse, it is undoubtedly a mutual feeling. Under these circumstances, your horse (or the horse you are training) will not put out that extra something for you that produces exceptional performance. Mutual respect and fondness for each other are necessary ingredients in selecting a horse that will do well for you in distance riding.

Tack and Accessories

All tack must fit well, be clean, and be trail-tested. The key word is *tested,* in respect to training. If you wish to use a Western saddle (it's heavy, but usually the weight is more evenly distributed than with the English type), your horse must be worked many miles in one. The new Flow-Form saddle pads by Crafters have pockets of urethane that form a self-contouring cushion between horse and saddle. Smooth, clean, well-fitted padding is essential. Saddle strings, a second cinch, saddle bags, and other accessory items must become familiar to the horse. If the terrain is mountainous and you've discovered that he should wear a breast collar, breeching, or crupper, be sure that he wears it often enough so that you have found out whether any of these items will rub or cause problems. You can make sheepskin tubes for your cinch, collar, and breeching that may either be brushed vigorously and kept clean or can be removed at the end of a day's ride and washed. They will then be clean and dry to save your horse from irritation the following day.

English saddles must also be tested and may also need a breast collar or crupper. It is not as easy to tie coat and extras onto an English saddle, but some semi-military saddles have convenient rings that may be used. If you have an English saddle that you plan to use exclusively for trail riding, you may find it worthwhile to take it to a harness shop and have it adapted for carrying extras.

Longe your horse in full gear, including canteen, tied-on slicker, rope

Ruth Chase Tyree and Dolly on the Tevis Cup Ride. Ruth wrote of this picture: "This mare, Dainty Rad 16406 (Dolly), 15 years, 14.2, has done all sorts of things—dressage, pleasure, trail class, costume, distance. But I feel that the 100-mile-in-one-day Western States Trail Ride at Auburn, California, has been a supreme training achievement. We were at the Emigrant Monument on top of the Sierra Nevadas, about 20 miles out. As you can see, we'd been working!" (Photo by Barieau, courtesy of Ruth and Woodson Tyree)

hobbles, and whatall, before riding if you are not sure of his reactions. Then ride him with all the necessary gear to make sure you have balanced the load correctly. Proper weight balance is especially important if you are on an overnight ride (not necessarily a competitive-type ride) and carrying sleeping bags, pots and pans, feed, or whatever. If you intend to use hobbles, he should of course have experience in wearing them. Take a poncho and extra jacket, along with hat, gloves, and other items to prepare for a weather change. Check Part II, Chapter 7, if your horse needs training to carry these and other items associated with distance riding.

Wear running shoes if you plan to "tail" your horse. In this case, you train your horse to work ahead of you, being guided by a line to his halter (or bit), while you are pulled up steep inclines by holding onto his tail.

Endurance riding allows you to "tail" your horse—have him move ahead of you and pull you up steep inclines as you hold onto his tail.

Will you use bridle or hackamore? What bit will you use? Many horses that go well in a riding ring in a snaffle bit will see all that distance in front of them on the trail and need more restraint than a snaffle can give. On the other hand, some horses that may need a full bridle for satisfactory ring work will enjoy the freedom of a snaffle on the trail. And some horses may do best in a hackamore, either Spanish bosal type or with hackamore bit. Experiment with and thoroughly test a variety of gear until you find the very best equipment for your distance horse. Make sure you know how to adjust it to control your mount properly and to afford him the greatest comfort.

Since there are no hard-and-fast rules as to kind of tack, some folks may use an English or cavalry saddle in conjunction with a Western hackamore, or invent some other combination. Many endurance riders take the saddle horn off a Western saddle; others may alter their Western saddle by putting the stirrup fenders under the skirt rather than over the skirt. Many riders use wide-tread, lightweight aluminum stirrups to let them stand in the stirrups more comfortably. Use whatever kind of outfit is most comfortable for you and your horse—performance is what counts.

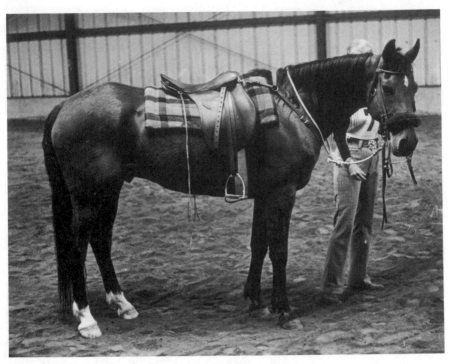

Experiment to find the tack that works best for you and your horse, whether English, Western, or a combination of the two.

Training and Conditioning
the Distance Horse

When your selection of a distance horse has been made, you may begin developing and promoting his special attributes. In this stage of specialized work, training and conditioning go hand-in-hand. As we stated earlier, everything you do is training: you must think of your conditioning program in this same light. Perhaps your horse loves to run up hills; since you feel this might help to muscle him up, perhaps you don't discourage him. But is this good training for the distance horse? Should he form the habit of running up every hill? If your answer is no (which it should be), muscle him up in another equally good way that will not confuse him in his training. Your riding habits and methods of training and conditioning must be sound and based on a firm foundation.

The horse that has been worked regularly will not need as much time to prepare as will the unfit horse. Similarly, the horse that has been out on range or a large pasture will take less time to condition than the stabled horse, assuming that both have had the same amount of work. When planning your training schedule, consider all the factors, such as age, need for more training, improving gaits, general condition of health, temperament, and the stress involved in the competition you choose. Decide how much time you can give *per day* and, depending on these factors, adhere to a schedule of weeks or months. Crash programs in this equine endeavor are not successful.

BASIC PROCEDURES OF
TRAINING PROGRAM

In Part II, Chapter 5, we proposed a daily program of longeing, arena work under saddle, and a short trail ride. This is an excellent beginning program for the distance horse.

Longeing. At this stage, longeing should be geared to improving the walk and trot. Longe with two reins as explained in Part II, Chapters 2, 3, and Part III, Chapter 1 (long-reining) if the horse needs work on lateral flexing or on walking out freely. In the trot, aim for a long stride and even tempo. Educated longeing can help the rough-gaited horse, unless the problem is due to conformation. It is not necessary to work on the canter unless you are having problems attaining the correct leads. Longeing at the trot will strengthen motor muscles and lung capacity.

Longeing need not be boring. When training for distance riding, include in the longeing: cavalletti work (Part II, Chapters 2 and 6) to improve balance and judgment of distance, as well as length of stride; and longeing over inclined and uneven terrain, as well as on various surfaces, such as sand, mud, through puddles, over a ditch, through tall grass or weeds, and so on. The horse will learn to pay closer attention to the ground, place his feet surely, and balance himself confidently. This will help him to maneuver over difficult terrain with the additional weight of a rider. When longeing, always use a large area and a long line; constricting a horse to a short longe line will shorten his stride.

Arena training. Again, improvement of the walk and trot under saddle is the main goal of your arena training. In order to conserve his energy over long distances, your mount must be able to travel a straight line, bend or flex laterally when turning, extend and collect when asked, work equally well on either diagonal or in either direction, and obey aids willingly and instantly. The overall conditioning time can be shortened by active ring work in the areas especially needed by your horse. To avoid wasted or aimless time in the arena, write out your lesson on a three-by-five card that you can stick in your pocket. Here is a sample card:

Walk around arena in both
directions, halting in predesignated spots

Change rein and walk large
voltes (15'-20'), bending horse
in both directions

Do some reverses, figure 8's

Walk down center, walk across
diagonals, halt

Circle half arena in both
directions at trot, changing
through the circle

Slow trot (collected—alternate
with extended trot on long sides
or through diagonals)

End with exercise he likes—
cavalletti work at walk and trot

You might carry the same card for several days, alternating your sequence and concentrating on those exercises that most need work. Chapter 5 in Part II, and Chapters 2 and 3 in Part III will help you to plan exercises for your horse that will not only improve his performance but will also keep him interested and alert.

On the trail. The last part of the training session will be out on the trail. Because most horses enjoy this tremendously after the concentrated effort of longeing and arena work, you will be contributing to an alert and receptive mental attitude as well as providing trail experience.

Most of his trail work had best be attempted alone; you and your horse are a team, and his concentration should be on you and your mutual effort. Occasionally, however, it is a good idea to ride with others, as this, too, is an important part of his training. While working with another rider, or a group, change your position within the group frequently. Your mount should be content to move in front, at the end, or in the middle. If you were to ride him always in the lead, he could learn to become frustrated at seeing horses ahead of him; he would tend to wear himself (and you) out, perhaps by pulling, jigging, and not keeping an effortless, even gait. The distance horse must be relaxed and not fret, which is a waste of his energy.

As you both progress in training and conditioning, you can "feel" your way along as to how much longeing or ring work you need. Gradually do more and more work out on the trail. One refreshing way to practice arena exercises is to find a level cleared area along the trail in which to work on figures, extension, collection, transitions, and so on. Eventually, the longeing and arena sessions may be used only on days when the weather makes trail riding impossible (if it's merely unpleasant, you should both get used to it), or on his vacation days, when you wish to relax the training without disturbing his metabolism. To allow unscheduled days of complete leisure will throw the entire program off balance when conditioning the athlete.

You will be gradually stressing your horse, increasing his ability to trot for long periods over varied terrain, including up and down steep grades, and developing his motor muscles, wind, and back muscles, as well as hardening the hide on his back.

See "Recommended Reading" for more on conditioning programs.

TEMPERATURE, PULSE, AND RESPIRATION—OR TPR'S

When a horse is under frequent stress, he must be checked regularly and thoroughly. Of course, you can tell that if he is losing condition, has a poor appetite, or is unresponsive, he is being overworked (unless you find a health condition causing this). But a more accurate daily check is needed, not only for health reasons, but also so that you can learn exactly how your horse operates—how best to use his potential while avoiding unnecessary stress. TPR's, the record of temperature, pulse, and respiration, are the indicators used today by riders, judges, and veterinarians to determine stress and its effects. These are not absolute figures, but, rather, relative figures; to be of use, they must be taken accurately and then be read accurately in relation to each other. Of the three indicators, pulse and respiration are used most often; temperature is not usually considered in today's competitive rides unless warranted by special circumstances. Nevertheless, the trainer should know how to use and evaluate temperature readings.

The goal of training for distance contests is to bring the horse to his peak of condition just about the time of the competition. Soundness and condition are interrelated but are not identical. Condition relates to the horse's recovery rate after stress, as indicated by his TPR's, desire to eat and drink, signs of fatigue, and signs of colic or azoturia. Soundness relates to his tendency toward lameness, tender back, saddle sores, filled tendons and to such basic conformation faults that stress would accentuate.

HOW TO TAKE TPR READINGS

Respiration—the rate of breathing—can be measured by watching the horse's flanks or nostrils. It is usually easier to watch the flanks and count either when the stomach comes up (inspiration) or when it goes down (expiration). Use a good watch with a second hand, and count the number of exhalations in one minute. Because it is difficult to keep a horse quiet for a full minute to get an accurate count, you'll probably want to count for 15 seconds and multiply by 4. Don't put your hand on the horse's flank, however, as this can be distracting.

About sixteen breaths per minute is *average;* your horse may be breathing normally at rest anywhere from eight to twenty-four breaths per minute. His normal rate will be higher when there is exciting activity around him than when he is home in his stall, even if he is standing completely at rest in both cases. Find the normal respiration for your horse under differing circumstances.

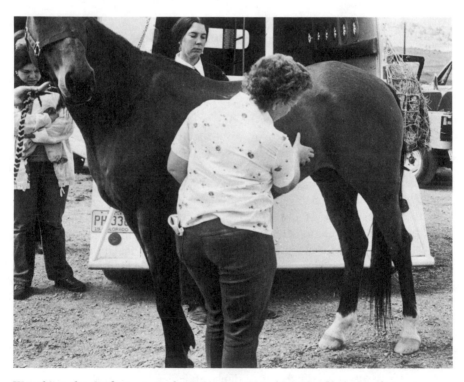

Watching the flanks to record respiration. Touching the flank can distract some horses and cause an inaccurate count; others won't mind.

Pulse, or heartbeat, can be measured with a stethoscope, or can be felt with the fingertips the way a person's pulse is measured at the wrist. One of the easiest places to feel the pulse is along the jaw where the external maxillary artery crosses the jawbone (feel along the bottom of the jawbone for a small cord—with light pressure on it, you should feel a steady beat). Another place is inside the left elbow with the back of your hand flat against the rib cage. Other points include the pastern above the heel bulb, the root of the tail, and the temporal artery near the eye.

Count for 15 seconds and multiply by 4 to find the number of beats per minute. Forty-two is about average for a healthy horse at rest. Again, there is a wide range of normal pulse rate, though it will usually fall within 28 to 50 beats per minute.

Temperature is taken rectally. Any rectal thermometer will do, but a veterinary thermometer is heavy-duty and longer than one made for humans; also, it has a loop in the end to which a string may be attached. Stand against the horse's left hip, pull the tail toward you, and gently insert the thermometer (coated with Vaseline) into the anus.

The normal temperature at rest averages around 100.0 degrees Fahrenheit. *Your* horse may be normal at 99.5 or 100.5; find out. When the temperature rises more than 1.5 degrees above normal, you should consult your veterinarian. Many problems can be controlled before they become serious if your vet is notified when the temperature starts rising.

UNDERSTANDING THE READINGS

When you know your horse's normal temperature, pulse, and respiration, you are ready to consider his TPR's (or P&R's) in relation to exercise. When under exertion, his TPR's will rise. Temperature may go up two or three degrees, respiration may go to 80 or 90, pulse may rise to 115 or more. What is important is the recovery rate—how soon they return to normal. When a horse is in good condition, his TPR's should return to normal (or nearly so) in 10 minutes.

What happens if a horse is overstressed? At rest, the ratio of pulse to respiration is about 3:1 or 4:1. If this P&R ratio closes at elevated levels, it is an indication that you are pushing your horse too hard. The danger level is reached as the P&R ratio closes or goes beyond 1:1—say, pulse 100, respiration 120—even after a 10-minute recovery period. This is called an inversion. At this point of exhaustion, the temperature could drop suddenly, becoming subnormal, and the horse go into shock. Inversions may occur at lower levels, and should be watched carefully, but are not usually dangerous if the horse recovers quickly. Be suspect of any abnormally high readings, even if the P&R ratio is not close. If TPR's have not dropped noticeably in 10 minutes, especially if there is an inversion, or

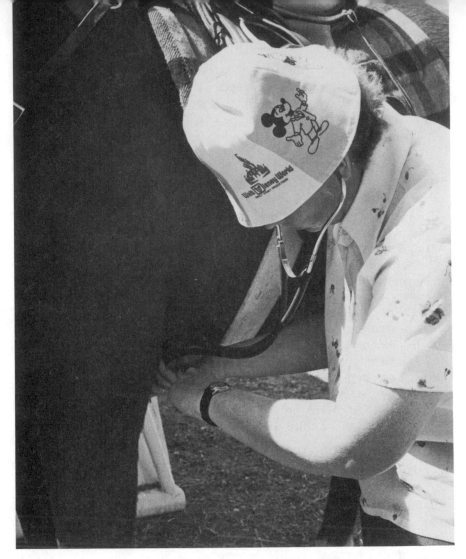

A P&R judge uses a stethoscope to measure pulse. (The hat isn't regulation equipment.)

if they increase, the horse is being overworked, and is possibly in danger. If the pulse does not drop to 70 or below after 45 minutes, you must re-evaluate either your horse or your training—maybe both.

USING TPR'S (OR P&R'S) AND OTHER INDICATORS
OF CONDITION

When conditioning a horse for distance riding, keep a close check on his progress by making a daily record. During the ride, record P&R's at stress points and after ten minutes; let him rest at any time he seems especially tired. After each ride, make a complete record of the stress TPR's, after-stress TPR's, distance traveled, stress factor of the ride (lots of uphill, rugged terrain, or easy flat work; half of ride at trot or most at walk), air temperature, humidity. Observe him closely as to attitude, appetite, muscle fatigue, or any peculiar reaction. Eventually a pattern will emerge. You will know whether he is progressing, standing still, or regressing.

You should also consider other indicators that determine condition. Examine the mucous membranes of eyes and mouth. When stressed, the color will be yellow and blue. Press your thumb against the gums and notice the time it takes for the blood to return which can give you an evaluation of circulation. You should also be concerned about dehydration. To evaluate this, notice the character of the sweat—it should be watery, not lathery. Pull the skin out away from the body and, if the horse is adequately hydrated, it will flow back into place. He should be taking nice, deep breaths with nostrils wide and even, indicating that an efficient exchange of oxygen is taking place. With a stethoscope, listen to his digestive system. If there are no sounds in the bowel area, this means that no digestion is taking place and the blood supply is being used elsewhere. This indicates that the horse is stressed; therefore do not feed heavily until recovery has taken place.

When in competition, a thorough knowledge of your horse's capabilities is vital. You should know just how much you can push him during strenuous exercise and under stress conditions. For instance, suppose that during your trail ride in the mountains, a hailstorm is building up and you are heading into it. You have ten miles to go. Do you know your horse well enough to decide that he is capable of trotting two thirds of the remaining distance, or that he could not arrive without overstress unless he walked? Overstress can lead to heart problems, leg problems, other permanent damage, and even death.

To condition your horse properly, you should establish—and write down—a definite schedule. Regular recording of TPR's, or at least P&R's, will help you to evaluate your program as you go—you may have to slow down, especially at first, for a longer period of primary conditioning, or you may be able to step up the exercise.

HINTS THAT WILL HELP YOUR HORSE MAKE THE MOST OF HIS ENERGY

Accustom your horse to stand contented for long periods while tied and saddled; he should be used to being tied to tree or trailer.

He should stand still while being mounted and dismounted from either side.

He should walk or trot—not jig and jog.

Know just how much you can stress your horse. Regal Fire Mist is lathering from strain on an uphill climb while the rider stays in a forward position to help him as much as possible. (Photo by Paul Hughes. Courtesy Ruth Waltenspiel and North American Trail Ride Conference)

He should be content to hold any position among a group of horses.

He should proceed on upgrades and downgrades at a sensible speed with good balance.

On winding trails, you should take him into switchbacks, not cut across.

Allow him to drink small quantities at each water crossing.

Don't let him crowd other horses; he should not kick or become upset if others pass too close.

He should not graze while being ridden.

Ride both in daylight and during darkness if you expect your competition to take part in the dark hours.

Improve his ability to trot for long periods and to walk freely with long strides.

He should be able to collect and extend. Collect him in steep, rough country; canter (or lope) on flat stretches. Keep the trot balanced by posting equally on both diagonals.

Familiarize your horse with all kinds of terrain.

He should enter a trailer willingly and ride in a relaxed manner so that you can trailer him to training terrain.

Vary your routine—ride in new areas and graduate to stiffer obstacles.

Experiment with different equipment during early training sessions, not during actual competition.

BETWEEN RIDES OR DURING SLACK PERIODS

Even if your distance horse is in pasture during slack periods, it is unwise just to turn him loose after an endurance or competitive ride. He should gradually be returned to normal activity. Short rides, longeing, arena work under saddle, cavalletti exercises, and free work (without rider) in the arena all help the horse to "let down" gradually. He has put out his best for weeks on the trail, so a change-of-pace activity is both necessary and welcome. Forced inactivity after a great deal of stress and movement could cause injury to muscles, or azoturia if the feeding schedule is not altered with the exercise. Some horses need disciplined exercise: If left to their own devices in a pasture, they will do nothing but stand. Knowing your animal's habits will help you arrive at a prescribed exercise regimen.

Remember that your attitude toward the distance ride is "catching" to your horse. Enthusiasm and a will to win generate that extra "something" in your mount. Negativism never generated anything but defeat; expect to make a good show. But most important—put your horse first!

Part V

———◆———

CORRECTIVE TRAINING AND SPECIAL PROBLEMS

CHAPTER 1

GENERAL CONSIDERATIONS
CONCERNING THE PROBLEM HORSE

Since every horse is an individual, every problem encountered by the trainer must be dealt with in an individual or special manner. And to handle any problem in the best way possible, the trainer must understand its cause. While it may not always be possible to determine the specific reason for a horse's actions, the trainer can use his knowledge of general equine behavioral patterns to assist in understanding the specific problem of a particular horse.

Many behavioral problems in horses are caused by interference with the natural instincts and drives that form the basis of their behavioral patterns. If a horse is unable to adjust to an experience or environment that is at odds with his basic instincts, the result is a behavioral problem that may well develop into a vice. In extreme cases, a horse may become totally unable to cope with the daily demands that would be expected of a normal, contented animal.

Other major causes or factors in the development of vices include frustration (due to conflicting demands), lack of mental growth, physical condition, unsuitability, and heredity.

The trainer may look for physical signs of stress, such as sweating, shivering, restlessness, abnormalities of appetite, or aggressiveness as indications of mental stress, and he should be willing to try to uncover the cause. Training can't proceed properly under such circumstances and ignoring the problem is more likely to allow a vice to develop.

Because prevention of problems and vices is so much more effective than any attempted cure, let's consider first how interference with basic behavioral patterns can provoke development of problems.

Influence of Basic Instincts and Characteristics
on Problem Behavior

In the first chapter, we considered the general characteristics of the horse (he is gregarious, imitative, sensitive, has an excellent memory, and so on), and throughout the book we've shown how the trainer can capitalize on these characteristics and use them to advantage in his training. Let's consider here the negative side—what can go wrong, or what vices can develop—when the trainer or handler fails to understand how these built-in instincts and characteristics influence a horse's behavior.

HUNGER

A large part of every horse's daily life is spent in his quest for food. On the range, this quest is under his own control, and most of his time will be spent grazing. When confined, the horse must depend on being fed. He learns to associate his handlers with food or tidbits, and this tends to make him less fearful and more willing to accept the human as the satisfier of his quest.

This urge is useful in catching horses, especially in a large area, because they will go to whomever they can depend upon to reward them with food. This can easily be turned in the wrong direction, however. Constant feeding from the hand encourages biting, nibbling, and general disrespect for the person handling the animal. Keep hand feeding to a minimum and be constantly aware of the effect it is having. Some horses should never be hand-fed at all; some stallions, for instance, can become obnoxious when fed tidbits too often. A kind word and stroking the neck can be just as effective and are far less apt to provoke a vice.

Food can keep a horse from rebelling at unpleasant ordeals such as clipping, trimming, shoeing, or treating a wound. Food can even change his attitude toward these experiences. As we noted, putting a little sweet feed on a wet bit makes accepting the bit more pleasant. Learning how to make each new learning experience pleasant to the horse should be one aim of the trainer. Food can play a large part in the prevention of resistances and vices, and it can be used with discretion in retraining.

FEAR AND THE URGE TO FLEE

Fear, of course, is a prime instinct, and it is the basic ingredient in many problems and vices. Being hard to catch is a common problem stemming from fear, and often the handler's "solution," while successful in one instance, only increases the problem for the future. The horse prefers to flee from the unknown, unpleasant, or dangerous. Whenever he feels insecure, he may show self-protective behavior. If the trainer understands this, he can cope with this behavior more effectively. It is easy to see that whipping or physically abusing a frightened horse will aggravate his fear, destroying any rapport that might have existed between horse and trainer.

Fear or the desire to flee from unpleasantness provokes the development of other vices also, one of which is halter pulling. Initially, the horse may have been startled by something—perhaps a cat jumping out in an unexpected place, or someone approaching without speaking when the horse is dozing. Once he has broken free successfully, his excellent memory comes into play, and he becomes more inclined to try it again—and it's only a short step to a confirmed vice.

Similarly, a horse may be startled or frightened while being led, and his first reaction is to jump away. If he pulls the lead rope from the handler, he learns he is stronger than the man, and this opens a wide range of problems. We have seen, in this kind of instance, the handler begin to yell and leap after the horse—with predictable results. By the time the horse is finally caught, the handler may be mad enough to punish him— adding more fear and confusion, and in effect teaching the horse that he does indeed have something to worry about.

The horse may also try to flee from unpleasantness when mounted, which develops into the vice known as bolting. An untrained rider may hurt the horse's mouth, and in pain and fear he may try to escape by running—the rider may haul on the bit, increasing the problem, and confirming in the horse's mind the need for escape.

In most of these problems, understanding the horse's instinctive behavior and taking sensible precautions can prevent the problem from occurring to begin with. But when it does occur, the wise trainer will immediately use his understanding to correct the problem without making it worse.

FEAR WHEN THE HORSE CAN'T FLEE

Most cornered animals will fight, and the horse is no exception. When all avenues of escape are cut off, he will resort to teeth and hoofs—and his size and agility make him a fearsome adversary. Charging, biting, striking, kicking, rearing, and bucking are the dangerous actions of a frustrated, cornered horse. If one or a combination of these actions succeed, he is intelligent enough to repeat the action in a similar situation. Because these actions give way to vices when they become habits, it is necessary for us as trainers not to force the horse into a potentially dangerous situation. Whipping, beating, and using cruel and unnatural methods and painful equipment are all ways to encourage vices. A horse trained with intelligent understanding will always outperform the horse that is trained through force. If you find that your horse is developing a dangerous vice in the course of your working with him, stop immediately and re-evaluate your program. If you're unsure of where the problem lies, or are unsure of how to correct it, get professional help from a trainer who has successfully trained and retrained many horses in a humane way. This is not something to fool around with!

MIMICKING OR IMITATION

A horse's tendency to mimic may work for or against the trainer. In the wild, or under range conditions, if one horse is startled by a paper flying in the wind, all the other horses will jump also. If one starts to run, so will the rest. This chain-reaction behavior is common to all horses. For instance, if one horse rears and pulls back on his halter, horses tied nearby will also become alarmed and try the same thing, some more effectively than others. Because this can be the beginning of a bad habit, don't tie an inexperienced horse near one that is inclined to halter pulling. Similarly, avoid such vices as cribbing, wind-sucking, and weaving in your barn, as young horses will imitate this type of behavior whether from fear or from mimicry. In trail training, we discussed the value of having an experienced horse as a companion, one that the green horse may imitate to good effect rather than a spook that will teach bad habits.

GREGARIOUSNESS AND SECURITY

Another natural urge of the horse is his need for other horses—he is gregarious by nature. Even the aggressive, seemingly unfriendly or loner-type equines generally stay near the herd. This is probably due to an inherent interdependence for survival in time of danger. As trainers, we should recognize this strong urge, as again it can work for or against us. A herdbound horse (also called a balky horse) refuses to be led or ridden away from the group. There is a certain security within the herd. Because a horse kept in a barn receives this feeling of security from his stall and barnmates, he may become barn sour (unwilling to leave the barn because of attachments to other horses or fear of leaving his security). How many times have we heard of horses burning to death because they refused to leave their stalls? They must be led out blindfolded, and even then, if not restrained, will rush back into the inferno.

Some horses will form very strong attachments to each other. Trying to ride one horse away from his companion can be a frustrating experience, and he may begin rearing, bucking, or balking in protest. This attachment could work for you as well. Riding a green horse out on the trail for the first time can be more pleasant if he's accompanied by an experienced equine friend. The security of companionship will deter him from shying and encourage him to walk out in a free and relaxed manner.

HERD INSTINCT AND SOCIAL STRUCTURE

The herd instinct influences social structure within any group of horses. There are dominant animals and submissive ones. Age, color, experience, and sex all have a part in determining the dominant horses. Surprisingly, size seems to have little to do with it. A pony can be the leader of a group of horses. The newcomers are inevitably picked on until they "belong." Usually, the dominant horses tend to have strong personalities as if "born to the station." They would be inclined to bite or kick at their fellows. Usually, these high-on-the-totem-pole horses will make their desires and resistances known to their handlers and trainers. The submissive horse does not seem to resent his more dominant herd member, but rather accepts his lot. So too, in the training process, he would be more apt to submit to bit and saddle, and be more tractable. Knowing your horse's place in the herd might give you more insight into his behavior and personality while being trained. In some cases, you must project yourself as the leader—in other words, take the place of the herd leader in the wild. You must enforce respect in a way the horse can understand and relate to. Some very powerful, dominant, and intelligent horses will never be suitable for a beginner or weak rider.

We should remember when purchasing a new horse that consideration should be taken in determining where that horse will live. Be careful when turning a new horse out with any established group, as he could be cornered, kicked, or driven through a fence or over a cattle guard with dire results.

Interference with the social structure of a herd may provoke a problem that could develop into a vice. We know of one old mare who is absolutely trustworthy under all circumstances except one: When the horses are out on winter pasture and are given their daily ration of cake (served in piles on the ground), she gets to sample each pile, stirring up the other horses until she has the pile she wants. They do not argue. If you attempt to interfere, by keeping her from one pile so that a "lesser" horse may have it, she might be tempted to kick. It is the only circumstance under which such an action would even occur to her. In another case, this time in a riding stable, stamping, kicking, and general turmoil at feeding time were eliminated when the horses were fed according to their own herd structure—boss horse first, and so on down the line—instead of according to location in the barn.

CURIOSITY

A horse's natural curiosity has a bearing on his behavior, and can be useful when training him. We can correct some cases of shying by using his curiosity: If our horse should shy at an object beside the trail, we ride strongly or lead him toward the object; usually his curiosity will do the rest. He will drop his nose, prick his ears, and slowly advance until he has identified it. When he discovers that the object is not harmful and his curiosity is satisfied, he will relax and go on his way.

Group or herd curiosity may be related to a horse's tendency to mimic. As an example of this, a group of horses were waiting impatiently for us to let them into a large corral for feeding. Suddenly one horse pricked his ears, raised his head, and faced east. The rest of the group did the same. We opened the gate, but now not even the hungriest one was interested in food. Instead, they trotted off, stiff-legged and heads high. What was bothering them? About three fourths of a mile across the highway was a large herd of Angus cattle. Although they usually grazed in groups around the pasture, they were now strung out in a long line, evidently walking to water. This strange moving line was something the horses could not identify. In this instance, we could say that curiosity, fear, uncertainty, and herd instinct all contributed to their behavior. As soon as they identified the cattle, satisfied their curiosity, and assured themselves that there was no danger, the horses returned and willingly entered the corral for their breakfast.

Amusing encounters with herd curiosity come about every spring when new foals make their appearance. We keep the mares in an enclosure near the house, where we can keep an eye on them. The first mare to foal has the privilege of showing her youngster off to the group of horses pastured around the enclosure. Without fail, every member of the herd is lined up at the fence watching the new baby, while the mare walks proudly up and down the fence with her foal. Sometimes their curiosity lasts the entire day. In this instance, we doubt that fear could be a factor in their behavior.

ATHLETIC AND NOMADIC TENDENCIES

A horse likes to move. Ignoring his need for exercise, or filling it only partially, is one of the greatest causes of problems and vices among today's horses. If a horse fails to get enough exercise, or if he is confined to a stall or small paddock, he becomes bored, frustrated, even frantic. Most stable vices have their origin in boredom or lack of exercise, and such problems as bucking, bolting, and general fractiousness under saddle may often be attributed to the horse's pent-up need to "get out and go." In this case, the problem is one of management, and the trainer should see to it that the horse has sufficient exercise and a sufficiently interesting environment. This is especially important for horses used to pasture living that must suddenly be stalled for training or for other reasons.

Other Causes of Behavioral Problems

CONFLICT OR UNCERTAINTY

Behavioral problems may begin when a horse is confronted with conflicting urges or uncertainty brought about by a problem he cannot solve. For instance, a young, green horse is ridden by a beginner who kicks him forward with his legs and at the same time pulls back on his mouth. What should a sensitive horse do? Often he might buck or bolt, ridding himself of his rider, thereby solving *his* dilemma for the moment, but beginning to acquire a vice.

MENTAL AND PHYSICAL UNREADINESS TO PERFORM

Pushing a horse, trying to hurry his training by introducing lessons that are too advanced—perhaps by using aids that are too subtle and then punishing him for misunderstanding—can cause behavioral problems. If the horse is physically or mentally unprepared, confusion and loss of confidence must result. In extreme cases, he will be on the defensive, restless, unhappy, and on the way to becoming vicious when the vice he chooses as a defense becomes habitual.

Similarly, a lack of mental growth in some areas may be a contributing factor. Throwing on a saddle, mounting, and riding an unprepared youngster can result only in panic, with consequent rearing or bucking—his instinct, you remember, being to throw off the mountain lion or other threat that has attacked him. Certainly he may be ridden out and eventually exhausted, but today's horses are sensitive and high-couraged, and the experience might color their actions for life. We insist on step-by-step training methods because we want our horses to develop without stress or fear; we want to make their progress pleasant and purposeful. Taking a horse too fast or leaving out basic steps frustrates and discourages him, gives him problems he cannot understand or solve.

PHYSICAL CONDITION OR INABILITY TO PERFORM

To respond to training, a horse must be healthy, not tired or ill. The trainer must be careful about diet, minerals, exercise, access to water, frequent worming—anything that will contribute to his general well-being. The unhealthy, unhappy animal will become confused easily and be without the will to co-operate or to work. Pushing such a horse will only frustrate him and promote lifelong bad habits.

Akin to this is physical inability to perform. We learned of a horse that bucked whenever mounted by his owner—a 350-pound rider. The man was advised to sell him since the horse could not and would not support him. With an average-size rider, the horse again became manageable.

UNSUITABILITY

Because of temperament, conformation, or other factors, some horses are unsuited to the task they are asked to perform, whether cutting, gymkhana, jumping, or whatever. When asked to perform in areas that cause fear or frustration, they will rebel in a variety of ways. Discovering the task best suited for the horse may return him to normal in a very short time.

HEREDITY

Heredity, in some cases, plays a large part in the development of problem horses. The young of mentally unstable parents will have a tendency toward the same problems, and in times of stress will break down more quickly than the offspring of normal animals. If you, as a trainer, know your horse's antecedents, you will know what to watch for, whether an inclination to balking, bolting, or other problem.

CHAPTER 2

CORRECTING THE PROBLEMS

It would be wonderful if our good training methods and complete understanding of equine psychology could prevent any problem from ever occurring. It would be equally wonderful if, whenever a problem did occur, we always knew what caused it, under what circumstances it first appeared, and consequently exactly how it could be cured. But of course problems occur even under the best of circumstances, and often we have no way of knowing a horse's background, how he was handled, or what precipitated his original fear or complex. All we can do is hope we guess correctly, and try to work on the habit sensibly and intelligently.

It would even be wonderful if, one way or another, all problems could be cured. Frankly, we do not believe that all horses with vices can be cured successfully for all time to come. Older horses with a profound and deep-seated habit will probably revert when the same situation presents itself, especially when in the same environment. In the case of the old firehorse, we doubt that he'd ever learn to walk slowly when he heard the fire alarm. The younger the horse is, and the sooner the problem is caught, the better the chance there is for complete correction and cure.

Retraining is always more difficult than training; it requires even more time and patience because you must sublimate the bad habit while teaching a desirable new response. The vice that was coupled with unpleasant experiences attending the old response must be surrounded by and submerged in new, pleasing experiences. Gradually the new habit supplants the old, but we should never lose sight of the fact that a mental incident is ineradicable and just one wrong stimulus might set it off again.

When faced with a retraining problem, begin with a vet check combined with your own careful observation. First eliminate the possibility of physical difficulty causing or contributing to the problem. Ovarian cysts in mares, and retained testicles in males (cryptorchid or monorchid) may cause unpredictable behavior. Hormone or dietary imbalance may cause problem behavior just as overfeeding and lack of exercise may result in boredom or excessive spirits. Eye troubles or partial blindness may make a horse appear balky. Happily, most physical problems can be dealt with in a direct manner—the mental or psychological problems take more time and are generally a more roundabout process.

As in the case of human neuroses, most treatment involves a period of rest away from the original agitation. Placing a horse out on pasture, giving him loving attention but demanding nothing, is a good way to begin this treatment. After several months of recuperation, depending on the severity of the vice, retraining may begin slowly, patiently, and sensibly, always realizing that the slightest misstep could trigger the return of the habit. The problem horse will need much encouragement and praise.

It will help if retraining takes place in different surroundings than his trouble-causing environment. The faulty behavior in most problem horses involves inept handling or bad riding. Once removed from the area, and under competent handling, the horse has a good chance of recovery. Often the problem is simply that the horse has been asked to perform a task for which he is temperamentally or physically unsuited. Discovering the activity best suited for this horse may return him to normal in a short time. We know of a gelding whose owner was determined to make a barrel racer of him. The more resistance he offered, the more practice he was given. He became sour, began balking and star gazing, and became increasingly irritable. He finally resorted to bucking and became unusable for any gymkhana event. We bought the gelding and placed him out on pasture for a season. When he was brought in to new surroundings, he was used only on the trail. At first he was ponied (without a rider), and later ridden slowly for short distances. Eventually he could be ridden successfully anywhere on a trail. However, we were careful never to let him see a barrel. He liked his new vocation and was both reliable and pleasurable.

What it all boils down to, then, is that in most cases, the problem horse has become that way because of problem handling. Professional trainers may be able to take the kinks out of a horse if they get to him early enough, but as soon as the horse is back home, he reverts to his old habit. The difficulty is obvious: The owner needs to be cured before the horse *can* be.

Knowing Your Own Limits

In the first chapter, we suggested evaluating yourself and your horse to determine whether you should attempt to train this particular animal. Throughout the training program, it is wise to make re-evaluations, and assess overall progress, appearance of problems, success in overcoming problems, and so on. Even the best trainers may not have the best answer or way of working with a particular horse, so don't *you* feel too proud or too smart to ask for help if you need it. If you don't feel capable of han-

Know your own limits when attempting to train a horse. Here a rank stallion, initially equipped with hobbles and sideline, has just broken the back hobble strap sideline. Professional trainers Lynn Richardson and Ken Serco have the know-how, equipment, and facilities to handle the problem. But do you? (Courtesy Dave Jones)

dling a given situation, ask for help. After all, each case is individual. If you're not sure, you may still do well to get assistance—you may learn something even if you've trained fifty horses.

How can you tell whether it's time to ask for help? Here are some suggestions:

•If you have a problem with a dangerous vice—kicking, striking, charging, bucking, rearing, bolting—you don't have a lot of time or room to fool around. You or someone else could be badly hurt. You may do best to sell the horse, or, if there's some excellent reason to keep him, at least send him to a professional prepared to handle the problem. If you wish to take on retraining a horse with these vices, you should have plenty of experience behind you, and good facilities to work with, as well as be an excellent rider.

•If you are not making progress, but rather seem to be falling farther behind even after re-evaluating your training program, ask an experienced horseman for suggestions. He may be able to pinpoint your problem, or may suggest turning the horse over to a more experienced trainer for a while.

•If you are somewhat—or very—afraid of the horse, he'll know it and you won't get anywhere. This can creep up on you—you may gradually be letting him get away with a few things because you're not sure how to correct him. This will lead to inconsistencies in your training (some days you'll feel tougher than others), and the situation can only deteriorate. Get help until you've regained confidence, or send the horse out.

•If you don't like the horse, don't try to train him. Professionals may have to take any horse that comes their way, but even so, if the chemistry is wrong, it won't turn out as well. It's better to find somebody else to do the job, or sell the horse.

•If you find yourself resorting too easily to gimmicks and paraphernalia, something's wrong. You're probably trying to rush the training, for one thing. Get professional advice—you may need lessons in advanced horsemanship.

•If you find yourself becoming generally impatient, frustrated, and inclined to rush, overdo, or push workouts to the limit, quit. If your horse doesn't have any vices so far, he soon will.

Above all, if you have trouble with a horse—if you just can't train him—don't give up for all time to come. Every professional has a list of failures behind him. That's why working with horses is such a challenge. Look forward to the next horse and be grateful for the experience you're gaining—it all helps.

One last point: We've been talking a lot about professionals here, but we don't mean just any professional trainer. There are quacks in this business just as in any other. Choose your professional trainer with care. Expect him to take time—if he promises thirty-day miracles, you'd probably better stay well clear of him. Watch him at work, and ask to see some of the horses he's trained. A good trainer—man or woman—will be pleased that you care enough about your horse to make sure he's in good hands.

Training Stallions

The key word in working with stallions is "respect," for both the trainer and the horse. As a trainer, you should respect his quick reactions, his pride, and his strength. And the stallion should respect you: He should have impeccable manners and be without vices.

Working with stallions is not a job for the novice trainer. You must have a thorough knowledge of equine behavior because, though a stallion is trained in the same way as any other horse, he is quicker, stronger, and more independent than a mare or a gelding. It requires experience, knowledge, and innate ability to handle the intelligent, virile, keen, and independent stallion.

A trainer should know the general characteristics of stallions, and he should be aware that a stallion is as individual as any mare or gelding. Within the province of their stallionhood, they can be lazy or energetic, friendly or antisocial, and so on. But overall, there is far less room for making mistakes when working with stallions.

What, then, are the distinguishing characteristics of a stallion?

His primary purpose is to breed mares. Because his mating urge is very strong, he tends to be easily distracted, especially by other horses (at a distance, he cannot always distinguish a mare from a gelding, but where there's life, there's hope!). He is quick, both in his thinking and in his physical reactions. He is proud and dislikes being humiliated. Because he is usually smart and sensitive, care and thought should be given to his training. He is powerful, exuberant, and "full of himself."

His training, then, whether in hand or under saddle, should be as thorough and successful as that of any well-trained mare or gelding. He should not crowd you in a stall or other small area, nor should he nip, bite, strike, or kick. He should stand quietly to be groomed, trimmed, shod, doctored, or tacked up. He should pay attention to you, and he should be expected to work obediently in a mixed group of horses.

From the very beginning, train a stallion to be obedient, and continue to expect obedience from him. Even as a youngster, discipline and respect are continually important; avoid either coddling or cruelty. It is not wise either to frequently feed a stallion out of your hand, or to fuss with him by incessantly patting his head or fondling his muzzle. Because he is proud, he should never be whipped or humiliated. Nor should he be picked at when being reprimanded; be firm, consistent, and decisive. A sharp word or slap on the neck with an open hand is usually sufficient when it is administered immediately in a firm but cool manner, and strongly enough to be effective. A kind word and gentle pat on the neck make good rewards. You don't want a stallion to be afraid to come near you, and you don't want him running all over you. There's a happy medium, and mutual respect is necessary to attain it.

As is true with any horse, don't try to train a stallion you don't like, or one that you fear. Know your limitations. Women trainers can work with stallions as well as men can; in either case, it is the trainer's experience, knowledge, ability, and horse sense that should determine his or her readiness to work with a particular stallion. If you feel unequal to the challenge, it is only sensible and safe for you to find someone able to help you or to do it for you. Abuse with a club or whip usually means that the handler is fearful and insecure; this will only spawn bad habits and meanness in a stallion, or, for that matter, in any horse. Stallions tend to get mad and fight back. Be fully aware, if you ever are confronted with an enraged stallion, that they fight mainly by striking and biting, rather than as a mare does by whirling and kicking, although they may do this also.

The way a stallion is kept and cared for relates directly to his training. The stallion, especially, needs adequate exercise, human attention, and friendship. He should be handled daily, both for exercise and to establish in him a feeling of well-being and security. He should see and be worked with other horses. To keep him exclusive or apart is an unnatural situation and tends to make him more excitable and unruly.

In leading a stallion from stall to training area, or training him for showing at halter, use the method explained in Part IV, Chapter 1, under "Training Your Horse to Show At Halter": two leads, one a chain through the halter, the other a regular lead attached to the halter ring. Not only are you in control if he becomes excited or spooked, but you are also instantly able to reprimand him for misbehavior, such as squealing or refusing to walk quietly. This method of restraint and chastisement helps him to respect you, yet is humane. (Take care that you know the degree of restraint your stallion needs; it is possible to jerk him so hard that he rears and goes over backward.)

Do's and don'ts of handling and training stallions:

1. Expect—and insist on—obedience and respect from the stallion.
2. Respect the stallion's strength, courage, virility, and pride.
3. Give him adequate exercise and human companionship.
4. Reprimand him firmly and immediately for nipping, crowding, squealing, and other bad manners.
5. Be kind, but firm, consistent, and patient.
6. Do not "pick" at him or tease him.
7. Don't "baby" a stallion by letting him nuzzle you or push at you, and don't feed tidbits by hand.
8. Do not abuse him or humiliate him.
9. Begin training the stallion in an enclosed area where outside influences are at a minimum, as his attention tends to wander more than that of mares and geldings. The techniques of training any horse are the same.
10. Use strong, comfortable tack.
11. Be patient—expect to take more time training the stallion than you would most mares and geldings.
12. Anticipate his actions and reactions.
13. When you begin his training, work with him every day and expect him to pay attention to you, whether on a lead shank or under saddle.
14. Always keep alert and don't take shortcuts.

Problems Resulting from Poor or Timid Horsemanship

Problems such as grass cropping, rolling, balking, and sometimes barn sourness often occur in hack stable horses—they are ridden more by nonhorsemen than by horsemen and they soon learn to do pretty much as they please. Such problems may also occur with dude and other resort-type horses. Sometimes a horse may follow another horse willingly but refuse to go anywhere on his own. Often these problems disappear magically when a strong rider mounts, but if ingrained, they will reassert themselves whenever the horse finds out he can take advantage of his rider. Sometimes such horses may be an advantage to school instructors—they can easily measure how much progress their students are making by how well they can manage the willful horse.

Problems Resulting from Boredom and Lack of Exercise

Cribbing, weaving, chewing, tail rubbing, wind-sucking, stamping, pawing, stall kicking, and related barn vices are not training problems. Usually they are caused by lack of exercise and boredom, often coupled with overfeeding or lack of bulk in the diet, mineral deficiencies, worms, and other physical problems. Sometimes horses will pick up the habit by mimicking another horse—and a whole barnful of problems will result. Begin with a good vet check, feed properly, and make sure your horse has plenty of exercise—in pasture or paddock if not under saddle or on the longe. If he must be stalled, arrange for him to be interested—with a Dutch door he can see other horses or watch your activities. If he's alone, find a companion for him; if not another horse, then a donkey, goat, cat— somebody!

Dangerous Vices

Kicking, striking, and charging are vices that should not be tackled by the inexperienced trainer. And such horses should not be kept by anyone, no matter how experienced, if children or novice adults are apt to enter barn or pasture. It's simply not worth the risk.

Kicking is a natural defense for horses. Almost any horse will kick if he is surprised out of a nap. Teach children and visitors basic safety rules if they are to enter your barn, stable, or pasture. A group of horses in a pasture will kick at each other, usually without great malice, and a person should be alert for such squabbles and stay out of the way. Occasionally they will get really mad for some reason, or may wish to discipline a new horse added to the group—this is serious business, and the blows horses can inflict are truly lethal. Although kicking should be reprimanded to prevent the development of a vice, a trainer should distinguish between what may be termed a justified reaction and deliberate maliciousness, and act accordingly.

Deliberate kicking at humans—when in the barn or when mounting—must be corrected immediately. Slap the horse on the leg and say "No!" If a young or green horse is touchy about his feet or other parts of his body, he may kick when this part is touched. See Part I, Chapter 2, under "Handling the feet." The older horse, however, may need to be thoroughly sacked out, and if the habit is well started, he may need to be Scotch hobbled or even thrown before he can be handled.

A variety of remedies are sold for confirmed kickers, which usually involve a chain or ball that is tied to the fetlock and hangs down so that the horse punishes himself when he kicks. When a horse kicks at others when being ridden, this is not the province of an inexperienced horseman. Such horses traditionally wear a red ribbon in their tail, but it is better not to ride them at all with a group.

Bucking and rearing have many initial causes, but when these actions become habits, the horse may be considered dangerous. If a usually well-mannered horse begins to buck or rear and the cause is not obvious, look for discomfort such as a bur or bee under the saddle, or his tongue over the bit. If the cause is clearly a basic hatred or fear of a particular activity, such as the gelding mentioned earlier that was temperamentally unsuited to barrel racing, the best solution is to find a task that the horse can perform without frustration and fear.

If a young or green horse experiments with bucking, it's important to stay calm, stay in the saddle, and give him no reason to feel he accomplished something he should repeat. Speak sharply to him (but not frantically), keep his head up if possible, urge him on with your legs, and turn him sharply in a circle. It may help your balance to lean back somewhat. If the experiment fails, he will probably not repeat it, and even if he does, his next try will be halfhearted and more easily corrected. If he should take you by surprise and dump you (he'll probably be very surprised to see you down there), and if you are hesitant about remounting, ask an assistant to hold the horse while you mount and then lead him until you're sure of control. You may ask the helper to longe the horse in both directions for several minutes while you ride.

If more experienced at bucking, and if more determined, the horse will need a strong rider who will gradually be able to supplant the bucking with correct behavior. If the horse is confirmed in the habit, however, he may never lose it entirely. Some old cowhorses would register their objection to being ridden by bucking every time they were mounted; once out of their system, they worked without a problem until the next time they were mounted. A "cold-backed" or very sensitive horse may need time to "buck out" in a corral or ring every time he is saddled. But as soon as his "fit" is over, he should be safe to mount and ride.

The rearing horse is especially dangerous as he may go over backward on his rider—keep his head low and urge him strongly forward, turning him in a circle. Give strong consideration to the type of bit used, and use your hands properly. Sometimes using a hackamore or hackamore bit will eliminate the problem. Retraining with longeing, suppling exercises, and emphasis on developing responsiveness and confidence may help both the bucker and rearer, but much depends on the history behind his resort to the vice.

Bolting is a vice that may develop if the horse was successful in his first few attempts at running away from the problem. When bolting, a horse will take the bit in his teeth, set his jaw, and run through anything. He may be cured if the initiative is taken from him—force him to continue running, preferably uphill, when he wishes to stop. Of course, this isn't always possible; if the rider uses enough force, he may be able to turn the horse into a circle, or keep him from returning to the barn or running into a fence, but this isn't easy. The initial cause is often pain in the mouth caused by a heavy-handed rider or wrong bit. The horse may be retrained to be more responsive to control, as explained later on under "Lack of Control and General Unmanageability."

Shying can sometimes be a dangerous vice, and a very nervous horse isn't much fun to ride. Suggestions for dealing with this problem appear throughout the chapter on trail training (Part II, Chapter 7). In some cases, a horse may not be suitable for riding on the trail. Young horses may be helped by the quiet establishment of greater confidence and improved responsiveness (see Part II, Chapter 5). Longeing near the source of the upset may also help by widening the horse's experience and base of familiarity.

Restraining Devices and Sacking Out

Restraining devices must sometimes be used even on well-mannered horses—for instance, if a wound must be treated. Older horses that grew up without human handling must be gentled before they can be worked with at all, and this usually involves some type of restraining device.

Remember that a blindfold is a helpful restraint, especially in an emergency where other equipment might not be available. A bandanna, shirt, jacket, burlap sack, saddle blanket—almost anything—may be used as a temporary blindfold. The horse will move very little when blindfolded.

For doctoring, a twitch is often used as a restraint. The twitch fully occupies a horse's mind so that he doesn't pay much attention to whatever else is happening to him. The one most commonly used consists of a loop of chain or rope attached to a short, stout stick. Usually the twitch is placed over the horse's upper lip. The stick is rotated, tightening the chain, until it pinches the lip. Pressure can be increased or relaxed as needed to maintain control. Other kinds include the one-man twitch, hand twitch, and hand pressure on the shoulder muscle.

Sometimes a kneestrap can be used to hold up a horse's forefoot. This can be an effective restraint, and is usually quicker to apply in an emergency than some other methods, providing the horse can be handled. A man's belt can do very well, or a stirrup leather. Pick up a forefoot, bending the leg at the knee as though to pick out the foot. Slip the closed belt over the knee, and the foot will be held up. This should not be used for more than a short time, because it is difficult for a horse to support the entire weight of his forehand on one leg.

The Scotch hobble is a traditional method of restraining a horse, and it has several advantages. For one, a hind leg can be held up for a much longer time than a foreleg without causing discomfort. It needn't be pulled high, just forward enough to be off the ground so that the horse can't kick and so that his mobility is limited. If he is difficult or dangerous to handle, he can be snubbed while the neck loop is tied, usually with a bowline; then

The Scotch Hobble

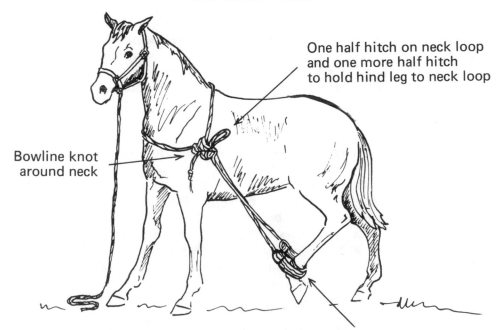

One half hitch on neck loop and one more half hitch to hold hind leg to neck loop

Bowline knot around neck

Use a cinch or 1-inch soft cotton rope (35 feet)

Ken Serco gentling a spooky one. Even if you can't spin a fancy loop, swinging a rope around a horse (without whapping him, please!), as one version of sacking out, is a good way to gentle him and prepare him for all-around usefulness. (Courtesy Dave Jones)

the long end of the rope can be thrown between the hind legs, or laid on the ground and his hindquarters hazed into position. The rope can be brought around, run through the neck loop, and the leg can be pulled up. Because this may cause rope burns, it's better to take another wrap around the pastern, or a cotton rope may be used. If the horse can be handled, a string cinch may be used as shown, or a leather hobble and D-ring.

A really rank horse may need to be thrown and tied before he can be handled—if you have one like this (how in the world did you get him?), call a professional and get out of the way.

Restraining devices, when used as training aids, keep the horse under control until you can teach him that he has nothing to fear, or that you are the boss—depending on the situation. Green horses must learn that you do not intend to harm them. When their fear is conquered, they are ready to turn their attention to pleasing you instead of fighting you. Any horse must learn to stand quietly, and a restraining device is one way to insist on obedience to "Whoa!"

"Sacking out" is the most common way of helping a horse to overcome his fears. Under restraint, he must simply accept the sacking and handling until he finally realizes that it won't hurt him and he becomes used to the feel of things touching him all around his body. Burlap sacks are the traditional tool, but a saddle blanket, piece of canvas, or anything else can be used—a slicker is particularly good. Wave it at him, slapping him gently on his back, legs, belly, all over. Wave it over his head and behind him. Using a soft cotton rope, run it back and forth between his legs, over his back, and let it slide over his rump. With the sack again, rub him with it, and finally rub him all over with your hands. Repeat the sacking lesson several times before removing the restraint, and again without it. Remember that the theory of sacking out is to gentle the horse and overcome his fear, and to teach him to stand quietly; if you are too rough, it will have the opposite effect. Praise the horse for proper response and talk soothingly to him as you would to calm a youngster.

If a horse has been thoroughly sacked out, especially with a variety of materials, he will be unlikely to shy or spook in any situation—he'll be safer, easier to train, and more pleasant to ride.

Problems in Pasture and Stable

HARD TO CATCH

This can be the most frustrating of vices, and really, what good to us is a horse that won't be caught? Fear is usually the main problem here— fear of an unpleasant time once the horse *is* caught. Youngsters may develop a hard-to-catch horse if, every time they want to ride, they run the horse the whole time. Sometimes a horse will learn the habit from pasturemates, though alone he was not a problem.

Food can be used to entice the horse to come, though of course care should be taken with hand feeding. Our horses know that they receive a grain reward in their manger every time they come in from pasture, and that they will have a pleasant time eating and relaxing for a few minutes— we have no trouble, and they will even come at odd times when called.

We bought Dixie as an older mare. She was half-Arabian, saddle-trained, intelligent, and wily. Catching her was a major project. We started by putting on a close-fitting halter and turning her into a fairly small corral. From the halter ring we had braided a foot-long piece of baling twine that hung down and made it easier to catch and hold her. We let her become acquainted with her surroundings for several days, during which time we talked to her, fed her grain in a bucket, and put hay in a manger, but never fed her quite enough to satisfy her. After several days, we offered her the bucket of grain while we held it. When she accepted this, we offered some grain from our hand, never trying to touch the halter or braided twine. From this we proceeded to hand-feed her often, other than at regular feeding times, and finally fed with one hand while stroking her neck with the other. By now she would come willingly to us for grain. Every time she came, she was rewarded. It became a simple thing to grasp the twine, reward her, lead her around a few steps, reward her again, and let her go. We worked on this several times a day for several days—yes, it was time-consuming, but each moment spent enforced the new desirable habit. If we had run all over the pasture each time we wanted her, the time spent would have been fruitless and frustrating, and actually would have helped her to learn new ways to outwit us. When we felt Dixie was ready, we turned her out in a pasture among easy-to-catch horses (to put her in with a group of wary horses would have been senseless). Again, we went up to her several times a day to catch her, lead her, and reward her. It took only five minutes a time, and after several more days, she was a different horse. With this particular mare, we often caught her, rewarded her, and let her go without riding her, so that she would not revert because of any previous unpleasant experiences.

Some trainers advocate "walking the horse down"—that is, walking after him in a small pasture until he's tired of having you as a shadow and will stop. This could entail hours and days, as you must stay with him until you are successful. We prefer the former method, but every horse is an individual and not all will respond to the same method. You may have to experiment and invent a system to solve the problem for a particular horse.

We watched one old-timer who wanted to catch a haltered horse in a large corral of spooky animals. Each time he'd walk toward the horse, the whole group would run. He held a long willow switch in his left hand, and when the horses ran, he would use the switch almost like a longe whip to keep them running longer than they wanted to. He would tell them "Whoa," and allow them to stop, then walk forward and reach out with his right hand for his horse. It was necessary to repeat this several times, but then he could go up to the group and catch his horse. As he said, never once were the horses allowed to think they were acting on their own —always they were made to believe they were obeying his wishes.

Remember that any horse can readily revert if he finds himself in a situation similar to his former unpleasantness or if someone he distrusts tries to catch him.

WILL NOT LEAD

A mature horse that will not lead willingly is dangerous since he is so much stronger than you. If he manages to get loose, it will make the habit even more difficult to correct. In a small enclosed area, lead this horse with a chain through the halter. When he tries to run off, jerk the chain; it will tighten under his jaw and bring his head under control. Then talk quietly to him, reward him when he comes forward with you, and actually work with him as you would a foal. However, you should punish him by tugging on the chain whenever he attempts to bolt away. Work with young and green horses as explained in Part I, Chapter 2, under "Leading" and "Leading from Horseback," Part II, Chapter 1, under "Teaching to Lead," and Part II, Chapter 7, under "Ponying."

HALTER PULLING

As mentioned earlier, pulling back when tied is an offense that stems from a desire to flee from unpleasantness. When a horse has used this defense successfully several times, it becomes a bad habit—one far easier to prevent than to cure. When training, always use equipment that fits well and is strong enough to withstand strain. A flimsy halter or rope will break easily even when your horse turns his head quickly to ward off a fly. Halter pulling is not only dangerous to you and the horse, but also expensive through breakage in halters, ropes, and snaps. The confirmed halter puller is difficult to retrain and cannot ever be entirely trusted.

One method of retraining is to use equipment similar to a bull halter —the long lead and halter are all one piece and made so that pressure is exerted on the poll area and around the muzzle whenever the horse pulls back. When he comes forward, the pressure releases. All equipment used on a confirmed halter puller must be very strong; if it breaks, the horse wins again and this habit becomes all the more difficult to erase.

If you do not have this type of halter, you can encircle the horse's body with a large soft rope tied with a bowline knot. The rope comes from between his legs, through the halter, to a stout tree or deep-set post. He punishes himself when he pulls back, as the rope tightens near the withers. It is safer than some methods because it's more difficult for him to rear and go over backward, and because he's less likely to get his front legs over the rope and become tangled. Usually this is effective for most horses, but the confirmed puller reverts as soon as the body rope isn't used.

Whenever you are working with ropes on a horse, it is always wise to have a sharp knife handy in case the horse must be cut loose to prevent injury. Never leave a horse to his own devices when tied—stay close by. Use knots that come loose easily; don't tie a slip knot on the horse when using the above method of retraining.

Another method, used by some old-timers, may work for confirmed pullers. It's called the head and foot tie. The halter rope is run through the manger hole or tie area and is tied around the cannon bone or pastern with half hitches. When the horse pulls back, he pulls his own foot forward. To put his foot down he must come forward. As a by-product, this method also teaches a horse to stand forward if his foot is caught, thus preventing him from pulling away and tearing himself up. However, the method can be dangerous when used on young horses or those that are particularly fearful or high-spirited; if they should panic, they could injure themselves severely.

Problems While Under Saddle

MOVING WHILE BEING MOUNTED

It is both unmannerly and unsafe for a horse to move while being mounted. If a child or inexperienced adult should try to ride such a horse, there is a good possibility he could be dragged or become thoroughly frightened. Usually the habit is one that a rider has contributed to at some time in the horse's past, often by jabbing him in the ribs with his boot toe when mounting or hitting him on the rump with his right foot, or by trying to imitate TV cowboys and take off at a run.

Face the horse into a wall or fence, or better yet, into a corner. Hold his reins fairly short, and talk to him quietly and calmly. Say "Whoa," and begin to mount. If he starts to move, give a tug on the reins and repeat the "Whoa" command. Be sure to show your displeasure if he moves. Mount smoothly, without digging him in the ribs with your left toe, or hitting him on the rump with your right leg. When you are mounted, make him stand quietly a minute or so before moving out. You may want to mount and dismount several times before moving out. Repeat this several times during a session and reward him with praise and pats for improved performance. As he responds, move back from the fence but continue to face it. Until the lesson has been thoroughly learned, don't try to mount in the open on a day when he is excited because of wind, a barking dog, a crowd, or other distraction; instead, use a wall or fence as a deterrent and reminder. And never make the mistake or urging him on before you are really settled in the saddle.

If the horse is more difficult, you may have to tie him in the corner and mount repeatedly. Even then, some horses won't co-operate. The Scotch hobble may be used to restrain the horse, sometimes in conjunction with hobbling the forefeet as well. If this method is necessary, sack him out several times before mounting to minimize the possibility that he might try to move and throw himself as he does. Be aware of the possibility, so that you can step aside if he does go down. Talk quietly to him, and mount and dismount repeatedly. It's a good idea to mount from both sides, reversing the Scotch hobble. Always sit quietly settled in the saddle for a moment or two before dismounting. When the horse accepts this, sack him out from the saddle. Keep your feet free of the stirrups so that you can step off easily if he goes down. Move around on top of him, lean one way and the other, slide over his rump. Eventually remove the Scotch hobble, but continue with the forefoot hobbles as you repeat the process. Finally, he should stand calmly for mounting (or anything else!) without restraint.

Be consistent in mounting smoothly, without kicking or jabbing the horse, in sitting down gently into the saddle, and in settling the horse before moving out.

BARN SOUR AND HERDBOUND

As mentioned earlier, this horse has placed his sense of security in his stall or with his companions; he doesn't want to leave them. A strong rider can insist on a good workout away from the barn. Whenever the horse turns toward the barn (or companions), turn him in the opposite direction and work fifteen minutes more (be prepared for a long day).

Generally, this problem is not found in a horse you've trained yourself. It can occur under certain circumstances, however, when the horse learns that the barn is a pleasant place to be, and what happens elsewhere is unpleasant. Reverse the situation. Instead of giving him grain in the barn, arrange to feed it out in the far pasture or off on a trail. Or at least dismount, feed him a small pile of cake, and talk pleasantly to him without demanding anything from him. Pay less attention to him at home, saving a bit of fussing and praise for away from home. Make sure that your work sessions are not overtiring or boring. The horse should enjoy going out, not just coming home.

PROBLEMS IN POSITION OF HEAD, REFUSAL TO ACCEPT CONTACT, TOSSING THE HEAD, OR LEANING ON THE BIT

Most of these head-related problems, whether active (tossing, lugging on the bit) or static (boring, head held too high or too low, behind or over the bit), evolve because the horse refuses to accept contact. As we discussed earlier, contact is a function of the entire body, not just the mouth, and proper correction of the problem involves the whole horse, not just the head.

First, of course, in order to correct any problem, you must determine its cause. It may be physical: A poorly adjusted curb strap may be causing discomfort, or the type of bit may fit poorly or be incorrect for the stage of training. Any animal (or person!) forced to perform in uncomfortable or painful gear rarely succeeds. If you do not know the cause of the head problem, it is sometimes wise to change the kind of headstall—perhaps riding the horse in a hackamore would help (try both hackamore bit and Spanish bosal). This would be especially true if the horse had been abused about the mouth or head.

A frequent cause of poor head set and active head problems is rushed training. The rider tries to collect the young horse before he is ready, and often does this incorrectly, by pulling the head into position rather than pushing the horse with seat and legs gradually up into the bit. The push should come from the horse's motor—the hindquarters. Forcing complete contact on the inexperienced horse produces lugging, throwing the head up or down, and hard mouth. Please read over the previous sections on methods of obtaining an educated mouth. This takes patience, time, and great tact on the rider's part, particularly when retraining.

Work on the longe can help correct this kind of problem, but again, much more time is required than when training the green horse. It may take weeks or months to gradually tighten the side reins (using bridle or hackamore) while driving him forward with the longe whip. The unbalanced horse will tend to slow down and speed up, cutting in on the circle or pulling out. Encourage him with the whip when he slows down, and give little tugs when he speeds up. The length of the sessions should be short, using the trot more than the walk or canter. If he has a tendency to throw his quarters out or turn his head away from the direction of movement, use two longe reins to give you control of lateral flexion. In the case of the horse that runs out of the circle with nose raised, use the longeing cavesson and work in an enclosed area.

When a horse carries his head too high, he is evading contact, often because he has been hurt in the mouth and expects to be hurt again. Control is difficult. The effects of this problem are easily seen on his whole body: hollow back with choppy gaits and poor balance. Work on the longe is valuable, as well as riding large circles and straight lines. Encourage free forward movement, relaxation as opposed to tension, and confidence. When the horse begins a choppy gait, use your legs actively to keep him going forward freely. Your actions should be firm, positive, and tactful. Eventually he will begin to stretch his neck and lower his head, thereby lengthening the rein. To reward him, lower your hands. He is coming up into the bit and now should be ridden actively with your legs, but without any forceful action from the reins. Give and take with your fingers ever so tactfully if any resistance is shown, but maintain a light contact with a straight line from elbow to bit. A martingale will keep you from being injured, but will not cure a poor head carriage or tossing head.

When a horse carries his head and neck too low (stretched toward the ground), he will have too much weight on his forehead and drag his hindquarters. This lazy, dull picture is unpleasant to ride. The rider is pushed into a forward position since the cantle of the saddle is raised, giving the feeling of perpetually riding downhill. When your horse has this tendency to be heavy on the forehand, keep your upper body and back straight, bracing your back while using your legs actively. Shorten your reins and, in the beginning stages, actively tug his head upward while using the driving force of your seat and legs to encourage engagement of the haunches and freeing of the shoulder for forward motion. As he responds, give and take with your fingers, and encourage him to carry himself rather than lean (lug) on his bit and your hands. Strive for sensitive, yielding, elastic rein contact. Keep in mind that the horse's disposition and temperament will affect your progress; insensitive force with the nervous, timid horse will make him more timid, while letting the stubborn, willful horse take advantage of his rider will also give poor results. Remember, too, that the young green horse is naturally heavier on the forehand; good basic training will cure this.

Use of cavalletti, also, will help to improve the sluggish, heavy-on-the-forehand horse. Whether on the longe or under saddle, this will involve his interest, make him watch his footing, and force him to lift his feet and engage his haunches, as well as be good gymnastic training. Cavalletti will help him to rebalance from forehand to hindquarters. When riding, take care that you are in balance with your horse and that you help him take even strides.

How can balance be improved? We have mentioned work on the longe. Under saddle, work with straight lines and circles, using driving aids on curves and making use of half-halts. You can also develop good balance by riding cross-country. Going up and down hills accustoms him to the aids for shifting his balance toward the hindquarters. Begin with gentle hills, and progress to steeper ones. Well-executed transitions from one gait to another help to improve balance, and the half-halt can be used to balance the horse on the downward transitions (trot to walk to halt). Use your body to cue him in these downward transitions—only when he doesn't respond should you use your hands. In this case, let him run into a restraining hand rather than a pulling one.

RUBBER NECK AND STIFF NECK

In the case of both rubber-necked and stiff-necked horses, the body will not flex laterally. The rubber-necked horse (neck bends too easily right and left) has learned that if he turns his head he can evade bending his whole body. His neck bends this way and that, without his body from poll to tail following the correct gradation of the curve. While making a circle to the left, his head will turn too far left, and his haunches will fall out to the right. The laterally stiff horse refuses to bend either neck or body.

As a rule, both problems stem from improper riding. The horse has been guided by reins alone, and in retraining, the rider must use his legs and seat actively to hold the haunches in the track of the forehand.

In reining the rubber-necked horse, the indirect rein should be the most important. This will restrict the bend of the neck, making it conform to the curve you are describing. Begin working in large circles and gradually diminish the size as response is obtained. In making a circle to the left, use your right leg behind the girth as actively as necessary to keep the haunches from falling out. The right rein should restrict overbending to the left, while the left rein guides lightly to the left. Your left leg is strong but quiet on the girth. You wish to wrap the horse around your inside leg, while asking him with seat and legs to move forward with some impulsion. Give and take with your hands if and when he rebels, and don't continue the exercise for long periods—vary it with straight-line posting trots and walks on a long rein.

For the stiff horse, most of the above applies, except that the stiffness of the neck will require you to lead the horse's head and neck into the correct curve. Use an opening rein. If the horse is too stiff or resistant to use the opening rein, you can resort to a sliding rein or draw rein. You will be able to counteract his resistance and use less force with your hands. The sliding rein is also helpful in cases where the horse refuses to halt, or refuses to flex at the poll. However, this method should only be used in re-

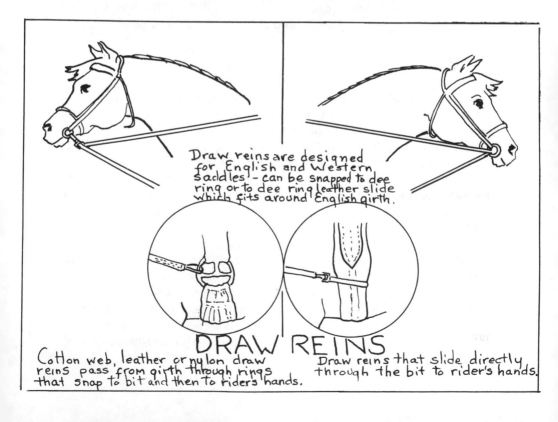

Draw reins are designed for English and Western saddles—can be snapped to dee ring or to dee ring leather slide which fits around English girth.

DRAW REINS

Cotton web, leather or nylon draw reins pass from girth through rings that snap to bit and then to rider's hands.

Draw reins that slide directly through the bit to rider's hands.

training when other methods have proved deficient. Be sure to relax the hand the instant flexion is obtained, and keep your hands as light as possible.

LACK OF CONTROL AND GENERAL UNMANAGEABILITY

Many horses have the habit of charging off when asked to canter. This problem is widespread, especially among "weekend" horses, and may be caused by one or more of the following situations:

•always riding at a gallop, never asking for a slower canter, as when using the horse only for gymkhana events such as barrel racing, pole bending, and other forms of racing;
•lack of a basic education, including ring work at all gaits, longeing, and cavalletti;
•physical discomfort arising from heavy hands, poor horsemanship, incorrect bit, or poor adjustment of tack. The horse will try to flee from discomfort, and eventually this may end up in bucking or rearing when he finds that he cannot escape the physical punishment;
•the horse's temperament: Some horses love to run and when given the slightest incentive will take advantage. In retraining a racehorse, we must sublimate this urge to run by giving him no opportunity or stimulus to run. Most rejected racehorses still have the breeding and temperament of racing stock, and this must be kept in mind when retraining.

What are some methods we can use to train or retrain a horse to take a slow canter? In all the above causes, excitement and tension play a great part. Strive for calmness and relaxation, returning to basic maneuvers and exercises at walk or trot that tend to relax and supple the horse. Longe in an enclosed area, with or without a longeing cavesson (depending on temperament), at a walk or trot. Follow up with some driving, unless driving lines would excite this particular horse. Working in a quiet indoor arena can be really helpful, since the closed-in feeling of the arena makes a horse reluctant to run, so you gain maximum mental and physical control. Longeing with two lines (long-reining) will give you control of the head and body.

Retraining for a slow canter (while riding) requires patience and tactful aids to produce relaxation. Use exercises in circles and straight lines (Part II, Chapter 5) at the walk and slow trot to promote obedience and response to the aids. Try for a relaxed but energetic walk. When he responds to the aids and seems willing and you feel he's ready for the canter, ask for the canter in an enclosed area for short periods. If he responds, work him in large circles and figure-eights with walks and other calming exercises in between. One excellent exercise is the circular spiraling in and out at the canter. It can be started large and made smaller or started small and become larger. The horse soon learns that he is not going anywhere special, and this in itself slows him down. Further, the nature of the circle makes it physically difficult for him to run "full out." When he becomes tractable in the enclosed area, take him on the trail after his ring work. Work him up and down hills at walk and trot, and take short canters up steeper slopes. Do not ride him with horses that will run ahead of him (especially if you are retraining a racehorse), but he could be ridden beside slow-cantering horses. Never let him find himself way behind and then try to catch up; always keep him beside a quiet, obedient horse with no chance that he can misinterpret the ride as a race.

A racehorse must be retrained to accept other horses in front of or behind him. Work in an enclosed arena with a well-trained companion horse. The companion follows behind, then walks or trots beside him, and eventually passes and leads, and finally falls back beside, and then behind. He continues to pass and fall back while the rider of the problem horse tries to keep a steady, even pace. Work for relaxation and calmness, and be free with praise.

Many riders have problems with neighing, cavorting around, and general inattention, especially when taking a horse to a new environment. In most cases, this behavior is due to lack of experience and concentration. The horse is actually on the point of flight and in some instances might go beyond this point and take off. He is reverting to his untamed state, as indeed his behavior shows. This horse must learn to trust his rider and obey his aids. Return him to the fundamentals. Gain his trust, help him to become obedient to your aids, and build a solid basic foundation before exposing him to exciting surroundings. This is a case where daily work is necessary—weekends are not enough. His attention span must be lengthened, and his experiences under saddle should be varied and numerous.

If we are to be successful trainers, our knowledge of horses must be thorough and sensitive. We must transmit our desires to the horse in a way he can understand, and in a way that causes him to desire to obey and please us. It's a tall order, but the rewards are worth our effort, patience, time, understanding, and love.

Recommended Reading

Applied Horse Psychology, Marion B. Williamson. Cordovan, 1974.

The Art of Dressage, Alois Podhajsky. Garden City, N.Y.: Doubleday & Company, 1976.

The Art of Long Reining, Sylvia Stanier. London: J. A. Allen & Co., 1974.

Basic Horsemanship: English and Western, Eleanor F. Prince and Gaydell M. Collier. Garden City, N.Y.: Doubleday & Company, 1974.

Breaking and Training the Driving Horse, Doris Ganton. North Hollywood, Calif.: Wilshire Book Company, 1976.

Cavalletti, Reiner Klimke. London: J. A. Allen & Co., 1974.

The Complete Training of Horse and Rider, Alois Podhajsky. Garden City, N.Y.: Doubleday & Company, 1967.

Creative Horsemanship, Charles de Kunffy. Cranbury, N.J.: A. S. Barnes & Co., 1975.

Dressage, Henry Wynmalen, M. F. H. Cranbury, N.J.: A. S. Barnes & Co., 1952.

Dressage Riding, Richard L. Watjen. London: J. A. Allen & Co., 1958.

Effective Horsemanship, Noel Jackson. New York: Arco Publishing Co., 1967.

The Endurance Horse, Ann Hyland. Philadelphia: J. B. Lippincott Co., 1975.

The Event Horse, Sheila Willcox. Philadelphia: J. B. Lippincott Co., 1973.

Golden Book of Arabian Horse Showing, The Arabian Horse Registry of American and the International Arabian Horse Association—seventeen booklets included as of 1967; new sections added periodically.

A Guide to Driving Horses, Sally Walrond. North Hollywood, Calif.: Wilshire Book Company, 1975.

Horse Packing in Pictures, Francis W. Davis. New York: Charles Scribner's Sons, 1975.

Horsemanship, Waldemar Seunig. Garden City, N.Y.: Doubleday & Company, 1956.

Horses, Hitches and Rocky Trails, Joe Back. Beverly Hills, Calif.: Sage Books, published by Alan Swallow, 1959.

The Mind of the Horse, R. H. Smythe. Brattleboro, Vt.: Stephen Greene Press, 1965.

My Horses, My Teachers, Alois Podhajsky. Garden City, N.Y.: Doubleday & Company, 1968.

NATRC Manuals (North American Trail Ride Conference, annual)

Practical Horse Psychology, Moyra Williams. North Hollywood, Calif.: Wilshire Book Company, 1975.

Practical Western Training, Dave Jones. New York: Arco Publishing Co., 1977.

Riding and Jumping, rev. ed., William Steinkraus. Garden City, N.Y.: Doubleday & Company, 1969.

Riding Logic, Wilhelm Museler. New York: Arco Publishing Co., 1976.

Side-Saddle, rev. ed., Doreen Archer Houblon. New York: Charles Scribner's Sons, 1951.

Trail Rider's Handbook, Equestrian Trails, Inc. Curtis and Curtis, 1971.

Trail Riding, International Arabian Horse Association, n.d.

Training the Driving Pony, Allan D. Conder. New York: Arco Publishing Co., 1977.

Training Your Own Horse, Mary Rose, F.B.H.S. London: George G. Harrap Publishing Co., 1977.

Training Your Own Young Horse, Jan Dickerson. Garden City, N.Y. Doubleday & Company, 1978.

Understanding and Training Horses, A. James Ricci. Philadelphia: J. B. Lippincott Co., 1964.

The Western Horse: Its Types and Training, rev. ed., John A. Gorman. Danville, Ill.: The Interstate Printers & Publishers, 1967.

Western Horse Behavior and Training, Robert W. Miller. Garden City, N.Y.: Doubleday & Company, 1975.

Western Horseman Series, published by *The Western Horseman.*

The Western Trainer, Dave Jones. New York: Arco Publishing Co., 1976.

Index

ELEANOR F. PRINCE grew up in New Hampshire and now lives on a ranch in Buford, Wyoming, where she raises and trains Arabian horses and teaches equitation at the University of Wyoming.

Originally from Long Island, New York, GAYDELL M. COLLIER lives in Sundance, Wyoming, where she and her husband operate the Backpocket Ranch.